Identities, Politics, and Rights

The Amherst Series in Law, Jurisprudence, and Social Thought

Each work included in The Amherst Series in Law, Jurisprudence, and Social Thought explores a theme crucial to an understanding of law as it confronts the changing social and intellectual currents of the late twentieth century.

Identities, Politics, and Rights

Edited by Austin Sarat and Thomas R. Kearns

Ann Arbor

THE UNIVERSITY OF MICHIGAN PRESS

First paperback edition 1997
Copyright © by the University of Michigan 1995
All rights reserved
Published in the United States of America by
The University of Michigan Press
Manufactured in the United States of America
⊛ Printed on acid-free paper

2000 1999 1998 1997   4 3 2 1

A CIP catalog record for this book is available from the British Library.

Library of Congress Cataloging-in-Publication Data

Identities, politics, and rights / edited by Austin Sarat and Thomas R.
   Kearns.
       p.   cm. — (Amherst series in law, jurisprudence, and social
   thought)
     Includes index.
     ISBN 0-472-10632-5 (hardcover : alk. paper)
     1. Civil rights. 2. Human rights. I. Sarat, Austin.
   II. Kearns, Thomas R. III. Series.
   JC571.I33 1995
   323—dc20   95-543
                                                                  CIP

ISBN 0-472-08473-9 (pbk. : alk. paper)

Contents

Acknowledgments

Identities, Politics, and Rights brings together essays that were first presented at a conference entitled "The Paradoxes of Rights." That conference, which was held at Amherst College in November 1992, took as one of its themes the need to reconsider liberal theories of rights. In this book we are pleased to present work that links rights and identities, on the one hand, and rights and politics, on the other. This work challenges liberal theory and suggests productive ways to imagine postliberal understandings of rights. We are grateful to the scholars whose work is contained in *Identities, Politics, and Rights* and to the Keck and Arthur Vining Davis foundations as well as the Massachusetts Foundation for the Humanities for their financial support.

Editorial Introduction

Austin Sarat and Thomas R. Kearns

As is now widely recognized, the subject of rights occupies an important place in liberal political thought.[1] Various strands of liberalism find the justification for rights in nature, in utility, or in the demands of justice and fairness,[2] but, throughout, liberal discourse about rights assumes two things. First, rights are assumed to be the entitlements of persons whose status as persons is fixed and from which rights are said to issue.[3] Rights-based theories "*presuppose* and protect the value of individual thought and choice" (emphasis added).[4] The essential attributes of persons are, in this account, ahistorical and universal; as a result, humans are, in their essential attributes, alike. Rights are said to be logically entailed by a recognition of those attributes. Thus, as Alan Gewirth argues, "Human rights are based upon and derivative from human dignity. It is because humans have dignity that they have . . . rights."[5] Or, as George Kateb puts it,

---

1. George Kateb, "Democratic Individuality and the Meaning of Rights," in *Liberalism and the Moral Life*, ed. Nancy Rosenblum (Cambridge: Harvard University Press, 1989). Also Colorado College Studies, *The Bill of Rights and the Liberal Tradition* (Colorado Springs: Colorado College, 1992).

2. Douglas MacLean and Claudia Mills, eds., *Liberalism Reconsidered* (Totowa, N.J.: Rowman and Allanheld, 1983).

3. A. I. Melden, *Rights and Persons* (Oxford: Basil Blackwell, 1977), chap. 6. See also Michael Meyer, "Dignity, Rights, and Self Control," *Ethics* 99 (1989): 520.

4. Ronald Dworkin, *Taking Rights Seriously* (Cambridge: Harvard University Press, 1977), 172.

5. Alan Gewirth, "Human Dignity as the Basis of Rights," in *The Constitution of Rights: Human Dignity and American Values*, ed. Michael Meyer and William Parent (Ithaca: Cornell University Press, 1992), 10. See also Joel Feinberg, "The Nature and Value of Rights," in his *Rights, Justice, and the Bounds of Liberty* (Princeton: Princeton University Press, 1980), 151.

> Public and formal respect for rights registers and strengthens awareness of three . . . facts of being human: every person is a creature capable of feeling pain, . . . is a free agent capable of having a free being . . . , and is a moral agent capable of acknowledging that what one claims for oneself as a right one can claim only as an equal to everyone else. . . . Respect for rights recognizes these capacities and thus honors human dignity.[6]

The second assumption of the liberal theory of rights is that rights stand outside of, and above, politics, where politics is understood in terms of the play of group preferences or state policy. One makes appeals to rights as a defense against those preferences and policies, to hold them at bay. The force of rights depends neither on the sentiments of electorates nor the desires of political elites. "The perspective of rights-based individualism," Kateb notes, "is suspicious of the political realm."[7] Rights are, in liberal theory, valuable since they entitle their holders willy-nilly to particular kinds of treatment. They provide an escape from the political realm because, in Dworkin's famous characterization, rights are "trumps."[8] If they are taken seriously, rights stop political argument and end political contest, and the recognition of a right removes the disputed claim from the political process. Thus, if taken seriously, rights make "the Government's job of securing the general benefit more difficult and more expensive."[9]

The essays in *Identities, Politics, and Rights* take up these two central assumptions of the liberal theory of rights by examining the extent to which rights constitute us as subjects and are, at the same time, implicated in political struggles.[10] In contrast to the liberal view in which rights are treated as a "unitary, universal analytic move and

---

6. George Kateb, *The Inner Ocean: Individualism and Democratic Culture* (Ithaca: Cornell University Press, 1992), 5.

7. Ibid., 25.

8. "Rights," Dworkin suggests, "are political trumps held by individuals. Individuals have rights when, for some reason, a collective goal is not sufficient justification for denying them what they wish, as individuals, to have or to do." *Taking Rights Seriously*, xi.

9. Ibid., 198.

10. For an interesting example of this view of rights see Neal Milner, "Ownership Rights and the Rites of Ownership," *Law and Social Inquiry* 18 (1993): 227. Also Mari Matsuda, "Law and Culture in the District Court of Honolulu, 1844–45: A Case Study of the Rise of Legal Consciousness," *American Journal of Legal History* 32 (1988): 16.

rhetorical practice," the essays in this collection emphasize that rights talk designates "a field of heterogeneous . . . practices that . . . help to constitute the array of subject moments or subject effects that comprise citizens and sovereigns."[11] These essays highlight both the context-specific qualities of rights and their constitutive effects.[12]

Taking context into account means recognizing the contingent quality of, and the contingencies associated with, rights.[13] As Milner notes rights are "demystified in this vision because the legal order's distinctiveness is minimized. If law cannot be separated from its social field, . . . [rights become] just another resource that can be used to convince others how to behave. . . ."[14] Examining their constitutive effects means inquiring into the way rights call into being, and enable, particular forms and expressions of personhood, as well as the way they disable others.[15] It means recognizing, as we have argued elsewhere, that "Legal-thought and legal relations . . . dominate self-understanding and one's understanding of one's relations to others. . . . [W]e have internalized law's meanings and its representations of us, so much so that our own purposes and understandings can no longer be extricated from them."[16]

The essays in this volume examine the varied roles that rights play in political struggles as well as ways they are mobilized in particular political contests and by particular political movements.[17] These essays recognize that political disputes in the United States

---

11. This contrast was suggested to us by one of the anonymous reviewers of this volume.

12. For a discussion of the constitutive effects of law and rights see Robert Gordon, "Critical Legal Histories," *Stanford Law Review* 36 (1984): 57.

13. Neal Milner, "The Denigration of Rights and the Persistence of Rights Talk: A Cultural Portrait," *Law and Social Inquiry* 14 (1989): 631.

14. Ibid., 634.

15. As Milner notes, "[R]ights talk is one way people frame and assess their worlds. . . . Because of their importance in American culture, rights play a powerful role in both accommodation and resistance." See "The Intrigues of Rights, Resistance, and Accommodation," *Law and Social Inquiry* 17 (1992): 322 and 330. See also Martha Minow, "Interpreting Rights: An Essay for Robert Cover," *Yale Law Journal* 96 (1987): 1860; and Morton Horwitz, "Rights," *Harvard Civil Rights–Civil Liberties Law Review* 23 (1988): 393.

16. Austin Sarat and Thomas Kearns, "Beyond the Great Divide: Forms of Legal Scholarship and Everyday Life," in their *Law in Everyday Life* (Ann Arbor: University of Michigan Press, 1993), 29.

17. See John Brigham, "Right, Rage and Remedy: The Construction of Legal Discourse," *Studies of American Political Development* 2 (1987): 303.

have increasingly been cast as disputes about rights.[18] As Mary Ann Glendon puts it,

> The marked increase in the assertion of rights-based claims, beginning with the civil rights movement in the 1950s and 1960s, . . . [is] sometimes described as a rights revolution. If there is any justification for using the word "revolution" in connection with these developments, it is not that they have eliminated the ills at which they were aimed. . . . What do seem revolutionary about the rights-related developments of the past three decades are the transformations they have produced. . . . in the way we now think and speak about major public issues.[19]

Moreover, with the fall of communism and the spread of democratization in Africa, Asia, and Latin America, the idea of rights has taken on new salience in political struggles in places where rights talk was formerly avoided or denigrated.[20] "In the years since the end of World War II," Glendon argues,

> rights discourse has spread throughout the world. At the transnational level, human rights were enshrined in a variety of covenants and declarations, notably the United Nations Universal Declaration of Human Rights . . . At the same time, enumerated rights, backed up by some form of judicial review, were added to several national constitutions. . . . Nor was the rush to rights confined to "liberal" or "democratic" societies. American rights talk is now but one dialect in a universal language of rights.[21]

Commentators here and elsewhere worry that reliance on rights in political struggles and by political movements invites a kind of legal imperialism, in which courts and lawyers take on an unhealthy promi-

---

18. Ronald Dworkin notes that "The language of rights now dominates political debate in the United States." *Taking Rights Seriously*, 184.

19. Mary Ann Glendon, *Rights Talk: The Impoverishment of Political Discourse* (New York: The Free Press, 1991), 4.

20. Jon Elster, "Constitutionalism in Eastern Europe," *University of Chicago Law Review* 58 (1991): 447.

21. Glendon, *Rights Talk*, 7.

nence.[22] As the "rights industry" flourishes and the export of American ideas of rights grows dramatically, from abroad we hear claims that the export of rights is the latest manifestation of neocolonialism.[23] Moreover, critics on both the political left and right attack rights as mystifying, alienating, and/or destructive of community.[24]

Critics from the left suggest that reliance on rights in politics disables disadvantaged or subordinated groups from mobilizing effectively,[25] that rights, as Mark Tushnet argues, are "contingent on social and technological facts . . . (so that) the set of rights recognized in any particular society is coextensive with that society,"[26] and that they do not prevent "violence, repression, and disciplinary subjection against individuals who have not acted to harm or to offend profoundly other persons."[27] From this, Tushnet and other critics of rights conclude that "once one identifies what counts as a right in a specific setting, it invariably turns out that the right is unstable; significant but small

---

22. Gerald Rosenberg, *Hollow Hope: Can Courts Bring About Social Change?* (Chicago: University of Chicago Press, 1991). See also Michael McCann, *Rights at Work: Pay Equity Reform and the Politics of Legal Mobilization* (Chicago: University of Chicago Press, 1994).

23. The debate at the Conference on International Human Rights in the summer of 1993 highlighted this critique. This debate illustrated the dialectic of nationalism and globalization in which national boundaries and traditions both are vehemently defended and, at the same time, give way to culture contact and the widespread circulation of images and ideas. In such an environment, does rights talk provide a global vocabulary that can respect local variation, or does the fact of globalization lose meaning if rights are adapted to the particular, the contingent, and the varied?

24. As Henkin notes,

From the perspective of some conceptions of the good society or the good life, the rights idea is selfish and promotes egoism. It is atomistic, disharmonious, confrontational, often litigious. . . . It is antisocial, permitting and encouraging the individual to set up selfish interests as he or she sees them against the common interest commonly determined. The idea of rights challenges democracy, negating popular sovereignty and frustrating the will of the majority. . . . The idea of rights, it is argued, is inefficient, tending to weaken society and render it ungovernable. Exalting rights deemphasizes and breeds neglect of duties. It imposes an artificial and narrow view of the public good. . . .

Louis Henkin, *The Age of Rights* (New York: Columbia University Press, 1990), 182. See also Martin Golding, "The Primacy of Welfare Rights," *Social Philosophy and Policy* 1 (1984): 121, 124.

25. Stuart Scheingold, *The Politics of Rights: Lawyers, Public Policy, and Political Change* (New Haven: Yale University Press, 1974).

26. Mark Tushnet, "An Essay on Rights," *Texas Law Review* 62 (1984): 1366.

27. See Richard Brisbin, "Antonin Scalia, William Brennan, and the Politics of Expression: A Study of Legal Violence and Repression," *American Political Science Review* 87 (1993): 914.

changes in the social setting can make it difficult to claim that a right remains implicated."[28] This is the claim that rights are indeterminate, that in every controversy the appeal to rights simply restates, though it gives the illusion of resolving, the fundamental tension in liberal thought between freedom and security.[29] As a result, Tushnet claims, "It is not just that rights-talk does not do much good. In the contemporary United States it is positively harmful."[30]

One important response to the criticism of rights made in the name of disadvantaged or subordinated groups has been advanced by scholars associated with those very groups. Thus Patricia Williams notes that while "rights may be unstable and indeterminate"[31] as Tushnet and others claim, "rights rhetoric has been and continues to be an effective form of discourse for blacks . . . (because) the subtlety of rights' real instability . . . does not render unusable their persona of stability."[32] The salience of rights, according to Williams, cannot be talked about without reference to the particular, historical situation of the group whose needs are in question. "For the historically disempowered," she claims, "the conferring of rights is symbolic of all the denied aspects of their humanity. Rights imply a respect that places one in the referential range of self and others, that elevates one's status from human body to social being. For blacks, then, the attainment of rights signifies the respectful behavior, the collective responsibility, properly owed by a society to one of its own."[33] As Williams sees it, the powerful effect of rights in constituting identity is inseparable from their utility in political struggle.

Conservative critics suggest that rights talk needs to be tempered with an awareness of civic responsibility, that Americans need to be a

---

28. Tushnet, "An Essay on Rights," 1363.

29. See Peter Gabel and Duncan Kennedy, "Roll Over Beethoven," *Stanford Law Review* 36 (1984): 1, 39.

30. Tushnet, "An Essay on Rights," 1386. See also Peter Gabel, "The Phenomenology of Rights Consciousness and the Pact of the Withdrawn Selves," *Texas Law Review* 62 (1984): 1563.

31. Patricia Williams, *The Alchemy of Race and Rights* (Cambridge: Harvard University Press, 1991), 148.

32. Williams, *Alchemy*, 149.

33. Ibid, 153. As Drucilla Cornell puts it, "If there is an obvious lesson of the last fifty years, it is that democracy does not fare well without the institutionalization of rights." "Should a Marxist Believe in Rights?" *Praxis International* 4 (1984): 45, 53–54. See also Michael McBride, "Rights and the Marxist Tradition," *Praxis International* 4 (1984): 57.

little less rights oriented and a little more attentive to the needs of the community as a whole.[34] Rights are criticized for introducing undue harshness and rigidity into political debate, for making necessary compromise and accommodation impossible, and for acting as barriers to efficient allocation of resources.[35] But it is to the language of community and responsibility that conservative critics of rights make recourse.[36] Reliance on rights constitutes a particular kind of subject; it encourages a strident, self-interested individualism and, according to this view, "contributes to the erosion of the habits, practices, and attitudes of respect for others."[37]

Examining the relationships among identities, politics, and rights suggests that rights persist and flourish, at least in part, because of, not in spite of, their many-sidedness and their paradoxical qualities. They turn out to provide a language to which many different persons and groups can attach themselves because they can, and do, mean many things at once. We now know that rights can be sources of empowerment and protection for persons against the societies in which they live,[38] yet they can constrain those same persons.[39] Additionally,

---

34. Richard Morgan, *Disabling America: The "Rights Industry" in Our Time* (New York: Basic Books, 1984). Glendon argues that "The American dialect of rights talk disserves public deliberation not only through affirmatively promoting an image of the rights-bearer as a radically autonomous individual, but through its corresponding neglect of the social dimensions of human personhood. . . . Neglect of the social dimension of personhood has made it extremely difficult for us to develop an adequate conceptual apparatus for taking into account the sorts of groups within which human character, competence, and capacity for citizenship are formed." *Rights Talk*, 109. It is, of course, true that the concern for community and the impact of rights on community is also prominent among scholars with a more politically progressive viewpoint. For example see Staughton Lynd, "Communal Rights," *Texas Law Review* 62 (1984): 1417. Also Minow, "Interpreting Rights," 1860, 1911.

35. As Glendon puts it, "Our stark, simple rights dialect puts a damper on the process of public justification, communication, and deliberation upon which the continuing vitality of a democratic regime depends." *Rights Talk*, 171.

36. These criticisms are sometimes made by scholars of a very different political stripe. See Robin West, "Narrative, Responsibility, and Death," in her *Narrative, Authority, and Law* (Ann Arbor: University of Michigan Press, 1993). Also Joel Feinberg, "The Nature and Value of Rights," *Journal of Value Inquiry* 4 (1970): 243.

37. Glendon, *Rights Talk*, 171. Also Alasdair MacIntyre, *After Virtue: A Study in Moral Theory* (London: Duckworth, 1981).

38. See David Richards, "Rights and Autonomy," *Ethics* 92 (1981): 3.

39. "[L]egal rights are interdependent and mutually defining. They arise in the context of relationships among people who are themselves interdependent and mutually defining. In this sense, every right and every freedom is no more than a claim

they can liberate and yet limit the imagination of the possible;[40] they can revolutionize and yet conserve. Rights authorize action and yet undermine authority's claims. They are, by definition, mandatory claims, yet they are fecund with interpretive possibilities.[41] They both constitute us as subjects and provide a language through which we can resist that constitution and forge new identities.[42]

Identities, Politics, and Rights is divided into two sections. The essays in the first, entitled "Rights and the Constitution of the Self," explore, in particular, the adequacy of the liberal conception of persons and the liberal theory of rights. They illuminate the constitutive power of rights and examine the way liberal subjects are brought into being. But they also show how rights can become vehicles through which persons try on, invent, and imagine new identities and new ways of being in the world.

Drucilla Cornell's "Bodily Integrity and the Right to Abortion" provides one example of this kind of scholarship. In this essay Cornell delivers a passionate defense of abortion rights, not for their legal value, but for their value in the sphere of cultural contestation in which the nature of women's subjectivity is defined. If women are to attain what she calls the "minimum conditions of individuation," abortion rights must be protected. Yet, contrary to the assumptions of liberalism, the protection of rights is neither an end in itself, nor a way of defending an already individuated subject.

Individuated selves come into being, Cornell suggests, only in a web of relations with others. However, unlike other scholars for whom such a recognition entails a rejection of rights,[43] Cornell believes it is possible, indeed essential, to hold onto rights discourse. She sees in the articulation of particular rights claims a new way of constituting selves and identities.

---

limited by the possible claims of others. . . . Rather than expressions of some intrinsic autonomy, property rights announce complex, and often overlapping, relationships of individuals and the larger community to limited resources." Minow, "Interpreting Rights," 1884.

40. See Duncan Kennedy, "Critical Labor Law Theory: A Comment," *Industrial Relations Law Journal* 4 (1981): 503, 506. Kennedy claims that rights "represent a liberating accomplishment of our culture" and that progressives do not "need a counter-theory that ends with rights."

41. See Minow, "Interpreting Rights."

42. See Milner, "The Denigration of Rights."

43. See Jennifer Nedelsky, "Law, Boundaries and the Bounded Self," *Representations* 30 (1990): 162.

Because individuation is not possible, Cornell contends, without the recognition and protection of what she calls a right to "bodily integrity," those who would limit abortion rights oppose the conditions of women's existence as individuals in the world. Their opposition perpetrates a serious "symbolic assault on a woman's sense of self." When abortion rights are denied, the female body and womb no longer are women's to imagine; they are, in essence, turned over to men. Cornell warns, however, that the defense of abortion rights must not reconfirm prevailing liberal conceptions of personhood. What is at stake in the abortion debate, as Cornell sees it, is a question of equality, equality of well-being, and of equal access to the minimum conditions of individuation. We must not, and cannot, take individuation for granted or fail to attend to its difficulties. Liberalism fails to attend to those conditions and, in so doing, fails to understand rights as constitutive of identity.

Wendy Brown uses Karl Marx's "On the Jewish Question" to take up Cornell's interest in the relationship between identity formation and rights claims. Through her reading of Marx, Brown shows how rights may, at one moment and in one context, operate to emancipate and enable the expression of identity in all its varieties while, at other times and under other conditions, rights may contribute to a regulatory project in which "deviant" identities are repressed. Rights, she argues, though they speak in a universalistic vocabulary, take on meaning only locally.

According to Brown, because Marx saw Jews making rights claims as Jews rather than as abstract, liberal subjects, his work remains relevant to contemporary identity politics. Rights emancipate, Brown argues, here following Marx, by constituting subjects in abstract terms, as formally free and equal. Yet such emancipation is, paradoxically, itself a form of subordination in which persons are required to disavow essential conditions of personhood. Claiming rights works to liberate by depoliticizing social existence.

For Brown, as for Marx, "subject position is social position." Unlike Marx, however, Brown suggests that subjects are not just positioned by power, but are formed and produced by power. Rights serve this project by naturalizing the identities so produced, but they also reduce the stigma associated with particular subject positions. She warns that rights discourse may seduce us into moving the debate about subjectivity and identity from the "highly accessible sphere of cultural contestation" to "the highly restricted sphere of judicial authority . . . and to confuse rights with equality, lawyers with potency, or legal recognition with emancipation."

Jane Gaines's essay heeds Brown's warning and explores the ways rights are implicated in the "sphere of cultural contestation." Gaines analyzes rights in aesthetic productions and explores the legal constitution of what it means to be a celebrity. Her work suggests that rights do not exist as things in the world, but are constructed as aesthetic productions themselves. She seeks to demonstrate that rights are always contingent claims that the state may or may not recognize.

Gaines takes Andy Warhol as the exemplification of celebrity and suggests that Warhol understood the possibility of producing celebrity without engaging in productive work. She notes that while celebrity is an empty signifier it is protected by an elaborate legal regime founded in copyright law and in the so-called "right of publicity." The former protects whatever work celebrity produces, while the latter constitutes the celebrity name and likeness as a right to exclusive use.

The right of publicity accords celebrities property rights in their own image and conveys to all of us property rights in our persons. "The fact that the . . . right of publicity actually contains within itself the possibility of our own celebrity . . . (suggests) that if we have no other property we have property in ourselves—that is, our name, voice and likeness." Rights become commodities and persons become commodities with rights; the distinction between persons and things is eroded. Attaching property rights to persons and to images of those persons reveals, in Gaines's view, "the vacuity of property rights." However, she notes that rights, vacuous though they may be, make us particular kinds of subjects, subjects for whom celebrity, property, and personhood become increasingly blurred categories.

A similar recognition of the duality of rights is amply displayed in Kirstie M. McClure's "Taking Liberties in Foucault's Triangle: Sovereignty, Discipline, Governmentality, and the Subject of Rights." Foucault himself, McClure notes, had a rather ambivalent relationship to rights.[44] He criticized rights as a language of humanism in which the image of the sovereign individual is invoked to serve the needs of

---

44. For a further exploration of this theme see Alan Hunt, "Foucault's Expulsion of Law: Toward a Retrieval," *Law and Social Inquiry* 17 (1992): 1.

sovereignty itself. And he expressed doubts about the capacity of rights to provide effective bases for resisting both sovereignty and discipline. Yet, as McClure notes, Foucault's rejection of rights was not total. He refused to relinquish the notion of rights entirely and, in fact, imagined the possibility of a "'new form of right, one which must indeed be anti-disciplinary, but at the same time liberated from the principle of sovereignty.'" Foucault's call for a new form of right requires, McClure argues, both a rethinking of rights and of the "notion of the autonomous 'individual' as their customary bearer."

McClure embraces this project while herself expressing some doubt about the adequacy of Foucault's conception of right. She suggests that a repositioning of rights can occur only if we take seriously both the deepening problem of "sovereignty-discipline-governmentality" in the late modern era and the diffusion of the idea of democracy. McClure believes that doing so complicates the relationship between rights and politics in a way that Foucault failed to see. Moreover, holding these two developments in tension provides a way of thinking about rights and the constitution of the modern individual that neither accepts an iron cage of limited political possibility nor embraces an uncritical optimism about democracy and liberation.

McClure criticizes Foucault for rendering the subject of rights a creature of law. She argues that the language of rights is properly polyvocal; it has a plurality of addressees who might make of it something other than it was intended to be. The subject of rights, McClure claims, "'lives' only in the manifold and multiple forms of its articulation." In fact, McClure argues that it is necessary to distinguish among different types of rights (e.g., positive liberty rights, negative liberty rights, and entitlement rights) to understand the way rights help constitute subjectivity. Positive liberty rights constitute an autonomous subjectivity, negative liberty rights a protected subjectivity, and entitlement rights a dependent subjectivity. Making these distinctions, McClure argues, helps account for "a continuing tension between invention and constraint," both of which need to be considered if we are to capture the "polyform historicity of the subject of rights."

Awareness of the tension between invention and constraint, between emancipation and domination, is at the heart of John Comaroff's account of the discourse of rights in colonial South Africa. In this essay Comaroff shows the role that modernist legal sensibilities and the language of rights played in the process of colonization. He shows how those sensibilities and that language were used to encourage both a "radical individualism" and a recognition of "primal sovereignty" in the indigenous population. Rights discourse, Comaroff notes, was part of the apparatus of colonial domination, confirming stereotypical views of African tribal life while, at the same time, introducing new sources of divisions among the native population. Yet rights discourse also helped create terms and spaces by which the colonized could resist colonial domination.

Rights discourse was used, among other ways, to regulate practices of the body and to reform conjugal customs as well as to introduce new forms of property relations. These processes were part of a complex process of class formation in which traditional relations were displaced by modernist assumptions. These assumptions were used to constitute the Tswana, the indigenous people Comaroff discusses, as a distinct ethnic group. The fact that the Tswana had their own elaborate repertoire of rights and practices of personhood went unrecognized. Yet attributing rights to persons by virtue of their membership in ethnic groups made it possible to remove those rights wholesale as the need arose. Rights discourse, like colonialism itself, promised equality while sustaining inequality. In so doing it both gave people new identities and effaced their own existing identity.

The second section of this book, "Rights in Political Struggles," carries forward the argument about the many-sidedness of rights developed by Brown, McClure, and Comaroff. It illustrates the many ways rights are taken up in politics, their utility in contests for human liberation as well as the way they are used by the enemies of liberation. The essays in this section remind us that rights seldom end political contests; instead they themselves become objects of struggle.

South Africa again provides the context for an examination of the politics of rights in the first essay in this section. In this essay Richard Abel contends that though modern South Africa has been a staunchly authoritarian state, law has played a central role in the now successful struggle against apartheid. Law was available as a resource for resistance because the white regime proclaimed its fidelity to rights and because all other avenues for resistance were effectively closed to blacks. In this sense, as Abel puts it, black South Africans had nothing left but rights with which to carry on their political struggles.

Abel notes that while black political groups sought recourse to the legal arena, the government often tried to politicize disputes. Law was used most effectively, Abel argues, as a "shield" rather than a "sword"; claiming violations of rights was more useful in preserving the status quo against greater government intrusions and escalating repression than in promoting change. Rights claims made a difference, in Abel's view, in that the black opposition was able to secure victories in court that it could not have won elsewhere. At the same time, the regime in South Africa prevented law from becoming too much of an obstacle to its policies by regularly instituting changes in laws that frustrated its will.

Abel draws a mixed lesson about the utility of rights in political struggles in South Africa. He claims, echoing E. P. Thompson,[45] that a government, even an oppressive government, that purports to rule through law will, in some ways, by constrained by law. Rights, Abel concludes, were neither "irrelevant" nor "essential" in the struggle against apartheid.

A comparable lesson about the utility of rights in political struggles emerges from Sally Engle Merry's "Wife Battering and the Ambiguities of Rights in a Post-Colonial Context." In this essay Merry considers the political movement against spousal violence in Hawaii. She argues that the mobilization against that violence has been heavily dependent on a rhetoric of rights. This is the case because in Hawaii, as in Abel's study of South Africa, women have used courts to resist oppression, in this case a gendered oppression that finds its locus in family relations.

Courts only lately, and reluctantly, have assumed any role in relation to domestic violence. Throughout the history of Hawaii they have been unresponsive to claims of domestic violence. Today though they are available to women, they provide a limited, but useful, arena in which to contest violence and highlight the conditions that give rise to it. For women the experience of going to court denaturalizes family violence and helps them define a sphere of autonomy apart from their abusers. Men, in turn, experience the disciplinary side of law, and they are taught a new way of understanding male-female relations and the inappropriateness of violence in those relationships.

For both women and men the claims of rights disorient and disrupt traditional roles. Women use law to assert autonomy and protect

---

45. E. P. Thompson, *Whigs and Hunters: The Origins of the Black Act* (New York: Pantheon, 1975).

themselves. Men experience law as coercion and constraint. Rights, Merry concludes, while they reshape the definition of selves for both the victims and perpetrators of violence, do not produce substantive change in the social conditions that produce violence. They supplement, but cannot replace, broad-based political activity.

One right in particular, namely the First Amendment's guarantee of freedom of speech, plays a key role in political struggle in the United States. This is the key claim of Steven Shiffrin's "The First Amendment and the Meaning of America." Shiffrin analyzes the First Amendment for the contribution it makes to the maintenance of a culture of dissent. He makes this argument in the context of the Supreme Court's decisions upholding flag burning as protected expression under the First Amendment. While he agrees with the result in those cases, Shiffrin suggests that the Court's reasoning revealed the inadequacy of a non-dissent-based understanding of the First Amendment.

Dissent, Shiffrin argues, has an important political role in a polity increasingly dominated by large interest groups and bureaucracies. It is, however, more than that. Dissent gives America its national identity. It is itself, paradoxically, a form of cultural glue that binds citizens to the community. Conservatives, Shiffrin states, do not understand the way in which protection of dissent actually produces political unity. Thus there is a political paradox at the heart of the First Amendment, a tolerance and protection for dissent that "masks the extent to which (even in America) dissent is discouraged and marginalized." The First Amendment's protection of dissent "forms a cultural ideology through which the society secures allegiance." Yet in the end Shiffrin defends a dissent-based conception of freedom of speech against not only political conservatives but also postmodernist critics of rights who, Shiffrin believes, undervalue their political utility.

Martha Minow's "Rights and Cultural Difference" notes the fear of disunity that marks many contemporary responses to identity politics. This fear is comparable to that generated in the First Amendment controversies discussed by Shiffrin. It is, she suggests, misplaced both at the level of cultural politics and at the level of the politics of rights. Like Shiffrin, Minow calls for greater openness to difference, and she warns that the language of unity is often a language of domination. In addition, she argues that the fear of group rights and cultural pluralism expressed in the vocabulary of rights is unfounded because while rights are ways of articulating difference, they also provide a vehicle through which unity can be forged.

Minow suggests that the very willingness of excluded groups to present their political demands in terms of rights draws them into a discourse designed by dominant groups and thus promotes unity. Furthermore, rights universalize political claims. They identify the interests of particular groups with the interests of everyone. Rights build bridges even as they articulate particular visions of the nature of the good, or the just, community. Rights channel political dissent into a consensual language and secure participation in the dominant structures of law. Thus the political struggles of disadvantaged groups are often marked by greater ambivalence toward rights and rights talk than is generally understood. It is only, Minow says, by attending to the history of political struggles against exclusion that we can accurately understand the role of rights in the dialectic of unity and difference.

Locating rights in this dialectic is the task of Elizabeth Kiss's "Is Nationalism Compatible with Human Rights?" In this essay Kiss ruminates about the rise of ethnic nationalism and the threat it appears to pose to the spread of human rights. As she puts it, "A specter is haunting the New World Order: the specter of violent and exclusionary nationalism. It alarms and discomforts those on both sides of recent debates over the validity of universal norms of justice and rights." The challenge nationalism poses to human rights restates, in a contemporary context, the paradox of universalism and particularism that has always plagued thinking about rights. Human rights, after all, are founded on the belief that humans have the same basic moral status wherever they happen to live. Advocates of human rights assert the primacy of the human community over any geographically localized association. Nationalism reverses this order of priority and thus would seem to challenge the basic premises of human rights.

In spite of this apparent opposition, Kiss insists that nationalism need not be incompatible with human rights. She believes that a commitment to respecting human rights can be one of the constitutive elements of nationalism. To recognize the claims of human rights, in Kiss's view, is to acknowledge the shared vulnerabilities all of us face. To protect us from those vulnerabilities humans must find shelter in various forms, and nations, united not by shared blood but by shared values, can provide one such shelter.

Kiss notes that human rights discourse has nothing to say about the proper boundaries of political community. She believes that the nationalist challenge requires new, creative thinking about the future of rights in the postcommunist world. She suggests that nationalist politics has played, and can continue to play, a critical role in securing respect for human rights for citizens of many nations. This is especially true when, as in the late modern world, we increasingly recognize ourselves as possessing multiple and overlapping identities. Celebrating difference, Kiss concludes, need not be antithetical to the maintenance of a "moral vocabulary of equality and universality."

The concluding essay, by Bruce Ackerman, notes the apparently paradoxical position of the United States in relation to the rights revolution that is occurring throughout the world. America, the first new nation, a nation born of revolution and of a revolutionary attachment to rights, faces a world of revolutionary upheaval. The question that will define our own political future as well as the future of rights around the world is how America will respond to that fact.

Ackerman argues that America must reclaim the idea of revolution and remake its identity as a revolutionary nation. He sees in liberalism a wellspring of revolutionary sentiment and argues that we should "respond to revolutionary vanguardism . . . by designing a constitutional system that subjects would-be revolutionaries to a series of fair democratic tests." This constitutional system, he contends, is fully compatible with an embrace of social justice that recognizes new rights for the most disadvantaged in the United States and abroad. It recognizes that "you and I are both struggling to find meaning in the world. We can—we must—build a civilized political life that allows each of us to respect the others' quest." Here Ackerman praises liberal revolutions even as he recognizes that "the revolutionary spirit in America is at one of its cyclical lows." Today is, however, a time when "proliferating ethnic, racial, and religious groups glory in their differences, a time when the liberating promise of individual freedom has given way to somber reflections over the paradoxical character of rights."

For Ackerman, and for the rest of us, such somber reflection not only alerts us to the challenges faced by rights in the late modern era but also reminds us of the fact that rights can both energize political engagement and provide a resource for defenders of the status quo.

Ackerman's essay shows that the political identity of an entire nation may be determined by its reaction to the revolutionary upheavals of the end of the twentieth century. It alerts us to the distinctive, albeit varied, roles of rights in both the constitution of identity and the play of politics.

Part 1. Rights and the Constitution of the Self

Bodily Integrity and the Right to Abortion

Drucilla Cornell

In this chapter, I will argue that the right to abortion must be guaranteed, as it is absolutely essential to the establishment of the minimum conditions for individuation.[1] My argument will proceed as follows: First, I will argue that the right to abortion should be treated as an equivalent right for women to what I will term "bodily integrity,"[2]

---

1. See Drucilla Cornell, "Equivalence and Equality: A Defense of Minimum Conditions of Individuation," in *The Imaginary Domain: A Discourse on Abortion, Pornography and Sexual Harassment* (New York: Routledge, 1995). The traditional conceptions of individuality offered by liberal thinkers mistakenly assume individuality as a given. Against this position, I argue that individuation is a fragile achievement, and one, as the word implies, that is necessarily dependent on constitutive relations with others. I therefore accept the communitarian insight that "selves" only come into "being" in a web of relations and sociosymbolic ties in which we are entangled from the beginning of our lives. However, I adamantly oppose the rejection of rights and the critique of "overindividuation" advocated by some "communitarian feminists."

Philosophical insight into how selves are constituted does not necessarily lead to any conclusions about the role of rights and the importance of individuation for those selves designated as women. As I have argued it is only if one ignores the significance of patrilineage as well as the legal and social institutions that implicitly or explicitly rest on patriarchy, and, therefore, on a specific form of stratified social differentiation, that one can wax sentimental about the value of family and community and warn against the corrosive powers of overzealous feminists and lesbian and gay rights activists. But if one rejects the idea that every individual or subject has a pre-given substantial core that, by definition, makes him—I use the word *him* deliberately because this very idea of the person has been criticized for its erasure of sexual difference—equal as a person before the law, then even the foundations upon which conceptions of rights or equality stand must be rethought. Any defense of the right to abortion that reinstates the reductionist alternatives I have described demands nothing less than the rethinking of these basic concepts.

2. My explanation of integrity is intended to encompass the concept of process of integration.

understood from within the context of mother right and reproductive freedom. The wrong in denying a right to abortion is not a wrong to the "self," but a wrong that prevents the development of the minimum conditions of individuation necessary for any meaningful concept of selfhood. I will provide a psychoanalytic account of how individuation demands the projection and the recognition by others of bodily integrity.

Second, I will argue that because the conditions of individuation are social and symbolic, the right to bodily integrity cannot be understood as a right to privacy, if that right is understood as a right to be left alone.[3] Thus, it is not enough for the state to refrain from actively blocking women's "choice" to have abortions. The right to bodily integrity, dependent as it is on social and symbolic recognition, demands the establishment of conditions in which safe abortions are available to women of every race, class, and nationality. I place the word *choice* in quotation marks because the word itself trivializes how basic the right to abortion is to women's minimum conditions of individuation. Moreover, it should be obvious that no woman *chooses* to have an unwanted pregnancy. If we could control our bodies, "ourselves," then we would not need state intervention to ensure conditions for safe abortions. The rhetoric of "choice" and "control" implies the much criticized dualistic conception of the subject as the king who reigns over the body. Distancing ourselves from the liberal analytic conception of individuality as a pregiven core or substance demands both a different political rhetoric and a redefinition of the content of the right to abortion itself.

The demand for new rhetoric also inheres in the effort to symbolize the feminine within sexual difference, a difference that is necessarily erased by a conception of the subject that defines itself as "above sex." This erasure underlies the difficulty in liberal analytic jurisprudence of conceptualizing abortion as a right: this right cannot be separated from some notion of ourselves as embodied and sexuate be-

---

3. The original analysis of the common law right to privacy was presented by Samuel Warren and Louis D. Brandeis. See Samuel Warren and Louis D. Brandeis, "The Right to Privacy," *Harvard Law Review* 4 (1890): 193. Warren and Brandeis advocated the protection of the "inviolate personality" of each person. Justice Brandeis set forth the basis for the modern right when he recognized a right to protection of one's private life from Government intrusion. He called it "the right to be left alone—the most comprehensive of rights and the most valued by civilized man." Olmstead v. U.S., 277 U.S. 438, 478 (1928) (Brandeis, J. dissenting).

ings.[4] This being said, we need to be very careful in how we conceive of the embodied self. The courts have too often relied on the "reality" of the womb as a pregiven natural difference in order to defeat equality claims under the equal protection doctrine.[5] We must find a way to resymbolize feminine sexual difference within the law so that such a resymbolization is not incompatible with claims of equality.

The attempt to resymbolize feminine sexual difference takes me to the third prong of my argument, which has two aspects. First, we need to account for how bodies come to matter. As Judith Butler shows us, the word *matter* has a double meaning. Bodies matter—that is, materialize and take on reality—while also carrying an implicit normative assessment. Bodies matter both as they materialize and as they come to have symbolic and ethical significance.[6] Butler's insight is useful for resymbolizing the feminine within sexual difference in the legal context. Second, I will use an analysis of how bodies come to matter to answer Ronald Dworkin's thoughtful defense of the justifiability of certain exceptions to any attempt to limit the right to abortion.[7] I will illuminate a virtually unpublicized political campaign that has been waged by some feminists in India to legally circumvent women's right to abortion.[8] The specific context of the legislation to circumvent women's right to abortion has been the context of

---

4. Luce Irigaray writes that as living, sexuate beings, our identities cannot be constructed without conditions of respect for difference and equality of rights to bring out such differences. Forced sexual choice denies us the most fundamental recognition of our differences and therefore the potential for the attainment of equality of rights. See Luce Irigaray, "How to Define Sexuate Rights?" in *The Irigaray Reader*, ed. Margaret Whitford, trans. David Macey (Oxford: Basil Blackwell, 1991) and Luce Irigaray, *je, tu, nous, Toward a Culture of Difference*, trans. Alison Martin (New York and London: Routledge, Chapman and Hall, 1993).

5. The Supreme Court has repeatedly upheld the regulation of reproductive freedom against equal protection challenges. In Geduldig v. Aiello, 417 U.S. 484 (1974), the Court held that state regulation of pregnancy is not sex based because such regulation does not categorically distinguish the class of women from the class of men. However, in Michael M. v. Superior Court, 450 U.S. 464 (1981), the Court suggested that state regulation of pregnancy by its nature cannot discriminate on the basis of sex, for such regulation pertains to a real and categorical difference between genders.

6. See Judith Butler, *Bodies that Matter: On the Discursive Limits of Sex* (New York: Routledge, 1993).

7. See Ronald Dworkin, "What is Sacred?" in *Life's Dominion* (New York: Knopf, 1993): 68–101, and Ronald Dworkin, "The Center Hold!" *The New York Review of Books* (August 13, 1992): 29.

8. Nivedita Menon, "Abortion and the Law: Questions for Feminists," *Canadian Journal of Women and the Law* 6 (1993): 103.

government-sponsored amniocentesis tests, which have had the effect of informing women of the sex of their fetus. Some women have made explicit decisions to use that information to abort their fetuses. The debate in India has turned on whether there should be legislation to circumvent the right of abortion, whether instead there should be legislation to restrict government-sponsored amniocentesis tests in the countrysides, or whether there should be an attempt to limit information from those amniocentesis tests. There has also been opposition to all three forms of legislation from within the feminist movement itself. I believe an examination of the terms of that debate can illuminate the difficulties inherent in Dworkin's analysis of which bodies matter in his sliding scale of morally better to morally worse abortions, a sliding scale he justifies through his argument for a metric of disrespect for the intrinsic value of life.

But my primary purpose in addressing the questions raised about the role of right in the feminist debate goes beyond my response to Ronald Dworkin. The Indian debate is crucial to feminists for at least two reasons. First, it addresses the question of whether or not we should insist on entitlement as opposed to duty, not only within development programs sponsored by governments but also as crucial to promoting the equality of women. My own position, as I argue elsewhere and as the notion of minimum conditions of individuation indicates,[9] will be that we must insist on entitlement rather than duty or the limit of entitlement in spite of the difficulties raised by the example of and the debate within India. Second, I address the question of India because its acknowledgment of the question of entitlement and its relationship to development programs has been an advanced and sophisticated contribution to the examination of both the power and the limitations of any theory of right.

I applaud Dworkin's timely defense of procreative autonomy as a fundamental right and the philosophical subtlety and doctrinal power of his defense of a woman's fundamental right to procreative autonomy under the First Amendment of the U.S. Constitution. Dworkin's argument that the heated debate over abortion has a religious dimension is made forcefully. I agree with him that one possible doctrinal defense of the protection of the right to procreative autonomy does

---

9. See Cornell, *The Imaginary Domain*.

come under the First Amendment clause, but I continue to disagree with his defense of a metric of disrespect of the intrinsic value of life. For Dworkin, such a metric of disrespect is based on the distinction between the state's encouragement of responsibility and the state's use of its coercive power. This distinction follows from Dworkin's recognition that the value he defends as the intrinsic value of life is a contestable value. Freedom of religion demands that we respect such a contestable value.

In spite of my appreciation for the doctrinal power of Dworkin's argument, I continue to disagree with him about the applicability of a metric of disrespect in the arena of abortion. Ultimately, our disagreement is threefold. First, I believe that we should defend the right of abortion as a matter of equality. A defense based on equality demands that we turn to an examination of exactly how women's bodies have been valued and devalued in the law. Such a reexamination is crucial because of its symbolic power. We have to face the way in which feminine sexual difference has been used to deny women equality. This difference is not just a matter of fact but a matter of evaluation. Thus, the reevaluation of feminine sexual difference is implicit in a legal defense of what Dworkin calls procreative autonomy. The focus on the valuation and the need for reevaluation of feminine sexual difference demands also that we reexamine, and indeed perhaps bring into visibility for the first time, the horrific wrong to women in the denial or the limitation of their procreative freedom and autonomy.

My second disagreement with Dworkin is based upon the denial and limitation of a woman's right to abortion as devastating to her achievement of the minimum conditions of individuation. Therefore, I defend abortion on demand while Dworkin does not. Again, we must understand this devastation within the context of the devaluation of feminine sexual difference more generally. Ironically, the reduction of the feminine within sexual difference to the maternal function downplays the overwhelming power and significance of maternity. Part of the recognition of the wrong to women not only demands that we reevaluate the feminine within sexual difference, it also demands that we reexamine the significance of the power of the maternal. I will suggest that it is precisely the power of the maternal and the terror of that power that have unconsciously influenced both the rhetoric and the heat in the abortion debate.

My third disagreement with Dworkin is that I would be much

more hesitant than he is to contend that we can bring moral recognition into the legal arena of abortion. My hesitancy is based upon allowing a woman's procreative autonomy to include the expression of her imaginary domain as the crucial determinant of the meaning of her pregnancy. It should be unnecessary for a state to encourage responsibility in women. The impact of a pregnancy on a woman's body forces her to accept that responsibility. If one looks at the studies of pregnant women, very few women take the decision to abort lightly.[10] Why do we need the state to encourage responsibility? We should not allow the state to encourage responsibility if it implies a view of women as irresponsible, as killing mothers who do not take maternity seriously. The encouragement of responsibility at the level of the state can itself be read as an inherent devaluation of women's own capacity for moral judgment. In like manner, it makes the state as important a determinant of the meaning of pregnancy as the woman herself. Thus my argument ultimately turns on the fundamentally liberal idea that it is the woman who must have narrative power over her own decision. The narrative power is as important for her "personhood" as the decision itself. Therein lies my third disagreement with Dworkin: the basis of how and why the feminine sex is thought to matter or not matter within the arena of the law.

This analysis of the devaluation of the feminine within sexual difference is crucial if we defend the right to abortion as based on equality. To rethink equality so as to deconstruct the difference/equality debate that is often mistakenly presented as an either/or,[11] we need to understand the symbolic and normative dimensions of how bodies come to matter. We need a theory of equality and of right based on the protection of minimum conditions of individuation. We can use this theory of equality to justify the measurement of feminine sexual difference as of equivalent value in relation to other expressions of sexuate "being." Equivalency, then, does not necessarily demand formal likeness or simple identity between men and women as the basis of equality. In conclusion, I will argue that we can only truly

---

10. Carol Gilligan, *In a Different Voice: Psychological Theory and Women's Development* (Cambridge: Harvard University Press, 1982).

11. Drucilla Cornell, "Gender, Sex, and Equivalent Rights," in *Feminists Theorize the Political*, ed. Judith Butler and Joan Scott (New York: Routledge, Chapman and Hall, 1992); and Joan Scott, "Deconstructing Equality versus Difference: Or, the Uses of Poststructuralist Theory for Feminism," in *Conflicts in Feminism*, ed. Marianne Hirsh and Evelyn Fox Keller (New York: Routledge, Chapman and Hall, 1990).

come to terms with the significance of abortion—both in terms of the psychic life of individual women and for a program of feminist legal reform—if we situate abortion within a context of mother right and reproductive freedom.

The Social and Symbolic Conditions for Bodily Integration and Individuation

My account of how and why individuation is an extremely fragile achievement, and one made possible only by spinning out a meaning for and image of a coherent self from a pregiven web of social ties, symbolic relations, and primordial identifications, is based on the writings of Jacques Lacan. Lacan relied on an interpretation of Sigmund Freud's notion of the bodily ego. I believe my presentation of Lacan's theory of how an infant comes to perceive himself or herself as a coherent whole or self is compatible with divergent psychoanalytic perspectives. It is not, however, compatible with philosophical positions advanced in political and legal philosophy that fail to give full weight to the social and symbolic constitution of the self. This is why my own account has a certain affinity with communitarianism and its critique of a version of radical individualism.

As I have argued before, insight into the relational and symbolic constitution of the self does not necessarily lead to any political and legal conclusions. But such insight does demand that we rethink the importance of protecting the symbolic, social, and legal conditions in which individuation can be maintained. The Lacanian account allows us to understand just how fragile the achievement of individuation is, and how easily it can be undermined, if not altogether destroyed, by either a physical or symbolic assault on the projection of bodily integrity. The denial of the right to abortion should be understood as a serious symbolic assault on a woman's sense of self precisely because it thwarts her projection of bodily integration and places the woman's body in the hands and imaginings of others who would deny her coherence by separating her womb from her self.[12] But before we can fully understand why the denial of the right to abortion can and should be understood as a symbolic dismemberment of a woman's

---

12. I am using the word *self* here to indicate what Lacan means by ego identity in the mirror stage (described in next paragraph of text). Jacques Lacan, *Écrits: A Selection*, trans. Alan Sheridan (New York and London: W. W. Norton and Company, 1977).

body, we need to explore Lacan's explanation of the constitution of selfhood.

For Lacan, there is an impressive singularity that distinguishes human beings from other primates: their reaction on seeing their mirror image. Between the ages of six and eighteen months, human infants display jubilation at the recognition of their mirror image. Lacan refers to this period as the mirror stage. In comparison, chimpanzees, for example, lose interest in an image of themselves as soon as they realize it is just an image and not another chimpanzee. The jubilation, according to Lacan, lies in the human infant's first experience of perceiving itself as a whole. This perception of wholeness occurs when the infant is, in reality, in a state of complete helplessness. Thus, the image functions both as a projection and an anticipation of what the infant might become but is not now.

This disjuncture between the reality of helplessness and the projection of a unified self is an effect of our premature birth such that our perceptual apparatus is much more advanced than our motor functions. In other words, during the mirror stage—which, I would argue, is not a stage in the traditional sense, because one never completes it— the infant can perceive what it cannot produce. The infant obviously cannot provide itself with the mirror image so that the experience can be repeated. Thus, the infant is completely dependent on others in order to have the experience repeated and its projected identity and bodily integrity confirmed. In this way, the sight of another human being, including the infant's actual image in a mirror, or in the eyes of the mother or primary caretaker, is crucial for shaping identity. This other, who, in turn, both appears as whole and confirms the infant in its projected and anticipated coherence by mirroring him or her as a self, becomes the matrix of a sense of continuity and coherence that the child's present state of bodily disorganization would belie.

It is only through this mirroring process that the infant comes to have an identity. The body's coherence depends on the future anteriority of the projection in that what has yet to be is imagined as already given. The infant, then, does not recognize a self that is already "there" in the mirror. Instead, the self is constituted, in and through the mirroring process, as other to its reality of bodily disorganization and by having itself mirrored by others as a whole.

The power that mirroring has over the infant is not, then, the recognition of similarity in the mirror, a "wow, that looks like me" reaction to the image; rather it is the *anticipated* motor unity associated with bodily integration. Thus, it is not the exact image, but the reflection of bodily integrity that does not match the infant's own body, that *matters*. In this sense, there is always a moment of fictionality, of imagined anticipation, in and through which the ego is constituted.

The sense of self-identity is internalized in the adult and continues to involve the projection of bodily integrity and its recognition by others. Our "bodies," then, are never really our own. The idea that we own our bodies is a fantasy that imagines as completed that which always remains in the future anterior. Therefore, to protect "ourselves" from threats to our bodily integrity and our sense of capability and well-being, we have to protect the future into which we project our unity and have our bodily integrity respected by others. To reduce the self to just "some body" is to rob it of this future anterior. This is the meaning of my earlier statement that the mirror stage is not really a stage at all because the self never completes it. As I understand it, the mirror stage is never simply overcome in a "higher" stage of development; it is a turning point through which the self must always come around, again and again, to guard continuously against social and symbolic forces that lead to dismemberment, disintegration, and total destruction of the self.

I want to turn briefly to Lacan's critique of ego psychology. Lacan's notion is that the self as an ego and not a subject is caught in a vicious circle of ego confirmation. This Lacanian circle of egoism is destructive, not only because it forever turns in on itself and is fated to be repeated, but because in its repetitions, which seek to realize the illusion of autoreflection as the truth of the ego, the Other upon whom this illusion is dependent is then erased. This moment of erasure is itself erased by a defensive posturing that reduces the Other to a mirror—an object that plays no active role in the constitution of the ego—and therefore cannot threaten the ego's imagined self-sufficiency by distorting or denying the truth of the ego's projected image of itself as self-constituted. Lacan explicitly connects what he calls "the era of the ego" with the objectification of women as mirrors who, as mirror objects of confirmation for men, must not be allowed to ascend to the position of subjects.[13] I will explore the full significance of this insight in explaining

---

13. See Teresa Brennan, *The Interpretation of the Flesh: Freud and Femininity* (New York and London: Routledge, Chapman and Hall, 1992).

why a feminist program of legal reform is so difficult to maintain and why it must include the rearticulation of the subject and, more specifically, of the subject of rights.

It would be impossible here to answer fully the question "Who comes after the ego?" or even what "the after" would mean if it were not to be thought of in a linear sense of temporality implied by the words *before* and *after*. But I can at least articulate "the beginning" of that other subject. I believe this must be done within a context that assumes the recognition of the alterity of the future from which the self has been constituted and on which, through a projection, it depends for its survival as a self and not just "some body." The feminist legal reform program I advocate depends on no less than the symbolic recognition of this specific egoistic form of misrecognition, particularly as it erases the mother and reduces women to objects that confirm the masculine ego as existing only "for itself." The egoism that finds its value only in its narcissistic investment, in its illusion of being for itself, is not only vicious, it is false. I am using the language of the Kantian moral critique of egoism deliberately.[14] The Kantian critique emphasizes that if people have value only for themselves, they are necessarily of a lesser order of worth because their worth is only narcissistic and thus only instrumentally valuable rather than valuable in itself.[15] Within the Kantian tradition, the "in itself" implies impersonal valuation of the person as a person. The legal system, if it is to be just, recognizes the inviolability that inheres in this impersonal evaluation that has already been given.[16]

I believe my psychoanalytic account is consistent with the rejection of the evaluation of persons based on narcissistic ego investment. As I have already argued, pure narcissistic ego confirmation is both impossible and based on an unethical erasure of the Other.[17] A more interesting point is to be made, however, by asking the question, "Can the value of a person just be 'there' in itself?" In psychoanalytic terms, such value, in the most primordial sense of even achieving a sense of oneself as a self, is always bestowed by the

---

14. See Thomas Nagel, NYU Law School and Philosophy Department, "The Value of Inviolability" (1992) (unpublished manuscript on file with author), for an excellent and succinct discussion of the significance of this distinction in Kantian morality and, more specifically, of how it relates to the value of inviolability.

15. Ibid.

16. Ibid.

17. See Drucilla Cornell, *The Philosophy of the Limit* (New York: Routledge, 1992).

Other. The mystery of impersonal evaluation of the person "in it-self" can be solved only if we remember the time frame of the heteroreflection that gave the person to the infant in order to be valued as a self, "in itself." This time frame is that of the future anterior, in which the self is always coming to be through the projection and the confirmation of the projection of what she or he has been given to be by others.

If we take this time frame, together with the role of the Other in constituting the person, we can begin to think of a legal system as a symbolic Other; a system that does not merely recognize, but consti-tutes and confirms who is to be valued, who is to *matter*. Moreover, if the legal system as a symbolic Other is also understood to operate through the future anterior, then its operations are transitive in that they participate in constituting what is recognized. Such an under-standing of the legal system as "active," as a symbolic Other, validates a feminist claim for legal reform. It allows for a fuller appreciation of how the denial of legal and social symbolization can be so significant to who is confirmed as a self, and, in that sense, guarantees what I have called the minimum conditions of individuation.

This conception also allows us to remove rights from their so-called basis in what has come to be called negative freedom, which traditionally has been defined as freedom from state intervention for already-free persons. But, because the self depends upon the Other for its sense of selfhood, if the state recognizes and confirms who is recognized as a constituted person, then there can never be any sim-ple negative freedom for persons. This move away from a pure con-ception of negative freedom is important in redefining the right to abortion to include conditions for safe abortions. Thus, the removal of state intervention from a woman's choice or right to privacy is not the only definition of abortion as a right, and defending a right to abor-tion need not be so restricted.

Let me now summarize before moving to a discussion of the precise wrong to women in the denial of the right to abortion, and of my argument for reconceiving the content of such a right. This notion begins with a rejection of the current viability analysis that has been used to curtail significantly the right to abortion.[18] First, the projection and confirmation of one's bodily integrity remains fundamental to the

---

18. Planned Parenthood of Eastern Pennsylvania v. Casey, 112 S. Ct. 2791 (1992).

most basic sense of self. The body is socially conceptualized at the very moment we imagine "it" as ours. This "body" is thus distinguished from the undifferentiated thereness, or what Charles Peirce called "Secondness" of the undifferentiated "matter" that subtends the imagined body.[19] Second, I believe the state and the legal system should themselves be understood as symbolic Other(s) that confirm and constitute who is established as a person. It is only from within such a psychoanalytic framework that we can see how other-dependent the sense of self is and why the time frame of its constitution through the future anterior demands the protection of the future self's anticipated continuity and bodily integrity. Without the protection of the future of anticipation, the self cannot project its own continuity. The denial of the right to abortion makes such an anticipation of future wholeness impossible for women. Finally, what is at stake in this loss is not only a loss to the self and the conditions of even a primordial sense of self (the critical significance of which I would not want to deny), but also of the good, dependent on individuation, that I have called the imaginary domain.

The Significance of Projection and Anticipation in the Context of Abortion

My intent is to rearticulate the wrong of the denial of the right to abortion by redefining it as an equivalent right and justifying its protection under the rubric of equality. I will do so by showing how the fragility of a coherent selfhood and the time frame of anticipation necessary for the projection of bodily integrity demand that we rethink this wrong. The ability to internalize the projection of bodily integrity so that one experiences oneself as whole is central to a conception of selfhood. Our embodiment makes this very projected sense of unity all too easy to lose. Throughout our lives, the disjuncture between what we have come to think of as mind and body is always latent, and we depend on it to remain so. In a case of physical assault, one's sense of projected unity is completely shattered. Physical violence imposes a horrifying dualism of the self. In a violent assault we are reduced to "some body," as other to our body. The representation

---

19. See Charles Peirce, *The Collected Papers of Charles Sanders Peirce*, vols. 5 and 6, ed. Charles Hartshorne and Paul Weiss (Cambridge: Belknap Press of Harvard University Press, 1960).

of the body as apart, as "made up" out of parts, is described by Elaine Scarry in her discussion of torture:

> But the relation between body and voice that for the prisoner begins in opposition (the pain is so real that "the question" is unreal, insignificant) and that goes on to become an identification (the question, like the pain, is a way of wounding; the pain, like the question, is a vehicle of self-betrayal) ultimately ends in opposition once more. For what the process of torture does is to split the human being into two, to make emphatic the ever present but, except in the extremity of sickness and death, only latent distinction between a self and a body, between a "me" and "my body." The "self" or "me" which is experienced on the one hand as more private, more essentially at the center, and on the other hand as participating across the bridge of the body in the world, is "embodied" in the voice, in language. The goal of the torturer is to make the one, the body, emphatically and crushingly *present* by destroying it, and to make the other, the voice, *absent* by destroying it.[20]

The self-betrayal of which Scarry speaks here is the betrayal of answering the torturer's questions "against one's will." I want to take Scarry's insight into just how shattering it is to have the factitiousness of the integrated body and the self's coherence so brutally exposed and place it into the context of abortion. At this point, I must also add a description of the full horror of this self-betrayal, of the ripping apart of the self and of undergoing both the apartness of the body and its dismemberment into parts in a self-inflicted abortion in which the hand operates against the womb.

In the novel *Nothing Grows by Moonlight*,[21] the anonymous voice of the woman narrator describes the anguish of a self-inflicted abortion in precise terms of the loss of self, as I have used the word, and of world, as Scarry uses it:

> Then I grabbed the knitting needle. I had to dry my hands. Drops of sweat were running down my temples. Then it growled again,

---

20. See Elaine Scarry, *The Body in Pain* (New York: Oxford University Press, 1985), 48–49.
21. Torborg Nedreaas, *Nothing Grows by Moonlight* (Lincoln: University of Nebraska Press, 1987).

the sound rose, the growling sprang loose from the horizon and flashed across the sky. Two sharp flashes of lightning, then a waterfall of rain. It clattered behind the mountain, reluctantly, subdued. It came like cannon fire, letting loose and being flung like flashing sheets of iron across the sky. There was a blinding light from a lightning flash, two flashes; then all hell broke loose. The sky exploded with a boom right above my head. The mountains on the other side of the fjord burst and collapsed. A thousand cannonballs fell and rolled around for a while across the earth made of iron. Lightning followed in their footsteps.[22]

The voice's raging despair blends with the narrator's remembrance of the storm's violence as it creates a surreal world around her, and as her own world collapses. Her remembrance is embodied in the metaphor of her own anguish as "the hell that broke loose in the storm." The voice continues:

I'd gotten one hand inside. The rest of my body was numb with fear. My tongue was without sensation and swollen in my throat. Nausea was sitting frozen in the back of my brain. The room was illuminated in blinding flashes, wiped away, and lit again. The white world was collapsing above me in a madness of noise.

My fingers had gotten hold of something. It was without sensation. But pains of fear were flowing through my fingers, which had found the uterus opening. I snarled through my teeth, 'God, God, let the earth perish. Now I'll do it, now I'll do it.'[23]

The self-betrayal here is the self-dismemberment undertaken to prevent the body from overtaking one's self. The body's potential overbearance is the pregnancy, which the narrator believes she cannot allow to come to fruition in light of her class impoverishment and the ostracization she and the child would endure because she is unmarried. The cruel contradiction is that dismemberment is the only way she can preserve the illusion that her body is her own, an illusion that is brutally shattered by the infliction of the unbearable pain by her own hand:

---

22. Ibid., 189.
23. Ibid.

Then I set to. Drops of sweat ran down the bridge of my nose, and I noticed that I was sitting there with my tongue hanging out of my mouth. Because something burst. I could hear it inside my head from the soft crunch of tissues that burst. The pain ran along my spine and radiated across my loins and stomach. I screamed [. . .] but there wasn't a sound. More, more, push more, find another place. It had to be wrong. And I held the very tip of the weapon between my thumb and forefinger to find the opening to my uterus once more. It was difficult but I thought I'd succeeded. The steel needle slid a little heavily against something[. . . .] More, more don't give up. Tissues burst. The sweat blinded my eyes. I heard a long rattling groan coming out of me while my hand let the weapon do its work with deranged courage.[24]

I recognize, of course, that not all illegal abortions are self-inflicted and thus do not necessarily represent the kind of self-betrayal the narrator describes. Yet, prior to *Roe v. Wade*,[25] there is no doubt that class, racial, and national oppression left many women with no option other than to endure a self-inflicted abortion.[26] This is why I deliberately rely on a working-class voice to tell the story of the anguish of a self-inflicted abortion. I also use the passive voice implied by the word *endure*, because it mocks the attempt to label this kind of terrible physical suffering a "choice."

Testimonials to the horror of illegal abortions have not changed the picture of the reduction of women to "some body" within the conditions of safety that legal abortions provide. The experience of splitting through the exposure of the factitiousness of bodily integrity still remains. One could argue that this kind of splitting that so effectively dismembers the "self," as it reduces the imagined unified body to its parts, is present in all experiences related to illness and medical treatment. But there are many studies that show that as the right of bodily integrity is accorded more respect, and the patient is treated more like a "self" and not just a diseased body, the primordial sense of self is assaulted less. As the self is attacked in its projected coherence by the splitting of illness, the sense of entitlement to a self

24. Ibid., 189–90.
25. *Roe v. Wade*, 410 U.S. 113 (1973).
26. Ibid., 149.

protected by the legal recognition of the right to bodily integrity is
even more necessary.

Of course, bodily integrity always remains imaginary. But there is
no self without this imaginary projection. Scarry makes this point
when she insists that violent assaults on the body always imply an
attack on the conditions under which the self had been constituted
and thus could be reconstituted. Rendering abortion illegal undermines the entitlement to a self at a time when it is most needed to
protect the necessary projection that there is a self that is still "there,"
and more specifically, that the womb is part of that self, not apart from
it. Wombs do not wander except in the wild imagination of some men
who have come up with very colorful stories of what a womb "is."[27]
To separate the woman from her womb or to reduce her to it is to deny
her the conditions of selfhood that depend on the ability to project
bodily integrity.

The denial of the right to abortion enforces the kind of splitting
that inevitably and continuously undermines a woman's sense of
self. Her womb and body are no longer hers to imagine. They have
been turned over to the imagination of others, and those imaginings
are then allowed to reign over her body as law. The wrong in denial
of the right to abortion is often thought to be that the women is
forced to turn over her body to the fetus as an invader. The wrong as
I reconceived it involves a woman, at a crucial moment, having her
body turned over to the minds of men. Judith Jarvis Thompson's
essay on abortion examples the first argument.[28] She argues that we
do not, under our law or moral institutions, believe that any person
should be forced to rescue another person. To draw out the implications of this position, Thompson uses the analogy of a person being
hooked up to a very talented violinist whose life is in danger, and
whose accomplishments and value to society are clearly established,
in order to save the artist's life. She argues that even in this situation,
we would not impose a duty to rescue. If we would not impose such
a duty in that case, why would we contradict our law and moral
institutions by insisting that women should be required to rescue
fetuses whose lives have yet to begin?[29] But Thompson's argument

---

27. Scarry, *The Body in Pain*.
28. Judith Jarvis Thomson, "A Defense of Abortion," *Philosophy and Public Affairs*
1:1 (Fall 1971).
29. Ibid.

itself involves an imagined projection of the relationship between the fetus and the mother, and one I believe should not be allowed to hold sway over our own imaginings, because the portrayal does not adequately envision the uniqueness of the condition of pregnancy. This failure is inseparable from the inscription of feminine sexual difference within the so-called human in which pregnancy is analogized with a relationship between two already independent persons. This formulation, in other words, assumes that the womb and the fetus is other to the woman rather than a part of her body. Such an assumption implies a view of the woman's body and her "sex" and a conception of the meaning of pregnancy that cannot be separated from imagined projections that erase the specificity of feminine sexual difference. If we reimagine the pregnant woman as her unique self, and also as pregnant, we get another picture. To quote Barbara Katz Rothman:

> Consider in contrast the woman-centered model of pregnancy I have presented: the baby not planted within the mother, but flesh of her flesh, part of her. Maybe, as very early in an unwanted pregnancy, a part of her like the ovum itself was part of her, an expendable or even threatening part, or maybe, as is most often the case by the end of a wanted pregnancy, an essential part of her, a treasured aspect of her being. If one thinks of pregnancy this way, then the rights argument is an absurdity. It is not the rights of one autonomous being set against the rights of another, but the profound alienation of the woman set against part of herself.[30]

How one "sees" a woman and her "sex" is central to understanding the status of the fetus. Although Rothman speaks explicitly of suits against the woman by her fetus, I am concerned here with her challenge to the prevalent image of pregnancy. Any analogy of a fetus to an already autonomous being rests on the erasure of the woman; it reduces her to a mere environment for the fetus. This vision of the woman is connected necessarily to one's view of the fetus, because the fetus can only be seen as a person if the woman is erased or

---

30. Barbara Katz Rothman, *Recreating Motherhood: Ideology and Technology in a Patriarchal Society* (New York: W. W. Norton & Co., 1989), 160–61.

reduced to an environment. Once the woman is put back into the picture, the pregnancy is no longer like any of the conditions to which it is analogized because, as I have already argued, it is unique. Thus, I agree with George Fletcher when he argues:

> The point is rather that any attempt to draw an analogy to abortion will be imperfect and deceptive. . . . The relationship between the fetus and its carrying mother is not like that between the dialysis-needy musician and a stranger with good kidneys. Nor is it like any other ingenious hypothetical cases that Kiss poses in an attempt to elicit our moral intuitions about killing and letting die. The fetus is not like a pedestrian whom a driver hits (when her brakes fail) in order to avoid hitting two others. Nor is it like the drowning boy whom a swimmer may save or not. Nor is it like a man overboard in a shipwreck whom we keep out of the overfilled lifeboat. These other standard characters make up the pantheon of moral philosophy as it has been plied at least since Carneades imagined the problem of two shipwrecked sailors fighting for the same plank to avoid drowning.[31]

All these examples involve cases of individuals who are clearly human beings. Fletcher's insight is to argue that whatever the fetus is, it is not a fully developed human being, and therefore the analogies, such as the one Thompson uses, to other justified or excused killings cannot hold. Abortion, then, is not killing in the traditional analytical sense and cannot be adequately discussed under that rubric. As a result, Fletcher concludes that we need another framework in order to adequately analyze abortion. I agree with him, and it is obviously my intention to provide such an alternative framework.

My addition here, however, is that the erasure of the uniqueness of the fetus, which Fletcher emphasizes, cannot be separated from the erasure of the uniqueness of the condition of pregnancy, which in turn cannot be separated from the failure of our legal system to symbolize and reimagine the specificity of the feminine within sexual difference. More sharply put, the status of the fetus comes into question once the uniqueness of pregnancy as a condition different from

---

31. George Fletcher, "Reflections on Abortion," unpublished manuscript on file with the author. Columbia University.

all others is recognized, and thus it turns on how the idea of the woman and her "sex" is viewed. The construction of the womb as a container, as an environment for the fetus, is just that—a construction—an imaginary projection that gives meaning to what cannot actually be seen. Here we have an extraordinarily clear example of how a woman's "sex" is constructed. To imagine a womb as a container is to imagine "it," not to know "it" in its truth. But for purposes of trying to provide an adequate framework to defend abortion as a right, we also need to "see" just how divergent constructions of the woman's sex, and particularly of her womb, will necessarily affect how the fetus is conceived and how abortion will be viewed. If we think of the womb as a part of the woman, if her body is respected as opaque, as bound, if the woman's "insides" cannot be forcibly "exposed" as an outside, then the idea that the woman and her body can be rendered transparent is denied. This view of the woman as a container for the fetus reduces her "sex" to a maternal function. Rothman, for example, reenvisions women as "whole selves" with reproductive power and creativity. As she notes, this redefinition changes the way abortion is conceptualized. If we reduce women (consciously or unconsciously) to the maternal function, then we "see" them as mothers, ironically, even as they seek, through abortion, to avoid becoming mothers. To quote Rothman:

> By creating this fetus, this unborn child as a social being, we turn this woman into "its mother"—defining her in terms of the fetus even as she seeks to avoid making a baby, avoid becoming a mother. If women controlled abortion, controlled not only the clinics, but the values and the thinking behind abortion, would we make such a distinction between contraception, not letting this month's egg grow, and abortion, not letting this month's fertilized egg grow? Or could we put early abortion back together with contraception, into the larger idea of birth control, and say that until we feel we've made a baby, an abortion is stopping a baby from happening, not killing one? Seeing women as creators, not containers, means seeing abortion as refusing to create, not destroying that which we contain.[32]

---

32. Rothman, *Recreating Motherhood*, 123.

Reducing a woman to the maternal function in the crude form of designating her "sex" as a container explicitly denies her the right of bodily integrity and thus the conditions of selfhood, in which a woman can project the meaning of her own "insides" as "hers." What is a woman under this fantasy of her "sex"? She is a *what*, a thing, a container, an environment, not a *who*, a self. We do not need to be essentialists to argue that the feminine "sex" is both more and other to this reduction of her "sex" to a container.

To summarize, the way in which a fetus and the woman is "seen"—and I put *seen* in quotation marks to remind us again of my argument that one does not see a woman directly but imagines her through projections of the significance or lack of same of her sex—is right at the heart of the abortion debate. This is a classic example of precisely why a feminist program of legal reform and the rearticulation of rights cannot proceed without the reimagining and the resymbolization of the feminine within sexual difference which takes back "ourselves" from the masculine imaginary.

Men and women create themselves by projecting the body as integrated, as being one's "own." The body matters as a psychic object, and its reality always has a phantasmatical dimension. Bodily integrity is actualized through the externalized fantasy one has of one's body, although this externalized idea of one's body as one's "own" can be effectively undermined. Any experience of illness graphically teaches us that lesson. But it is precisely the very fragility of bodily integrity that makes its protection so crucial. To deny women the conditions in which they can project bodily integrity by turning their bodies over to the projections of others is to deny them a basic condition of selfhood. There is also an important temporal dimension to the projection and anticipation of bodily integrity which can help us reemphasize how devastating the denial of the right to abortion can be to women, and which will also help us in understanding more deeply what is wrong with the image of maternal relationship that Judith Jarvis Thompson gives us in her discussion of abortion.

For Thompson the individual wakes up to find oneself—and I am using the word *oneself* to reflect the way in which Thompson's rhetoric removes the issue of abortion from "sex"—connected against one's will to a dialysis-needy musician. I have already argued that in order to develop an adequate analytic framework we have no choice but to confront "sex" and, more specifically, the way in which feminine sexual difference is both imagined and then symbolized in the law so as to reflect and reinforce such imaginary projections. The classic example is the image of the womb as a container. But there is a temporal dimension inherent in Thompson's analysis that it is also important both to note and to criticize. If one took the time frame implied in the suddenness of waking and finding oneself connected into the context of abortion, then it would seem that the wrong of the denial of abortion begins to take effect only at the moment that the woman finds herself connected and thus with the imposed duty to rescue. But under my analysis of how bodily integrity must be continuously confirmed, the wrong in the denial of the right to abortion begins long before that.

There are innumerable pre-*Roe* accounts of how the fear of unwanted pregnancies and illegal abortions haunted women's sense of themselves long before any woman herself actually became pregnant. As part of that generation, I remember the horrific stories of knitting needles, back-alley washrooms, lives lost, and long-lasting damage to the women's reproductive capacity. Sex was haunted by the specter and the fear of what an unwanted pregnancy would mean for the woman when abortion was illegal. I am aware that many right-to-lifers would defend the creation of such a specter as one of the advantages of rendering abortion illegal, since it might help prevent young people from engaging in the "sin" of unmarried sex. I want to reemphasize that what is at stake in the imposition of this specter is the serious undermining of women's ability to project their own bodily integrity over time. This undermining has serious implications because it becomes internalized as the inability to imagine oneself as whole. The very constitution of selfhood cannot be separated from the protection of the future projection of the woman's self as a whole body. The threat takes effect before any woman actually has to face an unwanted pregnancy. Here we have an important example of how the symbolization of a woman's "sex" has a constitutive effect on what we have to come to think of as selfhood. Not only is a woman's individuality not just given, it is limited in its very definition by certain symbolizations of her "sex" in the law. This reduces her to those definitions. To deny a woman the right to abortion is to make her body not "hers" at the same time that it reduces her to her "sex," limitedly defined as maternal function. Such restrictive symbolizations deny a woman her imaginary domain.

I have suggested that there is a truth implicit in Thompson's otherwise misguided comparison of pregnancy with an enforced relationship with a dialysis-needy violinist. In her presentation of the condition of the one who is forcibly tied to the musician we have an image of how imposed restrictions on bodily integrity affect a sense of self. Thompson's thesis is that one must be able to keep one's body for oneself as an essential aspect of one's very personhood. But because she desexualizes her own discourse, she undermines the power of her own argument in defense of that thesis. We can fully understand the wrong in the denial of abortion if we understand just how dependent a sense of self is on projections of bodily integrity. Put simply, there is no adequate way to think about abortion without having also to think about "sex." That point should be obvious. The reality that it has not been is reflected in the tortured and failed attempts to find an analogy of abortion in so-called human experience. My additional suggestion here is that this failure is not a coincidence but itself an expression of how the feminine within sexual difference has been subsumed in the human and thus erased or symbolized as the maternal function, a symbolization that makes it difficult if not impossible to defend the right to abortion. Once we understand that the conditions of women "being for themselves" have been systematically denied them by the dearth of symbolizations of their "sex," then we can see how perceptions of what a woman is have been shaped by the law and must be actively challenged in the validity of their meaning in a feminist program of legal reform. This challenge in the context of abortion demands that we rearticulate the right beyond its current encasement in an analytical structure that is inseparable, as I have already argued, from the reduction of feminine sexual difference to the maternal structure, a reduction necessary for the construction of the fetus as a social being different from other persons only because of its environment. Now that I have redefined the wrong of the denial of the right to abortion, let me turn to the rearticulation of the right that I believe flows from it.

The Rearticulation of the Right to Abortion

Abortion should be protected as an equivalent right necessary for the establishment of the minimum conditions of individuation for women, which must include the protection of the individual's projection of bodily integrity. I stress the word *individual* here to reiterate my argument that what the feminine within sexual difference "is" has been defined by the masculine imaginary, then resymbolized in law so that women are not representable as fully individuated beings with their own imaginary domain. The move from the objectification of the feminine within sexual difference as a "what," in the case of abortion, for example, as a container for a fetus, and to a "who," a sexuate being with her own imaginary dimension, is precisely what my own rearticulation of the right to abortion hopes to recognize.

The right to abortion should not be understood as the right to choose an abortion, but as the right to realize the legitimacy of the individual woman's projections of her own bodily integrity, consistent with her imagination of herself at the time that she chooses to terminate her pregnancy. Once the right is rearticulated in this manner, we can provide an alternative analysis that completely rejects the conclusion of *Webster*,[33] in which the Supreme Court stated that it is consistent with the right to abortion to allow states to enjoin public facilities and employees from providing abortions, because such an injunction purportedly does not place a governmental obstacle in the way of the right defined abstractly as "the right to choose." This alternative analysis rejects also the denial of Medicaid coverage for abortions, which was similarly defended as no impediment to "the right to choose."

We can further reject the "undue burden" analysis set forth in *Casey*[34] in which the Court upheld a series of state restrictions on both the exercise of the right to abortion and states' rights to determine who should shape the way a woman's decision to terminate her pregnancy should be viewed. My rearticulation of the right is consistent with the imaginary dimension of the projection of bodily integrity. Once we understand that the right to abortion is essential to bodily integrity and individuation, we can see that what is at stake in the states' efforts to regulate abortion is the woman's right to be insulated from state imposition of the views of others on her own imaginary. States have argued that their programs regulating abortion are intended to inform women of the seriousness of the act terminating pregnancy. Such efforts deny the woman's status as a fully individuated human being, capable of

---

33. Webster v. Reproductive Health Services, 492 U.S. 490 (1989).
34. *Planned Parenthood of Eastern Pennsylvania v. Casey*, 2791.

acting and of giving meaning to that action without help from the state. It is not only an issue of "who" can make the ultimate decision, as Justices Souter, Kennedy, and O'Connor argue in their opinion in *Casey,* that attempts to justify the legitimacy of certain of the provisions of the Abortion Control Act passed in Pennsylvania in 1982 in order to regulate abortion.[35] It is also "how" that decision may be exercised. The protection of "how" is essential for the establishment of respect for women as fully individuated sexuate beings with their own imaginary domain and thus their own understanding of what it means to end a pregnancy.

This rearticulation is transitive in that it hopes to promote the bringing into "being" of what has been both explicitly and implicitly denied as "true," the equivalent value of the feminine within sexual difference. This denial is particularly evident in court cases that have denied the validity of women's equality claims in the supposed name of recognizing a difference that is just "there" in its meaning prior to the evaluation. The debate over whether or not women should have the right to abortion as well as how that right is to be articulated forces us to face the truth that how a woman's body matters is inseparable from how "it" is symbolized and whether "it" is evaluated as of equivalent value to the masculine body. The reevaluation of the feminine within sexual difference as of equivalent value changes inevitably how a woman's body is thought to matter in the sense of both material reality and significance.

Privacy v. Equality Rethought

In *Roe v. Wade,* the Supreme Court first recognized the right of privacy to include the right to choose abortion as a limited right in which the state's interest in regulating abortion would gain ever greater legitimacy as the pregnancy approached birth. The Court argued against the appellant and some amici that the woman's right to abortion could not be absolute, even though it would take a compelling state interest to justify regulation, and even though there was much rhetoric in earlier privacy cases that the right of privacy was absolute in the sense that a state absolutely could not interfere with certain

---

35. Ibid.

zones of personal life. From the outset of its analysis, the *Roe* Court realized the difficulty of defining a right of privacy that would not be absolute in the aforementioned sense and yet would recognize how crucial the right to abortions was for women. The Court sought a compromise position through its viability analysis. To quote the majority opinion:

> Appellant's argument's that Texas either has no valid interest at all in regulating the abortion decision, or no interest strong enough to support any limitation upon the woman's sole determination, are unpersuasive. As noted above, a State may properly assert important interests in safe-guarding health, in maintaining medical standards, and in protecting potential life. At some point in pregnancy, these respective interests become compelling to sustain regulation of the factors that govern the abortion decision. The privacy right involved, therefore, cannot be said to be absolute.[36]

The Court's use of the phrase "at some point in pregnancy" meant that a specific point had to be located and fixed. But the Court had difficulty making this determination, once it rejected protection of the fetus as a person for purposes of the Fourteenth Amendment. The state's compelling interest thus could not be justified as protecting the rights of the fetus as against those of "The Mother." If the state was not concerned with protecting the fetus per se, then where exactly did its interest lie? The Court attempted to develop a compromise by finding a substantial increase in the state's interest as the fetus reached viability. Use of the word *viability* simultaneously allowed the Court to recognize that one cannot meaningfully speak of persons until the fetus is outside the mother's body, while recognizing that there is a point in pregnancy when the fetus could live outside the mother's body. It was at this point that the fetus's definition as a part of the mother no longer seemed to weigh in favor of the mother as primary decision maker. The point at which the fetus as a person could be realized took on normative significance for the justices who signed the majority opinion. But even once they had justi-

---

36. *Roe v. Wade*, 153.

fied why what they called viability should have normative significance enough to change the weight given to the state's interest in regulating abortion, they still had the difficulty of deciding when viability actually took place. The key was when the fetus could live outside the mother's body with the important qualification "with artificial aid."[37] The best definition they could derive once they had added the qualification "with artificial aid" included a spread: "Viability is usually placed at about seven months (28 weeks) but may occur earlier, even at 24 weeks."[38]

Thus, the point at which the state's interest seemed to gain greater weight was left unclear. Yet clarity was desperately needed for the framework of the decision because viability was supposed to serve as a crucial point in the Court's argument, which stated that the right to abortion could not be absolute even though the fetus was not a person for the purpose of the Fourteenth Amendment. Once the right was defined as not absolute, and the state's compelling state interest left imprecise, the possibility of justifying ever greater restrictions on the right to abortion was left open.

This possibility has now been actualized in post-*Roe* decisions.[39] The line of post-*Roe* cases with ever more elaborate and restricted readings of *Roe* makes it easy to forget the connection the Court at least tried to draw—admittedly with much waffling—between their viability analysis and the argument against making the right to abortion absolute. Prior to viability, the trimester division of the pregnancy could be interpreted to mean that until then the state had no compelling state interest to justify the regulation of abortion. Justice Blackmun's separation of viability and the trimester division should be noted here. The trimester approach allowed Blackmun to indicate, first, when the right to abortion could be rendered absolute, i.e., in the first trimester, and second, when concern for the woman's health would allow greater regulation of the abortion facilities provided for her. Greater regulation of facilities in the second trimester was to be

---

37. Ibid., 160.
38. Ibid.
39. See *Planned Parenthood of Eastern Pennsylvania v. Casey*, 2791. (Most post-*Roe* decisions define the issue of abortion rights as a battle between the fetus's rights and the woman's rights. *Casey*, however, has left the pregnant woman out of the picture entirely, instead focusing on the husband's right to notification.)

allowed. The second trimester begins before viability at least for the purpose of regulating health facilities in which women can have abortions. Viability, on the other hand, was used to analyze when the state's interest in protecting the fetus could be separated from the mother's rights. Viability and the trimester division have often been read in post-*Roe* decisions as if both analyses were solely addressed to concern for the fetus. But Blackmun used the trimester division to focus on women's health. Blackmun has consistently interpreted *Roe* this way in his passionate dissents in post-*Roe* decisions.

The Court's uneasiness and uncertainty over the enunciation of the right to abortion have made *Roe* famous for the equivocation of its language and an easy target for its critics. My suggestion here is that this uncertainty cannot be separated from the Court's recognition of the uniqueness of pregnancy, which seemingly made such a right an unlikely candidate for the privacy rubric since they did not feel fit to define the right as absolute.[40]

But the Court itself argues that because pregnancy and abortion involve a fetus and demand a medical procedure, they cannot be understood as private, at least in terms of the space in which abortion takes place if it is to be conducted safely.[41] One must differentiate the "situation" of abortion from the "situations" confronted in the other privacy decisions:

> The pregnant woman cannot be isolated in her privacy. She carries an embryo and, later a fetus, if one accepts the medical definitions of the developing young in the human uterus. See Dorland's Medical Dictionary 478–79, 547 (24th edition 1965). The situation therefore is inherently different from marital intimacy, or bedroom possession of obscene material, or marriage, or procreation, or education, with which Eisenstadt and Griswold,

---

40. One way out of this dilemma is to define the right to abortion as absolute in order to make its definition consistent with a strong interpretation of what the right of privacy entails. See Jed Rubenfeld, "The Right of Privacy," *Harvard Law Review* 102 (1989): 737, for an example of a powerful argument for this solution to defending abortion under the right to privacy.

41. It is difficult to define abortion as a completely private issue, considering that it is a surgical procedure that should take place in a public facility. Even RU486, a nonsurgical method of abortion, requires medical supervision and thus cannot be considered completely private.

Stanley, Loving, Skinner, and Pierce and Meyer were respectively concerned. As we have intimated above, it is reasonable and appropriate for a state to decide that at some point in time another interest, that of the health of the mother or that of the potential for human life, becomes significantly involved. The woman's right is no longer sole and any right of privacy she possesses must be measured accordingly.[42]

In the first trimester the "public" nature of the abortion led the Court to include only the doctor in the process of decision. Since later cases have rarely mentioned the significance of women's health in justifying certain restrictions on abortions, I will quote *Roe* again in support of the proposition that there was a sincere concern with the need to regulate later abortion in the name of providing women with safe facilities. Again to quote the majority opinion:

In respect to the State's important and legitimate interest in the health of the mother, the compelling point, in the light of present medical knowledge, is at approximately the end of the first trimester. This is so because of the now established medical fact, referred to above at 149, that until the end of the first trimester mortality in abortion may be less than mortality in normal childbirth. It follows that, from and after this point, a State may regulate the abortion procedure to the extent that the regulation reasonably relates to the protection and preservation of maternal health. Examples of permissible state regulation in this area are requirements as to the qualifications of the person who is to perform the abortion; as to the licensure of that person; as to the facility in which the procedure is to be performed, that is whether it must be a hospital or may be a clinic or some other place of less than hospital status; as to the licensing of the facility and the like.[43]

Blackmun has taken his concern for women's health expressed in *Roe* into all of his dissents in post-*Roe* decisions.[44] At the same

---

42. *Roe v. Wade*, 158.

43. Ibid., 162.

44. In *Rust v. Sullivan*, 111 S. Ct. 1759 (1991), the Court considered the constitutionality of a physician's "gag rule" concerning the option of abortion. Justice Blackmun's dissent pointed out that the effect of the gag rule is that a physician's advice is often "wholly unrelated to the [pregnant woman's] situation" *Rust v. Sullivan*, 1788.

time he has tried to separate the legitimacy of the kinds of restrictions listed above in the second trimester from the restrictions that have nothing to do with the woman's health but with the state's imposition of specific interpretations of the meaning of abortion in all stages of pregnancy. In his dissent in *Webster*, Blackmun appealed to the concern for women's health and the need to provide public facilities for abortion explicitly expressed in *Roe*. Unfortunately, this distinction in terms of the kinds of restrictions allowed in the arena of abortion has not been maintained. Instead, the language about the state interest has been stressed and reinterpreted at the same time that the viability standard has been rejected. In her dissent in *Akron v. Akron Center for Reproductive Health*,[45] which clearly influenced the analytical framework of Souter, Kennedy, and O'Connor in *Casey*, Justice O'Connor explicitly rejected the use in *Roe* of viability to determine the point at which the state could claim that it had a

---

In Ohio v. Akron, 497 U.S. 502 (1990), parental notification laws were considered. Blackmun's concern was that the notification requirement would cause up to 22 days delay in the procurement of the abortion. He criticized the majority, writing that "[t]he Court ignores the fact that the medical risks surrounding abortion increase as pregnancy advances and that such delay might push a woman into her second trimester, where the medical risks, economic costs, and state regulation increase dramatically." *Ohio v. Akron*, 520

Relying on the District Court findings in Webster v. Reproductive Health Services, 492 U.S. 490 (1989), Justice Blackmun criticized mandatory viability and lung maturity testing because the procedure has "no medical justification [and] imposes significant additional health risks on both the pregnant woman and the fetus." *Webster v. Reproductive Health Services*, 543. He further noted that

> if women are forced to carry unwanted pregnancy to term, hundreds of thousands of women, in desperation, would defy the law, and place their health and safety in the unclean and unsympathetic hands of back alley abortionists, or they would attempt to perform abortions upon themselves with disastrous results. Every year many women, especially poor and minority women, would die or suffer debilitating physical trauma, all in the name of enforced morality or religious dictates or lack of compassion, as it may be.

Webster v. Reproductive Health Services, 557.

In Planned Parenthood, Kansas City v. Ashcroft, 450 U.S. 398 (1989), the Court considered a statute that mandated that postviability abortions may not take place unless a second physician is in attendance to care for the fetus after it is discharged. The statute applied even where, in light of the abortion method used, it was completely impossible that a live child be born. Blackmun wrote, "[b]y requiring the attendance of a second physician even where the resulting delay may be harmful to the health of the pregnant woman, the statute fails to make clear that the woman's life and health must always prevail over the fetus' life and health when the two are in conflict." *Planned Parenthood, Kansas City v. Ashcroft*, 499.

45. Akron v. Akron Center for Reproductive Health, 462 U.S. 416 (1983).

compelling state interest in the regulation of abortion. To quote O'Connor:

> The choice of viability as the point at which the state interest in potential life becomes compelling is no less arbitrary than choosing any point before viability or any point afterward. Accordingly, I believe that the State's interest in protecting potential human life exists throughout pregnancy.[46]

I will return shortly to why there is a point "after" viability that is surely not arbitrary in the determination of when the state's interest in protecting a baby separately from its mother could become compelling. For now, I want only to emphasize again that *Roe* itself did not just define the state's interest in protecting potential life, but was also concerned with the health of the woman in the second trimester. The woman has completely dropped out of the picture as a source of concern in the post-*Roe* cases. I will strongly argue that the distinction between different kinds of restrictions, such as concern with proper facilities for later-date abortions, and imposition of particular views of women's bodies and their sexuality by state agencies who wish to discourage abortion, should be maintained. The former I will justify, the latter I will reject in accordance with the rearticulation of the right I have already offered. But first we need to return to the dilemma recognized in *Roe* that it is very difficult to justify the right to abortion under the privacy rubric because a "pregnant woman is not alone in her privacy."[47] Therefore, any adequate analysis of the right to abortion must enunciate exactly in which ways the state must both "keep its hands on" and "keep its hands off" in the protection of the right to abortion.

One can try also to expand the right to include a positive concept of liberty as Justice Douglas did in his concurring opinion in *Roe*.[48] But even the expanded definition that emphasizes choice "[i]n the basic decisions of one's life respecting marriage, divorce, procreation, contraception, and the education and upbringing of one's children" does not recognize the full significance of the reality "that a pregnant woman is not alone in her privacy." In the third dimension of what

---

46. Ibid., 460.
47. *Roe v. Wade*, 209.
48. Ibid.

Douglas refers to as the right of privacy and liberty established in the privacy precedents, he emphasizes "the freedom to care for one's health and person, freedom from bodily constraint or compulsion, freedom to walk, stroll or loaf."[49] The first prong of this third dimension comes very close to what I have called the right of bodily integrity. The problem with Douglas's analysis in terms of my argument is twofold. First, his view of the privacy and liberty right elaborated in the line of precedent beginning with *Griswold*[50] does not recognize fully the dependency in the area of health on the provision of public facilities. We need to provide certain conditions in order to have the "freedom to care for one's health and person."[51] This first limitation brings us to the underlying philosophical problem. Douglas's conception of autonomy rests on the view of the self as pregiven, in its autonomy, because the self is from the beginning "in-itself." Of course, Justice Douglas would not have put it that way. But his conception of the self reflects a philosophical conception of the person that underlies much of liberal jurisprudence and which I criticized in the second section of this chapter for failing to come to terms with the full legal significance of the self as a fragile and continuing process of internalization of a projected self-image that has been recognized by others in its coherence and bodily integrity. The other-dependence of the self for its constitution demands that we confront the social and legal conditions under which individuation can be achieved and, in the case of those sexuate beings who have been symbolically engendered as women, that we also confront the conditions for their equality of well-being and capability through the recognition of their right to the minimum conditions of individuation.

The shift in the conception of the self demands that we think of what Douglas has called the right to liberty within a more arching conception of equality. I have advocated that the view of equality is best understood as equality of well-being and capability because such a view is consistent with the "postmodern" critique of the pregiven self that purportedly does not need the establishment of certain conditions for the achievement of individuation. This view of the subject rests on a profound erasure of sexual difference and the complex social and symbolic network in which the engendering of the subject

---

49. Ibid.
50. *Griswold v. Connecticut*, 381 U.S. 479 (1965).
51. *Roe v. Wade*, 213.

there is a crucial connection between the two senses of matter that must be noted—and indeed have been noted in both the classical Greek and Latin definitions of matter—in analysis of the body and, more specifically, of the "matter" of sexual difference. To quote Butler:

> To speak within these classical contexts of bodies that matter is not an idle pun, for to be material means to materialize, where the principle of materialization is precisely what matters about the body, its intelligibility, significance and meaning. In this sense, to know the significance of something is to know how and why it matters, where "to matter" means at once "to materialize" and "to mean."[56]

It's not then just that the Court reasoned from the body but instead that they reasoned from a body already marked in its difference through its symbolic devaluation. The problem was not that difference was recognized, but that it was recognized as not being of equivalent value. In *Geduldig*, equivalent value meant equally worthy of being covered under the insurance program. This case is a classic example of how pregnancy is symbolized as a difference from men precisely so it can be devalued. But this measurement of pregnancy makes sense only within a relational concept of difference that takes men as the measure. To argue that pregnancy is a unique condition does not at all mean that it has to be "de-evaluated" in its differential worth. Indeed, the very use of the word *unique* denies that there is a basis for comparison on the so-called immediate physical level of the body—I use the term *so-called* here to remind the reader of my argument that the "sexed" body is engendered in a symbolic web of meaning, it is never just given. Feminine sexual difference is erased if it is reduced to a relational concept of difference.

Simone de Beauvoir argued this point when she insisted that a woman is defined as man's other and that as so defined she will be always evaluated as both inferior and not individuated.[57] But de Beauvoir could see no way to symbolize the difference of the feminine except within a relational conception of difference. For de Beauvoir, equal recognition of women demanded the repudiation of their "sex,"

---

56. Butler, *Bodies That Matter*, 32.
57. See Simone de Beauvoir, *The Second Sex*, trans. H. M. Parshley (New York: Alfred A. Knopf, 1974).

including its manifestation in pregnancy. The project of reimagining and symbolizing the feminine within sexual difference has to reject the relational concept of difference in which the feminine is devalued, at the same time that it must reject the alternative of neutralizing sex difference in an asexual notion of the human. This project then has nothing to do with either the analysis represented in *Geduldig* or with the differences approach that tries to find women's difference in any appeal to so-called physical "reality," including the "reality" of the body. At its heart is the reevaluation of the feminine so that it can matter as other than its reduction to matter.

If women matter only as the maternal function, then they matter only as matter, as a condition of the flesh and not as subjects. The recognition of pregnancy as a unique condition that must both be valued and symbolized in its uniqueness and in the power of the gift of birth must not reduce the definition of woman to her reproductive capacity. The question of how abortion is defined as a right can play an important role in the resymbolization of pregnancy which does not deny the power of maternity or define a woman only through her reproductive capacity. The denial of the right to abortion reenforces effectively the identification of women with the maternal function. Thus, an equality analysis need not, as Mary Poovey has suggested, "make reproductive capacity the defining characteristic of every woman."[58] It is the denial or restriction of abortion, not an equality analysis, that imposes that definition.

The Specific Justification of the Rearticulation of the Right to Abortion

My equality analysis does not rest on any direct comparison with men but rather on an analysis of the conditions for all sexuate beings to achieve the minimum conditions of individuation. I also wish to have women valued as beings who can constantly contest and reevaluate their own self-images in an endless process of recreation. Crucial to the specifically feminist aspect of this program is the corresponding recognition of the way in which the feminine has been either erased altogether, reduced to a unique physical condition, the maternal function,

---

58. Mary Poovey, "The Abortion Question and the Death of Man," in *Feminists Theorize the Political*, ed. Judith Butler and Joan W. Scott (New York: Routledge, Chapman and Hall, 1992), 241.

or symbolized only within a relational concept of difference. But the goal of this recognition is not the affirmation of a binary system of gender, which does try to encompass the feminine within a pregiven hierarchy. The insistence on equal evaluation denies the legitimacy of the hierarchy, which has, in turn, imposed a certain reality on sexual difference, limiting us in our sexual expression to our definitions as men and women within the framework of what gets called heterosexuality. We call for equal evaluation of the feminine within sexual difference knowing that this equality cannot exist within a system of hierarchy in which the feminine is devalued or simply erased in its specificity, a specificity that in the most profound sense cannot now be known but only reimagined and resymbolized.

The reasoning of *Roe* faltered because the majority opinion clearly recognized the dilemma it was confronting in abortion, which on the one hand involved the need for public facilities and the social and symbolic evaluation of the fetus, and thus seemed to undermine the privacy analysis, and on the other hand involved a condition unique to women, which then seemed to undermine the equality analysis. The Court recognized the dilemma but could not solve it because under the traditional conceptions of liberty and equality it may not be solvable. Thus, as I have argued, we need a framework that explicitly seeks to reevaluate the feminine within sexual difference within the definition of the right itself and then justifies the right as necessary to achievement of the minimum conditions of individuation, which in turn must be respected in the aspiration to conditions of equal well-being and capability. Under this understanding of equality the justification of the right to abortion would proceed as follows.

First, pregnancy may be a unique condition and one that should be valued so as not to create a barrier to women's equality of well-being and capability as in *Geduldig*. But even if pregnancy is valued, a woman must not be reduced to this physical capacity because such a definition identifies her with a function rather than as a self who projects and continuously reimagines herself and the meaning of her embodiment. Pregnancy may be a unique condition, but there is also a shared need for all human beings to project a self-image of bodily integrity. This projection includes the protection of some control over the divide between what is inside the body and out, what is to be publicly exposed in order to retain even the most primordial sense of self. Thus, it makes perfect sense to argue that if this protection of

bodily integrity is necessary for the minimum conditions of individuation for all sexuate beings, then women must not be denied these
conditions since to do so would mark them as unequal. To mark them
would mean for them to be reduced to a function that is then commanded for the use of others, for the use of the anonymous other of
the state, which imposes its own meaning on a woman's reproductive
capacity. This imposition denies women their ability to continuously
reimagine and redefine their sexual difference, so that they are also
denied their equality of well-being and capability.

   This process of giving meaning to their actions is crucial to the
respect for bodily integrity once the imaginary dimension of bodily
coherence is recognized. But it is also essential for women's well-being
and capability in a more subtle sense. In one of the few studies of
women's reaction to abortion, Graciela Abelin-Sas argues that it is
crucial for a woman's psychic well-being that she be able to tell her own
story about what the abortion has meant to her in the context of the
overall history and narrative constructions of her life. She directly connects the difficulty that women have in coming to terms with their own
abortions with its "demonization," which casts such a spell of shame
on the woman that it makes it difficult for her to articulate what the
abortion meant to her individually and not as it has been read through a
stereotypical grid of what kind of women have abortions. Abelin-Sas
argues that it is a serious error both in treatment and in understanding
to interpret a woman's decision through reductionist generalizations
about women and maternity. To quote Abelin-Sas:

> Rather than generalize about the meaning of abortion, such as
> connecting it with ambivalence toward the mother function or
> toward the woman's own mother or mate, I assess that the mean-
> ing of abortion is completely singular to the history and circum-
> stances of each woman.[59]

   Abelin-Sas's accounts from her many years of clinical practice do
not describe women who fail to take their decision seriously and
therefore need the state to show them films that will convince them
that deciding to have an abortion is a grave move. Indeed, these films

---

59. Graciela Abelin-Sas, "To Mother or Not to Mother: Abortion and Its Challenges," *Journal of Clinical Psychoanalysis* 1 (1992): 607.

and other materials are best understood as part of the "demonization" process that makes it difficult for women to truly integrate the decision to have an abortion into their own lives by developing their own accounts of their action.

Second, I would argue that what is being protected is not the abstract right to choose in the right to abortion as I have articulated it, and since abortion does involve the need for access to some kind of medical facility, the state may not prevent women from being able to live out their own self-image of themselves by making it either well-nigh impossible or unsafe for women to actually have abortions. The image necessary for selfhood is that of coherence and self-control. If one were truly in control of one's body then the problem of unwanted pregnancy would solve itself. What is being protected is not the actual power to control but the need to retain some image of coherence in spite of the loss of actual control that threatens a return to the experience of the body. It is at the point when one is most fragile in terms of the most basic sense of projected coherence that one needs to have one's self-image respected the most. Some forms of bodily integrity do not demand access to public facilities in order to be lived out. We can walk down the street and loaf without needing access to a public facility. If the state in practice denies access, demands delays, or imposes its own meaning against the woman's own self-image and understanding of her action, then it effectively undermines her sense of selfhood at the moment when it is most fragile. By engaging in such practices the state denies women minimum conditions for their individuation, turning their bodies over to the imaginations and symbolizations of others. Since a crucial aspect of the right to project one's self as a coherent whole is control over what is exposed to the public, the woman must be allowed to make the final decision of when and how the fetus is to be taken out of her body. The fetus is like no other being precisely because it is inside the body of the woman. Justice O'Connor is right that given constant change in technology, viability is at best arbitrary. Is it not arbitrary, however, to argue that there is a point of difference between when a fetus is in the woman's body and when it is born and thus outside by the process of birth? At this point only does the state's right in protecting a potential self outweigh the woman's decision to terminate her pregnancy. What is at stake here is the woman's most basic sense of self. The utilitarian argument, such as one made by Judge Posner that a woman's loss is less at the point of viability and the state's loss greater if the pregnancy is terminated at this stage, does not hold. Posner remarks, "[t]he killing of the fetus is peculiarly gratuitous if the fetus has developed to the stage where the mother is no longer required to devote her body to nurturing it. What does she lose if the fetus is extracted and allowed to live rather than killed?"[60]

The answer is her most basic sense of self. The argument that the woman has the right to get rid of the fetus at the point of viability—but not to prevent the state from trying to keep it alive—is to take away from the woman her right to keep a baby from happening. She is forced to give birth and be a mother. I agree with Rothman that once we put the woman back in the picture and allow her bodily integrity to count, abortion would be understood as keeping the baby from being born. The woman who has the fetus removed from her and then kept alive by the state has not been allowed to exercise her right. As I have discussed before, a crucial component of the projection of bodily integrity is the protection of control over what is "inside" from what is forced "out." To force the woman to have the baby denies her that protection. That is also why this loss cannot be calculated. It is a loss of the self, not to the self. Simply put, to deny women the right to have an abortion is to deny them equal protection of the minimum conditions of individuation.

Does this mean that there should be no regulations on abortion? My answer is no because I take very seriously the concern for women's health expressed in *Roe v. Wade*. Thus, I would allow the state to pass regulations to ensure basic conditions for safe abortions in second and third trimesters. Does this mean that I have no concern with the other state interest protected in *Roe*, the state's interest in fetal life? I recognize the importance of the concern. Nevertheless, I disagree sharply that the legal result of this concern should be the state's attempt to protect the fetus against the mother. I have argued already that in order to make sense of this legal conclusion one must imply both a view of the woman, and a vision of the woman's body, in which her womb is understood as a container and not part of herself. If, rather, both the womb and the fetus are envisioned as a part of the woman, then it is logical to argue that concern for the health of the

---

60. Richard Posner, *Sex and Reason* (Cambridge, Mass., and London: Harvard University Press, 1992).

Many states had liberal abortion laws . . . but no court declared that these laws violated the equal protection clause, or even that judges should regard them with suspicion or subject them to special scrutiny. Nor did any substantial number of politicians, even among those most savage in their opposition to abortion, suggest that these liberal laws were unconstitutional. . . . The best historical evidence shows that these laws were adopted not out of concern for, however, fetuses but in large part to protect the health of the mother and the privileges of the medical profession.[63]

A second piece of evidence is drawn from states that had restrictive abortion laws prior to *Roe v. Wade*. Again to quote Dworkin:

The structure and details of the anti-abortion laws show, that even the strictest states rejected the idea that a fetus is a constitutional person. Moreover, even the most stringent laws did not punish abortion as severely as they did ordinary murder. The difference was not explained as the consequence of applying some general exculpatory principle to abortion—it was not said, for example, that the moral wickedness of abortion is less because abortion is in some ways like self-defense. Rather it was simply assumed that even in principle abortion is not so serious a matter as murder. Nor did states that prohibited abortion try to prevent a woman from procuring an abortion in another state, when that was possible, or abroad.[64]

Dworkin also addresses another aspect of the derivative argument that would allow for states to forbid abortion. He addresses the argument of whether a state *may* make a fetus a person. Dworkin argues forcibly that a state cannot curtail constitutional rights by adding new persons to the constitutional population. Thus, a state can only make a fetus a person in such a way as to not diminish anyone's right under the national Constitution.[65] Both attempts, then, to draw a derivative defense of abortion as based on the fetus as a constitutional person fail.

Dworkin is also effective in his defense of Blackmun's own deci-

---

63. Ibid., 111–12.
64. Ibid., 112.
65. Ibid., 113.

sion against the charge that he "created" a right that does not exist in the Constitution. Blackmun applied the principle of judicial integrity that Dworkin believes is that hallmark of a good constitutional decision. As Dworkin argues,

> Justice Blackmun can not be charged with erring in treating *Griswold* as a precedent he was obliged to respect. But once one accepts that case as good law, then it follows that women do have a constitutional right to privacy that in principle includes the decision not only whether to beget children but whether to bear them. *Griswold* and the other privacy decisions can be justified only on the presumption that decisions affecting marriage and childbirth are so intimate and personal that people must in principle be allowed to make these decisions for themselves, consulting their own preferences and convictions, rather than having society impose its collective decision on them.[66]

As he concludes:

> A decision about abortion is at least as private in that sense as any other decision the Court has protected. In one way it is more so, because it involves a woman's control not just of her sexual relations but of changes within her own body, and the Supreme Court has recognized in various ways the importance of physical integrity.[67]

Thus, Blackmun's decision in *Roe v. Wade* can be defended as a correct adherence to the principle of judicial integrity. Yet we are still left with an unanswered question: How can we make sense of the seemingly vague language in *Roe v. Wade* that the state, at some point in the pregnancy, does have a compelling state interest in protecting human life? For Dworkin, we need to think more precisely about exactly what that legal interest entails. In order to do so we also have to rethink the moral objection to abortion.

Dworkin has a second objection to abortion that does not rest on a derivative claim that the fetus has rights:

---

66. Ibid., 106.
67. Ibid., 106–7.

The second claim that the familiar rhetoric can be used to make is very different: that human life has an intrinsic, innate value; that human life is sacred just in itself; and that the sacred nature of a human life begins when its biological life begins, even before the creature whose life it is has movement or sensation or interests or rights of its own. According to this second claim, abortion is wrong in principle because it disregards and insults the intrinsic value, the sacred character, of any stage or form of human life. I shall call this the *detached* objection to abortion, because it does not depend on or presuppose any particular rights or interests. Someone who accepts *this* objection, and argues that abortion should be prohibited or regulated by law for *this* reason, believes that government has a detached responsibility for protecting the intrinsic value of life.[68]

This detached responsibility flows from what he calls the "sanctity principle." Dworkin uses his sanctity principle in explaining why some abortions are "necessary" and are thus considered morally more acceptable than others. For Dworkin, both conservatives and liberals share moral intuitions about the intrinsic value of the life of the fetus. Again, to quote Dworkin:

We think a human life is sacred—that human life commands respect and protection no matter in what form or shape. This not because we respect or admire or love the person whose life it is: a human being's life is sacred, we think, quite independently of any knowledge at all. We treat human as sacred in that way because of the complex, fractioned investment it represents, because of our wonder that is, at the divine or evolutionary processes that have produced something so fantastic from as it were, nothing: at the miracle of reproduction that makes him both different from and yet a continuation of particular other people; at the processes of nation and community and language through which he embodies generations of human creation of forms of life and value: and finally at the process of internal creation and judgement, the way in which people make themselves, a mysterious, inescapable process in which each of us participates, and

_____
68. Ibid., 11.

which is therefore the most powerful and inevitable source of empathy and communion with every other creature who faces the same frightening challenge.[69]

Dworkin believes the sanctity principle can help us think more profoundly about abortion, and more specifically about certain exceptions to the right of abortion, if we view the principle as providing us with a metric of disrespect. This metric of disrespect includes a complicated notion of what "we" think of as the scale of disrespect of the sanctity of life. I put *we* in quotation marks because I offer a competing framework for the right to abortion, and I do not concur with Dworkin's assumption that "we" necessarily share these intuitions. I am not part of the "we" in a very basic sense. I reject the idea that it is a worse tragedy when a three-year-old child dies than when an infant dies. For me, there can be no standard of measurement for such a devastating tragedy. Note that this is a serious disagreement because it implies that such an overwhelming tragedy cannot be captured by Dworkin's concept of frustration. Dworkin describes his use of frustration as follows:

I shall use "frustration" (though the word has other associations) to describe this more complex measure of the waste of life because I can think of no better word to suggest the combination of past and future considerations that figure in our assessment of a tragic death. Most of us hold to something like the following set of instinctive assumptions about death and tragedy. We believe, as I said, that a successful human life has a certain natural course. It starts in mere biological development—conception, fetal development, and infancy—but it then extends into childhood, adolescence, and adult life in ways that are determined not just by biological formation but by social and individual training and choice, and that culminate in satisfying relationships and achievements of different kinds. It ends, after a normal life span, in a natural death. It is a waste of the natural human and creative investments that make up the story of a normal life when this normal progression is frustrated by premature death or in other ways. But how bad this is—how great the frustration—depends

69. Ibid., 6.

on the stage of life in which it occurs, because the frustration is greater if it takes place after rather than before the person has made a significant personal investment in his own life, and less if it occurs after any investment has been substantially fulfilled, or as substantially fulfilled as is anyway likely.[70]

Frustration is a concept of waste that does allow for measurement. We can talk about "more" or "less" frustration. But imagine one mother telling another that hers was the worse tragedy because she lost a three-year-old child rather than an infant. Such overwhelming losses in a person's life simply do not yield to comparison or measurement. To describe adequately such tragedies we need another word than *frustration*. I prefer *devastation*.

Dworkin, however, relies on his notion of frustration to provide us with a complicated notion of waste, because if we relied on the simplest notions of waste—either as loss of life or in terms of how much life is lost—we would be unable to make sense of some of our most fundamental intuitions. He offers several examples illustrating the notion of a waste of life as insufficiently complex to do justice to our moral intuitions.

If the waste of life were to be measured only in terms of how much life is lost, then early stage abortion would be morally worse, not better, than late-stage abortion, because the former wastes more life. But almost everyone holds the contrary assumption: that the later the abortion, the more like a child the aborted fetus has become, the worse what has happened is. We take a similar view about the tragedy of the death of young children, moreover. It is terrible when an infant dies; but it is worse, most people think, when a three year old does, and worse yet many people think when an adolescent dies.[71]

Thus, Dworkin's thesis requires the added conception of frustration to make sense of what he cites as examples that contradict these simple notions of waste.

Dworkin's notion of frustration is associated closely with the

70. Ibid., 87–88.
71. Ibid., 86–87.

ideas of investment and, I would argue, potential. Therefore, it would
be worse if a talented young painter were to die at age twenty-five
with only two painted pictures to her credit, because she would have
failed to bring to fruition the years she invested in learning her art,
than it would be if a fifty-four-year-old painter died after having produced hundreds of works expressing her early potential. For Dworkin, this idea of investment and frustration would justify the view
that late abortions are worse than early ones, because there will be
more frustration and waste. I have already argued against viability so
I will not repeat my argument here except to stress that even if I
agreed with Dworkin that there would be greater frustration in the
case of a late-term abortion, I would not accept this belief as the basis
for a limitation of the right. For other reasons, however, as I will argue
later, I would promote policies that would encourage early- rather
than late-term abortions.

I am sympathetic to Dworkin's argument that it is clearly in the
later stages of gestation that the fetus first shows signs of human
awakening and sensation. This argument does seem to be bolstered
by the evidence of embryologists, although there is considerable disagreement as to when the fetus is first sentient. Still, the very possibility of greater suffering would lead us to try to do everything we could
to discourage later abortions. However, given my view of women and
the undesirability of late-term abortions, I do not believe that it is
necessary to put the recognition of this suffering into law as a limitation of the right. We will come back to my discussion of the suffering
involved in a late-term abortion shortly. For now, I want to return to
the way in which Dworkin uses this concept of frustration to justify
exceptions to the prohibition of abortion that have been recognized.

Dworkin argues that his concept of frustration can help us in
comprehending why states have been allowed to abort deformed fetuses. The argument in defense of such an exception is that it allows
for the measurement to be made in terms of the frustration of the
future infant's life. For Dworkin, liberals are more likely to defend the
abortion of a deformed fetus because they are more likely, as he puts
it, to protect "life in earnest."[72] This defense has to do with the different value liberals and conservatives put on the natural and divine and
human investment in the creation of a human life. Liberals put greater

---

72. Ibid., 99.

stress on human investment. Thus, Dworkin argues that liberals believe that abortion is justified when it seems inevitable that the fetus if born will have a seriously frustrated life.

> That kind of justification is strongest, according to most liberals, when the frustration is caused by a very grave physical deformity that would make any life deprived, painful, frustrating for both child and parent, and in any case, short. But many liberals also believe that abortion is justified when family circumstances are so economically barren, or otherwise so unpromising, that any new life would be seriously stunted for that reason.[73]

Dworkin is careful to distinguish this liberal view from what he calls "loathsome Nazi eugenics."[74] He is not arguing that society would benefit by the death of such people. It is self-evident that disabled people have rights and that any harm to them would be as grievously wrong as to an "able bodied" person. But it is still important to note, and we will return to this point in my discussion of India, that for Dworkin "the liberal judgement that abortion is justified when the prospects for life are especially bleak is based on a more impersonal judgment: that the child's existence would be intrinsically a bad thing, that it is regrettable that such a deprived and difficult life must be lived."[75] The problem, as we will see, is that sex and race have played a very great role in whose life will be viewed as intrinsically "a bad thing." Indeed, race and sex have turned many people's lives into a difficult, arduous pathway—a pathway that has much in common with the suffering of those who have been physically as well as culturally handicapped. But then, all notions of handicap only become disabilities when they are translated into labor markets that value or devalue a particular person's bodily capacities. As a result, I question whether or not we want states to reinforce judgments about whose life counts, or even more strongly put, whose life is an "intrinsically bad thing," since such judgments are so intrinsically bound up with cultural prejudices. Let me use India as an example to demonstrate this danger.

Disability is a flexible notion: in India, women choose to abort

---

73. Ibid., 97–98.
74. Ibid.
75. Ibid.

female fetuses, because women and female children are not thought to have bodies that measure up to those of able-bodied men. As Nivedita Menon argues, the "devaluation" of female bodies is implicitly promoted by the Indian government's birth-control campaign, known as Net Reproduction Rate of One.[76] To quote Menon:

> Although the government does not openly advocate sex determination tests, the selective abortion of female fetuses seems to have been built into the population control policies of the Sixth and Seventh plans. These set a target of a Net Reproduction Rate of one. That is, one woman should replace her mother. This target along with that of two or three births per woman is expected to be achieved by 2006–2011. The implication of this is that "excess girls" will have to be killed at the fetal stage to maintain the NRR of one.[77]

It is important to stress that the net reproduction rate (NRR) of one is not explicitly targeted at women. Menon is arguing, however, that the effect of the government-sponsored program implicates the government in the promotion of that effect. Of course, the devaluation of female fetuses and infants is by no means unique to India. In her article on female infanticide in China, Sharon Hom has argued that:

> Female infanticide is no less than a gender based discriminatory judgement about who will survive.
> At the family and societal level at which the mother is subjected to enormous pressure to bear a son or face the consequences of abuse and humiliation, female infanticide is a form of policing and terrorist practice of control over women to keep them in their prescribed reproductive role as bearers of sons. Reminders of the reality of the persistence are present in media stories, in official pronouncements, and in the content of numerous education campaigns to eradicate these abuses. In the insidious and implicit message conveyed under the explicit condemnation of these abuses, female children, women and men may be

---

76. Menon, "Abortion and the Law," 4.
77. Ibid.

conditioned to accept the legitimacy, or perhaps worse, the inevitability of female life.[78]

Of course, I have made a distinction between infanticide and abortion, but the Indian program, which implicitly encourages the abortion of female fetuses *because* they are female, clearly expresses the same devaluation of female life. The Indian program brings out the possible danger of connecting such reasoning about whose body and life is to be valued, and thus more seriously frustrated by premature death, into the context of abortion. Explicit "femicide," even in the form of aborting female fetuses, is much more horrifying as a basis for abortion than simple abortion on demand. The India example brings home the tragic results of the devaluation of the female body. But it should also remind us that we should be extremely suspicious of a system that would utilize intuitions about whose body matters as its basis for allowing exceptions to an abortion prohibition. I do not believe that this kind of evaluation can be successfully separated from Dworkin's overall analysis of abortion, as it is based on an evaluation of life on a sliding scale of frustration and waste.[79]

It should be noted, however, that my argument so far has been to question Dworkin as to whether or not we can successfully use his conception of frustration to defend adequately a woman's right to abortion. The very idea of Dworkin's use of frustration in the area of abortion is to assume that abortion is always a moral wrong but that in certain circumstances it can be justified because the frustration to the woman's life will be much greater than the frustration to the fetus's life. This concept of frustration can then be used to justify certain exceptions to the overall legal disapproval of abortion. I stress the word *legal* deliberately because my main disagreement with Dworkin has to do with the role that the legal system and the law can or should play in limiting the right to abortion.

Dworkin, as I wrote earlier, is careful to distinguish a state law that encourages responsibility from one that enforces coercion. The key for Dworkin is whether or not such state laws actually put barriers between a woman and her ultimate decision, which must be protected as a fundamental right to have an abortion. States can encourage responsi-

---

78. Sharon Hom, "Female Infanticide in China: The Human Rights Specter and Thoughts Toward (An)Other Vision," *Columbia Human Rights Law Review* (1992): 259.
79. Dworkin, *Life's Dominion*, 87–94.

bility to the sanctity of life, but they cannot prevent any woman from exercising her procreative autonomy. Frustration gives us parameters to understand what responsibility entails. But, ironically, the introduction of the idea of frustration implies a kind of measurement that is difficult to fully justify from within a perspective that argues that life has an intrinsic value. When we begin to measure frustration, we inevitably look to external meaning, standardized evaluation codes, by which to comprehend that intrinsic value. As I have already suggested, I reject the idea that we can compare the loss of an infant to the loss of a three-year-old child. Of course, Dworkin could argue that he is not using frustration to attempt to comprehend the grief of the mothers. But my argument is that frustration implies some standardized notions of measurements about whose life is to count more or less and that we don't want such measurements encoded into law.

It is this standard of measurement that I would resist in its translation into a justification for any legal exceptions to abortion. But this does not mean that I would simply reject Dworkin's idea that there is an intrinsic value to human life. Dworkin could argue that my own defense of an absolute right of abortion as necessary for the achievement of minimum conditions of individuation is just another example of a liberal "taking the intrinsic value of life in earnest." Perhaps it can be so understood. To quote Dworkin:

> We can best understand some of our serious disagreements about abortion, in other words, as reflecting deep human differences about the relative moral importance of the natural and human contributions to the inviolability of individual human lives. In fact, we can make a bolder version of that claim: we can best understand the full range of opinion about abortion, from the most conservative to the most liberal, by ranking each opinion about the relative gravity of the two forms of frustration along a range extending from one extreme position to the other—from treating any frustration of the biological investment as worse than any possible frustration of human investment, through more moderate and complex balances, to the opinion that frustrating mere biological investment in human life barely matters and that frustrating a human investment is always worse.[80]

_____

80. Dworkin, _Life's Dominion,_ 91.

Am I arguing simply that I think that frustrating a mere biological investment in human life "barely matters," and that frustrating a human investment is "always worse"? The precise answer is that I am arguing that it is the woman, and not the state, who must ultimately make that balance. Making that balance for me cannot be comprehended in terms of simply allowing her to make the ultimate decision. It is crucial that we allow the woman to be the ultimate determinant of the meaning of her act. This view of the importance of meaning and not just the act is certainly compatible with Dworkin's own stress that a human life has an important creative aspect to its achievement. But I am also making a more basic argument. If we are to equally respect women as persons with their own imagination, and that personhood itself has such a crucial imaginary aspect to it, then we must allow them to be the determinants of the meaning of their act to have or not have an abortion. In this way, although I respect Dworkin's insistence that the state at most can only encourage responsibility and not enforce coercion on women's lives, I still reject the idea that state laws that demand that women endure waiting periods, or must see films, or must read certain materials, should be allowable. Such measures refuse to women their status as equal persons capable of moral judgment. It is because of my argument that women be recognized in their feminine sexual difference as equal that leads to my insistence that it be their imaginary domain that be allowed to determine the meaning of abortion for themselves at a particular time.

A woman may experience abortions differently, depending on what stage of life she is at, depending on how she views her relationship, and the like. But the assumption that we need states to encourage responsibility for women in this arena seems to me to reflect an overall view of women as less capable of moral judgments than men. For who is it that dominates the legislatures? This insistence that equality would encompass not only the allowance of the act, but the protection of the ability of the woman to be the ultimate interpreter of the act, is why I would defend the right of abortion under the rubric of equality rather than, as Dworkin does, under the First Amendment. This is not because I reject Dworkin's argument that the debate over abortion has an important religious dimension. I think it clearly does. Nor would I reject Dworkin's doctrinal defense of procreative autonomy as a First Amendment right as an important additional argument for the legal defense of abortion. We need as many sound arguments as we can develop. But there is no doubt that my defense under the rubric of equality puts much greater stress than Dworkin does on the woman being the ultimate determinant of the meaning of what she does when she has an abortion or chooses to proceed with a pregnancy. This insistence on equality has to do with my conviction that issues of abortion can never be separated from the perception of feminine sexual difference and the way its evaluation has been legally encoded and its definition legally restricted.

Thus, for example, I am much more suspicious than is Dworkin of the conservative defense of the exceptions to the prohibition against abortion in cases of rape and incest. There is for me an implicit moral message in these exceptions that I believe is reflective of fantasies about the sexuality of women who have abortions, whose abortions are not the result of exceptions. It is this message: Women who suffered incest and rape did not choose to have sex, and therefore should not be punished with an unwanted pregnancy. Put more simply, I am much more suspicious than Dworkin is about the moral intuitions that purportedly justify these exceptions. It may have less to do with the conservative commitment to the natural and divine nature of human life than the fear of female sexuality.

Such fear of female sexuality and the awesome power of reproduction is reflected in statements by right-to-lifers themselves. The image of the mother who aborts as the "killing mother" is the terrifying image held out by many who march in right-to-life parades. Such "killing mothers" and the fear of them seem to underlie much of the rhetoric that those of us who have been born would not have been born if our mothers had chosen to kill us. Dworkin philosophically demolishes the argument that the unborn have a prior interest in a life that they never achieve. He argues rightly that it is only from the retrospective position of those of us who are living that such an interest would even make sense. The incessant expression of that interest among right-to-lifers indicates the power and the terror of this image of the killing mother. It is undoubtedly because I do not share this perception that society needs to fear "killing mothers" that makes me believe it less necessary for the states to encourage responsible decision making on the part of women.

The debate, however, is not just over the image of the woman who aborts. The debate is ultimately over the content of the right itself and whether or not it must encompass the woman's capacity to determine the meaning of her own decision. Dworkin summarizes his bottom line as follows:

> I am defending the view that the debate over abortion should be understood as essentially about the following philosophical issue: Is the frustration of a biological life, which wastes human life, nevertheless sometimes justified in order to avoid frustrating a human contribution to that life or to other people's lives, which would be a different kind of waste? If so, when and why?[81]

For me, the debate over abortion is about whether or not women will be allowed to achieve minimum conditions of individuation. If they are not allowed the right to abortion, they will not be able to engage in the process of bodily integration I have argued is essential to and the very basis of what we legally think of as person. The loss of the self cannot be captured by the word *frustration*. Thus, ultimately, there is a disagreement between Dworkin and myself about just how devastating it is for women to have denied to them not only the choice to have or not have an abortion but also the process of imagining their own bodily integration. Perhaps in the end I am more liberal than Dworkin in my insistence that the meaning of the act, including the value that a woman gives to the act, must be left to her imaginary domain.

My thesis is that the right to abortion should be recognized as the right to bodily integrity, which includes realizing the legitimacy of the individual woman's projections of her own bodily integrity, consistent with the imagination of herself at the time she chooses to terminate the pregnancy. It is not only a definition of right that I am defending, but also the return of abortion to the sphere of rights. The sphere of right that I defend, however, is not that of the fetus. I am in complete agreement with Dworkin that the fetus does not have rights and that any derivative defense of states prohibiting abortion fails. We must continue to defend abortion as a right and to define abortion as within the sphere of rights.

---

81. Dworkin, *Life's Dominion*, 94.

How and Why Abortion on Demand Should be Defended as a Right

We now need to turn to the critique that some feminists have made of treating abortion as a right. To examine the reasons behind this critique I return the example of India. Feminists in India have been forced to ask the following question: Can we restate the right to abortion in the case of women who abort female fetuses? Menon has explicitly discussed the difficulty of making a distinction between disabled fetuses and female fetuses in delineating exceptions to a prohibition on abortion. Some feminists in India have argued that the solution to this practice would be either to restrict use of the amniocentesis test, or at least to restrict communication about the sex of the baby, so that such information would not become part of the decision to abort. Menon argues, however, that the specific practice of aborting female fetuses should be understood to be an aspect of the devaluation of bodies inherent in the perpetuation of a hierarchy that evaluates how bodies matter. To quote Menon:

> At this point, we reach another level of complexity if we consider the question of the morality of aborting handicapped fetuses, for the detection of which feminists continue to endorse amniocentesis. Once it is accepted that there can be a hierarchy of human beings on the basis of physical characteristics, upon which the right to be born can be withheld, then this reasoning can be extended to other categories, whether females, "inferior races," or any other. One feminist response to this is that since women would have to look after handicapped children, they should have the option not to have them. It hardly bears repeating that the identical argument is made about female children, that the social pressure to bear male children falls entirely on the woman and so she should have the right to abort female fetuses.[82]

As a result, limiting access to information about the sex of the fetus hardly seems to solve the problem if it stems from the perpetuation of a hierarchy that determines which bodies *matter*. Menon also argues forcefully against relinquishing control over the amnio-

---

82. Menon, "Abortion and the Law," 8–9.

centesis test to the state. She is concerned that attempts to limit directly the right to abortion will be made, as some feminists have already done, using right-to-life arguments on behalf of female fetuses. Menon notes correctly that such arguments could be used against the right to abortion itself. Menon notes further that the right to abortion has never been as controversial in the West because the state has successfully promoted population control. It is important to note here that the example of India obviously implicates a much wider discussion in the question of developmental economics and the program sponsored by the development to control population growth as crucial to such developmental programs. Amartya Sen has forcibly argued that such developmental programs must be based on a question of entitlement if they are to achieve quality of well-being and capability for women.[83] Thus, Sen has powerfully argued that questions of entitlement are inevitably implicated in how basic developmental decisions are made. It is precisely because of India's developmental program, which has included a program of population control, that the right of abortion has been much less controversial within the Indian context. Since feminists within India have understood the kind of argument made by Sen to be crucial to development programs, i.e., that entitlement will play a major role in the achievement of equality, their thinking of the question of right as it plays out in a broad sphere of social life has been both advanced and subtle. Due to the experience with the debate over questions of entitlement and development, the Indian example can help the feminists in the United States reexamine their own elaboration of the right of abortion.

For Menon this dilemma, of locating a limitation on the right to abortion in order to subvert the abortion of female fetuses while still maintaining the overall right to abortion, raises an even more basic problem about the very definition of "rights." Menon critiques the feminist analysis that situates the body in the realm of privacy, then justifies protection of the right to abortion as the right to be free from state intervention in that realm. For Menon the "body" clearly has a public dimension. I agree that the body always has a public dimen-

83. See Amartya Sen, "Well-Being, Agency and Freedom" in *Philosophy and Public Affairs* 19 (April 1985), and "Equality of What?" in *Choice, Welfare and Measurement* (Cambridge, Mass.: MIT Press, 1982). See also Isaiah Berlin, *Four Essays on Liberty* (London: Oxford University Press, 1969).

sion, in the sense that how the body matters cannot be separated from the symbolic order that signifies, and thus gives meaning to, bodies. I do not believe that we can ever simply "own" our bodies, and that the very idea that we do "own" them is in and of itself a fantasy. But this sense of one's body as one's "own" is a necessary projection for any sense of self. Thus, at least if I said no more, my defense of abortion as a right would not seem to solve the dilemma in India.

The amendment that must be made is that this right must be reviewed in the greater context of a legal reform that will systematically challenge devaluation of the feminine within sexual difference and, as a crucial aspect of this devaluation, the reduction of our "sex" to the maternal function. Menon argues that "a feminist manifesto on conditions of reproductive choice would have to recognize the materiality of cultural and ideological practices which constitute bodies and rights and even women."[84] She then adds that "this materiality cannot be tackled by law but a counter practice of ideology."[85] But if one understands law as one of the important systems of cultural symbolization, then law, and more particularly, rights, should not be dismissed. Certainly the masculine white Western definition of rights must also be challenged, since it cannot provide a coherent defense of the right to abortion. Traditional justifications for rights are then hardly justifiable as universal, since they are based on a very particular, incorrect conception of the subject and of the self. Recognition of this particularity does not demand that we switch to a cultural relativist conception of right, since what is crucial for feminists is the upward revaluation of the feminine within sexual difference, from its degradation by gender hierarchy. For example, Sharon Hom argues:

> For Chinese women, the relativist conception of rights is also problematic. By uncritically contextualizing a rights claim within the cultural and development goals of the country, women have no conceptual basis for challenging the legitimacy of the existing culture itself. The recent attention paid to abuses inflicted by traditional practices is illustrative of the beginning of a serious international effort to grapple with the political and methodologi-

---

84. Menon, "Abortion and the Law," 11.
85. Ibid., 11.

cal issues raised by the problem. In the Chinese context, female infanticide and preference for sons are clearly traditional and modern practices of Chinese culture.[86]

Indeed, one problem inherent in the justification of abortion in India was its definition relativized to the development goals of that country, without the explicit recognition of women's equal entitlement as subjects of right. Women were effectively valued as replacement mothers. Implicit in the plan was the evaluation that the numbers of mothers should not be reduced. Menon does not argue that "rights talk" should be completely forsaken or simply relativized to context; rather she warns us that rights do not exist as simple and self-evident facts, given to beings understood as atomized individuals. I agree that selves do not exist other than through symbolic formation and social constructions. But once the right of bodily integrity is recast, part of the feminist struggle is to protect the feminine imaginary domain, to allow us to take "ourselves" back from the masculine imaginary domain as it has been symbolized by law. This symbolization devalues Woman as the not-man and therefore defines her not as the subject of right but as an object of exchange. The governmental proposal that encourages women to replace themselves as mothers should be understood to reflect this symbolic construction that recognizes the prime value of women through the maternal function. It is the effect of the plan in its reinforcement of the devaluation of the feminine within sexual difference that Menon addresses in her own argument.

Of course, the explicit practice of aborting female fetuses is a horrifying example of this devaluation. But if we seriously contemplate protecting the woman's own imagining of the meaning of her abortion, then it would seem that we must include the woman who imagines her female fetus as so devalued that she would rather it were not born. It is also arguable that such practices in law reflect the systematic denial of the equivalent value of the feminine within sexual difference, i.e., the woman who imagines her female fetus as worthless does so because the feminine imaginary and the symbolization of the value of the feminine within sexual difference has almost been foreclosed.

---

86. Hom, "Female Infanticide in China," 293.

What does it mean to allow this practice under the protection of the rubric of the right to abortion if it denies equivalent value to the feminine within sexual difference? My preferred solution is to criticize all exceptions to abortion that turn on the perpetuation of hierarchies that evaluate whose body is to matter. This solution does mean that in a choice between protecting the right to abortion on demand and legally restricting the right in order to curb the practice of aborting female fetuses as a violation of the equivalent value of the feminine "sex," I would choose the former. This choice is, in part, because the resymbolization of women as subjects of rights for me forms one prong of the overall challenge to the devaluation of the feminine within sexual difference.

Gender hierarchy systematically denies women that status.[87] As we have seen in the American context, the regulation of abortion reduces women to objects, defines their "sex" as the maternal function, and further forecloses the play of the feminine imaginary by trying to define the meaning of abortion for the woman. The question becomes, how do we adopt or create a discourse that enhances what Hom has called women's "subject possibilities?"[88] To develop a discourse of the would-be female subject, whose imaginary domain can be symbolized in its own specificity, irreducible to the Other by which the man measures himself, necessarily has a utopian dimension, since it is precisely this position of the subject as woman that cannot be confirmed in a masculine symbolic. It is no coincidence that the projection of woman as a subject of rights challenges the traditional discourse of rights that has kept women captive in a patriarchal system of law that reflects and perpetuates the gender hierarchy in which women cannot be confirmed as subjects. The promise of the recognition of woman as a subject of rights is a promise toward an imagined future, in which sexual difference could be articulated as other than its definition within the gender hierarchy and its limited duality upon which the normalization of heterosexuality is justified. That promise must be reexpressed in the rearticulation of rights. The discourse in which such a promise can be expressed must also be created. Such a

---

87. Drucilla Cornell, "The Philosophy of the Limit: Systems Theory and Feminist Legal Reform," in *Deconstruction and the Possibility of Justice*, ed. Drucilla Cornell, Michel Rosenfeld, and David Carlson (New York and London: Routledge, Chapman and Hall, 1992), 68.

88. Hom, "Female Infanticide in China."

discourse, then, does not rest on the so-called universalist premises that turn us toward the past of gender, national, and racist hierarchy that disguises the particularity of the Western man. As we imagine women reimagining themselves, our captivity by a discourse that has told us what we are as women is also challenged. Recognizing the right to abortion challenges the discourse that legitimizes our social status as objects to be manipulated, since it insists that it is women who must be empowered to define and reimagine what maternity means to them.

Conclusion

Abortion must ultimately be placed in the context of mother right if we are to seriously embark on taking the feminine within sexual difference back from the masculine imaginary domain. Another aspect of my definition of the right to abortion includes protection of a woman's own understanding of her abortion. Advocates of "choice" are often accused of downplaying the tragic significance that an abortion may have in a woman's life. In a class society like our own, the right to be a mother can itself seem a class privilege. Class position can force women to abort their fetuses when this is the last thing they would freely choose to do.[89] I return once more to Nedreaas's novel, *Nothing Grows by Moonlight,* in which the "voice" articulates her terrible suffering over her second self-inflicted abortion precisely because she has already imagined her fetus as a baby. Unable to have access to a hospital, she gives "birth" alone and in a graveyard:

> I sneaked down between the graves and hid in the toolshed. I put the hook on the floor and stayed there until dusk arrived in the evening. I sat on the floor with chattering teeth, quietly moaning. I kept it in my handkerchief. I had gathered it up and hidden it inside my handkerchief.
>
> It wasn't big. No more than a slimy lump of blood that smelled bad. Nevertheless, I thought my stomach, my brain and my heart and everything, would be driven out of me when it came . . .

---

89. Mary Elizebeth Bartholemew's insightful analysis of mothering as a class privilege, and our discussions regarding her forthcoming paper on this topic, have informed my thinking here.

Half crazy with pain and my face frozen with tears, I buried it. I found a poor, neglected grave with a crooked wooden cross with a tin sign where the name was almost erased. You could only read "With Faith in her Saviour," and the first name Marie.

That's where I buried the tiny, little fetus.[90]

The narrator's pain was not only the pain caused by the condition of her abortion, an allegory for the death of "her-self" that she had to impose, but included her grief over the loss of a baby she deeply wanted, but as a single, unemployed, working-class mother, did not feel she was entitled to have. I use the word *entitlement* deliberately to reemphasize that the so-called glorification of women as the maternal function has nothing to do with their achievement of the subject position in which they would feel entitled to their selves.

The "voice" in *Nothing Grows by Moonlight* emphasizes the hypocrisy of those who try to forbid abortion at the same time that they rail against the sexual shamelessness of unmarried women who find themselves pregnant. Her horror at her own gesture to abort cannot be separated from her profound desire to keep the baby in conditions in which she would not be forced to pass on the so-called shame of her "sex":

Something is greedily absorbing nourishment, something that has already, from the first moment, been given its talents and abilities from an unknown number of ancestors, yes, a surprise package full of talents that is eternal. And this must be killed. This piece of eternal life is killed every day. Oh, yes, yes, they may well forbid us to remove it, in the name of morality and the Bible. At the same time they force us to remove it in the name of God and the Bible.[91]

Earlier I suggested that, though I would not place legal limitations on the right of abortion, I would promote a social program that would actively aid women in locating safe and supportive abortion facilities, because I am concerned with the trauma that may be brought on by second-trimester abortions.

---

90. Nedreaas, *Nothing Grows by Moonlight*, 193.
91. Ibid.

Some years ago when I worked as a union organizer, I sat through several saline abortions that were conducted in what I would consider to be extremely unsafe conditions. The women whose abortions I witnessed were nonunionized Hispanic workers without green cards or insurance, with no access to the English language, and whose husbands and lovers were abroad in their native lands and therefore unavailable for financial and emotional support. These women did not "choose" to undergo late-term abortions. They had no access to information, facilities, or money needed for a first-trimester abortion. Eventually, their only recourse was to seek help from a stranger—a union organizer—who seemed to them to be their only way of locating information and finding social services.

I will never forget the horror of one particular saline abortion that I witnessed. The woman went through the labor of an induced miscarriage without anesthesia and suffered labor pains for several hours without medication. I will never forget the horror of waiting, the fetus being "born," the "mother's" heartbreak, and my inability to find a doctor to help us as I ran up and down the hospital halls. Like the mother in the Nedreaas story, this woman also named the fetus and held it in her arms, weeping desperately while I went for the doctor.

What were we doing alone in that Long Island hospital room? In 1976 doctors were already intimidated by the activities of the fledgling right-to-life lobby and were performing second-trimester abortions with great reluctance. As a result, the quality of care was inconsistent, and doctors tried to have little to do with those abortions and the poor women who were forced to have them. It is not surprising, given how horrifying this experience was for me, that I take Blackmun's concern for the health of women who have abortions in the second trimester so seriously.

I use Nedreaas's novel and my own story to emphasize how class position enforces both meaning and reality. The woman must abort, in part because of the shame given to her "sex" in which her right to be a mother is not fully protected. Such a right would include the conditions for healthy mothering. But there are other situations less starkly compelling in which women have abortions and only later realize the depth of their sadness. In discussing her women patients' difficulty in mourning their abortions, Abelin-Sas connects mourning with the demonization of abortion. A crucial part of their difficulty is that the decision to have an abortion is read through a pregiven grid by which they are stereotyped. The women's loss of words cannot be dissociated from the much larger problem of the dearth of symbols for women as subjects, in which they can imagine, and then articulate, their experience. Some women clearly suffer over their abortions, and they are forced to suffer in a silence so profound that it erases the experience from conscious life, leaving its traces in other forms of unconscious expression. Abelin-Sas's case studies detail the repercussions of enforced erasure in her patients' futures.

By contrast, not all women experience abortion as a serious loss, or as any loss at all. All sorts of factors, including the woman's age, her experience, her desire to have a baby, and the presence of a lover, will affect the meaning of a woman's action. But nothing in the right to abortion necessarily trivializes the meaning a woman gives to her pregnancy or to her decision to terminate it. My emphasis is on empowering women to do just that—give their own meaning to their abortions, to imagine their own bodies, and to represent their "sex" with joy within sexual difference.

Rights and Identity in Late Modernity: Revisiting the "Jewish Question"

Wendy Brown

> For the historically disempowered, the conferring of rights is symbolic of all the denied aspects of their humanity: rights imply a respect that places one in the referential range of self and others, that elevates one's status from human body to social being. . . .
> —Patricia Williams, *The Alchemy of Race and Rights*

> [I]t is not through recourse to sovereignty against discipline that the effects of disciplinary power can be limited, because sovereignty and disciplinary mechanisms are two absolutely integral constituents of the general mechanism of power in our society. If one wants to . . . struggle against disciplines and disciplinary power, it is not towards the ancient right of sovereignty that one should turn, but towards the possibility of a new form of right, one which must indeed be anti-disciplinarian, but at the same time liberated from the principle of sovereignty.
> —Michel Foucault, *Power/Knowledge*

> Minority people committed themselves to these struggles [for rights], not to attain some hegemonically functioning reification leading to false consciousness, but a seat in the front of the bus, repatriation of treaty-guaranteed sacred lands, or a union card to carry into the grape vineyards.
> —Robert A. Williams, Jr., "Taking Rights Aggressively"

What is the emancipatory force of rights claims on behalf of politicized identities in late-twentieth-century North American political life? If, historically, rights have been claimed to secure formal emancipation

for individuals stigmatized, traumatized, and subordinated by particular social identities, to secure a place for such individuals in a humanist discourse of universal personhood, what does it mean to deploy
rights on behalf of identities that aim to confound the humanist con-
ceit? What are the consequences of installing politicized identity in the
universal discourse of liberal jurisprudence? And what does it mean
to use a discourse of generic personhood—the discourse of rights—
against the privileges that discourse has traditionally secured?

In pursuing these kinds of questions about the contemporary
deployment of rights, I am not asking whether rights as such are
emancipatory. Nor am I concerned with the theoretical question of
whether the sovereign subject of rights can be squared with contemporary deconstruction of such subjects.[1] Rather, I want to begin by recognizing rights as protean and irresolute signifiers, varying not only
across time and culture, but across the other vectors of power whose
crossing they are sometimes deployed to effect—class, race, ethnicity,
gender, sexuality, age, wealth, education.[2] I want to acknowledge the
diverse, inconstant, even contradictory ways that rights operate
across various histories, cultures, and social strata.[3]

But an inquiry into the relationship between identity formation
and rights claims in late-twentieth-century politics requires register-
ing more than the indeterminacy and contingency of rights. Those
concerned with emancipatory political practices in our time confront
as well a set of paradoxes about rights, perhaps the central one of
which is this: The question of the liberatory or egalitarian force of
rights is always historically and culturally circumscribed; rights have
no inherent political semiotic, they carry no innate capacity either to
advance or impede radical democratic ideals. Yet, rights necessarily
operate in and as an ahistorical, acultural, acontextual idiom: they

---

1. Drucilla Cornell offers one of the most interesting speculations on this topic in
"Bodily Integrity and the Right to Abortion," in this volume.

2. See, on a related but somewhat different point, Laclau and Mouffe, who argue
that "the meaning of liberal discourse on individual rights is not definitively fixed."
Ernesto Laclau and Chantal Mouffe, *Hegemony and Socialist Strategy* (London: Verso,
1985), 176.

3. Consider: rights as boundary, and as access; rights as markers of power, and as
masking lack; rights as claims, and as protection; rights as organization of social space,
and as defense against incursion; rights as articulation, and as mystification; rights as
disciplinary, and as antidisciplinary; rights as a mark of one's humanity, and as a
reduction of one's humanity; rights as expression of desire, and as foreclosure of desire.

claim distance from specific political context and historical vicissitudes, and they necessarily participate in a discourse of enduring
universality rather than provisionality or partiality. Thus, while the
measure of their political efficacy requires a high degree of historical
and social specificity, rights operate as a political discourse of the
general, the generic and universal.[4]

This paradox between the universal idiom and the local effect of
rights itself transpires on both a temporal and spatial level. On the
temporal level: while rights may operate as an indisputable force of
emancipation at one moment in history—the American civil rights
movement or the struggle for equal rights by subjects of colonial domination such as black South Africans or Palestinians—they may become at another time a regulatory discourse—a means of obstructing
or co-opting more radical political demands or simply the most hollow
of empty promises.[5] This paradox is captured in part by Nietzsche's
insistence that liberal institutions cease to be liberal as soon as they are
attained.[6] It is expressed as well in the irony that rights sought by a
politically defined *group* are conferred upon depoliticized *individuals;*
at the moment a particular "we" succeeds in obtaining rights, it loses
its we-ness and dissolves into individuals. On the spatial or social
level: rights that empower those in one social location or stratum may
disempower those in another. The classic example is property rights,
which not only buttress the power of landlords and capital but also
help constitute the subjects called tenant and worker. Less obvious
examples would be the right to free speech, which some feminists
argue fortifies the "speech" of pornographers that in turn "silences"
women; or the right to privacy, a highly ambiguous right that differentially serves those differentially situated in that murky sphere demar-
cated as "the private." The point is that rights converge with powers
of social stratification and lines of social demarcation in ways that

---

4. To put this matter in an old-fashioned way, rights work within the dissimu-
lating ideology of modernism, and in this regard, there will always be something of a
chasm between the discourses of rights and their concrete operations.

5. I take this to be the force of Derrick Bell's argument in *Faces at the Bottom of the Well*
(New York: Basic Books, 1992), namely that whatever extraordinary historical and political event the Civil Rights movement was at the time, the emancipatory power of civil
rights practices *and* ideology does not necessarily endure over time. See also Kristin
Bumiller's *The Civil Rights Society* (Baltimore: Johns Hopkins University Press, 1992).

6. Friedrich Nietzsche, "Twilight of the Idols," in *The Portable Nietzsche*, ed.
W. Kaufmann (New York: Viking, 1954), 541.

extend as often as attenuate these powers and lines. And, when the temporal and spatial dimensions of the paradox of the universalistic idiom and particularistic force of rights are combined, we can see quite clearly the impossibility of saying anything generic about the political value of rights: It makes little sense to argue for them or against them independently of an analysis of the historical conditions, social powers, and political discourses with which they converge or which they interdict.

The universal-local paradox of rights is itself paradoxical insofar as the "discovery" that the value of rights is tethered to history, and that the political efficacy of rights shifts according to which social group is wielding them and what social powers situate them, is a discovery that occurs as "history" unravels and social "identity" destabilizes. Thus, we historicize rights in late modernity even as we discredit history as such, and we try to take the measure of the political effectivity of rights according to an analysis of social stratification even as we place in question the "structures" and fixity of the identities that such measurement presumes. And within this paradox lies still another: the late-modern effort to critically rework the individualist and universalist legacy of rights for a formulation that offers a potentially more fecund form of political recognition, namely "group rights," rights of "difference," or rights of "cultural minorities," is an effort also beset by the contemporary historical, geopolitical, and analytical destabilization of identity upon which such formulations depend. Here we circle back to the first paradox: If contemporary rights claims are deployed to protect historically and contextually contingent identities, might the relationship of the universal idiom of rights to the contingency of the protected identities be such that the former operates inadvertently to resubordinate by renaturalizing that which it was intended to emancipate by articulating? In the context of this paradox, our question acquires an analytic as well as a historical form: If, as Robert Meister paraphrases Hegel, "for itself, representation is a means for the people to transform the state [while] in itself, it is a means for the state to control the people," when do rights sought by identity "for itself" become "in themselves" a means of administration?[7] When does identity articulated through rights become produc-

7. Robert Meister, *Political Identity: Thinking Through Marx* (Oxford: Blackwell, 1990), 172.

tion and regulation of identity through law and bureaucracy? When does legal recognition become an instrument of regulation, and political recognition become an instrument of subordination?

Here is yet another way of casting this paradox: Historically, rights emerged in modernity both as a vehicle of emancipation from political disenfranchisement or institutionalized servitude and as a means of privileging an emerging bourgeois class within a discourse of formal egalitarianism and universal citizenship. Thus, they emerge both as a means of protection against arbitrary use and abuse by sovereign and social power and as a mode of securing and naturalizing dominant social powers—class, gender, and so forth. Not only did bourgeois rights discourse mask, by depoliticizing, the social power of institutions such as private property or the family, they also organized mass populations for exploitation and regulation, thus functioning as a modality of what Foucault termed "biopower."[8] But, like the others, this paradox is not only of anachronistic interest. How, we might ask, does this historical function of rights as operating both to emancipate and to dominate, both to protect and to regulate, resurface in contemporary articulations of rights, especially those sought for subjects recently, and patently, produced through regulatory discourses—subjects such as welfare mothers, surrogate mothers, or lesbian mothers?[9]

---

8. In this regard, I am taking slight distance from Foucault's suggestion that historically, disciplinary discourses displace or converge with discourses of rights, and I am suggesting instead that rights are from the beginning a potentially disciplinary practice.

Rosalind Petchesky and Eli Zaretsky have both argued that the juridical recognition of women in the late nineteenth century corresponded with expanded state and medical control over women's reproductive and sexual conduct. See Petchesky, *Abortion and Women's Choice: The State, Sexuality, and Reproductive Freedom* (New York: Longman, 1984); and Zaretsky, "The Place of the Family in the Origins of the Welfare State," in *Rethinking the Family: Some Feminist Questions*, ed. B. Thorne (New York: Longman, 1982). Through Michael Grossberg's study of nineteenth-century family law, Martha Minnow makes a similar point about the effect of children's rights in enlarging state power over both children and adults. Minnow cites Grossberg's *Governing the Hearth: Law and the Family in Nineteenth Century America*, 287–307, in "Interpreting Rights: An Essay for Robert Cover," *The Yale Law Review* 96 (1987): 1882, note 82.

9. If the traditional left critique of rights focuses on the law's decontextualization of persons from social power, the critique of contemporary legal efforts to *achieve* such contextualization, to recognize subjects as "effects" of social power, might be precisely that it reifies these effects, that it marks with a reactionary permanence the production of social subjects through, for example, "race," "gender," or "sexuality." A critique of contemporary efforts to install difference in the law would worry as well about the

I begin with this nest of paradoxes not to resolve them—paradox designates a condition in which resolution is the most uninteresting aim—but to avoid misconstrual of my critical engagement with contemporary rights discourse. I do not want to participate in an argument for or against rights as such—as the argument between critical legal studies thinkers and critical race theorists appears to have transpired—precisely because such an argument eschews the significance of historical timing, social power, and political cultural context in adjudicating the emancipatory value of rights discourse. Rather, I want to reflect upon the place of rights in the politics of politicized identities—rights of "inclusion" as well as rights of "difference" currently sought for people of color, homosexuals, and women in the late-twentieth-century United States.

In the service of such reflection, let us reconsider the critique of "political emancipation" embedded in Karl Marx's essay "On the Jewish Question." Arguably one of Marx's most philosophically and politically complex, and least programmatic, pieces of writing, the "Jewish Question" was and remains an occasion to inquire into the formulations of identity, state, and law configured by modernity, by liberal constitutional polities, and by capitalist economies. The quest for Jewish citizenship in a Prussian, Christian, or even ostensibly secular state raised for Marx, and for his left Hegelian protagonist Bruno Bauer, an ensemble of questions about the nature of religious identity, the state, citizenship, political consciousness, and political freedom. Do Jews want political recognition and rights as Jews or as persons? How does the demand for recognition construct Jewishness, personhood, and citizenship? How does this demand figure the state and political life—what is the state being asked to see or recognize, to disregard in its seeing, and to disavow in itself? Do Jews seeking emancipation want to be free from Judaism, free of Judaism, or free to be Jewish? What does it mean to turn to the state for such emancipation? What is the relationship between political representation, political identity, social identity, and religious identity? How does the nature of the political state transform one's social identity when one

---

analytical slide from social construction and constructions of subjectivity to social position and constructions of identity. It would worry about the conversion of articulations of modes of power complexly and temporally constitutive of subjectivity into static analyses of social position, which are then installed in the ahistorical discourse of the law.

turns to the state for political resolution of one's subordination, exclusion, or suffering? What kind of subject is being held out to the state for what kind of redress or redemption?

If there are, however, substantial riches to be mined from an essay concerned with such questions, there are also stumbling blocks in approaching "On the Jewish Question" to reconsider the formulations of identity, rights, and the state it poses. These include the anti-Semitism evinced in the essay, an anti-Semitism that has led some to dismiss it (and Marx) altogether, and others to eschew the extent to which the essay is concerned with Jews and Judaism by treating it either as an immanent critique of Hegelian philosophy or as a critique of liberal constitutional precepts, and for which, in either case, the Jewish question is only a heuristic device.[10] I will try to steer a third

---

10. While Marx goes well beyond the question of Jewish demands for political recognition and civil rights in his essay, he also comments directly on these demands and about "the nature of Jewishness." Some, but not all, of these remarks are anti-Semitic insofar as they heap scorn upon Jewish religion, deride Jewish culture, and traffic in degrading Jewish stereotypes. (At other moments, as we shall see, Marx's effort to use contrasts between Jewish and Christian sensibilities to understand the relationship between state and civil society is productive and incisive; however limited as religious history, it makes interesting political theory.) The question then, which admits of no simple answer, is how to handle this feature of Marx's critique of the movement for Jewish political emancipation in the Prussian state.

Provisionally, I want to say two things in order to proceed with the analysis of rights and identity I want to consider here. First, as quickly as I concluded that Marx's essay (and other essays and letters by him) includes anti-Semitic sentiments, nothing inherent concludes from this, any more than Hegel's sexism, Sartre's misogyny, or even Heidegger's ostensible Nazism constitutes the conclusion rather than the beginning of a discussion. Since there is good evidence that Marx was more racist than he was anti-Semitic, and it is a certainty that he took Jewish men more seriously than he took any woman, we need to ask *ourselves*, what precisely vexes us here? Is his anti-Semitism at issue because he was writing *about* the "Jewish Question?" Or is it the possible specter of self-hatred and dissimulation within the quest for assimilation that produces anxiety here? Why isn't J. S. Mill's sexism as bothersome to us? Is the problem anti-Semitism, Marx as a Jew, or Marx as a Jewish anti-Semite writing on the Jewish question? Related to this, if Marx's putative anti-Semitism pertains to his disparaging remarks about Judaism as "huckstering," what of his disparaging remarks about Christianity? Insofar as Marx criticized religion as such and criticized Christianity with vehemence, what specifically constitutes his critique of Judaism as anti-Semitism? These questions are not intended to defend Marx but rather to suggest that in objecting to his anti-Semitism, I am not certain that we know the nature of our objections, what unique place the charge of anti-Semitism occupies in our psyches, what psychic place is held by the self-hating Jew, and above all, why it is this and not Marx's terrible remarks about Africans or silences about women that are at issue.

course: Particularly in light of twentieth-century formations of European anti-Semitism, including those of the present, Marx's rough distillation of Judaism into "practical need, egoism,"[11] is certainly disturbing, as is his consequent resolution of the "Jewish Question" into the "general question of the age"—the domination of civil society by capital. But this is not the whole story of his treatment of Judaism in the essay, nor can his critique of Judaism be isolated from his more general critique of religion—his caricature of Christianity is at least as savage.

But rather than inquiring into the anti-Semitic elements of the Jewish assimilationist formulations of which Marx's essay is a particular expression, I want to consider the essay's characterizations of Judaism along different lines. The variations on "the Jewish question" across European states spurred Marx to attempt to diagnose politically, and resolve theoretically, the historically specific making and meaning

---

The second point responds to the impossibility of the answering the first in anything short of a separate study of the problem. If there is something of potential value in Marx's essay, but it is not easily extricable from the deprecations of Judaism and Jews, then we need to proceed with the double consciousness such a paradox demands, a consciousness quite familiar to critical race theorists, feminists, and postcolonial intellectuals who work in the humanities. In this kind of consciousness, one attends both to the exoteric argument or narrative of a novel or philosophical work, and simultaneously, to the effect of the anti-Semitism on the shape and turns of this argument. This reading strategy offers not simply a mode of "correcting" Marx's prejudice but, even more important, of learning, rather than preconceiving, how this prejudice operates both as philosophy and as politics. Indeed, one can learn a great deal about colonialism from reading Marguerite Duras, but that is not all that one acquires from her novels, nor finally, all that they reduce to. On the other hand, her love stories cannot be separated from their colonial settings and colonial narratives.

Sources on this issue: A careful, if somewhat cranky, consideration of the anti-Semitism in Marx's work, including a lengthy historical contextualization of the writing and its audience, is provided by Julius Carlebach, *Karl Marx and the Radical Critique of Judaism* (London: Routledge and Kegan Paul, 1978). Carlebach adjudicates the question of Marx's putative anti-Semitism this way: "If criticism leads to a denial of the right of the Jew to exist as a Jew, then the critic has become anti-Jewish. . . ." (6). A more recent contribution to the question of Marx's relationship to Judaism is provided by Dennis K. Fischman, *Political Discourse in Exile: Karl Marx and the Jewish Question* (Amherst: University of Massachusetts Press, 1991). For analysis of the *content* of Marx's writing about Jews, Fischman substitutes a study of the "Jewish patterns of thought" that shape Marx's concerns, perspectives, values, and formulations. And an interesting contribution to the problem by Isaiah Berlin, "Benjamin Disraeli, Karl Marx, and the Search for Identity," can be found in a collection of his essays, *Against the Current: Essays in the History of Ideas*, ed. H. Hardy (London: Hogarth, 1979).

11. Karl Marx, "On the Jewish Question," *The Marx-Engels Reader*, 2d ed., ed. R. Tucker (New York: Norton, 1978), 50.

of the Jewish quest for political membership in a variety of states, some
of which bore tacit rather than explicit Christian investments.[12] And it
is this formulation of the problem that may be of use in thinking about
contemporary campaigns by feminists, gay activists, indigenous peoples, and people of color for emancipation through and for rather than
in spite of their "difference," for recognition from a state whose
masculinism, heterosexism, and whiteness is also frequently tacit
rather than explicit. In other words, precisely because Jews sought
political rights as secular Jews in Christian as well as "secular" states,
precisely because the "Jewish question" does not issue from a wholly
liberal claim to generic personhood on the part of the historically
disenfranchised, Marx's essay has potentially rich contemporary resonance. Insofar as the analysis concerns the complex political claims and
aspirations of a marked identity not constituted *solely* through subjugation and exclusion, not reducible to a social-economic category, not
figurable as a "difference" entirely attributable to a form of social power
as class is attributable to property relations, the quest for Jewish civil
and political rights in European nation-states in the nineteenth century
bears some (incomplete) parallels to antiassimilationist juridical claims
generated by contemporary identity politics.[13]

Marx begins with a notoriously ungenerous engagement with Bruno
Bauer's own attempt to "resolve" the Jewish question. But Marx is
ultimately less interested in the left Hegelianism Bauer espouses than
in the historical condition of which Marx takes Bauer (as well as Hegelianism, right and left) to be a political and philosophical symptom.
For Bauer, the Jewish question arises as a consequence of the unemancipated *consciousness* of Jews on the one hand and the state on the
other: as long as the Jew privileges his Judaism (his partial nature)

12. See Carlebach's *Karl Marx and the Radical Critique of Judaism* for a discussion of
the ways in which assimilation in general, and conversion and baptism in particular,
figured in both the background and foreground of "the Jewish question" in Marx's
time.

13. This, notwithstanding Marx's own effort to reduce Judaism to an "empirical
essence of . . . huckstering and its conditions," and thus to render Judaism as a "historically produced need" and "the Jewish question" as a *symptom* of an age materially
dominated by relations of capital and spiritually dominated by Christianity. At the
extreme, Marx casts Judaism as the avatar of "material egoism" and civil society, dialecti-
cally opposed to Christianity, as the avatar of "spiritual egoism," imaginary transcendence, and the state ("Jewish Question," 52).

above his universal personhood, and as long as the state privileges its Christianity above its universal (secular) nature, this partiality (in both senses of the word) prevents the recognition and realization of "the universal humanity of man."[14]

Marx's objection to Bauer's formulation is that within its terms, both the state and the Jew could give up their religious "prejudice" and in so doing be "politically emancipated" without being emancipated from religion. What, Marx asks, is the nature of the emancipation Bauer advocates such that it addresses only the way the state and the Jew respectively *represent* themselves, the way each *thinks* of itself in a political way, such that the formal secularism demanded from each in no way affects the "actual religiosity" of either? What does it mean to render "prejudice" a matter of attitude and freedom, a matter of words and representation, a matter of pose? And why does Bauer's (idealist) formulation of freedom so closely resemble that represented by the state itself? Is it significant that the left Hegelian formulation of freedom as a problem of consciousness, representation, and state proclamations is precisely the formulation of freedom animating and legitimating the liberal constitutional state?

In contending that the "actual religiosity" of the state and its citizens is undiminished by the declared irrelevance of religion to politics, Marx is concerned not simply with the religious *belief* harbored by Jews or the state, but, more importantly, with the conditions that give rise to religious consciousness, the conditions that produce and require religion. While Marx and Bauer share a view of religious consciousness as "a defect," Marx regards this consciousness, and the state's participation in it (expressed in the very declaration that it is *free* of religion when it ceases to determine political membership on the basis of religion), as historically necessary rather than contingent. To the extent that religious consciousness is historically produced rather than freely adopted, it cannot, as Bauer would have it, be "cast off like snake skins." Here is Marx:

> The question is: What is the relation between *complete* political emancipation and religion? If we find in the country which has attained full political emancipation [the United States], that religion not only continues to exist but is fresh and vigorous, this is

---

14. Marx, "Jewish Question," 28.

proof that the existence of religion is not at all opposed to the perfection of the state. But since the existence of religion is the existence of a defect, the source of this defect must be sought in the nature of the state itself. Religion no longer appears as the basis, but as the *manifestation* of secular narrowness. That is why we explain the religious constraints upon the free citizens by the secular constraints upon them. We do not claim that they must transcend their religious narrowness in order to get rid of their secular limitations. We claim that they will transcend their religious narrowness once they have overcome their secular limitations. We do not turn secular questions into theological questions; we turn theological questions into secular ones.[15]

Critical here is Marx's effort to reveal the metalepsis in Hegelian thinking about the relation between religious and secular life, consciousness and institutions. This effort is most apparent in his insistence that religious consciousness is a *manifestation* of, rather than the *basis* of, what he calls "secular narrowness"—the social and political constraints upon substantive freedom, equality, and community. This, in a vernacular foreign to the one we now speak, is Marx's method of de-essentializing in order to deconstruct political expressions of cultural, ethnic, or religious identity. Reading religious consciousness as a political symptom, even a site of injury and despair about freedom in *this* world, Marx seeks to avoid responding to it as a political demand issuing from fixed political identities or interests.

What Marx calls religious narrowness, what we might term investments in particular identities, is not blamed by him as it is by Bauer upon those who have such investments and fail to understand their place in the world of universal humanity, nor upon the state's failure to look beyond such investments to the universal humanity of its subjects. Marx's critique of Bauer's Hegelian emphasis upon the independence of consciousness—either in individuals or in the state—turns on his derivation of "religious narrowness" from the specific political

---

15. Ibid., 31. Marx's point about the "fresh, vigorous" character of religion in the United States was repeated on September 16, 1992, almost verbatim, by Governor Bill Clinton on the presidential campaign trail as he argued for the continuation of religious tolerance and separation of church and state. "In no other advanced nation," Clinton remarked, "is religion so widely practiced, do so many people go to church, synagogues, temples, and mosques."

conditions that require this "narrowness"—conditions that are obscured rather than redressed through formal emancipation, through acquisition of the right to be free of the political stigma of this narrowness. In fact, Marx argues, the limits of political emancipation "appear at once in the fact that the state can liberate itself from a constraint without man himself really being liberated."[16]

The political "constraint" to which Marx refers is the state's vulnerability to *reproach* for a religious bearing, for its appearance of failed or incomplete secularism. Yet the state is no more liberated from religion by declaring itself religiously tolerant than it is liberated from private property through the "abolition of the property qualification" for suffrage.[17] Insofar as Marx *de-literalizes* both religion and secularism, he is able to establish the state's religiosity as inhering not in express religious statements but in its transcendent ideology, its representation of universal humanity above the mortal particulars of civil society. The constitutional state he is analyzing is homologically Christian in its reduction of freedom to pronouncements of freedom, in its equation of equality with the declaration that it regards us as equal, in its creation of equality through its ideology of popular sovereignty— in short, in its *idealist* resolution of our relative lack of freedom, equality, and community.

The "constraint" from which political emancipation "frees" the individual is politicized identity—the treatment of a particular social identity as the basis for deprivation of suffrage, rights, or citizenship. But, Marx repeats, emancipation from this "constraint" does not liberate the individual from the conditions constitutive or reiterative of the identity. To the contrary, it is only in abstraction from such conditions that the individual can be "emancipated" by the universal state:

> [M]an frees himself from a constraint in a political way, through the state, when he transcends his limitations, in contradiction with himself, and in an *abstract, narrow, and partial way.* Furthermore, by emancipating himself politically, man emancipates himself in a *devious* way, through an intermediary, however necessary this intermediary might be.[18]

16. Marx, "Jewish Question," 31.
17. Ibid., 33.
18. Ibid., 32.

Marx's characterization of political emancipation as "devious" does not constitute a moral objection to the evident hypocrisy of the liberal state. Such an objection would remain within the rubric of liberalism in which certain attitudes or postures on the part of the state become eligible for moral criticism and potentially, reform; this is exactly the kind of criticism in which Marx considered left Hegelians like Bauer to be wrongheadedly engaged. Rather, "deviousness" here signals a ruse of power necessitated when the requisites of power's legitimacy generate a promise upon which they cannot deliver; deviousness connotes the political culture of *indirection* and *mediation* inherent within, rather than accidental to, this political condition.[19]

In Marx's account, the ruse of power peculiar to liberal constitutionalism centers upon granting freedom, equality, and representation to *abstract* rather than concrete subjects. The substitution of abstract political subjects for actual ones not only forfeits the project of emancipation, but also *resubjugates* us precisely by emancipating substitutes for us—by emancipating our abstracted representatives in the state and naming this process "freedom." The subject is thus *ideally emancipated* through anointment as an abstract person, a formally free and equal human being, and is *practically resubordinated* through this idealist disavowal of the material constituents of personhood, through disavowal of that which constrains and contains our freedom. Thus, it is because we are in this way subjugated by the very discourse of our freedom that liberal freedom is structurally, not merely definitionally, ambiguous. The notion of "representative" and the process by which we "author" the state in Hobbes's *Leviathan* exemplifies this condition, and Rousseau makes a similar point in his critique of representative government in the "Discourse on Inequality" and the *Social Contract*.[20] Marx himself develops this point through an analogy *between* the state and Christianity:

Religion is simply the recognition of man in a roundabout fashion; that is, through an intermediary. The state is the intermediary

19. Using the notion of the camera obscura, Marx will offer a more substantial account of this feature of political power in the theory of the relationship between consciousness and power developed in *The German Ideology*.

20. Thomas Hobbes, *Leviathan*, ed. C.B. Macpherson (Harmondsworth: Penguin, 1968), chap. 16, and Jean Jacques Rousseau, "Discourse on Inequality," *The First and Second Discourses*, ed. Roger Masters (New York: St. Martin's Press, 1964) and *The Social Contract*, ed. M. Cranston (Harmondsworth: Penguin, 1968)

between man and human liberty. Just as Christ is the intermediary
to whom man attributes all his own divinity and all his religious
bonds, so the state is the intermediary to which man confides all his
non-divinity and all his human freedom.[21]

Here again it becomes clear why Marx not only considers political
emancipation partial, narrow, and contradictory, but also why he insists that the "secular" state is Christian in character: As Christ represents man's holiness, the state represents man's freedom, and in both
cases, this representation abstracts from the unfree and unholy conditions of man's actual life. Moreover, these unfree and unholy conditions are the basis of both state and Christianity—as the conditions of
real as opposed to abstract human beings, they are the conditions that
necessitate the state and Christianity. As Christianity consecrates a
ghostly ideal of man as divine and leaves actual man to suffer on
earth, so the state liberates its ideal of man and abandons actual man
to the actual powers that construct, buffet, and subject him.

In one of his earliest formulations of the *political* structure of
alienation in modern society, Marx then argues that both Christianity
and the constitutional state require that "man lead not only in
thought . . . but in reality, in life, a double existence—celestial and
terrestrial";[22] this "double existence" is one in which heavenly life is
inaccessible and earthly life is degraded. Insofar as Christianity and
the bourgeois state are the available discourses for self-understanding
and political articulation, it is in what Marx calls "real life"—life in
civil society and on earth—that man will be most illusory to himself,
while the "imaginary domains" of the state and heaven articulate the
"real nature" of man:

> [Man] lives in the *political community,* where he regards himself as
> a *communal being,* and in *civil society,* where he acts simply as a
> *private individual,* treats other men as means, degrades himself to
> the role of a mere means, and becomes the plaything of alien
> powers. The political state, in relation to civil society, is just as
> spiritual as is heaven in relation to earth. It stands in the same
> opposition to civil society, and overcomes it in the same manner

---

21. Marx, "Jewish Question," 32.
22. Ibid., 34.

as religion overcomes the narrowness of the profane world; i.e., it has always to acknowledge it again, re-establish it, and allow itself to be dominated by it . . . In the state . . . where he is regarded as a species-being, man is the imaginary member of an imaginary sovereignty, divested of his real, individual life, and infused with an unreal universality.[23]

In the political state, "man treats political life, which is remote from his own individual existence, as if it were his own true life"— this formulation constitutes the religious consciousness of the state. However, Marx also insists that "religion is here the spirit of civil society" insofar as it "expresses the separation and withdrawal of man from man" and insofar as "every man is considered a sovereign being, a Supreme Being, but it is alienated man, man lost to himself. . . ."[24] The Christian dimension of the liberal ideological formulation of the state and civil society ordered by capitalism rests here: although anointed as a sovereign, even a supreme being, man's sovereignty is ghostly, alienated, and finally, punishing, insofar as it casts this isolated and impotent creature as fully accountable for himself. Man is proclaimed king but limited by his powerlessness and alienation; his crown ultimately serves to bewilder, isolate, and humiliate him.[25]

Remarking that "the political elevation of man above religion shares the weaknesses and merits of all such political measures,"[26]

---

23. Ibid.

24. Ibid., 39.

25. If Marx's analysis is difficult to follow at this point, this is because he is doing three things at once: he is criticizing religion and the state, establishing a homology between them, *and* establishing their philosophical, as well as material and historical, presupposition of each other. This is Marx, in other words, in his least economistic and most deconstructive mode, but it is deconstruction in a historically progressive motif, governed by the dialectic, reason in history, and analytically coherent, if contradictory, social totalities. While it is Marx's genius to sustain the analysis on all three levels at once, it may also be this genius, steeped in Hegelianism, that leads Marx to overstate the theological dimension of the constitutional state. Here is the extended passage from which the citation in the text is drawn:

The members of the political state are religious because of the dualism between individual life and species-life, between the life of civil society and political life. They are religious in the sense that man treats political life, which is remote from his own individual existence, as if it were his true life; and in the sense that religion is here the spirit of civil society, and expresses the separation and withdrawal of man from man. ("Jewish Question," 39)

26. Marx, "Jewish Question," 33.

Marx makes clear that he is not against political emancipation, which he deems "a great progress . . . the final form of human emancipation *within* the framework of the prevailing social order,"[27] but, rather, seeks to articulate the historical conditions of its emergence and its consequent limitations. The "deviousness" of political emancipation—its removal of a stratifying social power from political standing—calls not for refusal of this form of emancipation, but for analysis of the kind of social and political relations engendering and engendered by it. In particular, Marx is interested in how the state's "emancipation" from particular social powers operates as a form of *political suppression* and thus *tacit legitimation* of these powers, and how, at the same time, this process itself *constitutes* the power and legitimacy of the liberal state. Thus, for example, the elimination of the "property qualification" for citizenship constitutes the "ideal abolition" of private property since the "property qualification is the last *political* form in which private property is recognized." Yet

> the political suppression of private property not only does not abolish private property; it actually presupposes its existence. The state abolishes after its fashion, the distinctions established by birth, social rank, education, occupation, when it decrees that [these] are *non-political* distinctions; when it proclaims, without regard to these distinctions, that every member of society is an *equal* partner in popular sovereignty . . . But the state, none the less, allows private property, education, occupation, to *act* after *their* own fashion, namely as private property, education, occupation, and to manifest their particular nature. Far from abolishing these *effective* differences, it only exists so far as they are presupposed; it is conscious of being a *political* state and it manifests its *universality* only in opposition to these elements. . . . Only in this manner, *above* the *particular* elements, can the state constitute itself as universality.[28]

If civil society is striated by forms of social power that the state declares politically insignificant, and the state's universality or "perfected secularism" is premised upon its transcendence of the particu-

27. Ibid., 35.
28. Ibid., 33.

larism of civil society, then the state is premised upon that which it pretends to transcend; it requires that which it claims to abolish; it reinforces by politically suppressing (removing from political discourse) that which grounds its raison d'être. But in addition to its legitimacy, the state achieves a good deal of its power through its "devious" claims to resolve the very inequalities it actually entrenches by depoliticizing. Achieving its "universality" and reinstantiating the "particularity" of civil society through this depoliticization, by this ruse it also acquires its own "right" to govern—to legislate and adjudicate, to mobilize and deploy force.[29]

If, according to Marx, the bourgeois constitutional state is premised upon depoliticized inegalitarian social powers, if it depends upon naturalizing egoistic civil society and abstract representations of equality and community, *rights* comprise the modern political form that secures and legitimates these tendencies. Rights emblematize the ghostly sovereignty of the unemancipated individual in modernity. In order to see the connections as Marx makes them, we must return

---

29. It may be appropriate here to mark the way in which Marx's critique of universalism, and the constitutional state's embodiment of it, differs from many contemporary critiques, particularly those trafficking under the sign of postmodernism, post-Marxism, or poststructuralism. For Marx, the false universalism of the state presupposes *and* entrenches unresolved particulars, stratifying social powers that not only enact subordination and sustain poverty, but also estrange human beings from one another and divide us against our respective selves. The unreal communal life of the state presupposes the general egoism of civil society and enforces a dualism between "political man . . . abstract, artificial man, man as an allegorical, moral person," and "man in his sensuous, individual, and immediate nature, man as a member of civil society" ("Jewish Question," 46). For post-Marxist critics of liberal universalism, the problem is of a different order: universalism is less an unrealized political ideal than an unrealizable one, a bad political metonymy in which particular kinds of humans and positions masquerade as generic or universal. Marx is not without sympathy for this position—indeed, his appreciation of the extent to which universalist discourse is always strategically deployed by the dominant or the would-be dominant is cogently expressed in *The German Ideology*: "For each new class which puts itself in the place of one ruling before it, is compelled, merely in order to carry through its aim, to represent its interest as the common interest of all the members of society, that is, expressed in ideal form: it has to give its ideas the form of universality, and represent them as the only rational, universally valid ones" (*German Ideology, The Marx-Engels Reader*, 2d ed., ed. R. Tucker [New York: Norton, 1978], 174). But especially for the early Marx, history is making its way toward true, as opposed to strategic, universalism; while for most post-Marxist critics, universalism is unredeemable insofar as it is always one with the hegemonic aims of the historically dominant.

briefly to his engagement with Bauer on the question of Jews' entitlement to rights.

According to Marx, Bauer argued that the Jew could neither
acquire nor concede to others the universal rights of man because his
"Jewish nature," and more particularly his avowal of its effect in
separating him from other men (gentiles), prohibited his entitlement
to rights that *associate* all men with each other.[30] In Bauer's view,
"man has to sacrifice the 'privilege of faith' in order to acquire the
general rights of man," in order to acquire membership in the community that delivers these rights.[31] But why should this be, Marx
asks, when the rights of man are nothing more than the rights of "a
member of civil society . . . of egoistic man, of man separated from
other men and from the community?[32] Nothing about these rights,
Marx notes, pertains to human association, membership, or participation in political community; consequently there is no basis for with-
holding them from anyone, regardless of particulars of social station,
faith, or consciousness.

It is within this analytical vein, where rights are figured as both
manifestations and entrenchments of a specific historical production
of egoistic man in civil society, that Marx proffers his (in)famous
critique of bourgeois rights. This critique is not a condemnation but
an exposure of the way rights encode rather than emancipate us
from the social powers and social formations that are the conditions
of our unfreedom. Thus, Marx calls the constitutional right to liberty
the right of "separation" from other men, the "right of the circumscribed individual, withdrawn into himself."[33] The right to private
property, as the "practical application of the right of liberty," is only
"the right of self-interest."[34] And equality, putatively the most profound political achievement of liberalism, Marx identifies as a "term
which has no political significance" since it is "only the equal right to
liberty [in which] every man is equally regarded as a self-sufficient
monad."[35] Liberal equality, insofar as it neither constitutes political
community nor achieves substantive equality, guarantees only that

---

30. Marx, "Jewish Question," 40.
31. Ibid.
32. Ibid., 42
33. Ibid.
34. Ibid.
35. Ibid.

all individuals will be treated *as if* they were sovereign and isolated individuals. Liberal equality guarantees that the state will regard us all as equally abstracted from the social powers constituting our existence, equally decontextualized from the unequal conditions of our lives.

Marx concludes this brief assessment of rights with a consideration of the constitutional guarantee of security, "the supreme social concept of society; the concept of the *police.*"[36] Imprecisely termed a right but underpinning the basic bargain of the social contract in which we largely surrender to the state the power to protect our lives and our property, the concept of "security" reveals the essential character of this society and the historically configured obsession of its members: "The concept of security is not enough to raise civil society above its egoism. Security is, rather, the *assurance* of its egoism."[37] The state founded on the promise to secure its members against each other is thus the state that provides an antipolitical "resolution" of the historically produced Hobbesian character of civil society. Like rights themselves, the state's constitutional guarantee of security, embodied in "the concept of the police," reifies a historical condition as an ontological one, naturalizing rather than redressing it.

Certainly Marx's polemical treatment of the civil liberties foundational to the liberal state could be criticized for the undeconstructed binary oppositions it deploys: ideal versus material, theological versus secular, state versus civil society, mediated versus unmediated freedom, egoism versus association, universal versus particular. It could also be impugned for presenting as immanent critique what is actually bound to a panoply of normative referents: radical egalitarianism, "real" popular sovereignty, and "true" political community unmediated by the state. Moreover, insofar as rights are not tethered to the values Marx endorses but serve other ends, he could be faulted for demanding from them what they were not intended to figure or deliver. His criticism of the liberal state for reducing the political to a "mere means" glosses the possibilities that, on the one hand, rights need not be the *end* of liberal political states, and that, on the other, liberal

36. Ibid., 43.
37. Ibid.

individuals, even socially subordinated ones, may want nothing more than state-secured rights and protection—they may bear no desire for radical freedom or community.

We shall return shortly to the problem of binary oppositions and progressive historiography in Marx's critique. For the moment, I want to suggest that while Marx's critique of the "egoism" of rights is fueled by ideals of political and economic life which exceed liberal aims, its force is not wholly dependent on these norms nor on the extent to which liberalism forecloses them. Rather, it depends upon a critical reading of the form of political life produced by the social relations of capital; it depends upon understanding the domination and alienation entailed in capitalist social relations as simultaneously reiterated and obscured by the political life they generate.

In Marx's view, the transition from feudal monarchy to bourgeois democracy entailed a form of economic and political revolution that "abolished the political character of civil society," that is, put an end to the ways in which "elements of civil life such as property, the family, and types of occupation had been raised, in the form of lordship, caste and guilds, to elements of political life."[38] The European political revolutions that abolished monarchy at the same time shattered the expressly political form of social and economic stratifications, the estates and corporations. "The political revolution therefore *abolished* the *political character of civil society*" such that "a specific activity and situation in life no longer had any but an individual significance."[39] Marx is again underscoring how certain modalities of social and economic domination are less eliminated than *depoliticized* by the political revolutions heralding formal equality, although these modalities are transformed by virtue of being depoliticized, losing their formal representation in the state as estates. At the same time, Marx is seeking to articulate the extent to which the modern *individual* is produced by and through, indeed *as*, this depoliticization and in the image of this depoliticization. He is proffering a political genealogy of the sovereign individual, a genealogy that features the depoliticization of social relations as the crucial site of production of this sovereignty. Put the other way around, Marx exposes the modern formulation of sovereignty as itself a modality of discursive depoliticization. Power as circulating

38. Ibid., 44.
39. Ibid., 45.

and relational—as located not in the state but in social relations and the movement of history—is ideologically suppressed in the congealed and static persona of sovereignty.

Marx's criticism does not stop with depicting the political emancipation or declared sovereignty of the individual as its effective depoliticization. He also posits the depoliticization of civil society as the "consummation" of the materialism of civil society and the removal of political community to the realm of the state as the "consummation" of the idealism of the state.[40] Community is figured in a ghostly way in the state, and social atomism is the concrete reality of civil society. But in becoming celestial and otherworldly, abstracted from the real character of its subjects, the state also figures its future overcoming, its future irrelevance. And in becoming thoroughly material and egoistical, civil society forecasts its disintegration:

> The bonds which had restrained the egoistic spirit of civil society were removed along with the political yoke. Political emancipation was at the same time an emancipation of civil society from politics and from even the *semblance* of a general content.[41]

Establishing the breakup of the feudal state as that which "frees" civil society in a double sense—from feudal bondage but also from the bonds of association that express our ontological sociality, "from even the semblance of a general content"—Marx signals the ambiguousness that for him characterizes not only bourgeois rights but also the spirit of capitalism. (Recall that this double freedom is also how Marx ironically frames the condition of the proletariat in *Capital*. In contrast with the serf, the proletarian is free to sell his labor power to any buyer but is also "free" in the sense of being unburdened and deracinated: he lacks any means of survival other than selling his labor power. The proletarian's "freedom" is thus the source of his radical exploitability *and* of his expanded political capaciousness.) Similarly, when Marx refers to the representation of man in the political state as the "ideal" of man, he is identifying the state representation of community and equality as directly contradicted by the egoism of rights-bearing sovereign individuals in the depoliticized domain of civil society. And he is

---

40. *Vollendung*, which Tucker translates as "consummation," means completion, termination, ending, and perfection.
41. Marx, "Jewish Question," 45.

identifying rights as fundamentally ambiguous: both a marker of our unfreedom and of our expanded political capaciousness.

What should be evident by now is that in contrast with some critical legal studies scholars' anxieties about the individualism of rights, Marx's analysis in the "Jewish Question" is neither a moral critique nor an ontological claim about the "nature of rights." Rather, Marx's characterization of rights as egoistic rests on a reading of the ways in which the historical emergence of the "rights of man" naturalize and thus entrench historically specific, unavowed social powers that set us against each other, preoccupy us with property, security, and freedom of movement, and stratify us economically and socially. "The liberty of egoistic man, and the recognition of this liberty . . . is the recognition of the *frenzied* movement of the cultural and material elements which form the content of his life."[42] In other words, the kind of liberty that bourgeois rights discourse casts as natural is actually the *effect* of the historically specific elements constitutive of life in civil society. Through rights discourse, bourgeois social relations are reified as bourgeois man, and the rights required by this "frenzied" (*zugellosen*, actually "unbridled") social order are misapprehended as required by and confirming the naturalness of the man it produces.

For Marx, then, the political culture of "egoism" and rights produces not mere individualism but anxious, defended, self-absorbed, and alienated Hobbesian subjects who are driven to accumulate, diffident toward others, obligated to none, made impossibly accountable for themselves, and subjected by the very powers their sovereignty is supposed to exude. "Egoism" also connotes the discursive depoliticization of this production; it connotes a discursive order of sovereign, self-made, and privatized subjects who subjectively experience their own powerlessness as their own failure vis-à-vis other sovereign subjects. In sum, even as they emancipate certain groups and certain energies from historical suppression, bourgeois rights codify the social needs generated by historically specific, traumatic social powers as natural, unhistorical, and permanent.

Marx's criticisms of bourgeois rights might be distilled thus:

1. Bourgeois rights are rendered necessary by the depoliticized material conditions of unemancipated, inegalitarian civil soci-

---

42. Ibid.

ety, conditions that rights themselves depoliticize rather than articulate or resolve.

2. They entrench by naturalizing the egoism of capitalist society, reifying the "frenzied movement of the material elements" of this society as the nature of man, thereby masking social power and mistaking its effects—atomistic individuals—for its wellspring and agents.

3. They construct an illusory politics of equality, liberty, and community in the domain of the state, a politics that is contradicted by the unequal, unfree, and individualistic domain of civil society.

4. They legitimize by naturalizing various stratifying social powers in civil society, and they disguise the state's collusion with this social power, thereby also legitimating the state as a neutral and universal representative of the people. They disguise the actual power constitutive of both civil society and the state through the ruse of establishing fictional sovereignty in the domain of civil society, and illusory liberty, equality, and community in the state.

Marx's *enthusiasm* for political emancipation, including bourgeois rights, could be distilled thus:

1. Being regarded by the state *as if* we were free and equal is an improvement over being treated as if we were naturally subjected and unequal vis-à-vis stratifying social powers. Insofar as personhood and membership in community are ideally cast as unconstrained by these social powers, political emancipation constitutes *progress*. (Here, a discerning contemporary eye might see an analysis concerned with the way ideological idealism masks social power slide into one that emphasizes the discursive production of political possibility.)

2. The ideal of freedom, equality, and community in the bourgeois state figures the (historically unrealized) *desire* for these goods, and, in a historical process governed by dialectical materialism, they will be realized through the establishment of the material conditions for them.

3. Related, political emancipation in the form of civil and political rights can be embraced precisely because it represents a

"stage" of emancipation. In dialectical analysis, the failure of rights to procure "true human emancipation" is made manifest in our experienced unfreedom and alienation, and is overcome by the development of forms of association appropriate to a society that has "revolutionized its elements" and transcended its egoism.

Marx's essay produces two sets of questions for contemporary political struggles waged under the rubric of identity politics. First, if the desire for rights in liberalism is, in part, a desire to depoliticize or unmark one's social existence, to be free of the politicization of subordinating social powers, and if, in this respect, rights entail a turn away from the political, how do they also advance a political struggle to transform the social conditions of one's making? What, if anything, guarantees their instrumental deployment in this direction? Moving Marx's account into a more Foucaultian register, to the extent that the egoism of rights, their discursive formation of the sovereign individual, obscures the social forces *producing* rather than merely marking particular groups *or* behaviors as subhuman, rights appear to discursively bury the very powers they are designed to contest. To the extent that the "egoism of society" both provokes rights claims and is entrenched by them, the social relations iterating class, sexuality, race, and gender would appear to be individualized through rights discourse, ascribed to persons as attribute or internal content rather than social effect. If rights thus reify by individualizing the social power they are designed to protect against, what are the political implications of doing both? What happens when we understand individual rights as a form of protection *against* certain social powers of which the ostensibly protected individual is actually an *effect*? If, to paraphrase Marx, rights do not liberate us from relations of class, gender, sexuality, or race, but only from formal recognition of these elements as politically significant, thereby liberating them "to *act* after their own fashion," how does the project of political emancipation square with the project of transforming the conditions against which rights are sought as protection?

The second set of questions pertains to the place of rights in legitimating the humanistic dimensions of liberal discourse. To what extent is the power of a humanist fiction of universality affirmed as the mantle of generic personhood sought by the historically disenfranchised? How is the metonymic operation of the generic person obscured by the increasingly wide distribution of his political attributes? How can the invidious dimensions of universalist claims be contested even as the historically disenfranchised seek a place under their auspices?

These questions become more vexed when the progressive historiography presumed by Marx is excised from his critique of rights, when the contradiction between "political emancipation" and "true, human emancipation" is no more likely to erupt as radical consciousness or be transcended through revolution than various contradictions within capitalism are likely to explode into a socialist alternative. Absent this teleology, instead of rights constituting a "historical stage" of the progress toward emancipation, they figure a political culture that daily recapitulates its value in anointing and protecting personhood, and daily reiterates the "egoism" out of which rights emerge. Operating as a "discursive regime" rather than a "stage" in the history of emancipation, rights appear as political ends rather than historical or political instruments. And situated within the larger context of Weberian rationalization in modernity, a process whereby instrumental rationality cancerously supplants all other values, whereby all means become ends, the so-called "litigious culture" disparaged across the contemporary political spectrum appears as more than a contingent item for political criticism.[43] In this recasting, rights discourse appears in opposition to—rather than a stage in the progress toward—alternative modes of redressing social subjugation expressed as politicized identity. When "history" is no longer regarded as driven by structural contradictions and tethered to the telos of freedom, the delusion is no longer possible that "every emancipation is a restoration of the human world and of human relationships to man himself."[44]

---

43. The political range of critics of the "litigious society" is quite wide: from George Bush's 1992 campaign attack on "trial lawyers" to Mary Ann Glendon's *Rights Talk: The Impoverishment of Political Discourse* (New York: Free Press, 1991), to Ben Barber's worry over the contemporary privatizing turn of rights discourse ("Constitutional Rights: Democratic Institution or Democratic Obstacle?" in *The Framers and Fundamental Rights*, ed. R. Licht [Washington, D.C.: AIE Press, 1992]) and Michael Walzer's kindred worry in *What It Means to Be An American*, especially the essay therein entitled, "Constitutional Rights and the Shape of Civil Society" (New York: Marsilio, 1992).

44. Marx, "Jewish Question," 46. There is a question, at least in my mind, about whether poststructuralist critiques of historical metanarrative are themselves appropriately historicized such that only *in our time* does progressive historiography collapse, or whether to subscribe to the stronger claim that all progressive notions of history were

Yet it is also the case that when we cease to regard history as composed of coherent social totalities and single threads of progress, and view it instead in terms of converging and conflicting discourses and genealogies, a different order of political thinking becomes possible. Consider the difference in the relationship between history and freedom conceived by Marx and by Foucault: For Marx, political promise inheres in the dialectical movement of history toward freedom. (Animated generally by a drive to overcome scarcity expressed in the developmental aspect of modes of production, history is specifically powered by the class struggles that occur at the point of contradictions between the means, mode, and relations of production.) Thus, for Marxists, history voided of a teleological project (achieved by exposure of the religious Hegelian metanarrative at the core of Marxist historiography) implies the political nightmare of nihilism or of eternal daylight, of time frozen. The forfeiture of historical design implied by the "end of history," by the bankruptcy of the principle of temporal (dialectical) movement forward, signals the political crisis of a total present. It heralds totalitarianism insofar as the pervasive domination in the social totality Marxism depicts is without a principle of self-overcoming. Marxist critique absent redemption through dialectic, it may be recalled, was precisely the logic structuring the dark conclusions of Marcuse's *One Dimensional Man*.

For Foucault, on the other hand, the "end of history" is less a political problem than a political relief. The critique of metanarrative offers reprieve not only from humanist conceits but from temporal or structural models of power: economistic models, in which power is figured as a wieldable commodity, and repressive models, in which power is figured as suppressing the capacities of a transcendent subject. The critique of teleology in history releases us as well from models of the political subject framed in the (global) narrative of identity, subjugation, and redemption. Reason in history, which requires both the fiction of social totalities and the fiction of epochal periodization, is made to give way to genealogical analyses of selected regimes of truth, analyses that make no claim to spatial or temporal comprehensive-

---

thoroughgoing fictions. I remain enough of a Marxist to find it difficult to surrender the notion of "development" in an economically driven historiography that accounts for the "transition" from feudalism to capitalism, from competitive capitalism to corporate capitalism, and from industrial to postindustrial capitalism in the global economic core (Europe and North America).

ness. We are also incited to conceive the problematic of power in spatial yet nonstructural terms and temporal yet nonlinear terms: space is refigured as the domain in which multiple and contestable discourses operate, and time as a domain of imprecise and refigurable repetition. Intervention or resignification is possible in both dimensions insofar as power is reconceived outside discourses of laws of history, structures, and even hegemony. In this regard, Foucault's insistence on the spatialization of power means that "history" finally becomes human even as the "human" becomes a relentless production.

Yet if Foucault's critique of progressivist historiography offers reprieve from historical and political perspectives tethered to social totalities and temporal stages, thereby varying and widening the field of political intervention, his investigations into the nature of power also thicken the problem posed by depoliticizing discourses such as those of rights. In his concern with disciplinary power, in his articulation of how certain discourses are forged into *regimes* of truth, and in his formulation of power as that which *produces* subjects rather than simply suppressing or positioning them, Foucault conjures a political field with relatively little open space and none of the tricks of self-overcoming, of forward motion, contained in Marxist historiography. This Foucaultian discernment of power where neither Marxism nor liberalism perceives it forces a rethinking of the Marxist formulation of politicized identity and rights claims. The Foucaultian discernment not only severs "political emancipation" from a phantasmatic progress of emancipation, it also problematizes the Marxist presumption that the quest for such emancipation issues from historically subordinated or excluded subjects seeking a place in a discourse of universal personhood. It suggests instead that these claims may issue from contemporary productions of the subject by regulatory norms, productions which may be entrenched as much as challenged or loosened through political recognition and acquisition of rights. In other words, the collapse of a progressivist historiography becomes more weighty given the extent to which contemporary discourses of rights converge with the disciplinary production of identities seeking them, given the extent to which contemporary discourses of political emancipation may be a product not simply of stratified and egoistic civil society, but of disciplinary modalities of power producing the very subjects whose rights become a method of administering them. Here, one additional comparison between Marxist and post-Marxist social theory will indicate how certain limitations in Marx's formulation of power interact in a complex way with his problematic historiography.

For Marx, subordination is a function of social position, of where one is positioned within hierarchical relations of power constitutive of a social order. At its most economistic, the Marxist formula for measuring subordination involves ascertaining a subject's relationship to the means of production within a particular mode of production. In its less economistic moments (for example, in the "Jewish Question" or "The Holy Family"), elements of social power other than production may be considered relevant, but the issue remains one of positioning. The problem of political consciousness thus becomes one of accurately apprehending one's social positioning and hence the truth of the social totality, a matter that requires "piercing the ideological veil" in which the order is shrouded and in particular, reversing the "camera obscura" by which it disguises its power. Political consciousness in inegalitarian societies is thus a matter of perceiving the power by which such societies are objectively stratified, a perception that depends upon a critique of the ideological mystification and especially naturalization of stratification in order to recognize its achievement by power. (This process is mapped in the discussion of ideology in the "German Ideology" and is modeled in the discussion of commodification in Volume 1 of *Capital*). For Marx and in many social theories heavily indebted to Marxism, for example, Catharine MacKinnon's, subject position is social position; determined by social relations that structure stratification, it follows that subject position can be apprehended through scientific discernment of these relations, a science elaborated in various incarnations of standpoint epistemology.

While critical theories of gender, race, and sexuality probably cannot dispense entirely with a notion of "subject position," the formulation of power and of the subject entailed by this notion are also inadequate to the aspirations of such theories. Consequently, much contemporary critical theory has moved to augment the Marxist account of subordination as a function of social positioning. Post-Marxist feminist theory, for example, figures the political problem of women both as a problem of constructed subjectivities (local, particular, unfixable, always exceeding the denotations of woman or women) *and* as one of social positioning (nameable, tangible yet always abstract, a potent designation evacuated of any particular inhabitant). If "identity" "occurs," is named or produced, at the point where these touch, where the particulars of subject formation intersect with vectors of social stratification such as race or gender, then the richest accounts of racial formation or gendering will prevail when subjectivity and social positioning are figured simultaneously.[45] More than simply recognizing the importance of both analytic registers, this requires interlacing them such that social "positioning" is formulated as part of subject production and the construction of subjectivity is formulated as an element in the making of social hierarchy and political domination.

What are the implications for the emancipatory potential of rights of replacing an account of subjugation as subject position with an understanding of "subject formation," and with an understanding of power as "something which circulates . . . which is never appropriated as a commodity or piece of wealth . . . [but] is employed and exercised through a net-like organization"?[46] What happens when we come to understand subjects as not only positioned *by* power, as not only created out of the expropriation or exploitation of their powers, but as *effects* of power, as formed or produced by power, *and* as "simultaneously undergoing and exercising . . . power"?[47] What happens when we understand subjects of racial or sexual domination to be the partial effects of *regimes* and *formations* of race and sexuality, rather than positioned within and fully comprised by totalizing *systems?* What is implied for rights when we understand politicized identity as a regulatory production of a disciplinary society and not only as political consciousness of one's "social positioning" in orders stratified by hierarchical social power? Might rights then appear as both a means

45. Yet this project is made difficult by virtue of the articulation of subject positioning and formations of subjectivity in such different registers: While subjectivity is local, particular, psychoanalytic, concerned with the problem of consciousness and unconscious, body and psyche, desire and culture, social positioning invariably refers to orders or structures of power and involves reading them historically and deducing how subjects are located within a field of power rather than how subjects are formed by specific operations of power. Many (but not all) contemporary battles about the "discursive" versus the "material" elements of power are drawn over this line, where those most concerned with subjectivity insist that all is discourse while those who see only social positioning insist on the pre- or extradiscursive materiality of that positioning. Resolution on this matter will undoubtedly require a more thoroughly developed notion of discursive materiality, and the different valences of, for example, political discourses of race and discourses of racial subjectivity.

46. Michel Foucault, "Two Lectures," in *Power/Knowledge*, ed. C. Gordon (New York: Pantheon, 1980), 98.

47. Ibid.

of contesting state power or asserting individual autonomy and more deeply articulating identity by forgetting the social norms and regulatory discourses that constitute it? Do rights affixed to identities partly function to imprison us within the "subject positions" they are secured to affirm or protect?

Contemporary reflection on Marx's critique of right casts its value as mixed. On the one hand, a number of Marx's operative assumptions are called into question by post-Marxist theory: the "real universality" embodied in "true human emancipation"; the progress toward this universalism secured by a Hegelian historiography rooted in the resolution of systemic contradictions through dialectic; the ontological, historical, and epistemological distinctions between state and civil society, politics and economy, ideal and material orders; and the distinction between social position and subjectivity presumed by the possibility of scientific critique and rational consciousness. On the other hand, the experience of late modernity poses questions about the emancipatory function of rights never entertained by Marx: these include attention to disciplinary power, subjectivity, subject production; political culture understood in spatial rather than temporal dimensions; and power and politics formulated in the metaphor of "battle" or permanent contestation rather than the metaphors of contradiction, progress, and transcendence.

Yet for all the limitations and aporias in Marx's formulation of rights and political emancipation, there are strong claims to be made for its contemporary relevance. In fact, the suspension of certain Marxist assumptions and the addition of certain Foucaultian insights may, rather than vitiate the Marxist critique of rights, intensify its weight. Indeed, post-Marxist theory permits us to understand how rights pervasively configure a political culture (rather than merely occupy a niche within it) and discursively produce the political subject (rather than serving as the instrument of such a subject). It also permits us to grasp the way in which disciplinary productions of identity may become the site of rights struggles that naturalize and thus entrench the powers of which their identities are the effects.[48]

48. See note 6. The point here is that naming may be *simultaneously* a form of empowering recognition and a site of regulation—this is the ambiguity about identity that Foucault articulated in his concern that we might be excavating only to then intern insurrectionary discourses. Moreover, the emancipatory function of rights cannot be

But to suggest that rights sought by politicized identities may cut two (or more) ways—naturalizing identity even as they reduce elements of its stigma, depoliticizing even as they protect recently produced political subjects, empowering what they also regulate—is not to condemn them. Rather, it is to refuse them any given place in an emancipatory politics and to insist instead upon the importance of incessantly querying that place. I want to proceed with such querying now by reflecting on the formulation of rights by two of their progressive exponents in contemporary law and politics, Patricia Williams and Catharine MacKinnon.

What happens, in the kind of culture Marx diagnosed as producing the need and desire for rights, to those without them, or to those largely sequestered in domains marked "private" or "natural" where rights do not apply? What happens in the ontological basement and exterior to the "frenzied" order of egoistic civil society where those subordinated via race, sexuality, gender, or age are routinely exploited or violated by those armed with rights, social power, and social legitimacy? What happens when the lack of a right to property or speech, bodily integrity or sexual conduct, is conjoined with the vulnerability and dependence created by relative social powerlessness and marginalization?

This is the perspective, in her terms "the subject position," from which black law professor Patricia Williams's defense of rights issues in *The Alchemy of Race and Rights*. This defense is mindful of critiques from the left wing of the legal establishment as well as of the failure of civil rights acquisition to substantially augment the socioeconomic condition of the majority of blacks in the United States. It is also a defense that de-emphasizes the enmeshment of the emergence of rights with the triumph of the bourgeoisie in postfeudal Europe, with capital's pressing need for the free circulation of land and labor, with individual propertied male ownership of the members and elements of his household. It is a defense that eschews the way that historically,

---

adjudicated in abstraction from the bureaucratic juridical aperture through which they are negotiated. Who, today, defends their rights without an army of lawyers and reams of complex legal documents? In this regard, rights, rather than being the "popular and available" currency depicted by Patricia Williams, may subject us to intense forms of bureaucratic domination and regulatory power even at the moment that we assert them in our own defense.

rights discourse legitimated the new class formations as well as a constitutional state designed to secure and naturalize them. Williams's account begins already inside this history, presumes the Hobbesian/Adam Smithian culture it figures, and dwells upon the experience of those explicitly deprived of rights within it, those whom, *Dred Scott* opined, "were so far inferior . . . they had no rights which the white man was bound to respect."[49] For Patricia Williams, in whose analysis of the law "subject position is everything,"[50] thinking about rights is relentlessly tethered to the experience of those historically denied them in a political culture where political membership; civic belonging; bodily, emotional, and sexual boundary; social respect; legitimacy as an actor; capacity as a transactor; autonomy; privacy; visibility; and generative independence are all negotiated through the language and practice of rights and rightlessness.

While the importance of this tether cannot be overstated, neither can its partiality, for deprivation on this scale is not merely lack but also the creation of desire through lack. As homosexuals may crave the legitimacy conferred by the institution of marriage from which we are debarred—and thus reinscribe the very mechanism of our subjection in our yearning for that which is *premised* on our exclusion, Patricia Williams's defense of rights on the basis that it is "a symbol too deeply enmeshed in the psyche of the oppressed to lose without trauma and much resistance" poses a similar conundrum.[51] What if this deeply enmeshed symbol operates not only in but also against that psyche, working as self-reproach, depoliticized suffering, and dissimulation of extralegal forms of power? To see how this might be the case, I want to consider three strands of Williams's argument in *The Alchemy of Race and Rights:* her critique of the phenomenon she calls "privatization," her analysis of black women's cultural positioning, and her effort to proliferate and resignify the meaning and distribution of rights.

For Patricia Williams, the "over-expanded mental state we call 'privacy'" is among the most pernicious and subtle enemies of contemporary democracy, as well as a powerful mode of legitimizing class and race inequalities. "The tyranny of what we call the private," she argues,

---

49. Patricia Williams, *The Alchemy of Race and Rights* (Cambridge: Harvard University Press, 1991), 162.
    50. Ibid., 3.
    51. Ibid., 165

risks reducing us to "the life crushing disenfranchisement of an entirely owned world where permission must be sought to walk on the face of the earth."[52] Williams spies the corrosive effects of privatization in contemporary arguments about "reverse discrimination" and for "employer preference," in Supreme Court decisions permitting states to determine levels of indigent support, in police commissioner complaints about being singled out for media attention during police brutality investigations, in John Tower's promise to give up drinking if confirmed as President Bush's defense secretary. Criticizing not only privatization of public functions *by* the economy (workfare or school vouchers), Williams also assails increased privatization *of* the economy represented by restricted access in commerce. The latter frames an incident in which a young white Benetton salesman refused her entry to a buzzer-controlled shop in New York and characterizes as well a sign she saw in a Greenwich Village boutique—"Sale! $2 overcoats. No bums, no booze"—which commodifies poverty while excluding the poor.[53]

Williams also traces forms of privatization that, like the design of corporate parks and shopping malls, effectively resegregate populations along lines of race and class. Reflecting on Mayor Koch's plea for black compassion toward white Howard Beach residents unhappy about an interracial protest march through "their" streets, she writes:

> Koch was, in effect, pleading for acceptance of the privatization of public space. This is the de facto equivalent of segregation; it is exclusion in the guise of deep-moated property "interests" and "values." Lost is the fact that the object of discussion, the street, is public.[54]

Williams also examines how the language of privacy and its cousin, "choice," are used to mask state coercion as private desire. When defendants in child abuse or rape cases are "offered a 'choice' between . . . jail and sterilization . . . the defendant is positioned as a purchaser, as 'buying' . . . freedom by paying the price of her womb"

---

52. Ibid., 43.
53. Ibid., 42.
54. Ibid., 69.

or by "choosing castration."[55] This repackaging of state domination as the market freedom of individuals, she argues, imperils both public morality and the meaning of citizenship. It vandalizes a language of public obligation and at the same time legitimizes the de facto racism, misogyny, and hatred of the poor that, in her analysis, it is the task of the political to mitigate. In short, "privatization" violates public space, depoliticizes socially constructed problems and injustices, exonerates public representatives from public responsibility, and undermines a notion of political life as concerned with the common and obligating us in common.

How is this searing political critique reconcilable with Williams's unalloyed defense of rights? Rights in liberal capitalist orders, Marx reminds us, are bits of discursive power that quintessentially privatize and depoliticize, that mystify and reify social powers (property and wealth but also race, sexuality, and gender) as the natural possessions of private persons, that analytically abstract individuals from social and political context, indeed, that are *effects* of the social power they obfuscate. To the extent that rights discursively mask stratifying social powers through their constitution of sovereign subjects rendered formally equal before the law, they would appear to be among the most basic strategies of the privatization Williams condemns. As the last decade has made clear, rights discourse is precisely what furnishes the claims of reverse discrimination and employer preference, the justifications for school voucher systems, regressive tax reform, union busting, the prerogatives of store owners and neighborhoods to restrict access. Rights discourse in liberal capitalist culture casts as private potentially political contests about distribution of resources and relevant parties to decision making. It converts social problems into matters of individualized, dehistoricized injury and entitlement, into matters in which there is no harm if there is no agent and no tangibly violated subject. And if we shift here from Marx to Foucault in querying the incommensurability of Williams's critique of privatization and defense of rights, we can ask: What more thoroughly obscures domination by regulatory norms— the "whiteness" or "maleness" of certain standards of excellence— than the figure of the sovereign subject of rights? And what would more neatly converge with the late-modern disciplinary production

---

55. Ibid., 32.

of identity, and regulation through identity, than the proliferation of rights Williams counsels?[56]

None of this is to suggest that those without rights in a rights-governed universe should abandon the effort to acquire and use them. Williams and others make clear enough that such counsel, especially from white middle-class academics, is strategically naive and disavows its cultural prerogatives.[57] But to argue for the importance of having rights where rights are currency is not yet an assessment of how they operate politically nor of the political culture they create. Rather, that argument underscores the foolishness of walking into a pitched battle unarmed and the crippling force of being deemed unworthy of whatever a given culture uses to designate humanity. The question Williams's defense leaves unasked is whether the proliferation of rights she advocates might not abet the phenomenon she calls privatization, the encroachment of an entirely owned world, the disintegration of public obligations and a political culture of responsibility. It also leaves uninterrogated the relationship between the promise of rights for black people as "an illusion [that] became real for only a few"[58] and the function of rights in depoliticizing economic power, in privatizing economic circumstance—in short, in disguising the workings of class.

Williams's defense of rights veers away from this question and instead focuses on the historical deprivation of social, sexual, and physical integrity that rightlessness conjured for blacks in the United States. With Robert Williams, she argues that if rights function to individuate, separate, and defend individuals, if they grant individuals a sphere of bodily integrity and privacy, if they announce our personhood even in abstract fashion and our membership even in an abstract community, then these may be exactly what is needed and

56. Ibid., 165.

57. See both Williams's account of mental experiments she undertook to see if she could get help for her enslaved great-great-grandmother without the discourse of rights (*Alchemy of Race and Rights*, 157–58) and her account of the different subject positioning that led her and a white male colleague to very different relationships to formal legal arrangements (146–49). See also the essay by Robert Williams, Jr., "Taking Rights Aggressively: The Perils and Promise of Critical Legal Theory for Peoples of Color" (*Law and Inequality: A Journal of Theory and Practice* 1 [May 1987]) in which he argues that critical legal studies scholars' critiques of rights and those who clamor for them involve a certain condescension, even racism, in their blindness to the privileged position from which they make their arguments.

58. Williams, *Alchemy of Race and Rights*, 163.

wanted by those denied them in a culture that marks its "others" through such deprivation.[59] "Where one's experience is rooted not just in a sense of illegitimacy but in being illegitimate . . . then the black adherence to a scheme of . . . rights—to the self, to the sanctity of one's own personal boundaries—makes sense."[60] Given the history of violent "familiarity" and "informality" with which blacks have been treated by whites in the United States, some distance, abstraction, and formal rather than intimate recognition might be an important remedy. "For me," Williams argues, "stranger-stranger relations are better than stranger-chattel."[61]

Elaborating this argument, Patricia Williams delineates the dilemma of "exposure and hiding" as the constant experience and measure of subjugation of black women. The choice between humiliating exposure and desperate hiding is the nonchoice that configures the drama of Tawana Brawley, Anita Hill, Williams's own "exaggerated visibility and invisibility" as a black female law professor, black women as slaves ("teeth and buttocks bared to interested visitors"), and black women's present positioning in a racial-sexual economy that routinely marks their sexuality as unbarred availability.[62]

This unnavigable "choice" between exposure and hiding clearly calls for redress through social practices that accord black women autonomy and privacy, agency and respect. But perhaps, heeding a Foucaultian appreciation of subject formation, this violent legacy also takes shape as a complex form of desire in the subjects it creates, a desire symptomized in Patricia Williams's deeply personal and quasi-confessional writing. Indeed, how else to explain her production of our *intrusion* into her morning toilette—her *exposure* of how with astringent, mascara, and lip glaze she "hangs her face in contradictions" to "deny pain . . . be a role model . . . pave the way for her race"—in this way restaging the scene of invasion, the absence of bodily privacy that is the history of African American women? How else to explain the revelation of bouts of depression, humiliating teaching evaluations, unedited dreams and nightmares, long hours of suffering in her terrycloth bathrobe and vanity before the mirror? Perhaps this historically produced desire—for the right

59. R. Williams, "Taking Rights Aggressively."
60. P. Williams, *Alchemy of Race and Rights*, 154.
61. Ibid., 148.
62. Ibid., 18, 92–93, 175–77, 196.

to expose oneself without injury, and for the right to hide without recrimination—undergirds a certain desire for rights, those implements that promise, as liberalism does more generally, to guard exposed subjects and legitimize hiding. But rights could only fulfill this promise if they could bring into view the complex subject formation consequent to a history of violation, precisely the articulation they thwart in figuring desire as natural, intrinsic and unhistorical.

Thus, as with the relationship between rights and privatization, it may be that the very condition that designates liberalism's "others"—being condemned to exposure or hiding (here homosexuality also comes to mind)—is both intensified and redressed by rights: the same device that confers legitimate boundary and privacy leaves the individual to struggle alone, in a self-blaming and depoliticized universe, with power that seeps past right and with desire configured by power prior to right. It may be that the discourse of rights, Maxine Thomas's stock in trade, is precisely what could not protect her from, and indeed what stole the political language for, the unlivable contradictions that finally made this stunningly accomplished black female judge "split at the seams and return to the womb . . . exploded into fragments of intelligence and scattered wisdom."[63] It may be that the withdrawal that rights offer, the unmarking or destigmatizing they promise, has as its cost the loss of a language to describe the character of domination, violation, or exploitation that configures such needs. Indeed, what if the desire for withdrawal into the buffered and enclosed space of liberal personhood marked by rights is *symptom,* and what if treating the symptom covers over by distracting us from its generative source? What if, as Marx put it, the "right of the circumscribed individual, withdrawn into himself" responds to the socially produced condition of exposure or hiding, excessive vulnerability or invisibility, humiliation or death, by codifying that condition as natural and installing it in the law?[64]

There is still another strand to Williams's defense of rights: as the historically and currently existing social form of freedom, they are both concretely available and "magic in the mouths of black people." Yet, even as Williams insists upon the immediate political efficacy of rights and contrasts this efficacy with the "timeless, formless

63. Ibid., 196–97.
64. Marx, "Jewish Question," 42.

futurism" held out by rights critics, she also makes a fierce argument
for the exploitability of the indeterminacy of rights:

> The task . . . is not to discard rights but to see through them or
> past them so that they reflect a larger definition of privacy and
> property: so that privacy is turned from exclusion based on self-
> regard into regard for another's fragile, mysterious autonomy;
> and so that property regains its ancient connotation of being a
> reflection of the universal self. The task is to expand private prop-
> erty rights into a conception of civil rights, into the right to expect
> civility from others. . . . Society must give rights away . . . to
> slaves . . . to trees . . . to cows . . . to history . . . to rivers and
> rocks . . .[65]

The risk here is that appreciation of the power and flexibility of
the word afforded by recent literary theory may have converged with
what Marx identified as liberalism's theological impulses to exagger-
ate a sense of what it is possible to do with words. How resonant of
Bauer's understanding of civic emancipation is Patricia Williams's
proclamation that "the problem with rights discourse is not that the
discourse itself is constricting but that it exists in a constricted referential universe."[66] In literalizing the promise of rights on the one hand
and lifting them from historical and social context on the other, an
analysis so dependent upon floating signifiers appears to end up
intensifying the idealist tendencies of liberal thought. Indeed, how
could "extending to all of society's objects and untouchables the
rights of privacy, integrity and self-assertion" contest the steady
commodification of the earth and of public life that Williams also
decries? Might words be more mutable, more subject to alchemical
fire, than the political histories that generate rights, the political economies in which they operate, and the subjectivities they fashion?
    In this sense, what Williams calls the "magic" of rights may per-
tain less to their transmutational capacities than to the fact that while
they formally mark personhood, they cannot confer it; while they
promise protection from humiliating exposure, they do not deliver it
(hence the Benetton incident, which no truckload of rights can amelio-

---

65. Ibid., 164–65.
66. Ibid., 159.

rate or redress). The necessarily abstract and ahistoricizing discourse of rights mystifies the conditions and power that delimit the possibility of achieving personhood, while their decontextualizing force deprives political consciousness of recognition of the histories, relations, and modalities of power that produce and situate us as human.

Thus, if provision of boundary, and protection from "bodily and spiritual intrusion"[67] offered by rights are what historically subjugated peoples most need, rights may also be one of the cruelest social objects of desire dangled above those who lack them. For in the very same gesture with which they draw a circle around the individual, in the very same act with which they grant her sovereign selfhood, they turn back upon the individual all responsibility for her failures, her condition, her poverty, her madness—they privatize her situation and mystify the powers that construct, position, and buffet her. In this respect, perhaps they not only failed to save Judge Maxine Thomas— perhaps they also intensified the isolation of her struggle with all the contradictory forces of power and freedom that rights disacknowledge in their occupation of the field of justice. If rights are all that separate Williams from her bought-and-sold, raped-and-abused great-great-grandmother, they are also the device that demeans Clarence Thomas's now infamous sister, which permits him to ratify a larger social presumption that if he could become a Supreme Court justice, then so could they both, and only her laziness, her lack of moral fiber or industriousness, or her corruption by "welfare culture" accounts for the difference. Perhaps Williams's contrast of the concrete, immediate, and available character of rights discourse with the "timeless, formless, futurism," the "unrealistic . . . unattainable, or other-worldly" characteristic of other emancipatory political projects is, finally, a false contrast dependent on a false concreteness: under the guise of the concrete, what rights promise may be as elusive, as otherworldly, as unattainable as that offered by any other political myth.[68]

Catharine MacKinnon's effort to rectify the masculinism of the law and redress women's inequality depends upon taking seriously Marx's critique of rights, bending it in a feminist direction, and incorporating

---

67. Ibid., 164.
68. Ibid., 163–64.

it into a form of jurisprudence that Marx never entertained. Unlike
Marx, MacKinnon seeks to make visible *within* the law, and particularly within rights discourse, precisely the kind of social power that
Marx argued was inherently obscured by bourgeois rights discourse.
For MacKinnon, the project of feminist jurisprudence, especially in
the domain of sexual harassment and pornography, is to make rights
articulate and respond to rather than mask the systematic workings of
gender subordination.

In MacKinnon's analysis, gender is the congealed effect of a patriarchal organization of sexuality as male dominance and female submission. A specific organization of sexuality creates gender as a specific organization of work creates class, and a politics that redresses
gender inequality is therefore a politics that makes visible the construction and enforcement of women's subordination through the appropriation, commodification, and violation of female sexuality. Sexual
harassment, rape, battery, and pornography in this way appear not
simply as violations, but as violations that specifically reduce persons
to women, that iterate and reiterate—indeed, perform—the category,
women, and thus constitute a violation of women's civil rights,
women's right to civic and political equality. In Althusserian terms,
MacKinnon regards these practices not simply as hurting but as *interpellating* women as women, where woman is analytically conceived
as only and always an effect of male dominance constituted by and
operationalized as sexual dominance.

MacKinnon criticizes legal claims to objectivity as inherently
masculinist, casting the law's claimed aperspectivalism and universalism as "male" in substance as well as form: "In the liberal state, the
rule of law—neutral, abstract, elevated, pervasive—both institutionalizes the power of men over women and institutionalizes power in its
male form."[69] In arguing that point-of-viewlessness *is* the law's maleness, she adapts for feminism the Marxist view that universal
discourse—the discourse of liberal constitutionalism—in an unequal
social order is a ruse of power, presenting as generic what actually
privileges the dominant. More specifically, she argues that the universalism of the state masks its masculinist substance through the
(masculinist) aperspectival form, a form that covers the law's male-

---

69. Catharine MacKinnon, *Toward a Feminist Theory of the State* (Cambridge: Harvard University Press, 1989), 238.

ness just as the "universality" of the state both comprises and legitimizes the state's bourgeois character.

MacKinnon thus seeks to make the law "gender-equal" precisely
by prying this project loose from one of "gender-neutrality," indeed,
by opposing gender equality to gender neutrality. Arguing that the
law is most gender biased where it is most gender blind, she seeks to
make the law "gender-sighted," in part by bringing to light its gendered perspective. MacKinnon's effort to use the law as a means of
recognition and *rectification* of gender subordination depends upon forcing the law to recognize and reform its own masculinism. This she
aims to achieve by establishing both the partiality and the veracity of
women's "perspective," a perspective rooted in women's experience
of sexual subordination and violation.

MacKinnon seeks to realize the universal claim of liberal equality
not by expanding the law's range of inclusion but by installing within
the law the capacity to recognize stratifying social power, which its
formal categories ordinarily make invisible and which rights discourse
in particular depoliticizes. Thus, MacKinnnon does not abandon the
universal formulation of justice claimed for the present by liberals and
anticipated in the future by Marxists, nor, however, does she post-
pone the realization of true universal equality and liberty to a
postliberal, nonstate millennium. Rather, MacKinnon aims to force
the law to fulfill its universalist promise by forcing it to recognize and
rectify relations of domination among its subjects, and in particular by
making it recognize gender as a relation of domination rather than a
benign or natural marker of difference.

If the law can be made to articulate rather than mask social domination, if it can be made to reveal gender as the effect of eroticized
male dominance, then perhaps substantive rather than merely formal
equality can be won through civil rights law. This is what MacKinnon
seeks to achieve through a jurisprudence that equates women's equality with women's rights *against* the incursions of male sexuality,
against what MacKinnon posits as the *material basis* of female subordination. The project is ingenious in the parsimony and radicalism of its
basic formula: If sexual subordination defines the category, woman,
then sexual subordination—whether through rape or marriage, incest
or harassment, abortion restrictions or pornography—must be legally
construed as a violation of women's civil rights in an egalitarian legal
order, a violation of women's right not to be socially subordinated. In

this way, sexual harassment and pornography become issues of gender equality, rather than issues of gender "difference," and rather than gender-generic issues of obscenity, assault, or labor relations.

In this effort to install an *analysis* of women's sexual subordination *in* the law, MacKinnon attempts to resolve the chief Marxist ambivalence about rights and legal reform, namely, their potential mystification of the "real, material basis" of subordination even as they offer formal protection to marked subjects. MacKinnon resolves this dilemma by refusing it, by installing *within* legal discourse an analysis of the material basis *of* women's subordination. Thus, rather than emancipating women abstractly while leaving intact the substantive conditions of their subordination, MacKinnon's legal theory and legislative proposals seek to emancipate women from these conditions by making the conditions themselves illegal, by *politicizing them in the law.* Put the other way around, instead of emancipating us abstractly by denying the relevance of sexuality to gender and gender to personhood, a move which, to paraphrase Marx, "emancipates sexuality to act after its own fashion, namely *as* male dominance and female subordination," MacKinnon insists that the emancipation of women *is* the right of women to be free from sexual incursion, violation, appropriation, and subordination. She would thus seem to be doing precisely what Marx thought could not be done, namely, employing rights discourse to expose and redress inequalities that its abstract formulations of personhood and equality are thought to obscure and depoliticize.

With due admiration for MacKinnon's analytic achievement, there are a number of political and strategic questions to be posed about this work, many of them now sufficiently familiar to be summarized rather than detailed here:

First, if MacKinnon aims to write "women's experience into law," precisely which "women's experience(s)," drawn from which historical moments, which culture, and which racial and class strata, is MacKinnon writing? Certainly many women have argued that MacKinnon's depiction of pornography as "the graphic sexually explicit subordination of women" that violates women's civil rights squares neither with their experience of being female, their experience of pornography, nor their ambivalence about the legal regulation of porn. Similarly, many feminists have protested MacKinnon's reduction of gender to sexuality, arguing that motherhood or other gendered practices are at least as constitutive of their subordination through gender.

Second, what does it mean to write historically and culturally circumscribed experience into an ahistorical discourse, the universalist discourse of the law? What happens when "experience" becomes ontology, when "perspective" becomes truth, and when both become unified in the Subject of Woman and encoded in law as women's rights? Moreover, what if the identity of women as keyed to sexual violation is an expressly late-twentieth-century and white middle-class construction of femininity, consequent to a radical deprivatization of sexuality, on the one side, and erosion of other elements of compulsory heterosexuality, such as the sexual division of social labor, on the other? What does it mean to install in the universalist discourse of law an analysis of women's subordination that may be quite historically and culturally circumscribed?

Third, does a definition of women *as* sexual subordination, and the encoding of this definition in law, work to liberate women from sexual subordination, or does it, paradoxically, reinscribe femaleness as sexual violability? How might installation of "women's experience" as "sexual violation" in the law reiterate rather than repeal this identity? Foucault (along with certain strains in psychoanalytic thought) reminds us that the law *produces* the subjects it claims to protect or emancipate. How, then, might a formulation of women's civil rights as violated by pornography or sexual harassment produce precisely the figure MacKinnon complains we have been reduced to by sexism, a figure of woman wholly defined by sexual violation, wholly identified with sexual victimization?

Fourth, insofar as MacKinnon's attempt to legally encode "women's experience" *interpellates* woman *as* sexually violable, how does this effectively deny the diversity and complexity of women and women's experience? Might this interpellation be particularly unemancipatory for women whose lived "experience" is not that of sexual subordination to men but, for example, that of sexual outlaw? How does the encoding of women's civil rights as rights against male sexual violation reaffirm the operations of exclusion enacted by the heterosexually normative category, woman?

Fifth, by returning to the analogy with class that inaugurates MacKinnon's analysis of gender and feminist jurisprudence, we can see from yet another angle how her effort to achieve substantive equality through rights may reiterate rather than resolve the opposition between rights and equality articulated in Marx's critique. MacKinnon's method of installing within rights discourse an analysis of the social power constitutive of gender ought to be applicable to class, that form of social power from which her analysis took its inspiration. But to render class exploitation illegal, to outlaw its conditions as MacKinnon seeks to outlaw the conditions of gender domination, would entail circumscription, if not elimination, of the right to private property, one of the most fundamental rights of liberal capitalist orders. (As Marx reminds us, real emancipation from private property requires the abolition of private property, not the abolition of political distinctions based upon property ownership.)

Now if substantive economic equality, the abolition of class, is incompatible with private property rights, might it be the case that substantive gender equality as MacKinnon defines it is equally incompatible with rights of free speech? If, as MacKinnon argues, sexual dominance is in part a matter of speech (e.g., sexual harassment) and representation (e.g., pornography), then is it any surprise that MacKinnon's effort to "get equality for women" comes into direct conflict with the First Amendment? Here it would appear that MacKinnon has not so much countered as extended and affirmed Marx's critique of rights as masking power and social inequalities. Her analysis *confirms* rather than resolves the opposition Marx articulates between "the rights of man" on one side (property, freedom of expression, of worship, etc.) and the substantive equality (which she calls the civil rights) of women on the other. Appropriating a discourse of civil rights to procure equality for women, MacKinnon opposes the liberties secured by constitutional universalism and in this sense reaffirms rather than reworks Marx's formulation of the opposition between political emancipation and true human emancipation, between liberal universalism and domination in civil society, between bourgeois liberty and real equality.

On the one hand, MacKinnon seeks to encode the "experience" or "subject position" of a fiction called '"women" in the timeless discourse of the law, such that women are produced as the sexually violable creatures the law says we are. On the other hand, she appears engaged in a critique of rights in the name of women's equality. Together these efforts may reveal the extent to which deployment of a

Marxist critique *of* liberal universalism *as* law, rather than *against* the law, paradoxically breeds a politics of severe unfreedom. Legally codifying a fragment of history as a timeless truth, interpellating women as unified in their victimization, and casting the "free speech" of men as that which subordinates women, MacKinnon not only opposes bourgeois liberty to substantive equality but also potentially intensifies the regulation of gender and sexuality through rights discourse and abets rather than contests the production of gender identity as sexual. In short, as a regulatory fiction of a particular identity is deployed to displace the hegemonic fiction of universal personhood, we see the discourse of rights converge insidiously with the discourse of disciplinarity to produce a spectacularly potent mode of juridical-disciplinary domination.

Perhaps the warning here concerns the profoundly antidemocratic elements entailed in transferring from the relatively accessible sphere of popular contestation to the highly restricted sphere of juridical authority the project of representing politicized identity and adjudicating its temporal and conflicting demands. MacKinnon's ingenious and failed effort at appropriating Marx's critique for legal reform may also stand as a more general caution against installing identity in the law, where inevitably totalized formulations of identity converge with the individuating effects of rights to produce levels of regulation through juridical individuation not even imagined by Foucault. Her failure may caution too that even as the generic man of the universal "rights of man" is problematic for the social powers it discursively cloaks, the specifications of identity in late-twentieth-century rights discourse may be equally problematic for the social powers it discursively renaturalizes. In this regard, Marx's critique of rights may function most importantly in an era of proliferating politicized identities as a warning against confusing the domain of rights with the domain of political contestation, against confusing rights with equality or legal recognition with emancipation.

What if the value of rights discourse for radical democratic project today lies not in its potential affirmation of difference, not in its guarantees of protection, circumscriptions of autonomy, or as remedy to social injury, but in the (fictional) egalitarian imaginary this discourse could engender? Might rights campaigns converge most effectively with "prepolitical" struggles for membership or postpolitical dreams of radical equality? Certainly the contemporary right-wing reading of campaigns for equal rights for gays and lesbians as campaigns for "special rights" suggests that the political disruptiveness, the democratizing dimension of rights discourse, may pertain precisely to the sustained universalist fiction of this discourse. The moment at which, through the discourse of rights, lesbians and gays claim their personhood against all that would disallow it is a radically democratic moment, analogous to those moments in U.S. history for white women and African Americans.

If, as Marx argued 150 years ago, the democratizing force of rights discourse inheres in its capacity to figure an ideal of equality among persons qua persons, regardless of socially constructed and enforced particularities, then the political potency of rights lies not in their concreteness, as Patricia Williams argues, but in their idealism, in their ideal configuration of an egalitarian social, an ideal contradicted by substantive social inequalities. Such a claim further implies, with Marx, that the democratic *value* of political emancipation lies partly in its revelation of the *limits* of political emancipation. But where Marx counted on a progressive dialectical process for such revelation, it now becomes a project for discursive struggle whose parameters are invented rather than secured in advance and whose outcome is never guaranteed.

If rights figure freedom and incite the desire for it only to the degree that they are void of content, empty signifiers, and without corresponding entitlements, paradoxically, they may be incitements to freedom only to the extent that they discursively deny the workings of the substantive social power limiting freedom. In their emptiness, they function to incite possibility through discursive denial of historically insedimented and institutionally secured constraints, by denying with words the effects of relatively wordless, politically invisible, yet potent material constraints. Still more paradoxically, when these material constraints *are* articulated and specified as part of the content of rights, when they are "brought into discourse," rights are more likely to become sites of the production and regulation of identity as injury than vehicles of emancipation. In entrenching rather than loosening identities' attachments to their current constitutive injuries, rights with strong and specified content may draw upon our least expansive, least public, and hence least democratic sentiments. It is, rather, in their abstraction from the particulars of our lives—and in their figuration of an egalitarian political community—that they may be most valuable in the democratic transformation of these particulars.

Reincarnation as the Ring on Liz Taylor's Finger: Andy Warhol and the Right of Publicity

Jane Gaines

What I want to do here is to look at a productive coincidence—the coincidence of the life and work of Andy Warhol and the development of a peculiarly American right—the right of publicity. In 1954, following the important U.S. Supreme Court decision in *Haelan Laboratories, Inc. v. Topps Chewing Gum, Inc.* (1953), Melville B. Nimmer interpreted the new "right of publicity" encoded there as a right due everyone, going beyond the general understanding of this emerging entitlement as a "right" whose advantage should only accrue to the person who has attained celebrity.[1] Arguing the "impracticality of drawing the line" at the "achievement of celebrity status," Nimmer suggested that "it should rather be held that every person has the property right of publicity . . . "[2] In Nimmer, then, we find a strange premonition of Warhol's prediction that "in the future everybody will be famous for fifteen minutes," a condition that the artist illustrated in the life he made of his work and in the work he made of his life. And I do mean condition. In Warhol, celebrity is not only a person, it is a condition, a condition of reproduction and production, but also of existence and, as he lived it, a real relation to a completely imaginary

---

1. Haelan Laboratories, Inc., v. Topps Chewing Gum, Inc., 202 F.2d (2d Cir. 1953). See my discussion of this case in *Contested Culture: The Image, the Voice, and the Law* (Chapel Hill: University of North Carolina Press, 1991).
2. Melville B. Nimmer, "The Right of Publicity," *Law and Contemporary Problems* 19 (1954): 217.

condition. Certainly Warhol both lived and understood the paradox that is celebrity, which is this: the desire to be really something is the desire to be nothing. He lived as well the corollary to the paradox of celebrity, the principle that there is only a shade of difference between wanting mass adulation and wanting to be alone, for Warhol wanted to be alone as much as he wanted to be subsumed by his admirers. Warhol's grasp of celebrity as absolutely everything and absolutely nothing at all is also there in his unapologetic and unconditional adoration of the "heroes of consumption" of his age: Marilyn Monroe, Elizabeth Taylor, and Elvis Presley.[3] We see it in his personal and heart-felt collection of the residue of glamour as well as in his fascination with the mechanisms of the production of celebrity—from the subcultural base of gossip to the main cultural superstructure of public relations and advertising.

In his celebrity icon work, Warhol's basic move was to transfer star photos from the cheap entertainment milieu to the high-culture museum. The physical move (as much as or more than his imprimatur) produced "works of art" out of throwaway publicity ephemera— posters and stills. Critics have often remarked on this inversion—the low elevated and the high brought low—but I want to look at something quite different although nonetheless related. I also find Warhol's life and work located at the intersection of copyright and "right of publicity." His life/work, as we might call it, is an essay on two doctrines that coexist somewhat precariously—the former a limited monopoly on cultural reproduction and the latter an unlimited monopoly on the same thing. I find the Warhol life/work at this intersection, and I also find that from this crossing point one can follow him one way or the other. For the sake of my analysis, I want to take the right of publicity route, to some degree following his own lead, but I will finally suggest where copyright and right of publicity might meet. Although it is certainly productive to read Warhol's disinterest in authenticity as a critique of the high art enshrinement of the original work of art as well as copyright law's fortification of the art world's system of value, I want to put this reading on hold and take the less obvious approach instead. In doing this, I'm actually taking my cue from Warhol himself who, when asked if he wanted to be a great artist, replied, "No, I'd rather be

3. The term *heroes of consumption* was coined by Leo Lowenthal, "The Triumph of Mass Idols," in *Literature, Popular Culture, and Society* (Englewood Cliffs, N.J.: Prentice-Hall, 1961).

famous." So it is his own insight about the separability of authorial work and acclaim, the possibility of spooning off the cream of authorship—of producing celebrity without engaging in productive work—that leads me to link him first with the right of publicity.

It is the way the culture holds celebrity in such low esteem, at the same time that celebrity itself is the product of esteem and doesn't know the difference between low or high esteem, that attracts me to the issues that arise out of the development in this century of a right of publicity. What I want to argue is that, against commonsense notions of fame as spontaneous public choice or personal self-promotion, there is a legal foundation for the production of mass culture notoriety.[4] By legal foundation I mean less a determining set of rules than an equivalent basis in an adjacent realm, and here it is difficult to spatialize the legal realm since it is able to appear as both base and superstructure.[5] Neither is the law a realm set apart from the rest of the culture since the culture both constitutes and is constituted by it. This is then to advance a theory of law as absorbed into the very pores of a culture, itself made up of densely packed and oftentimes indistinguishable layers.

The commonsense notion of celebrity as spontaneous public choice has a complementary set of ideas in two prevalent misconceptions about property. As C. B. MacPherson describes it, in contemporary usage, property tends to mean *things* and is treated as synonymous with *private* property. While the former misconception is nothing more than a popular misuse, he says, the latter is a more problematic misunderstanding. Both, however, he links to specific historical conditions, in particular, the development of capitalism in the last century. But more relevant to our discussion, MacPherson notes that while these popular conceptions of property have had a grip on public consciousness that began to take hold as early as the seventeenth century, they are now both becoming and may become obsolete.[6]

And in this period during which we will probably witness the

---

4. By commonsense knowledge here I mean something more synonymous with ideology and less aligned with "good sense." For background on the use of the concept in Marxist cultural studies, see Stuart Hall, Bob Lumley, and Gregor McLennan, "Politics, and Ideology: Gramsci," *Working Papers in Cultural Studies* 2 (1977): 45–76.

5. See *Contested Culture*, 17, for a discussion of the relationship between the law and the mode of production.

6. C. B. MacPherson, "The Meaning of Property," in C. B. MacPherson, ed., *Property: Mainstream and Critical Positions* (Toronto and Buffalo: University of Toronto Press, 1978), 2.

obsolescence of property as thing, a mirrored confusion between property as "thing" and property as "value" appears. This surface confusion has its support in a deeper conundrum within legal doctrine, that is, that although property is technically a "right" because it can be enforced as a claim, it is not the enforceability of a claim that gives credence to property as a "right"; rather, it is the belief that property is a natural "right." MacPherson puts it this way: "Property is not thought to be a right because it is an enforceable claim: it is an enforceable claim only because and in so far as the prevailing ethical theory holds that it is a necessary human right."[7]

Of course, much of the time this confusion (in daily life as well as legal doctrine) is opaque to us. But at some moments, most notably in the ideological upheaval of a legal dispute that gives rise to a significant case, such a confusion becomes apparent. For instance, at the very moment of a production of a new "right" (in unfair competition law, in the middle of the twentieth century), we are able to glimpse the confusion between "property," "value," and "right" within legal doctrine, a confusion that has a past as well as a future. Before I go further into the history of this confusion, I want to review the significance of *Haelan v. Topps*, the case to which I referred at the outset. In this case involving the photographs of baseball players on trading cards, the question of the protectability of the photographs arose. Here the issue of right to reproduce rested on the players' exclusive agreements with one chewing gum manufacturer; however, these agreements were based on a personal right to seclusion. In its resolution of a legal dispute, the Court produced a cultural contradiction. What was essentially a privacy right became the basis for transferring rights and consequently for authorizing publicity—that is, for authorizing mass reproduction.

Although the point of law in *Haelan* arose in the context of the settlement of a trade dispute between two competing companies, Topps Chewing Gum and Haelan Lab's Bowman Gum, these same questions are pertinent here. Judge Jerome Frank, circumventing the question of the impossibility of transferring a personal right of privacy (the right to be let alone), declared that he found in operation a "new right" that might be called a "right of publicity." In acknowledging a new right he was essentially acknowledging the capital investment in

---

7. MacPherson, "Meaning of Property," 3.

career building, or the sports celebrity practice of trading on exclusive rights to their own names and likenesses, whether for advertising endorsements or other commercial artwork. In the words of Nimmer, *Haelan* was one of a significant number of cases that began to show that "publicity values [were] emerging as a legally cognizable right protectable without resort to the more traditional legal theories."[8] Here, Nimmer's enthusiasm for trends in the law that would favor growth in the entertainment industry is barely concealed.

But the key question for us is which came first, the right or the economic value of that right. Historically, U.S. courts have equivocated in unfair competition disputes, in an endless postponement of resolution: The law creates the right, the right creates the value, the value creates the right, the right preexists in the property, which is recognized by law, which is none other than the right itself. As early as the 1930s, the Legal Realists noticed the circular reasoning characterizing unfair competition law. Remarked Felix Cohen, "It purports to base legal protection upon economic value, when, as a matter of actual fact, the economic value of a sales device depends upon the extent to which it will be legally protected."[9]

So at midcentury, this shift from the personal privacy "right to be let alone" to a property right "to exploit one's image," this complete about-face within the same doctrine, can be fleetingly observed in the arguments made within *Haelan*, the 1953 Supreme Court case where they had their last rehearsal. For one moment, in this branch of the law, there is a clear yielding to the needs of capital expansion, a yielding that is less clear to us in the arguments of the Law and Economics School of legal thought closer to the end of the century when the desire for celebrity is assumed or, rather, appears as a cultural given. It is now possible, then, for Richard Posner to argue that very few people "want to be let alone" and therefore that prying could be seen as having as much value as privacy. To quote Posner, "People are assumed not to desire or value privacy or prying in themselves, but to use these goods as inputs into the production of income of some other broad measure of utility or welfare."[10] This position leads

---

8. Nimmer, "Right of Publicity," 204.

9. Felix Cohen, "Transcendental Nonsense and the Functional Approach," *Columbia Law Review* 35, no. 6 (1935): 815.

10. Richard Posner, "The Right of Privacy," *Georgia Law Review* 12 (1978). See Duncan Kennedy, "Cost-Benefit Analysis of Entitlement Problems: A Critique,"

us to wonder, at the end of the century, if individuality (which has had its sway over Western culture since the eighteenth century at least), may be losing ground to opportunism, since it seems that privacy no longer has anything to do with individuality but instead has to do with economic opportunity.

To attain some distance on the contemporary situation, I want to drop further back in history to the period when "property" and "right" had a somewhat different relationship, which requires us to look more closely at seventeenth-century England, where it was widely agreed that property was a right in something, whether liberty, land, or life. Because people often held various and different rights in the same land, that land didn't appear to them as a "possession," especially since an owner couldn't sell or deed it outright. This situation changed significantly with the advent of the capitalist market economy after the seventeenth century. The emergence of absolute property, in Blackstone's terms, characterized now by unlimited rights (as opposed to the earlier limited rights) produced a new relation between persons and their property: "It appeared to be the things themselves, not just the rights in them, that were exchanged in the market."[11]

Morton Horwitz, in his history of American law from 1879 to 1960, picks up where MacPherson leaves off. In the nineteenth century, U.S. courts began to expand the definition of property right violation to encompass any action that had as its consequence the reduction of market value, and this included labor conflicts that threatened to reduce profits. As new kinds of intangible properties (such as goodwill) grew in number and kind, land as the model for the conception of property began to disappear. What emerged, then, was the "abstraction of property into market value," which, although it relieved the legal system from the old reliance on physical trespassing in property, also "brought to the surface many more fundamental difficulties that a concrete and tangible conception of property had been able to avoid."[12] Over the last two centuries, as rights became marketable commodities, "limited and unsaleable rights *in* things

---

Stanford Law Review 33 (February 1981): 387–445, for an excellent discussion of the incoherence of the efficiency standard appplied by the law and economics school.

11. MacPherson, "Meaning of Property," 7–8.

12. Morton Horwitz, *The Transformation of American Law, 1870–1960: The Crisis of Legal Orthodoxy* (New York: Oxford University Press, 1992), 149.

gave way to unlimited rights *to* things."[13] Today the modern corporation produces rights to markets and offers shareholders rights to revenue. And in this new situation, as MacPherson concludes, "property as things becomes unrealistic."[14]

In the contemporary period, then, we see a circling back to property as rights but with a difference. Now, in a period in which corporate investors hold that they have a "right" to a return on their money, we also see a new kind of "intangible" propertyless property—exemplified by the franchise and the merchandising right. Rights have become capital assets, and formerly untransferable entities ("goodwill," the celebrity's "right to be let alone") become transferable.[15] This transferability is accompanied at once by a new divisibility, a feature that more than anything describes the abstraction of property into rights (not things). Here we find the celebrity name and likeness, constituted as rights to use, divided into periods, markets, and media manifestations. "Marilyn Monroe" as a line of shoes, swimsuits, clocks, lamp bases, and bath towels, which may be permitted in Switzerland but not Germany, in Japan but not in Brazil. These rights superimposed over rights may resemble the precapitalist rights to land, which allowed multiple productive use of the same concrete property, but whereas the earlier rights were limited and could not necessarily be sold, contemporary rights are unlimited, the consequence of which is rights severed by rights—internally conflictual networks of entitlements.[16]

I have earlier been interested in the political economy of availability, that is, the degree to which the legal divisibility of popular icons produces them as for or not for their fans. With merchandising, it would seem that the same mechanism that produces availability also produces unavailability. So on the one hand, the multiple entitlements (each held by a different small manufacturing company licensee)

---

13. MacPherson, "Meaning of Property," 2.

14. MacPherson, "Meaning of Property," 7–8.

15. On the new "intangible" property, see Kenneth Vandevelde, "The New Property of the Nineteenth Century: The Development of the Modern Concept of Property," *Buffalo Law Review* 29 (1980): 325–67.

16. See my discussion of contemporary merchandising as it depends on the right of publicity in *Contested Culture*, chap. 6; the leading treatise on this doctrine is Thomas J. McCarthy, *The Rights of Publicity and Privacy* (New York: Clark and Boardman, 1988), but also see Gregory J. Battersby and Charles W. Grimes, *The Law of Merchandise and Character Licensing* (New York: Clark Boardman, 1985).

multiply the points of intersection between fan and star. And yes, merchandising *is* a kind of artificially induced swell of excitement or, as in the case of the dead celebrities, a reenactment of excitement, a commodified nostalgia. This is not to diminish the appeal of these stars, really, since "Sex is nostalgia for sex," as Warhol once said. On the other hand, the private property status of celebrity icons works as a built-in censoring device. For example, in California, the 1985 civil code that legislated a state right of publicity, constituting the name and likeness of a celebrity as inheritable property, effectively returned these rights to the descendants of popular figures.[17] Family members could and did exert their inherited rights, particularly when the gay subculture claimed the images of matinee idols. Predictably, Clark Gable's relatives objected to the greeting card substituting a man for Scarlett O'Hara in Rhett Butler's arms, and John Wayne's family was outraged at the postcard image of the Western hero touched up with lipstick. Considering gay subculture from this somewhat different vantage, the work of camp is not only the work of reclamation but is also a battle to wrest these images from their private protectorates, to liberate them from the clutches of private property.[18]

Introducing Warhol into the history of the constitution of popular images as divisible property or a network of rights gives us a new stage, a missing link in this history. Clearly the year 1985 is a high-water mark in the development of a specifically American law of merchandising, a comeback from an earlier heyday in the 1930s.[19] But Warhol had already given us a premonition of the 1980s in his most memorable 1960s portraits—the images of Marilyn, Liz, and Elvis—anticipating, as these works did, the lives of performers extended and enlarged through merchandising. To some degree, the circulation started with the covers of *Time* and *Life*, with Marilyn and Liz vying with each other for more covers.[20] Warhol's multiples, then, reiterate not only the frame-by-frame imagistic plethora of the motion picture strip but also the aesthetic opulence of newsstands stacked with mass

17. See Roz Brassel and Ken Kulzick, "Life After Death for the California Celebrity," *Los Angeles Lawyer* (January 1985): 12–15; McCarthy, *Rights of Publicity and Privacy*, 6.24–6.25.

18. See the discussion in *Contested Culture*, 229–30, 237–39.

19. See Weston Anson, "A Licensing Retrospective and Glimpse into the Future," *Merchandising Reporter* 3, no. 5 (June–July 1984): 4–5.

20. Sidra Stich, *Made in USA: An Americanization in Modern Art, the '50s & '60s* (Berkeley: University of California Press, 1987).

circulation magazines. However, the achievement of an aesthetics of ever-presence is neither purely spontaneous nor exactly calculated. Ever-presence in this age of reproducibility is also a by-product of the underlying rights that attempt to make these publicity images cohere. And I do mean "attempt," since coherence can never be insured. Witness the imbalances in the Presley and Monroe images produced by scandal as an effect of the real. Consider how, during and after their deaths, the arteries of public relations, media coverage, and fan appropriation pumped new life into these images.[21]

It would be fruitful to ask (by way of contrasting copyright with right of publicity) if the semiotic binding that the right of publicity attempts to produce resembles in any way the binding of the authorial rights Warhol might be said to have in the images of Presley and Monroe as "original works." It could be said that in part because of the special attachment of the publicity right to the person (as opposed to copyright's attachment to the work), the pattern of contracts and claims enforced in the former is more wide-ranging, constituting a greater threat to image coherence (which both contract and person attempt to rectify). In the 1960s, these star images were constituted in part by contractually organized exclusive rights to the same star property, held by different parties including competing motion picture studios, subsidiary companies with various partners (as in Presley's case), and the stars themselves.[22] This situation is particularly relevant in relation to Presley since the silver Elvis series is a mutation of a publicity poster for a motion picture feature. What one finds on closer consideration is that the division of rights around star images does not organize, simplify, or reduce but, rather, multiplies contradictions. The larger question here, which I will not have space to address, has to do with the question of whether or not meanings tend to accumulate and shift irrespective of property rights. Instead, I want to

21. For the best theorization of the relationship between "real" events and the construction of public personas, see Richard Dyer, "*A Star is Born* and the Construction of Authenticity," in *Star Signs*, ed. Christine Gledhill (London: British Film Institute, 1981); the fundamental work in this field is Richard Dyer, *Stars* (London: British Film Institute, 1979), which builds on the earliest sociology of stardom, Edgar Morin's *The Stars*, trans. Richard Howard (London and New York: Grove Press, 1961). Note that Warhol had a copy of Morin's book: See Peter Wollen, "Raiding the Icebox," in *Andy Warhol: Film Factory*, ed. Michael O'Pray (London: British Film Institute, 1989), 24.

22. I discuss the merchandising arrangements made by Boxcar Enterprises, the company Elvis started with Colonel Tom Parker, in *Contested Culture*, 203–5.

turn to what is for me a new investigation—the possibility that we can consider rights in intellectual property according to the high-low culture hierarchy.

While low-culture entertainment law exclusive rights historically insured the sufficient substantiality of the photo ephemera on which Warhol worked, guaranteeing its existence and preparing the ground of signification through the circulation of these apparently "free" and immediate image properties—Liz, Marilyn, and Elvis—high-culture authorial rights now insure something else. From the point at which Warhol first smeared green paint on Marilyn Monroe's eyelids, his high-culture rights insured a cancellation of the consequences of unauthorized "taking" in the realm of trademark law, the realm of Coca-Cola and Mickey Mouse.[23] After all, as these images entered the realm of copyright and left the low-culture realm of trademark, their transformation into a new work became (magically) all that mattered. What matters more for us, however, is not so much Warhol's irreverent "theft" (of what was widely available anyway) but the incidence of high culture prevailing over low. It would seem here that high-culture copyright preempts low-culture unfair competition law in the move from the drugstore newsstand to the museum.

At the same time that Warhol managed a rights coup, overriding Campbell Soup's trademark by adding no requisite authorial touch of "originality" (which critics would persist in searching for and even finding), he performed a parody of the ideas/expression dichotomy.[24] At the same time that he used the underlying "idea" of Marilyn, Liz, and Elvis, Warhol reconceived of these popular "ideas" as "paintings," rendering them in substantially different expressive forms. And yet, despite his rendering they remained totally familiar forms, not-so-new expressions. The gesture of "painting" such "found" images, not unlike his gesture of "buying" the dollar bill idea from another artist, is a kind of performance art parody of rights transactions, suggesting that what is free and available should be paid for, and that rights can be bought and sold just like any other property, especially when they are rights to the most used and ever available (but never available enough)

23. For background, I suggest Thomas J. McCarthy, *Trademarks and Unfair Competition*, 2d ed., 2 vols. (Rochester, New York: Lawyers Co-op Publishing Company, 1984).

24. For an overview and critique of the ideas/expression dichotomy in intellectual property, see Justin Hughes, "The Philosophy of Intellectual Property," *Georgetown Law Journal* 77 (1988): 288–366.

of signs—the basis of rights exchange as well as all signification in U.S. culture—money.[25]

What I am trying to do is to dramatize the difference between what I am calling high and low culture rights, a distinction neither seen nor recognized in intellectual property doctrine. Indeed, the high-low culture distinction that might have informed this doctrine was checked early in the history of intellectual property law in the 1903 U.S. Supreme Court decision in *Bleistein v. Donaldson Lithographic Co.* In this 1903 U.S. Supreme Court decision, Justice Oliver Wendell Holmes Jr., for the majority, held that even a form as low as the circus poster was protectable under copyright law. The operative dichotomy in cases where the protection of such forms was at issue, he argued, should not be between high and low culture but between "the arts" and commerce. To quote Justice Holmes: "The antithesis to 'illustrations or works connected with the fine arts' is not works of little merit or of humble degree, or illustrations addressed to the less educated classes; it is 'prints or labels designed to be used for any other articles of manufacture.'" [26]

While Justice Holmes's decision for the majority may be read as indicating a generous inclusiveness and an unwillingness to refuse protection to low forms because of the class of persons to whom they appeal, Holmes was not taking a position against aesthetic elitism but was, rather, bending to meet the needs of the expanding market. Reversing the decisions of the Circuit Court of Appeals as well as the trial court, Holmes essentially argued that commercial value took precedence over the "intrinsic value" that the lower courts had wanted to see. In the long run, of course, he was awarding copyright protection to the circus posters on the theory of the need to protect an author, but here the issue of whether or not the "value" of the work as advertising justifed its service in the "promotion of the useful arts" eclipsed the issue of authorship. It is hard to ignore Holmes's ambivalence in his written opinion, and perhaps he was torn between the tastes of his own elite class and the requirements of an evolving commercial law. If nowhere else, his ambivalence, if not his reluctance to extend copyright protection, is evident in this passage: "Yet if they command the interest of any public, they have a commercial value—it

25. David James, *Allegories of Cinema: American Film in the Sixties* (Princeton, N.J.: Princeton University Press, 1989), 61.

26. Bleistein v. Donaldson Lithographic Co., 23 S. Ct. 298 (1903).

would be bold to say that they have not an aesthetic and educational value—and the taste of any public is not to be treated with contempt. It is an ultimate fact for the moment, whatever may be our hopes for a change."[27] After *Bleistein* a "mere advertisment" was on a par with any other "original work of authorship" in U.S. copyright law, and any test of aesthetic value was considered inappropriate and irrelevant in deciding whether copyright protection should be extended.

And yet, as I have argued elsewhere, in the current century there is evidence of an instability in this theory evolving from *Bleistein*, which came down as a strict stand behind protection of all cultural forms as authorial "works" (no matter what the aesthetic value). What I mean by "instability" here is the always existing possibility of a judicial eruption of an aesthetic bias against low forms such as soapbox designs, canned good labels, and even popular cartoon imagery. This foreseen possibility has produced a kind of retreat from copyright law (with its "original work of authorship" requirement) to the shelter of trademark law.[28] In this century, trademark doctrine can be seen as favoring the accumulation of capital, especially given its perpetual monopoly provision, which has meant an official declaration that commercial designs and images are exactly what they are: signs indicating the commercial interest standing behind them. So in terms of preferred theory of protection, it is the copyright versus trademark law dichotomy that evidences the distinction between high and low culture, that works itself out as high as opposed to low culture rights. And although, in theory, intellectual property law does not know the difference between the high-culture aestheticized object and the low-culture functional object, the divide between the two doctrines effectively shores up the existing cultural hierarchy (wherever possible), although not with consistency since this is an area in which the official cultural values are at odds with the needs of capital, a discrepancy that reproduces the deep asymmetry Raymond Williams sees as characteristic of capitalist societies.[29]

Warhol's celebrity icons as well as his consumer culture images

---

27. *Bleistein v. Donaldson*, as quoted in Melville B. Nimmer, *Cases and Materials on Copyright and Other Aspects of Entertainment Litigation—Including Unfair Competition, Defamation, and Privacy*, 3d ed. (St. Paul: West Publishing Co., 1985), 4.

28. See the discussion of the history of Superman in copyright and trademark law in *Contested Culture*, chap. 7.

29. Raymond Williams, *Culture and Society: 1780–1950* (New York: Columbia University Press, 1983).

test this hypothesis about high as opposed to low culture rights, illustrating the way in which high-culture copyright could be seen as pre-empting low-culture trademark rights. Whether by design or by chance (it doesn't matter which), Warhol's shifting of vigilantly protected popular images into the realm of "art" moved him out of the line of fire of possible infringement claims and gained him an automatic defense against charges of unauthorized "taking."[30] Ironically, such a defense always presumes the very ideal to which Warhol was most indifferent—the ideal of transcendant authorial genius, an ideal manifested in the originating "touch" of the master. While art critics looked for Warhol's evidence of presence and mark of difference under microscopes, he engaged his mother to sign his works and employed workers to render them. While it would be completely possible to argue that a larger percentage of the artistry in the (mostly derived) work he produced was "taken" and a relatively small percentage "added" by the artist, working as Warhol did, under the protection of the charmed art world, this issue was held at bay. This art world charm made it possible for Warhol to make the kinds of outrageous and offensive visual statements (through a broad reinflection of the common object and the star image) that you or I would not be able to make if we set up a small factory to produce Marilyn Monroe's image in Day-Glo for discount merchandising chains such as Wal-Mart and Revco. Certainly no small novelty manufacturing business has historically been able to treat the Campbell's soup can label or the Coca-Cola bottle with such irreverence. In Warhol's case, however, such high-low inversion produced the artist's famed critique of the avant-garde's obliviousness of their own complicity in commerce. But after the establishment of the Warhol

---

30. In no way do I mean to suggest that the lawyers who advised Warhol would have been inclined to use this or that defense, and my argument doesn't attempt to conform to any account of legal claims against Warhol. Neither is this to say that the empirical evidence is not significant, and here one must deal with the difference between lawsuits threatened, lawsuits filed, and settlements out of court. Certainly, beginning with the challenge from the designer of the Brillo box in 1964, Warhol was aware that his work would raise legal issues (see "Boxing Match," *Time*, 15 May 1964, 86). Between the 1960s and the 1980s, both the litigation climate and his attitude toward permissions changed. In the early years of his career, Campbell Soup Company representatives wrote to him with objections to his use of their trademark, but eventually they resigned themselves to a position that allowed them to see the publicity value of Warhol's rendering of the can. In the 1980s, Warhol actually secured clearance from the Disney company to use the image of Mickey Mouse (telephone conversation with Vincent Fremont, executive manager of the estate of Andy Warhol, February 8, 1993).

reputation, the artist's work almost completely escaped the silencing effected by the kind of corporate censorship so often extended in the interests of warding off the "tarnish" of unwanted semiotic associations.[31] Perhaps Warhol stopped short of a truly radical critique (at once a defiance of private property and the elite enshrinement of art), which could have been performed by selling his celebrity icons and Coca-Cola bottle works in the street.

I want to return to something that Warhol's work does not know but should know about its own status as original reconception of the low, as authorial makeup that "gussies up" the ordinary object. But I want to make my argument in reference to the right of publicity where the development of the new property as rights is more subtle, given that we don't automatically think of personhood as property. This is an argument that the celebrity image material on which Warhol worked is already multiply worked over—not only by the culture that has originally claimed Liz, Marilyn, and Elvis but also by the publicity teams that produced the stars' motion picture appearances (both on and off the screen) as exclusive. So it is finally the nature of the exclusive right that I want to consider. No matter how the star actor asserts him- or herself as biological being, as the star image has evolved, that image is a legally effective monopoly conveniently based on a belief in human nature and natural assets, in individual personhood and separateness from others—nothing more.[32] The star monopoly is an inviolable corner on one's inalienable self, a self-cancelling redundancy, but nevertheless an unassailable position.

Property, as MacPherson has told us, always implies a political relation between persons.[33] Recall that against the commonsense notion that property is things, he reminds us that historically in both logic and law, property is rights "in" or "to." So it is these rights "in" or "to" that define the relationality—the near or far, the having or not having—being certain not to forget that these rights are between persons and not between a person and a thing. The fact that property rights are always between persons, however, is made clear only when

31. I refer to the literal legal term *tarnish* that is basic to unfair competition doctrine in relation to the question of competing use of a trademark that might somehow reflect adversely on the protected mark.

32. See the discussion of star image and star monopoly in *Contested Culture*, 33–41.

33. MacPherson, "Meaning of Property," 4.

properties are in dispute. The question may also arise whether a similar relationality obtains when one is talking about civil law where the rights to speak out, to have a fair trial, or to congregate freely are understood as "liberties" accruing to persons. Are these rights only rights in relation to the state and not in relation to other persons? It may be that the relationality factor in unfair competition law is best analogized with criminal law. And yet it is not that rights of persons are weighed—one against the other in unfair competition doctrine. The right to exclude, based on an enforceable claim, the foundation of those branches of the law in which property is a key category always seems to overwhelm the more timid right to "use." In "Property and Sovereignty," a classic essay written more than sixty years ago, legal realist Morris Cohen cautioned against identifying property right with physical possession, aligning it instead with enforcement. Properly, he asserted, "A right is always against one or more individuals." While we may imagine that the law functions to insure our enjoyment and use of what we think that we possess, the law of property, says Cohen, "helps me directly only to exclude others from using the things which it assigns to me."[34] It can therefore be said that since property is the right to enforce, property always contains the "threat of force."[35]

Certainly the brutality of the exclusive right is difficult to see in intellectual property, where the physical manifestation of the protected work itself is, more often than not, circulating in a public realm and is never actually in the private possession of its owner. Copyright, we always need to recall, is only a right to copy, a right not necessarily coincident with possession of a manuscript, a photograph, or a piece of sculpture. The publicity right as well doesn't always coincide with either the physical body or its representations (although it may originate in the body of the celebrity). In both copyright and right of publicity, the "right" only manifests itself in the exercise of a claim against an infringer. Until then, it is unseen, or as one judge characterized the right of publicity, until exercised, that right is "dormant."[36]

The curse of the private property right is difficult to see in

---

34. Morris Cohen, "Property and Sovereignty," *Cornell Law Review* 35, no. 6 (1927): 12.

35. MacPherson, "Meaning of Property," 3.

36. Lugosi v. Universal Pictures, 160 Cal. Rptr. 323 (1979), 342.

intellectual property, and any other kind of property that might be commonly held is difficult to imagine. Common property, as MacPherson defines it, always implies the right "not to be excluded," which in effect, negates the curse.[37] Yet we tend to think of common property less in terms of culture and more in terms of state-owned parks and public buildings. The notion of an arena where exclusionary rights cannot be enforced seems not to apply to common culture, unless, perhaps, we understand the public domain as common property. From a legal point of view, however, that space is thought to be more a junkyard of finally "abandoned" properties than a popular, shared "live" space.[38] Given that collective rights as a concept is underdeveloped in Anglo-American law, it may seem that there is no foothold in intellectual property for any kind of common property.

Theoretically, the publicity right ought to contain some knowledge of its debt to the common. It is, after all, a private right maintained in the public eye—a contradiction, it would seem—but one that the right of publicity doctrine takes care of for us. As I have said, the right of publicity is actually a personal monopoly for a numbered few, but since these few have been "selected" by the many, the exclusivity goes unnoticed. Neither has anyone noticed the rarity of collective ownership defenses in unfair competition disputes. However, at least one of the hundreds of cases in the last fifteen years involved a right of publicity defense. The question of the right to Elvis Presley's image arose in one of a group of cases in which Boxcar and its licensees sought to rein in the runaway production of "Elvis" products rushed onto the market immediately following the singer's death. In *Memphis Development Foundation v. Factors, Inc.* (1980) the city of Memphis, Tennessee, was enjoined by Boxcar's licensees from producing statues in the image of their favorite son.[39] The Memphis argument, in effect, amounted to a demand for an accounting that took fans into consideration in the production of celebrity, particularly in their question, "Who is the heir of fame?" In the final outcome, however, *Mem-*

---

37. MacPherson, "Meaning of Property," 4.

38. The implications of the legal concept of *abandonment*, whether of a trademark or a work of art, are that the expiration of protection, for whatever reason, is a kind of abdication of parental responsibility, which is to say that a negative judgment is made against an irresponsible owner who would "leave" a cultural property in the public domain.

39. Memphis Development Foundation v. Factors, Inc., 616 F.2d 956, 205 U.S.P.Q. 784 (6th Cir. 1980).

phis Development was decided in line with the other cases that awarded damages to Elvis's company and its licensees, his corporate heirs. So it would seem that under the unfair competition umbrella, since there is no way to calculate socially produced assets, cultural property value under this doctrine must always accrue to a human or a corporate "person."

Here again, Andy Warhol provides an object lesson in his profound grasp of the mechanism of celebrity creation. Critics have often noted that he seemed to want to be nothing more than the mirror of his followers. The sociology of The Factory might be described as a range of gender offenders and semiotic provocateurs looking into the mirror at the center. Or, as one critic described the scene, "This world of 'freaks' gravitated around a central figure who had himself called the 'boss' but who made it a point of honor never to seem to have the slightest individuality, never to be anything but the mirror of his entourage, the xerox of what his courtiers wanted him to be."[40] The mirror shows nothing, except to those who hover around it, looking for themselves in it, and who, seeing themselves, recognize the image of the star. This theory of fandom spells disappointment for those anticipating their fifteen minutes of fame, implying as it does that if there is a moment for each of us in the limelight, it will only be a vicarious one. The formula for celebrity, after all, is that the fame of one depends on the complete obscurity of others. The exclusive right requires their exclusion.

And yet the law keeps the fantasy alive. Echoing Warhol's prediction, the common law right of publicity actually contains within it the possibility of our own celebrity, however "dormant" the right. From this law we also learn that if we have no other property, we have property in ourselves—that is, our name, voice, and likeness. While we might be led (by judges in celebrated cases involving well-known personalities, if nowhere else) to think that our "name" is the most valuable thing we have, we should be skeptical. If we recall what actually constitutes this "property," we realize that we are not left with much.

My example of the right of publicity as property, where the notion of "property" can be more easily seen as hollow, is meant to bring

---

40. Thierry De Duve, trans. Rosalind Krauss, "Andy Warhol, or The Machine Perfected," *October* 48 (Spring 1989): 4.

home two lessons about the vacuity of property rights: (1) that all we ever really have in entitlement to property is the right to enforce a claim, and (2) that such a right finds its origin not in the labor of the producer nor even in the intrinsic value of the property itself (whether material or immaterial), but in the will of the state. But perhaps the last thing that we want to be told in the West at this time in history is that a "property right" is given to us by the state.

If Warhol's genius was his ability to produce works that could be confused with their reproductions, it would follow that his sayings could be similarly confused with their quotation. One of the best examples of the latter is *Village Voice* critic Gary Indiana's report that one of the eulogies at Warhol's funeral contained a reference to the artist's statement that he wanted to be "reincarnated as the ring on Liz Taylor's finger." While I have yet to find a reference to Warhol's having said this in any of the published works by or about him, I have found in the collection of his wit and wisdom the statement that "it would be very glamorous to be reincarnated as a big ring on Pauline de Rothschild's finger."[41]

In one move he seems to have resolved the dilemmas of the human work requisite to the production of property, the instability of intellectual property, the valuation of rights, the origin of value, and the fate of celebrity after death. Warhol has wished himself reincarnated as an indisputable thing, against the general belief that bodies are reincarnated as other animal or human bodies. Neither is he incorporated into the body of the celebrity Liz Taylor. However, he seems to have come back as something better—as something that she coveted. At last, a truly unambiguous property. A ring. A thing.

---

41. Andy Warhol, *The Philosophy of Andy Warhol (From A to B and Back Again)* (New York and London: Harcourt Brace Jovanovich, 1975), 113; Gary Indiana, "I'll Be Your Mirror," *Village Voice*, 5 May 1987, 2.

Taking Liberties in Foucault's Triangle: Sovereignty, Discipline, Governmentality, and the Subject of Rights

Kirstie M. McClure

SALUS POPULI SUPREMA LEX
VOX POPULI VOX DEI

By repetition across time and place old slogans have a way of taking on new meanings, new referents and resonances, new implications. With the emergence of what Tocqueville called "the democratic revolution" and, more particularly, with its articulation through the institutions of representative government, we might say that variations on these two were wedded into the hypothetical conditional of popular sovereignty: if the purpose of government is the good of the people, then the voice of the people must command the government. Sedimented as this is by now into the common sense of liberal democratic cultures, there may seem little need for evidencing either its virtue or its relationship to the language of rights. And yet, a variety of recent theoretical perspectives suggest the necessity of rethinking that common sense in fundamental respects. Michel Foucault, for example, argues that the legal-juridical frame of sovereignty within which rights make political sense has been not only colonized by new apparatuses of disciplinary knowledge, but deeply and complexly imbricated with "governmentality," with techniques of power concerned not with the obligations and liberties of rights-bearing juridical subjects but with the management of "population," with the "convenient disposition" of people and things.[1] These new forms of power, on his account, are sufficiently distinct from the questions of rightful resistance to oppression that circulate through the discourse of sovereignty as to preclude effective recourse to the language of rights.[2]

And yet, curiously, even Foucault refused to relinquish the notion of "right" entirely. "If one wants," he observed, " . . . to struggle against disciplines and disciplinary power, it is not towards the ancient right of sovereignty that one should turn, but towards the possibility of a new form of right, one which must indeed be anti-disciplinary, but at the same time liberated from the principle of sovereignty."[3] What such a new form of *right* might have to do with claims to *rights* is by no means clear. But what is crystalline above all else is that it calls not only for a rethinking of rights but a rethinking as well of the notion of the autonomous "individual" who is supposed to be their necessary bearer. And it is this potent challenge, Foucault argued, that constitutes "the political, ethical, social, philosophical problem" of the present. As he posed it, the task is not to "liberate the individual from the state and the state institutions, but to liberate us both from the state and from the type of individualization which is linked to the state. We have to promote new forms of subjectivity through the refusal of this kind of individuality which has been imposed on us for several centuries."[4]

Foucault's work, however, is not the only quarter from which we are urged today to rethink the relationship between sovereignty, resistance, and the language of rights. Concurring with his refusal of "the subject" as a unified and unifying essence, agreeing as well with his contention that "wherever there is power there is resistance," Ernesto Laclau and Chantal Mouffe pose a similarly provocative challenge by pointing to "the democratic revolution" as a series of historical struggles embracing successively broader and more dispersed fields of social

---

1. "Two Lectures," in *Power/Knowledge: Selected Interviews and Other Writings 1972–1977*, ed. Colin Gordon (New York: Pantheon/Random House, 1980); "Governmentality," in *The Foucault Effect: Studies in Governmentality*, ed. Graham Burchell, Colin Gordon, and Peter Miller (Chicago: University of Chicago Press, 1991); "Reason and Politics," in *Michel Foucault Politics/Philosophy/Culture: Interviews and Other Writings 1977–1984*, ed. Lawrence D. Kritzman (New York: Routledge, 1988); "The Subject and Power," in *Michel Foucault: Beyond Structuralism and Hermeneutics*, 2d ed., ed. Hubert Dreyfus and Paul Rabinow (Chicago: University of Chicago Press, 1983).
2. "Two Lectures," 108.
3. Ibid.
4. "Subject and Power," 216.

antagonism and political contestation.[5] From workers' and women's struggles, to struggles for the civil rights of ethnic and racial minorities, to contemporary resistances around questions of sexuality and environmental politics, they argue that the historical expansion of that revolution has effected a series of displacements of the line of demarcation between public and private, bringing various forms of subordination once considered "private" into question. On Laclau and Mouffe's account, however, the possibility of sustaining such radicalizations of democratic possibilities takes the form not of a refusal but of a contestation of the meanings conventionally attached to the language of rights. And for them, the political challenge of the present requires not only the production of a new form of individual but the generation as well of a new way of posing the problem of rights.[6]

If we are interested in the possibility or, should this be credible, the efficacy, of the language of rights as a language of resistance, this juxtaposition of Foucault and Laclau and Mouffe presents both a problem and a possibility. The problem might be suggested most broadly by noting the extent to which their differing estimations of the language of rights take the form of significantly different historical narratives, each of which weighs differently on one's sense of political possibilities in the present. Like questions of rights, to be sure, questions of democracy rarely appear in Foucault's work. Indeed, without exception his historical researches attempted both to diminish the significance of the sovereignty problematic and to shift political attention away from a long-standing modern fascination with the French Revolution and its aftermath. But for Laclau and Mouffe that revolution—or, more properly, the democratic and egalitarian imaginary it put into play at the level of effective history—was a pivotal but incomplete beginning in the struggle for democratic possibilities. Between the two, however— that is, between Foucault's account of the insinuation of governmentality, discipline, police, and security apparatuses into the crevices of the social, on the one hand, and Laclau and Mouffe's account of the historical deepening and diffusion of the democratic revolution, on the other—politics from the late eighteenth century to the present seems to live two disparate and separable lives across a single temporality. In a

---

5. Ernesto Laclau and Chantal Mouffe, *Hegemony and Socialist Strategy* (London: Verso, 1983), chap. 5.

6. Ibid., 184.

word, the politics of the past two centuries appears nothing if not schizophrenic.

We might do well, though, to resist the temptation of seeing this as a choice between two distinct and mutually exclusive alternatives, as an invitation, that is, to embrace *either* "the democratic revolution" *or* what Foucault refers to as the "triangle" of "sovereignty-discipline-government."[7] Instead, we might ask if it is possible to think the two simultaneously, if it is possible to think "democratic revolution *and* governmentality," as a point of departure for the project of reposing the problem of rights. In this chapter I offer three partial and preliminary ruminations on that possibility. With an eye on the sovereignty problematic, the first juxtaposes Foucault's skepticism about rights with a contemporary historian's postfoundationalist defense of rights as rational conventions. The second is a broad reflection on the peculiar historicity of the Anglophone language of rights. With an eye, in particular, to the variegations of rights claims in relation to the rise of national states, it focuses attention on the multiplicity of "subjects of rights" enunciated through claims to negative liberty rights, positive liberty rights, and entitlement rights. The third rumination offers a closer consideration of an extended moment in that history in light of Foucault's "triangle" of "sovereignty-discipline-government." Focusing on Malthus's *Essay on Population*, Robert Owen's *New View of Society* and other writings, and a variety of William Hazlitt's critical essays, it suggests some of the tensions and disjunctions between these sorts of rights as they circulated through reform polemics on politics, population, and popular liberties in Britain in the first decades of the nineteenth century. The chapter ends, rather than concludes, with a note on the insistent equivocality of what "taking liberties in Foucault's triangle" might mean for the project of reposing the problem of rights.

But a Right Is Not a Rose: Discourse, Sovereignty, and the "Subject of Rights"

Let me begin with a question Foucault presumed settled: What is "the subject of rights"? In the broadest sense, he suggested, it is the subject of humanism, which from its roots in Roman law has historically

---

7. "Governmentality," 102.

generated "individuality" as one among many forms of "subjected sovereignty." "Humanism," he argued, "invented a whole series of [such] subjected sovereignties: the soul (ruling the body but subjected to God), consciousness (sovereign in a context of judgment, but subjected to the necessities of truth), the individual (a titular control of personal rights subjected to the laws of nature and society), basic freedom (sovereign within but accepting the demands of an outside world and 'aligned with destiny')."[8] Or, more narrowly, he might say the "subject of rights" is the given, the product of juridical discourse, "the sovereign individual with sovereign rights" generated and invoked by "reference to a certain theory of sovereignty."[9] And this, indeed, is precisely why he found recourse to the language of rights ineffective as a strategy of resistance to the configurations of power/knowledge typical of disciplinary society and the "governmental" state. For although, in the eighteenth and nineteenth centuries, the theory of sovereignty became "a permanent instrument of criticism of the monarchy," it nonetheless simultaneously permitted "a system of right to be superimposed upon the mechanisms of discipline in such a way as to conceal its actual procedures, the element of domination inherent in its techniques, and to guarantee to everyone, by virtue of the sovereignty of the state, the exercise of his sovereign rights."[10]

To invoke a distinction distant from the terminology of Foucauldian genealogy, the "subject of rights" for Foucault is a bearer of "subjective rights"—but only as a creature birthed from the womb of the state, with the latter figured as the source of "objective right" or law.[11] It is a subject produced by the discourse of "law, rule, or

---

8. "Revolutionary Action: 'Until Now,' " in *Language, Countermemory, Practice: Selected Essays and Interviews*, ed. Donald F. Bouchard (Ithaca: Cornell University Press, 1977), 221–22.

9. "Two Lectures," 108.

10. Ibid., 105.

11. That Foucault is not operating within the legal discourse or cultural parameters of Anglophone jurisprudence is worth noting. That this may be rather more than a problem of accurate translation might bear attention as well. Why, we might ask, is there such a ruckus in the Anglophone world about poststructuralist critiques of the language of rights? One account, well removed from contemporary pyrotechnics, might be found in Paul Vinogradoff's discussion of the curiosity of the English usage of *right*: "The English language brings forcibly to our attention the fact that legal situations can be considered from two different points of view. We distinguish between law and right, while in most European languages both notions are combined in generic terms and have to be distinguished by the help of adjectives. When we speak of law in English we mean the legal order instituted and enforced in a community; when we

sovereign will," a subject for which subjectivity and subjection are flip sides of the same coin, a subject that owes the equivocality of its being to the sovereignty of the law. It is not, then, perhaps accidental that of Anglophone writers Bentham figures so prominently in Foucault's various accounts of the intimacies shared by sovereignty, discipline, and governmentality. Bentham repudiated "subjective right" as a matter of individual judgment and insisted, rather, that the "subject of rights" owes its life wholly to the power of law. Such "subjected sovereignties" may, in fact—that is, empirically in practice—resist that law, but never licitly under the sign of "rights." Where the state has not granted rights by positive declaration, neither rights nor a "subject of rights" can exist in any meaningful sense.[12]

For a theorist and historian reputedly obsessed with ruptures, fissures, and discontinuities, this seems a strangely solid, continuous, and monolithic response. But it also suggests a question. If the "subject of rights" is an artifact of the discourse of sovereignty, what sense does it make to speak of a "discourse of rights"? As an object of theoretical inquiry and concern, a discourse entails patterns and regularities, rules of formation proper to itself that orchestrate the dispersion of its ele-

---

speak of right we mean usually a power exercised by each person under this legal order. In Norwegian the term ret covers both things and we have to distinguish between "den objective ret" and "den subjective ret" if we want to render the contrast between law as order and right as power. The same is true of the German Recht, of the French Droit, of the Slavonic Pravo. Such peculiarities of expression are not accidental nor superficial; they point to important distinctions . . . connected with a fundamental problem of jurisprudence. Law, den objective Ret, is evidently a creation of society acting by means of the State, or through some other channel of social organization, e.g. the Church or an autonomous community. But what is to be said of right? Why is right contrasted with law in English, while Recht stands both for right and for law in German, Jus in Latin, droit in French, pravo in Slavonic languages? Obviously the nations of Continental Europe laid stress in their terminology on the unity of legal order, on the fact that it is constituted, governed and directed by the general authority of the Commonwealth. On the other hand the English-speaking nations distinguish in terms between two aspects of the juridical arrangement—between the public settlement of law and the consciousness of right rooted in the last instance in the conviction of each individual member of the community and influencing his will to exercise his power." Custom and Right (Oslo: Institutte for Sammenlignende Kulturforkning, 1925), 65–66.

12. Hobbes, too, might appear a prime source for the "subjected sovereignty" of the modern individual. But contrary to the conventional view of Leviathan as bent on the thoroughgoing subjection of its subjects, Hobbes's development of civil society left a far from insignificant remainder of "subjective right" as a continuing reservoir of private judgment. For a duly provocative appreciation of this, see Richard E. Flathman, Thomas Hobbes: Skepticism, Individuality, and Chastened Politics (Newbury Park, London, New Delhi: Sage Publications, 1993), esp. chaps. 4–6.

ments. If there is a patterned historicity of rights claims, and if this, as Foucault suggests, owes its existence to the rules of formation that drive sovereignty, it would seem that we have not so much a "discourse of rights" but, again as Foucault would have it, the "discourse of right," the discourse of law, the discourse of sovereignty by another name. But this in turn may raise the question of whether Foucault has not significantly circumscribed the political valences and potentials of the language of rights definitionally at the outset. Ironically, by accepting the privilege accorded "objective right" by a monistic account of sovereignty, "subjective rights" are not only captured but domesticated—one might even say, subordinated or subjugated—by the sort of statist logic that Foucault otherwise, and usually quite effectively, was at such pains to avoid. In short, if for Foucault "a right is a right is a right and by any other name feeleth as foul," the problem may be of his own making—or, perhaps more precisely, may be itself a discursive effect of the very theory of sovereignty that he sought to displace.

In this, however, Foucault is not alone, for the sovereignty problematic similarly, if more subtly, inflects discussions of rights on this side of the Atlantic as well. As an example of that inflection, we might consider Thomas Haskell's recent essay, "The Curious Persistence of Rights Talk in the 'Age of Interpretation.' "[13] Haskell's postfoundationalism would seem a different sort of creature than Foucault's. Certainly it would seem far more encouraging on the question of "rights": while it refuses "rights" the status of eternal verities secured by metaphysical foundations, it nonetheless defends them as historically and culturally specific "rational conventions." The absence of foundations for rights talk, on this account, is a cause neither for alarm nor celebration. Rather, it is simply the disappearance of an illusion. And this, as it happens, is finally not such a bad thing, for it leaves us "rights-talkers" with a clearer and perhaps more humble view of what we've been doing all along. Contingently secured as "rational conventions," "rights here and now," we might say, "may not be rights there and then, may not be rights anywhere tomorrow, but by the same name they smelleth as sweet."

Anticipating one of the central themes of this conference, Haskell poses a paradox of rights: the real "puzzle" about rights, he suggests,

---

13. In David Thelen, ed., *The Constitution and American Life* (Ithaca: Cornell University Press, 1988).

"is why talk about rights should continue to flourish in the West after well over a century of widespread . . . skepticism about the soundness of its foundations."[14] Admitting "the plain truth . . . that no one at present can offer any entirely satisfactory justification for the idea of a right, or for the . . . vital principle on which it depends, the idea of objective moral obligation," Haskell confesses "ambivalence and anxiety" about his own insistence that rights talk "for all its liabilities, refers to something real," that it is "a valuable cultural practice" that "we ought to encourage."[15] Where that anxiety comes out perhaps most trenchantly is in his recognition of the ways in which that century-long critique of metaphysics has proved a powerful historical solvent for the presumption of objective moral knowledge in any form. The paradox presented by the persistence of rights talk in such a context, he suggests, far from being contained within the domain of rights, extends "across the entire spectrum of ethics and morality."[16]

Why? Because "the idea of a right, after all, is only one variation on the claim to objective knowledge about morality."[17] And where the latter has been called into question, we find ourselves "unable to distinguish" not only between saying we want something and saying we have a right to it, but between "any form of moral utterance" and "statements of merely personal preference." Fraught with a similar uncertainty, he suggests, is any attempt "to explain the difference between 'You *ought* to do y' and 'I want you to do y.' "[18] Haskell condenses the pathos of this recognition into an extended metaphor:[19]

> Having begun by noticing something paradoxical about the persistence of rights in modern society, it now seems that what we have stumbled across is a fragment of a ruin so extensive that it stretches to our farthest cultural horizon. It is as if we have found ourselves standing before an ancient building, visibly weathered and beginning to tumble down, which squatters inhabit and even use ceremonially, but whose founders have vanished, and whose true function and purpose become hazier in the minds of each

14. Thomas Haskell, "The Curious Persistence of Rights Talk in the 'Age of Interpretation'," 238.

15. Ibid., 324.

16. Ibid., 334.

17. Ibid., 335.

18. Ibid.

19. Ibid.

succeeding generation. The ruin is the very idea of moral obligation. We are the squatters.

Haskell, however, resists the siren song of a return to a world we have lost, whether that be the classical rationalism of Strauss or the longing for premodern teleological conceptions of virtue favored by MacIntyre. Squatting amidst the ruins, it turns out, is not the worst of all possible worlds to inhabit.

But it is, Haskell insists, a condition that puts us on our mettle to provide plausible justifications for our claims to rights—justifications that acknowledge the impossibility of secure foundations, that appreciate the conventionality and hence historicity of all such claims even as they refuse the slippery slope of radical historicism. Referencing Hume's resignation "to the imperfections of reason" and his shift of "trust to social conventions and common sense," Haskell points to a middle way.[20] "We are," he suggests, "free to decide where to stand."[21] Shifting metaphors, we squatters in the ancient ruin are now reinscribed as travellers in a not entirely new land, explorers whose belated recognition of the conventionality of "rights and other kinds of moral obligation" need not drive us into Nietzsche's waiting arms:[22]

> Once we have ventured out into this sparsely settled land, far from the seductive, but unreal, comforts of Reason, and uncomfortably close to the maelstrom of History, the next question is whether the ground is stable enough to build on.

Having left the ruin of "the very idea of moral obligation," one might say, we are now free to reinvent it— this time, perhaps, with a bit more humility. And perhaps, too, with a bit more civility, since we will now be wary of claims to self-evidence and universality. We might even be astute enough to understand that rights claims have an inescapable, in the sense of culturally sedimented, linkage to political contestation, for they "will be a perpetual object of struggle between rival groups with strong vested interests, both ideal and mate-

---

20. Ibid., 344.
21. Ibid.
22. Ibid.

rial, in one interpretation or another."[23] And, best of all, once we accept the conventional character of rights claims, we might finally abandon the desire for the certainty of closure. We might finally recognize that the conventions marshaled by rights talk "promise only a continuation of the endless, but usually bloodless, wrangling to which bourgeois societies are already well accustomed."[24] Nothing much, really, would change; "everyday practice already implies no more than that."[25] Indeed, on the best-case analysis, a broad public recognition of the conventional character of rights would encourage toleration, with the wholly laudable consequence that "rights debates might take on a less sanctimonious character" when they "concern conventions, rather than Truth."[26]

A hopeful picture, a picture that limns not the "Reason" but the reasonableness of rights talk as a conventional way of settling moral claims and obligations. And yet—as Haskell's own confession of ambivalence might suggest—there is a brooding shadow that haunts its edges. Alongside his support for the idea that rights claims are secured by conventions, perhaps, looms another question, a question never explicitly addressed, a question not of morality but of politics— one might even say a question of power: what is to secure the conventions that secure rights claims? At this level of generality, when it is not busy refusing the question as necessarily Nietzschean, Haskell's essay is silent. Its concern is neither with the referents of particular rights claims nor with their mode of practical enforcement but, rather, with the conventionality of rights as a referent—with the right, we might say, to have rights, with the right to talk rights talk at all. But if, as Haskell suggests, all "rights talk" is conventional, it would not seem inappropriate to consider the conventions governing his own.

The paragraph from which the account of Haskell's hopeful picture was drawn, for example, is a significant turning point in the language of his presentation as a whole. It is here that the philosophical abstractions of Reason and rationalism, History and historicism, give way to a more pointedly political vocabulary. It comes, in fact, as the second paragraph following the metaphorical invocation of a "sparsely settled land," and the discussion inserted between the two

23. Ibid., 345.
24. Ibid.
25. Ibid.
26. Ibid.

provides a series of tropological bridges between that territorial meta-phor and the happy picture attending the recognition that all rights claims are conventional. Each bridge, however, is caught up in the circulation of power: rights are things that must *"win . . . loyalty"*; conventions have a *"power"* not only to "project an uncontestable givenness into the most contingent arrangements" but also "to *impose* a heavy burden of proof on those seeking change."[27] So understood, it turns out that rights as conventions may even be a bit *too* durable. As a consequence, they must "be open to rational criticism" and capa-ble not simply of winning loyalty but "of *commanding* rational alle-giance."[28] And this, as Haskell observes, produces an "inescapable tension" at the heart of rights talk. The more durable such a conven-tion is, "the more like a tradition it becomes, and the less rational human allegiance to it is likely to be"; while "the more open to ra-tional criticism it is perceived to be," the more likely it is to be "open to change or the possibility of abandonment."[29] Although the refer-ents of such rights remain coded as moral claims and obligations, and although there is no doubt that the exit of foundations has rendered all such rights claims inescapably contestable, the terrain and stakes of that contestation remain as yet unnamed.

But not for long. Following upon this, the section I quoted from selectively deserves reproduction in full, for my initial gloss did not do justice to the referential claims and strategies of the original. Con-sider, for example, the ways in which that hopeful picture figures its "subjects of rights":[30]

> Clearly rights as rational conventions will lack some of the quali-ties that have traditionally been claimed for rights. They will not be self-evident or eternal. And every attempt to apply them be-yond the boundaries of *one's* own culture will carry grave risks of injustice through the unwitting effects of parochialism and ethno-centrism. Far from being fixed once and for all in a constitution or a bill of rights, the definition of rights will be a perpetual object of contention between rival groups with strong vested interests, both ideal and material, in one interpretation or another. Far from

27. Ibid., 344–45 (my emphasis).
28. Ibid., 345 (my emphasis).
29. Ibid.
30. Ibid. (my emphasis).

allowing *us* to escape from interpretation into a realm in which moral judgment becomes a matter of fact, rights understood as conventions promise only a continuation of the endless, but usually bloodless, wrangling to which bourgeois societies are already well accustomed. Few changes would accompany a general acceptance of the idea that rights are conventions, because *our* everyday practice already implies that they are no more than that. At best *one* might hope that if the conventional nature of rights ever became widely understood, rights debates might take on a less sanctimonious character, as *people* recognize that *their* differences concern conventions, rather than Truth.

The "subjects of rights" offered here at the beginning seem both laudable and familiar: the unmarked "one," wary of risking injustice and respectful of the rights of others; the inclusive "us" that beckons an implicit "we," already accustomed to wrangling over rights in "our" everyday practice. By the end, however, that language of "we" and "our" rather oddly gives way to something different: finally, it is not "we" and "our differences" that become subjects of less sanctimonious rights debates, it is "people" and "their" differences. A glimmer, perhaps, of the political unconscious at work? Might those "people" not effectively mean "*those* people"—people who take their differences and contentions over rights claims too seriously? Could this not be taken as an indication that such "people" are somehow less rational than *we* who recognize the conventionality of all such claims? Although *we* may be unaccustomed to thinking of tolerance itself in such terms, I cannot but wonder if *our* rational acceptance of the conventionality of rights claims has proven such an effective guard against sanctimoniousness. Perhaps "rationality" doesn't require the mantle of Truth to be sanctified; perhaps convention itself can serve that function. If, as Haskell suggests, the notion of rights as rational conventions reflects what is already the case in common practice—if rights talk is, in fact, always already conventional—can we discern the governing convention implicit in this odd shift of referents?

Haskell's subsequent elaboration of his position suggests that there is such a convention, and that that convention has to do not only with a particular construction of the political stakes of rights but, more specifically, with the political character of "rights" understood as moral obligations in relation to something not unlike "objective right." And yet, curiously, where Foucault suggested that the problem with rights talk was its historical complicity with modern techniques of power and strategies of social discipline, Haskell's worry appears quite the opposite: "Can rights that do not pretend to be eternal verities," he asks, "provide public life with sufficient order and continuity?"[31] But as the remainder of the essay spins out an affirmative answer to that question, in part by reference to abortion rights, in part through a discussion of Thomas Kuhn, it leaves ample room for the possibility that Foucault might be right after all. For present purposes it will suffice to consider only the first of these.

Adapting to his own purposes Mark Tushnet's hypothetical case of the effects of technological change on abortion rights, for example, Haskell concurs that the achievement of technologies for extra-uteral fetal development would radically alter the terms of the abortion debate. As Tushnet put it, "no one would care about a woman's decision merely to remove a fetus from her body, because that act would not have the consequence (i.e. the death of the fetus) that troubles many people today."[32] Haskell agrees: "[O]nce the technology was in place, a statute requiring the removal, rather than the destruction of the fetus would probably meet with no significant resistance on grounds of privacy or anything else."[33] Here, unsurprisingly perhaps, the idea of rights as rational conventions finally finds its real referent, along with its teeth and its power of enforcement, in statutory law. But it finds that power in ways that remove contestations over rights from the domain of politics— in ways, that is, that render rights talk indebted not to the vicissitudes of public opinion and discussion, but to the presumptively obvious rationality of a technological solution. That "solution," to be sure, is of Tushnet's devising, and Haskell duly notes that it would resolve one dilemma only to spawn others, among them being what to do with the resultant children.[34] And yet, it is Haskell's own language that rivets his rational conventions to scientific rationality, for it is precisely this connection that saves his rights

---

31. Ibid.

32. Mark Tushnet, "An Essay on Rights," *Texas Law Review* 62 (May 1984), 1366. Quoted in Haskell, "Curious Persistence of Rights Talk," 346.

33. Haskell, "Curious Persistence of Rights Talk," 346.

34. The fantasy of such a solution to contestations over reproductive rights, however, is rather more general, and finds expression in feminist writings as well. See, for example, Shulamith Firestone's *The Dialectic of Sex* (New York: Morrow, 1974) and Marge Piercy's *Woman on the Edge of Time* (New York: Fawcett Crest, 1976).

as conventions from the charge of arbitrariness. That the members of that hypothetical society quickly "abandoned the right to abortion as it is defined today and adopted statutes guaranteeing the protection of the fetus by the new technology," he suggests, "is reassuring testimony that even when rights are admitted to be conventions, they retain a kind of objectivity: debates concerning them can be rational; there is a basis for discriminating between better and worse conventions."[35] But in this case, the basis for that discriminating judgment— the rationality, that is, that guarantees the new convention—is not a characteristic of its "subjects," much less a characteristic or even a product of political discussion and debate. Rather, it is an artifact of the "kind of objectivity" proper to science, and the "rational convention" that objectivity secures is, in the first instance, statute. Bluntly put, the referent of Haskell's rational conventions is not rights but law. If rights are to be accounted rational it would seem to be only as a donation of the rationality of law, itself secured by the luminous objectivity of science.

In effect, Haskell's "subject of rights," like Foucault's, not only owes its life to the force of law and the power of the state, it is similarly unencumbered by any connection to democratic politics. Interestingly, however—and quite unlike Foucault—Haskell's account makes no reference to sovereign will. Indeed, it may be that the notion of rights as rational conventions functions precisely to avoid the implications of arbitrariness resident within a theory of sovereignty as "objective right." Instead, the objectivity of the law that ensures the right to have rights is secured by the authority of science, an authority presumptively external to the contentiousness of politics, and indeed, finally, an authority to which politics itself is subjected. But here, far from avoiding Foucault's dismal conclusions with regard to the potential of rights as a language of political contestation or resistance, Haskell's account seems rather to support them—and support them quite effectively, in this example, by instantiating the assimilation of sovereignty to biopolitics, to the authority, that is, of new complexes of power/knowledge in the form of biomedical technologies. What sense, after all, could it make to contest the truths of science in the name of one's rights?

What I am suggesting here is that despite Haskell's ostensibly

---

35. Haskell, "Curious Persistence of Rights Talk," 347.

friendlier conclusions with regard to the future of rights talk, his defense of rights as rational conventions and Foucault's skepticism about rights as counters to modern power have much in common. For different reasons, of course, and from very different theoretical and historical perspectives, both presuppose law, *droit*, *Recht*—in effect, the objective right of the state—as the singular source and privileged origin of "rights" in any meaningful sense of the word. And in so doing, both render the "subject of rights" a creature not of will, but of law, however felicitously or infelicitously each may view the assimilation of the law to modern scientific rationality. Both, in other words, underwrite their estimation of rights with a theory of sovereignty that marks their "subject of rights" from the outset as preeminently a product rather than a producer, much less a potential contester, of law. Both, in short, would seem to agree that the discourse of rights, finally, is indeed nothing less than the discourse of law. And nothing more. Effecting the containment of rights by law, both sing a single refrain: "a right is a right is a right, and wherever so named it smelleth the same." And what it smells of is order. From the standpoint of the present, in short, it may be more than merely possible to think both "governmentality" and "the democratic revolution." It may be unavoidable.

But perhaps it is not the name of rights that is to blame here. Perhaps, rather, the problem has to do with the specific form here attributed to the linkage of rights and law, with the discursive complicity between the two on the model of sovereignty. On that model, where law is about obligation and rights are about liberties, their specifically political valence is produced by the complex reciprocity of their mutual relation. Politically speaking, in other words—in accord with the old saying—as law without liberty is tyranny, so is liberty without law license. This, of course, is the doubled sense in which Foucault spoke of the modern discourse of sovereignty—as a "permanent instrument of criticism" of monarchical power and as the source of that "subjected sovereignty," the modern individual. And yet it is precisely this reciprocity, I would suggest, this mutual relation guaranteed by sovereignty, that subtends the notion that rights are susceptible to formalization either as "rational conventions" or as a "discourse" subject to discernible rules of formation. Where rights per se are conceived as patterned regularities produced by law, in other words, the conventional mapping of such dichotomies as law/right, obligation/liberty, constraint/freedom is not only sustained, but sustained in ways that necessarily subject rights claims, implicitly or explicitly, to a rule governed logic with the state as its ultimate source and singular guarantor. *Pro et contra*, supportive or critical of either the sovereign state or the sovereign subject of modernity, the specifically political logic of rights appears the same. And if this is so, if we are interested in reposing both the problem of rights and the question of resistance, we might begin by seeking a theoretical term of art less thoroughly or less securely wedded than "discourse" or "convention" to the governance of law or rule.

My own preference is to speak not of a "discourse" but of a "language of rights." Here, however, I mean to suggest something rather messier, more protean, than a system of philosophical concepts, something perhaps friendlier to rhetoric than to a general grammar. Indebted in large part to the work of Bakhtin, I mean to gesture toward something articulated differentially in time and place through diverse usages and disparate practices, something more labile, more polyvocal and polyvalent, than a "discourse."[36] Something, further, that presumes a plurality of addressees who may well make of it something other than they were intended to receive; something itself variously embroiled in the centripetal and centrifugal forces of diverse speech genres, both within a broader linguistic context and over time. Finally, and precisely by virtue of such heteroglossia, multiplicity, and generic differentiation, by thinking of rights as a language in this sense we might better imagine it as a potential problem for, rather than a necessary product of, sovereignty. More to the point, perhaps, my hope is that thinking of a language of rights in these terms might open a space for considering not the history but the historicity of rights claims, a space for acknowledging both the startling resiliency of the language of rights and its successive complicities and resistances, ravelings and unravelings, within and without what might be styled as the life of the law.

To close this section, then, let me return to its beginning: What is the subject of rights? If we can think of a language in the terms but vaguely limned above, it is a subject neither wholly commanded by

---

36. See especially "The Problem of Speech Genres," in *Speech Genres and Other Late Essays*, ed. Caryl Emerson and Michael Holquist, trans. Vern W. McGee (Austin: University of Texas Press, 1986) and "Discourse in the Novel," in *The Dialogic Imagination*, ed. Michael Holquist, trans. Caryl Emerson and Michael Holquist (Austin: University of Texas Press, 1981).

the discourse of sovereignty nor wholly captured by the philosophical discourse of modernity, a subject discernible only in the vicissitudes and contestations of the languages in which it both speaks and is spoken. In these terms, it is a subject neither necessarily prior to nor a consequence of law, though in different times and places it may be variously articulated as either, or both, or perhaps something else altogether. At the level of effective history, in other words, it is a subject that "lives" only in its manifold and multiform articulations. And in this respect it is a subject perhaps not of "rights" as such, but of their multiple, contingent, contestatory, and historically specific enunciations.

Recollections

If, in the context of a formally democratic constitutional order, Haskell's defense of rights can be seen to exemplify their assimilation to "governmentality," this might nonetheless provide an occasion for re-thinking rather than simply accepting Foucault's skepticism regarding rights. In this context, for instance, we might mark an important differ-ence between their respective estimations of the language of rights as a language of political contestation. If Foucault suggests the historical complicity of rights claims with governmentality and discipline, Has-kell's project seems informed by the contrary presumption, specifi-cally, by the presumption of a certain unruliness to rights talk, a certain resistance or even threat to the order and continuity of public life. In defending rights as rational conventions, in other words, Haskell's confinement of rights to legal permissions seeks to ensure the subordi-nation of rights talk to the necessities of public order. From Foucault's perspective, however, such an argument should be unnecessary—that subordination is presumed already long secured, "imposed on us for several centuries."[37] This difference, I think, is more than curious. And I suspect that it may have more than a little to do with the fact that historically the Anglophone language of rights has been repeatedly at odds with the construction of sovereign right that informs Foucault's analyses.[38] Bare suggestion though this may seem, it nonetheless

---

37. "Subject and Power," 216.

38. This is not to say that such constructions are absent from the Francophone context. See, for example, such exemplars of Francophone "pluralism" as Georges Gurvitch's *l'Idee du Droit Social* (Paris: Librairie du Recrueil Sirey, 1931) or *Sociology of*

raises a not uninteresting possibility. If it can still be conceived as necessary to contain rights claims firmly within the necessity of public order and continuity, perhaps this is because the political valences of the language of rights have not yet been so wholly or so effectively subordinated to the discourse of sovereignty as Foucault presumed. This possibility, in turn, suggests more specific questions. What conceptual and historical problematics have attended Anglophone articulations of the language of rights in relation to the rise of state sovereignty? And what bearing might such problematics have upon the historical development and elaboration of "the democratic revolution"? Although space prohibits a detailed exploration of such things, a few general observations are nonetheless possible.

In conceptual terms, what I've referred to as the language of rights is by no means an undifferentiated whole. In contemporary articulations of the language of rights, for example, we might distinguish between three kinds of rights: positive liberty rights, negative liberty rights, and entitlement rights. Philosophers, to be sure, might want to argue about which of these are "properly" rights.[39] But to the extent that the effective meanings generated and contested within the language of rights have to do less with its philosophical coherence than with its usage and deployments in practice, these different sorts of rights may suggest more about the political character of rights-claiming subjects than philosophical analyses can adequately discern. By positive liberty, of course, is meant the right of active citizenship in the body politic. The very stuff of the democratic revolution, and yet preceding it wherever representative institutions had been historically established, positive liberty rights entail participation in the processes, however institutionalized, by which the sovereign will of the community is supposed to be translated into law. Negative liberty

---

Law (New York: Philosophical Library and Alliance Book Company, 1942), or Leon Duguit's earlier *Traite de Droit Constitutionnel* (Paris: E. de Broccard, 1921–25).

39. See, for example, Wesley N. Hohfeld's differentiation of rights as claims, liberties, powers, or immunities in *Fundamental Legal Conceptions*, ed. Walter Wheeler Cook (New Haven: Yale University Press, 1919). Later philosophical arguments often emphasize one or another or some combination of these as rights properly understood. In *Consent, Freedom, and Political Obligation* (London: Oxford University Press, 1938/ 1968), for example, J. P. Plamanatz emphasized rights as powers, while Joel Feinberg stresses rights as justifiable claims. For various formulations of the latter sense, see "The Nature and Value of Rights," *Journal of Value Inquiry* 4 (1970) and "Duties, Rights, and Claims," *American Philosophical Quarterly* 3 (1966).

rights, by contrast, long antedate not only the emergence of democratic sovereignty, but the modern state as such. Referenced to a
sphere of private judgment and individual independence, negative
liberty entails rights of protection or defense, of personal security
against violence, injury, or unwonted interference from others, including government itself. Finally, entitlement rights. In their secular form
historically coincident with the democratic revolution, entitlement
rights are rights to public provision, guarantee, or support, in particular in the form of claims to the public supply of specific goods, services, or income. Empirically, of course, and precisely because these
various sorts of rights are artifacts of historical contestation as well as
of legal and constitutional mechanisms, there are tremendous differences between the substance and extent of such rights in particular
political orders. Who has which rights, under what conditions, with
what effects, with what sanctions or modes of enforcement for their
violation: all these vary not only among and between nations but also
within specific national histories. And yet, despite such variation, we
might nonetheless discern in these formal categories rather different
figurations of the "subject of rights," as well as differences in their
respective modes of relationship to law or to political institutions
more generally.

With the positive liberty rights of citizenship, for example, we
seem to encounter the autonomous self-determining subject of modernity, Foucault's "subjected sovereignty" in its modern democratic
mode, the active subject willing laws that it will in turn be obligated to
obey. The protectionism of negative liberty, on the other hand, by no
means requires the universalism of the citizen-subject, as might be
suggested by the juridical systems of various early modern European
polities as well as by some forms of colonial administration. Negative
liberty rights, for instance, may be as general as securities against
bodily injury or guarantees of some form of property rights. Or they
may be as particularistic as customary recognitions of dower rights
and peasant gleaning rights, or statutory regulation of the conditions
of industrial labor. Historically speaking, however, the subject of such
rights need not be a citizen-subject in the political order and may or
may not be credited as an autonomous subject in the domain of social
practices and institutions more broadly. Typically, though, whatever
shape the subject of negative liberty rights may assume in other respects, in juridical terms some portion of its identity as a social subject

is an object of legal definition and protection. Lastly, the subject of entitlement rights: while its relationship to the order that guarantees its provisioning may range across varying degrees of dependency, its distinguishing characteristic is that of dependence.[40] Like the subject of negative liberty rights, its connection to the citizen-subject is contingent rather than necessary. As the history of poor relief or the establishment of public orphanages might imply, one need not have the right to vote to receive some form of public support. Similarly contingent, it would seem, and consequential for the extent and character of its dependency, is the substance of what the subject of entitlements is entitled to, as well as the manner in which various sorts of entitlements place or mark their respective subjects within structures of economic stratification and cultural or ideological valuation. Dependence upon public provision for basic needs, for example, in some cultural contexts could (and in the United States arguably does) produce a subject of entitlement rights rather different from that generated by the public provision of veterans benefits, retirement pensions, or grants for higher education. But however it may be configured in particular cases, the hallmark of the subject of entitlements is its reliance upon public supply.

In sum, three sorts of rights, three sorts of right-bearing subjects: one autonomous, one protected, one dependent. Excessively formalist as this might seem, what is at work in these variegations of the language of rights lacks the neatness of a worldly logic, for neither the categories nor their denizens are mutually exclusive. While one might be tempted to discern in this description the juridical glimmer of a liberal democratic imaginary—a state in which universal participation both provides for the unprovided for and secures all from violence or harm—I hope its emphasis upon the contingency of such rights in particular times and places intimates something other than a utopian impulse. To suggest what that might be and why it might be pertinent to questions of resistance, perhaps a brief historical observation will lend these conceptual differences something of a political edge.

If the effective history of rights is the product of social con-

---

40. To use this term is already to mark this discussion with a specific cultural location—if not, indeed, to install a political difference—because the sorts of provision that in the United States are referred to as "entitlements" are in many European countries characterized as "social rights." For present purposes, however, I will simply mark rather than pursue the conceptual and political fecundity of the distinction.

testations in particular times and places, for example, we might consider the ways in which these different sorts of rights receive differential articulation and substance in the history of specific juridical orders. In the Anglophone context in particular, we might begin by noting a certain peculiarity of the language of rights in the history of English political discourse. There, as elsewhere, subjects of rights were creatures of law; there, as elsewhere, various forms of negative liberty rights long preceded the emergence of popular sovereignty and the positive liberty of the citizen-subject. As artifacts of common law and custom, however, the centrality of rights to political discourse was established significantly before the rise of the modern state and the institutions through which its statutory law was made, promulgated, and enforced. As a consequence, historically speaking, such institutions have been recurrently confronted by the articulation of rights claims presumed antecedent to the positive law of the state. Whether framed as "customary rights," "ancient liberties," "natural rights," or something else entirely, in the English context the language of rights has functioned as a language of dissent, a language that has authorized various forms of opposition to the discourse of sovereignty and resistance to the enterprise of state building from the Renaissance to the present. That history, to be sure, is marked as well by repeated attempts to render all rights dependent upon positive law—unsuccessfully in the seventeenth century by arguments from divine right, more successfully later through the state-centrism common to utilitarian, positivist, and Hegelian philosophies of law. But even these latter philosophies were contested by recourse to a notion of rights antecedent to the state, most recently in the first decades of this century by English pluralist conceptions of group rights immanent within the diversity of associational life and social experience.[41]

In pointing to these conceptual and historical problematics, I don't mean to imply anything like a continuing "tradition" of resistance right. Rather, in light of the heteroglossic dimensions of the language of rights noted in the foregoing, these broad observations are meant to suggest that, historically at least, the relationship between the Anglophone language of rights and the discourse of sovereignty may be more complicated, less settled, and more contestatory

---

41. I have discussed this pluralist conception in more detail in "On the Subject of Rights: Pluralism, Plurality, and Political Identity," in *Dimensions of Radical Democracy: Pluralism, Citizenship, Community*, ed. Chantal Mouffe (London: Verso, 1992).

than Foucault's invocation of "the ancient right of sovereignty" would appear to allow. And this, in turn, might suggest that, whatever their contemporary relationship, the historical connections between sovereignty, discipline, governmentality, and the language of rights may have been less securely settled and less clearly complicitous as well. Although it is well beyond the scope of this essay to extend this suggestion into the present, it might nonetheless be possible to identify a point of departure for such a broader exploration.

Righting the Triangle: "Governmentality" and the Democratic Revolution

In the 1978 lecture on "Governmentality," Foucault traced the successive emergence of three economies of power in the West—sovereignty, discipline, and governmentality—each of which was implicated with a specific figuration of the state and a corresponding type of society. First, sovereign power, with its juridical institutions, is associated with the territorial state, "the state of justice," and with a "society of laws . . . involving a whole reciprocal play of obligation and litigation."[42] Second, disciplinary power—articulated through such institutions as schools, armies, factories, prisons, and asylums—is linked to "the administrative state" and a corresponding "society of regulation and discipline."[43] Finally, the power of "governmentality," a regime devoted to the management of population and the economy, is identified with "the governmental state" and with "a type of society controlled by apparatuses of security."[44] Each form of power, Foucault suggested, historically supplements or complicates, rather than supplants, its predecessor. "Accordingly," he argued, "we need to see things not in terms of the replacement of a society of sovereignty by a disciplinary society and the subsequent replacement of a disciplinary society by a society of government; in reality one has a triangle, sovereignty—discipline—government, which has as its primary target the population and as its essential mechanism the apparatuses of security."[45]

Rather than consider Foucault's account as a whole, I would like to focus on one moment in its elaboration, the moment at which the

42. "Governmentality," 104.
43. Ibid.
44. Ibid.
45. Ibid., 102.

connection between "governmental" power and the sciences of population and political economy most clearly distinguishes "governmentality" from the juridical frame of sovereignty. Around the middle of
the eighteenth century, Foucault argued, the "ultimate end" of government was transformed. Unlike sovereign power, for which the purpose
of governance was "the act of government itself," government became
concerned with "the welfare of the population, the improvement of its
condition, the increase of its wealth, longevity, health, etc."[46] The
means used to achieve these ends were "all in some sense immanent to
the population" and linked to the formalization of new knowledges of
population and political economy. But in Foucault's elaboration of this
process, I think we can identify a point at which his reliance upon
sovereignty and objective right might elide the contestatory possibilities of the language of rights in a cultural context for which the discourse of sovereignty remained unsettled. Let me quote one part of
that account at length: with "governmentality," Foucault suggests,[47]

> it is the population itself on which government will act either
> directly through large-scale campaigns, or indirectly through tech-
> niques that will make it possible, without full awareness of the
> people, the stimulation of birth rates, the directing of the flow of
> the population into certain regions or activities, etc. The popula-
> tion now represents more the end of government than the power
> of the sovereign; the population is the subject of needs, of aspira-
> tions, but it is also the object in the hands of government, aware,
> vis-à-vis the government, of what it wants, but ignorant of what is
> being done to it. Interest at the level of the consciousness of each
> individual who goes to make up the population, and interest con-
> sidered as the interest of the population regardless of what the
> particular interests and aspirations might be of the individuals
> who compose it, this is the new target and the fundamental instru-
> ment of the government of population: the birth of a new art, or at
> any rate of a range of absolutely new tactics and techniques.

Put in such general terms, the description is indeed plausible. Broad
familiarity with the work of the Physiocrats, the Manchester school,
or Utilitarianism sets up strong resonances with this account of a

---

46. Ibid., 100.
47. Ibid.

transformation of the character, function, and *savoir* of government. Similarly, although remote from Foucault's theoretical agenda, Tocqueville's scrutiny of the *cahiers de doléances* for *The Old Regime and the Revolution in France* would appear to support the claim that the articulated wants of the "population" as subjects were quite compatible with substantial ignorance of what effects the operative techniques of governmentality were working upon them as objects of policy. But in the English context at the turn of the nineteenth century, such resonances are not without remainder or exception. And thereby, I suspect, hangs a tale worth telling, for there are a range of indications that the public discourse and political polemics of the period not only registered cognizance of the new techniques of power, but did so in ways that variously engaged and articulated the question of their relation to the language of rights and liberties. Again, it is beyond the scope of this essay to discuss these in detail, much less to explore the variegated connections between them, but a few brief examples might nonetheless suffice to illustrate the point.

We might begin by instancing Thomas Malthus's *Essay on the Principle of Population*, a pivotal text for the development and elaboration of the science of population across the nineteenth century. Malthus's thesis—that the asymmetry between the arithmetical increase of the means of subsistence and the geometrical increase of population rendered moot various Enlightenment schemes of human perfectibility—is well known, as is his more specific stance regarding the futility of direct public ministrations to social distress. What is less commonly brought to the fore, however, are those elements of the *Essay* that contest the Poor Laws in terms drawn from juridical notions of law and liberty. These, to be sure, are marginal elements in the context of Malthus's more general arguments, and they are easily figured in retrospect as part and parcel of laissez-faire economics. But what is at issue in the *Essay* may be something more than this. Consider, for example, the terms in which Malthus articulates not the scientific but the political character and basis of his opposition to the Poor Laws. However benevolently intended, the *Essay* suggests, those laws not only failed to relieve the misery of the poor. Beyond this, the "positive institutions" of parish relief created "dependent poverty."[48] What is at stake here, however, is less the practical

---

48. Thomas Malthus, *An Essay on the Principle of Population* (New York: Viking Penguin, 1985), 99.

question of alleviating distress than the broader implications of public provision for the subject of negative liberty. "One of the principal objections" to the poor laws, Malthus argued, was that parish assistance mandated that "the whole class of the common people of England . . . [be] . . . subjected to a set of grating, inconvenient, and tyrannical laws, totally inconsistent with the genuine spirit of the constitution."[49] The objection, in other words, had to do not only with the knowledge requisite to such power, but with its specific bearing on the liberty of individuals:[50]

> If assistance is to be distributed to a certain class of people, a power must be given somewhere of discriminating the proper objects and of managing the concerns of the institutions that are necessary, but any great interference with the affairs of other people is a species of tyranny, and in the common course of things the exercise of this power may be expected to become grating to those who are driven to ask for support. The tyranny of Justices, Churchwardens, and Overseers is a common complaint among the poor, but the fault does not so much lie in these persons, who probably before they were in power were not worse than other people, but in the nature of all such institutions.

In addition, then, to the creation of a "free" market in labor by eliminating the restrictions on geographic mobility imposed by the Poor Laws, the abolition of such institutions would eliminate a species of "tyranny"; it would "give liberty and freedom of action to the peasantry of England which they cannot be said to possess at present."[51] Indeed, and precisely because on Malthus's account social distress was beyond human control, to retain such institutions was not simply to promise the impossible, it was to impose a penalty on the poor in the same breath:[52]

> We tell the common people that if they will submit to a code of tyrannical regulation, they should never be in want. They do

---

49. Ibid., 100. See also his analogizing of the knowledge he deemed necessary to Condorcet's schemes of credit and insurance to an "inquisition," 122.

50. Ibid., 101.

51. Ibid.

52. Ibid., 103.

submit to these regulations. They perform their part of the contract, but we do not, nay cannot, and thus the poor sacrifice the
valuable blessing of liberty and receive nothing that can be called
an equivalent in return.

Here, as elsewhere in the *Essay*, the invocation of "liberty" is not
expressly enunciated in the language of rights. And yet Malthus's
valorization of liberty as individual independence, as well as his identification of the emergence of such liberty with the elimination of
personal dependence, is consistent with what today might be called
negative liberty rights.[53]

Similarly, and courting the same risk of anachronism, Malthus's
repudiation of the dependency attributed to the operation of parish
relief, his refusal, that is, of any *rightful* claim to the public provision
of necessities, could equally well be construed as a refusal of entitlement rights. And yet, the anachronistic phrasing of entitlements
aside, such a position would seem to be consistent with the historicity
of the Anglophone language of rights noted previously, and more
specifically with the priority and privilege accorded negative liberty
considerations in relation to the authority of the state. Baldly put, on
Malthus's account the fact that the Poor Laws were laws carried no
prima facie legitimacy. That fact, indeed, was itself an object of criticism not only from the standpoint of the emergent "science of population" but from the juridical frame of individual liberty as well. To recur
to Foucault's formulation, what is at issue here is precisely the equivocality of the complication of juridical power by the problem of population, for the latter is itself interwoven both with the partial and provi-
sional rearticulation of negative liberty rights in a new, or at least

---

53. In speaking, for instance, of the "evil effects" of dependence for all parties
involved, Malthus rejects the spirit of benevolence as not simply impractical as a general remedy for distributive injustice. Admitting agreement with Godwin on the "evil of
hard labour," he continues: "yet I still think it a less evil, and less calculated to debase
the human mind, than dependence, and every history of man that we have ever read
places in a strong point of view the danger to which that mind is exposed which is
entrusted with constant power." Following this, the language in which Malthus describes the wage relationship resonates with notions of independence and corruption
current in much eighteenth-century political discourse: "the man who does a day's
work for me confers as great an obligation on me as I do upon him. I possess what he
wants, he possesses what I want. We make an amicable exchange. The poor man walks
erect in conscious independence; and the mind of his employer is not vitiated by a
sense of power." Ibid., 179.

different, idiom and with the repudiation of entitlement rights.[54] In effect, Malthus's *Essay* evidences the intricacy of the linkage Foucault suggested between political institutions and governmentality, for it not only articulates the necessary laws of "population" as a limit or boundary to the effective operation of law, but simultaneously re-inscribes the older opposition between the "free" individual and tyr-anny as a limit as well.

In Malthus's *Essay*, in other words—to adopt Graham Burchell's characterization of the "system of natural liberty" theorized by Scot-tish political economists—"[l]egal and economic forms of subjectivity are formally heterogeneous"; they "involve different relations with the political order and appeal to distinct principles for limiting the exercise of sovereign power."[55] Malthus's simultaneous deployment of scientific knowledges and juridical principles is in this regard largely consistent with Burchell's example of contrasting forms of subjectivity and the political address respectively implied by each: "The legal subject of rights says to the sovereign: 'You must not do this, you do not have the right.' The economic subject of interest says: 'You must not do this because you do not and cannot know what you are doing.' "[56] In the space between the two—as Burchell, following Foucault, notes—arises a distinctively liberal political rationality that links the activities of government "and the principle of their necessary self-limitation, to the naturally self-regulating processes of what must be governed."[57] Insofar, however, as the juridical liberty of individu-als to pursue private interests is constitutive of the latter, that liberty becomes "a technical requirement" for governing presumptively natu-ral social processes:[58]

---

54. See, for example, Malthus's critique of Godwin's contention that a common agreement on the part of the lower classes as a whole to reduce the hours of labor might still produce sufficient commodities. Malthus agrees, but adds that empirically, some laborers will require more than others to support larger families and may desire to exchange a "greater quantity of labour" for a "greater quantity of subsistence." What, Malthus asks rhetorically, is to prevent this, since it "would be a violation of the first and most sacred property that a man possesses to attempt, by positive institutions, to interfere with his command over his own labour." Ibid., 181.

55. Graham Burchell, "Peculiar Interests: Civil Society and Governing the 'System of Natural Liberty,' " in his *The Foucault Effect: Studies in Governmentality* (Chicago: University of Chicago Press, 1991), 137.

56. Ibid.

57. Ibid., 139.

58. Ibid.

> The security of laws and individual liberty presuppose each
> other. . . . Liberty . . . is positively required as the necessary cor-
> relate and instrument of a government whose task is to secure the
> optimal functioning of natural processes: liberalism requires a
> proper use of liberty.

What is distinctive about liberalism in this account is the way in which
it ties governmental rationality and the exercise of political power "to
the freedom and self-interested rationality of the governed themselves."[59] In this respect the liberal "rule of law" precludes the arbitrary exercise of political power identified with sovereign will as objective right, while the participation of interested citizen-subjects "in a
legally constituted democratic or 'representative' parliamentary system" offers "the most effective system for providing a rational check
on governmental activity within a unified system of legal-political
sovereignty."[60] Hence the complicity of rights with 'governmentality,'
and one Foucauldian answer to the question of how to think "governmentality" *and* the democratic revolution.

But as a telephoto lens collapses the distance between objects in its
frame, so too does this genealogy of governmental techniques com-
press theoretical articulations into a more solid series than a broader or
more extensive archive might support. If, as I have suggested, the
Malthusian science of population also articulated an incompatibility
between negative liberty and entitlement rights, and if, as would seem
to be the case, it tended to marginalize the question of the positive
liberty rights of suffrage, there may be some missing chapters in the
story of the complicity between "governmentality" and the democratic
revolution. On the supposition of such a possibility, it might be useful
to return briefly to that Malthusian "individual liberty" with an eye not
only to its place in the elaboration of the science of population, but to
the public responses it spurred in the popular polemics of the period.
Some of the more curious counters to Malthusian authority, not least of
all for the extremity of their resonance with Foucault's formulation of
disciplinary institutions, are provided by Robert Owen's many contributions to post-Napoleonic controversies over social reform, political
democracy, and the question of individual liberties.

---

59. Ibid.
60. Ibid., 140.

First, Malthus. The *Essay on the Principle of Population*, to be sure, has little to say about individuals as such, save for the centrality of "self-love" as a necessary spring to action. As a species characteristic, however, on this account the self-concerned desire of individuals to court pleasure and avoid pain produced salutary consequences, as the competition it produced amidst scarcity was linked to whatever improvement of conditions was possible. If no one "could hope to rise or fall, in society, if industry did not bring with it its reward and idleness its punishment," things might be worse than they were. While the few may rise to entertain "enlarged motives," on Malthus's formulation it was "the narrower motives that operate on the many" that were responsible for "the various useful discoveries, the valuable writings, and other laudable exertions" of the species.[61] Attempting to contain such motives by legislation was, from the standpoint of the *Essay*, like spitting in a tempest. Spit, perhaps, we must, but self-interest and foresight would suggest the necessity of first discerning our position relative to the prevailing winds. On Robert Owen's account, however, this presumptive naturalization of individual liberty manifested not knowledge but ignorance, and an ignorance, more specifically, that failed to acknowledge the historicity of the isolated and competitive "individual" it valorized. In language evocative of but other to Foucault's own, Owen roots the "errors" besetting the "past and present state of society" in the processes through which individuals were "individualized." "[I]ndividuality and distinctness of character," Owen argued, were not the products of self-making but the consequences of social fashioning. Subjected from infancy to a variety of prejudicial "mental atmospheres" that frame perception, individuals so constituted "soon discover that they do not see objects alike; and, wholly unconscious of the real cause of difference between them, an opposition of *feeling* as well as of seeing, is created; extending from a slight degree of dislike, to anger, hatred, revenge, death, and destruction in every form and shape."[62] Such "differences of opinion," framed by sect, class, party, and country, have "separated man from man" and "compelled" all to remain strangers to their fellows.

61. Ibid., 206–7.
62. Robert Owen, "A Sketch of Some of the Errors and Evils Arising from the Past and Present State of Society" (1817), in *Robert Owen: A New View of Society and Other Writings*, ed. Gregory Claeys (New York: Viking Penguin, 1991), 161–62.

Here as elsewhere Owen reserves particular scorn for the notion that "individuals" form their own character and command their own affections, for the notion, that is, that "individuals" are the cause rather than the consequence of broader social processes, conditions, and institutions. Characterizing these latter as no more than "ever-changing insanity," Owen argued that it was "folly" to expect improvement without the removal of such circumstances and the form of individuality they generated:[63]

> Happiness is not one jot nearer the grasp of a single individual *now*, than it was at the period when we have the first records of man. Born in ignorance, he imagined first, and has ever since been systematically taught, that he himself created the motives for his own actions: his mind has been formed on this base; it has been and is now, the very foundation of his thoughts; it has been combined into all the associations of his ideas; and only doubt, disorder, and confusion of intellect could follow.

Under such conditions, each "is individualized, and made openly or covertly, to oppose every other human being."[64] To remedy such effects, each "mind must be born again," must be "discharged of all the inconsistent associations which have been formed within it"; its "foundations must be laid anew" and a new "superstructure raised of just and useful proportions. . . ."[65] What Owen called for was the creation of new social institutions and practices, based on the recognition that only rational training through rational institutions could constitute new individuals properly attuned to their social capacities and responsibilities. The prototype was his own "institution for the formation of character" at New Lanark.

Like Malthus, Owen had little to say about the sorts of individual liberties conventionally associated with the language of rights, but unlike Malthus nothing Owen had to say was particularly favorable.[66]

---

63. Ibid., 162. See also, in the same collection, "An Address to the Inhabitants of New Lanark," 123, and "A New View of Society," 43.

64. Owen, "Errors and Evils," 163.

65. Ibid., 162.

66. By the late 1830s, however, Owen had begun to deploy a variation of "natural rights" language to elaborate and justify his criticisms of existing institutions. Here, and not uninterestingly, the equality of such "natural rights" is a consequence of human agents' natural ignorance at birth and their common dependence upon receiving rather

Indeed, as the foregoing might suggest, Owen's "new view of society" cast the subject of such rights and liberties as a problem to be overcome, if gradually and with great care, by new forms and institutions of rational discipline. Functioning not through mechanisms of legal coercion and punishment but through the provision of incentives for the reformation of individual desires and habits, Owen's schemes looked to the voluntary internalization of rational norms of productivity, sanity, and benevolence. In this respect, though they celebrate possibilities that Foucault regards with dismay, Owen's contributions to the "condition of England" question are strongly resonant with the latter's account of the intersection of disciplinary power and "governmentality." Where Owen does speak of the implications of his proposals for rights and liberties more conventionally understood, however, there looms a significant disjuncture between the language of rights, "governmentality," and emergent pressures for popular governance. While sanguine about the immediate consistency of his proposed villages for "unity and mutual cooperation" with established property rights, for instance, Owen cautioned against Malthus's alternative of simply eliminating existing pauper legislation, as well as any other reform that did not begin with the task of reforming and training individuals. To do otherwise, he argued, "would inevitably create immediate revolution"; it would exacerbate existing passions and stimulate violence, with the consequence that not only Britain but "all of Europe and the Americas would be plunged into one general scheme of anarchy and dreadful confusion, of which the late French Revolution will give but a faint anticipation."[67] Not only would the condition of the "individualized" individuals of the present not be improved by ensuring them the negative liberty rights Malthus had urged, such a move would place in "imminent hazard" both "the lives and properties of the well-disposed" and "the safety of the State" as a whole.[68]

This invocation of the danger presented by freeing the "interested individual" to the mechanisms of the market suggests a significant

---

than creating knowledge. When it comes to specifying such rights, Owen's formula is a simple one: "No man has a right to require another man to do for him, what he will not do for that man; or, in other words, all men have equal rights." See "Six Lectures Delivered at Manchester" (1839), *Robert Owen*, 344.

67. Robert Owen, "Letter Published in the London Newspapers of August 19th, 1817," *Robert Owen*, 188.

68. Robert Owen, "Second Address to the City of London Tavern," August 21, 1817, *Robert Owen*, 192.

distrust of what Burchell characterizes as "the freedom and self-interested rationality" of the population.[69] To the contrary, rather than an effective "rational check on governmental activity," such "interested" subjects appear on Owen's account as likely to be quite disruptive. Further, though, and suggestive of a decisively political wrinkle in the smooth cloth of "governmentality," Owen linked the danger of such "individualized" subjects to a corollary danger attending the increasing influence of public opinion on the processes of governance. Because the "Government . . . cannot now resist the influence of the public voice," Owen warned, it "was of the highest importance . . . that the public should not be superficially trained or instructed, but that it should be substantially well informed, and that effective means should be devised to train it as human beings intended to be rational ought to be trained."[70] On Owen's account, we might say that the juridical liberty of "interested" subjects could function, *pace* Burchell, as a "technical requirement" of the system only on the condition that such subjects be duly trained to the rational exercise of that liberty. The imperative, in other words, of reforming the character of "individualized" individuals extended well beyond the indirect governmental management of the population as presently constituted. Under the conditions created by the increasing prominence of public opinion, it required the prior constitution of a manageable population.

In this formulation we might discern not one but two disjunctures or fissures in the language of rights as it comes into contact with Owen's popularized variant of the sciences of population and political economy. While subsistence, productive employment, and education in useful knowledge appear as public entitlements or guarantees, their effective provision requires the *elimination* of the "interested" individuals of traditional negative liberty rights and their replacement by more rational individuals, individuals *trained* to perceive "the inseparable connection . . . between individual and general, between private and public good" and capable of disciplining themselves accordingly.[71] In the absence of such a transformation, the "interested" juridical subject of negative liberty rights as conventionally conceived is an obstacle to the reforms envisioned by the Owenite populariza-

---

69. Burchell, "Peculiar Interests," 139.
70. Owen, "Second Address to the City of London Tavern," 192.
71. Owen, "A New View of Society," 61.

tion of the new human sciences. Further, though, it is a threat as well
to the development of the sort of rational public opinion necessary to
the smooth governance of the country more generally. And in this
respect the "individualized" individual Owen excoriated would appear to be a potentially dangerous subject of positive liberty rights as
well.[72] In both regards, Owen's writings may look forward to the
"subjected sovereignty" of Foucault's disciplined modern individual,
but they also suggest considerable trepidation that that individual had
yet to be produced by modern institutions.[73]

To the extent that such a possibility is credible, the question of
the historical complicity between "governmentality" and the democratic revolution would seem to merit further investigation. In this
context, the difficulty has to do not with any essential characteristic
of the language of rights but rather with the possibility, suggested
as much by Malthus's defense as by Owen's fears, that at least
some articulations of the "subject of rights" at the turn of the nineteenth century posed a problem for the new techniques of power
that Foucault triangulated as "sovereignty—discipline—government."
Because Malthus's and Owen's contributions to the popular polemics on the population question are themselves implicated in the
elaboration of disciplinary and governmental power, we might want
a more positive instance of such a contestatory democratic subject,
as well as evidence of its stance toward the new techniques of
power. One final example, then, this time of an intervention more
clearly invested in the emergence of "the democratic revolution,"
might be worthy of note.

Equally critical not only of Owenite "new harmonies" and Malthusian warnings but of Utilitarian reform as well, a variety of essays
by William Hazlitt might suffice as a marker of a different axis of
contestation, a different perspective on the question of taking liberties

---

72. Indeed, Owen expected his model communities eventually to replace government as it had been traditionally known. His villages were to be governed by what
he accounted the "natural" elite of an age cohort, not by anything so messy as public
opinion or representative institutions, let alone more extensive forms of popular
participation.

73. Recent historical accounts of such disciplinary institutions as the penitentiary
and the asylum in England would seem to confirm the point. See Roy Porter, *Mind-
Forg'd Manacles: A History of Madness in England from the Restoration to the Regency* (Cambridge: Harvard University Press, 1987) and Michael Ignatieff, *A Just Measure of Pain*
(New York: Penguin, 1978).

in Foucault's triangle. A fictive dialogue between a "Rationalist" and a "Sentimentalist," for example, has the latter voice equating scientific enthusiasm for managing public happiness with the religious enthusiasm of an earlier epoch. Excoriating the "modern sciolists" who preached the "greatest happiness of the greatest number" as promoters of an administered asceticism, Hazlitt asked,[74]

> Where is the use of getting rid of the trammels of superstition and slavery, if we are immediately to be handed over to these new ferrets and inspectors of a *Police-Philosophy;* who pay domiciliary visits to the human mind, catechise an expression, impale a sentiment, put every enjoyment to the rack, leave you not a moment's ease or respite, and imprison all the faculties in a round of cant phrases—the Shibboleth of a party?

Implying that Utilitarian reformers liked nothing "else better than they like Government," Hazlitt's "Sentimentalist" accused them of being "equally at war with the rich and the poor," of giving scope to their "troublesome and overbearing humour" by lecturing the poor, and this seemingly as a compensation for "having failed . . . in their project of *cashiering kings.*"[75] Overemphasizing human frailties and neglecting human strengths, such proponents of rational reform dogmatically promulgated "a discipline of humanity"; they "thank God in their hearts for having given them a *liberal philosophy,* though what passes with them for liberal is considered by the rest of the world as very much akin to illiberality."[76] The antipathy suggested here toward Utilitarian reform is extended, in a number of Hazlitt's essays, to Malthus and Owen as well, both of whom he portrayed as sacrificing liberty to necessity. Malthus, for example, "cut up liberty by the roots by passing 'the grinding law of necessity' over it, and entailing vice and misery on all future generations as their happiest lot."[77] To Owen's "new view of society," on the other hand, Hazlitt ascribed considerable age: it "is as old," he insisted, "as society itself," as old as "attempts to reform it by shewing what it ought to be, or by teaching that the good of the whole

74. William Hazlitt, "The New School of Reform: A Dialogue between a Rationalist and a Sentimentalist," in *Works,* ed. Percival Presland House (London: J.M. Dent and Sons, Ltd., 1930–34) 12: 181.

75. Ibid., 182.

76. Ibid., 184, 188.

77. William Hazlitt, "On the Jealousy and Spleen of Party," *Works,* 12: 374.

is the good of the individual, an opinion by which fools and honest men have sometimes been deceived but which has never taken in the knaves and knowing ones."[78] Hazlitt's criticism of both, as well as of alternate schools of reform, was more often than not phrased as a defense of liberty, but in terms that tended to privilege such liberty less as an abstract principle than as a viscerally embodied capacity linked to both individual will and conscience.[79]

The connection of such liberties to conscience, however, is in Hazlitt's writings far from a platitudinous reminder recalling one to the strictures of duty or obligation, much less an incitement to guilt or self-recrimination. To the contrary, such liberties were more often than not invoked as powers, particularly as powers of individual judgment in the trenchant immediacy of social and political contestation. In a satirical jibe at Malthus, for example, Hazlitt imagined a world constituted in conformity to the *Essay's* refusal of entitlements and charitable provision in the name of independence:[80]

> the poor would no longer be dependent upon the rich, the rich could no longer wish to reduce the poor into a more complete subjection to their will, all causes of contention, of jealousy, and of irritation would have ceased between them, the struggle would be over, each class would fulfill the task assigned by heaven; the rich would oppress the poor without remorse, the poor would submit to oppression with pious gratitude and resignation; the greatest harmony would prevail between the government and the people; there would be no longer any seditions, tumults, complaints, petitions, partisans of liberty, or tools of power. . . .

Instead, "we should all have . . . the same happy spirit of resignation that a man feels when he is seized with the plague, who thinks no more of a physician, but knows that his disorder is without cure."[81] Such a world, Hazlitt submitted, would not last long. Those who were "convinced by arithmetical or geometrical ratios" might resign themselves to their fate, but others would wax troublesome. Those not easily

---

78. Review of Owen's "A New View of Society" and "An Address to the Inhabitants of New Lanark," August 4, 1816, in William Hazlitt, *Political Essays* (London: Printed for W. Hone, 1819), 97.

79. See, for example, "Capital Punishments," July 1821, *Works*, 19: 216, 226.

80. William Hazlitt, "On the Application of Mr. Malthus' Principles to the Poor Laws," *Political Essays*, 431.

81. Ibid.

seduced by abstractions, those who were "more governed by their feelings than calculations" might prefer the facts before their eyes, might question in particular the disparity evident in the starvation of the poor and the waste of the well-to-do. By the end of Hazlitt's fable, a mob has confronted Malthus in person, a mob that "impatient for an answer, and not finding one to their minds, might proceed to extremities."[82] A similar refusal of abstract generalities marks Hazlitt's reaction to Owenite reform: Owen's schemes are "remote, visionary, inapplicable," tolerated by the powerful precisely because of this, and because his "cant against reform in Parliament . . . serves as a practical diversion in their favor."[83] Taking official suppression as a litmus for the credibility of proposals for reform, Hazlitt finds Owen suspect: "when we see Mr. Owen brought up for judgment . . . , or standing in the pillory, we shall begin to think there is something in this *New Lanark Scheme* of his."[84] A similar result, he suggests, would ensue—even if Owen continued to speak in vague generalities—if in fact any significant portion of the public were to take up his ideas in earnest, for were that to occur all the reputable elements of the country would turn against him as a "Jacobin, a leveller, an incendiary."[85]

It would be easy enough to figure Hazlitt as a sort of intellectual Luddite bent on destroying the conceptual machinery of the emergent human sciences. But this, I think, would be to miss the more provocative aspects of his connection to "the democratic revolution," for his persistent inscription of reform schemes as antithetical to "liberty" is infused with an English Jacobin imaginary of popular judgment, an imaginary quite distant from the measured rationality and self-limiting calculations of the "system of natural liberty." Recalling Owen's dread of undisciplined individuals, for example, consider Hazlitt's description of the "true Jacobin":[86]

> To be a true Jacobin, a man must be a good hater; but this is the
> most difficult and least amiable of all the virtues. . . . The love of
> liberty consists in the hatred of tyrants. The true Jacobin hates the

---

82. Ibid., 432–33.
83. Hazlitt, Review of "A New View of Society," 103.
84. Ibid.
85. Ibid., 104.
86. William Hazlitt, "On the Connexion Between Toad-eaters and Tyrants," Jan. 12, 1817, *Political Essays*, 167–68.

enemies of liberty as they hate liberty. . . . His memory is as long, and his will is as strong as theirs, though his hands are shorter. He never forgets or forgives an injury done to the people, for tyrants never forget or forgive one done to themselves. There is no love lost between them. . . . He makes neither peace nor truce with them. His hatred of wrong only ceases with the wrong. The sense of it, and the barefaced assumption of the right to inflict it, deprives him of his rest. It stagnates in his blood. . . . It settles in his brain—it puts him beside himself.

Refusing the authority claimed by the various schools of reform to speak for the well-being of the people, Hazlitt accorded a similarly visceral privilege to the *vox populi*, with all its warts. His inscription of "the People" is particularly striking for its manifest corporeality. "The People" appears neither as a population to be managed nor as an abstract collectivity whose *salus* is simply the object of policy, but as the embodied severalty of a political public. To the question "What is the People?" he replied:[87]

Millions . . . like you, with hearts beating in their bosoms, with thoughts stirring in their minds, with the blood circulating in their veins, with wants and appetites, and passions and anxious cares, and busy purposes and affections for others and a respect for themselves, and a desire of happiness, and a right to freedom, and a will to be free.

Hazlitt credits such people with the capacity to know when they are harmed, "to feel their wrongs."[88] They have "as much common sense and sound judgment" as any other sector of society. "When they judge for themselves, they in general judge right"; and in any case, even if they have erred, "the way to improve their judgment in their own concerns . . . is not to deny them the use and exercise of their judgment altogether."[89] Indeed, "if they do not judge for themselves, they will infallibly be cheated both of liberty and property, by those who kindly insist on relieving them of that trouble."[90]

---

87. William Hazlitt, "What is the People?" March 7, 1818, *Political Essays*, 307.
88. Ibid., 328.
89. Ibid., 329.
90. Ibid.

Heady stuff, to be sure—in a rhetoric long out of fashion. But it may nonetheless mark a site of political contestation and a deployment of the language of rights not only at odds with the "ancient right of sovereignty" but resistant as well to the new techniques of governmentality. It is not, of course, an appeal to the "objectivity" of rights, but neither is it indebted to natural law. And the "common sense" it invokes has more to do with felt sensation, with embodied perceptions of injury or abuse, than it does with the stabilizing conventions of a community favored by the Scottish Enlightenment. The "subject of rights" it inscribes is a prickly creature, wary and willful, attuned to what is close at hand, to its needs and its desires. It is, one might say, an unruly subject, at once undisciplined and unorganized, a subject suspicious of those who claim to speak in its name. It is a subject, to recall Owen, that has not yet been trained to perceive the connection "between individual and general, between public and private good," at least not from the Archimedean point occupied by the emergent sciences of population and political economy. Finally, and perhaps precisely by virtue of its skeptical relationship to the emergent human sciences, it is a subject for which the language of rights offers an open space for private judgment— a "subject of rights" for which "subjective right" is neither a permission of law nor a product of sovereign largesse but, rather, as Vinogradoff had it, the "consciousness of right rooted in the last instance in the conviction of each individual member of the community and influencing" their will to exercise their power.[91]

Remainders

If, amidst the rubble of foundationalisms, the contemporary proliferation of rights claims smacks of paradox, it is a paradox that may turn its implicit truth in more than one direction. From one point of view, to be sure, it may beckon us toward more modest and contextually nuanced accounts of the "rational" basis of rights. As the first of the foregoing ruminations sought to suggest, however, such accounts may rescue rights from the flames of metaphysical doubt only to subject them to the tempering mercies of the governmental forge and the legal ministrations of scientific rationality. From another perspective, though, we might glimpse in that paradox something of an affinity between the

---

91. Vinogradoff, *Custom and Right*, 66.

subject of rights and the bracing air of political skepticism. Rights may be, as it were, the legal tender of democratic exchange, but to the extent that politics is "before the law"—with all the robust equivocality such a phrase implies—this possibility should be less than surprising. And this, in turn, might suggest "subjects of rights" that are "before the law" in a similarly equivocal sense—variously within and without the discourse of sovereignty, at once indebted and excessive to the forms of subjectivity and self-assertion made licit by legal guarantee. Our brief excursions into the historical vicissitudes of the language of rights would appear to suggest this much, at least.

But they might be taken to imply, further, that this equivocality harbors the scent of subjectivities variously at odds with the equivalential logic by which Foucault joins the subject of rights and the modern individual under the sign of "subjected sovereignty." Taken in the latter sense, of course, the subject of rights is indeed equivocal—but that equivocality appears as an ironic residue of the discourse of sovereignty rather than a protean consequence of contingently articulated disjunctures within the language of rights itself. Here, if Foucault's genealogical impulse seems to have succumbed to a more monologic historiographical convention, if in this respect it falls short of its ostensibly Nietzschean inspiration, perhaps compensation can be sought in a momentary return to that source. By way of paraphrase, for instance, we might analogize the question of rights to Nietzsche's observations on punishment. It is impossible, we might say, to say with certainty today *why* people have rights: "all concepts in which a whole process is semiotically condensed elude definition; only that which has no history is definable."[92] No less a product of semiosis than the notion of "punishment," we could say, the notion of "rights" is susceptible to differential appropriations, redeployments, and condensations as it comes into historical contact with other discursive constellations, and in this sense is a site of multiple and by no means mutually consistent significations. That a "subject of rights"–as–"subjected sovereignty" has been historically articulated in conjunction with the emergence of the modern state and the discourse of sovereignty—or, *pace* Haskell, with various accounts of "the idea of objective moral obligation"—is hardly to be denied. But this is no basis for presuming that the political

---

92. "The Genealogy of Morals," Second Essay, section 13 in *On the Genealogy of Morals and Ecce Homo*, ed. Walter Kaufmann (New York: Vintage/Random House, 1967), 80.

character of "subjects of rights" is somehow captured or contained, much less exhausted, by such contingent articulations, however hegemonic. Indeed, as the more historical of the preceding ruminations might suggest, such formulations have been not only shadowed but interrupted by counterarticulations, by alternative figurations variously impertinent not only to the discourse of sovereignty but to emergent disciplinary and governmental techniques as well.

In drawing these reflections to a close, however, I am wary of committing the same mistake in reverse. If, in other words, we can discern archival traces of something in excess of Foucault's "subjected sovereignty," this too should be read as a product of contingent articulation—not as an essential characteristic of the language of rights per se, much less a resurrection of the autonomous subject as an ontological given. But if there is a conclusion appropriate to the foregoing ruminations, this is only its leading, its most obvious, and hence perhaps its least interesting edge. More to the point, as exemplified previously by various reform polemics on politics, population, and popular liberties at the turn of the nineteenth century, to the extent that such traces suggest tensions and disjunctures between various aspects of the language of rights, so too do they suggest subjects of rights neither wholly at odds with nor wholly subordinate to the constellation of discursive practices triangulated by Foucault as "sovereignty-discipline-governmentality."

Instead, as I have broadly suggested, far from crystallizing different facets of the language of rights into a singular claimant, Malthus, Owen, and Hazlitt appropriated, shifted, and redeployed diverse elements of that language to significantly different and yet internally heterogeneous political effect. Albeit in different ways, by variously elevating or reducing the political valence accorded to negative liberty, positive liberty, or entitlements, each forwarded subjects of rights drawn differentially along multiple axes of contestation within the language of rights itself, subjects variegated in their relationships to emergent regimes of disciplinary and governmental power as one or another of their political faces turned to the fore. Antagonistic to the notion of entitlements and agnostic on the question of citizenship, the Malthusian emphasis on negative liberty rights was complicitous with the development of governmentality even as it opposed the disciplinary apparatus of the Poor Laws as tyranny. Owen's defense of the rationality of disciplinary institutions, on the other hand, was as strident in its support of entitlements as it was critical of conventional views of negative liberty—and, as a consequence, such institutions were offered not as supplements but as alternatives to the operations Foucault theorized as "governmentality." Further, and pointing to yet more intense disjunctures within the language of rights, Owen's "new view of society" resisted the egalitarian imaginary of democratic citizenship as not only dangerous in practice, but inconsistent in principle with the rationality he ascribed to "natural" hierarchies of age, talent, and gender. Finally, if there is nothing particularly pretty about Hazlitt's irritable and insouciant democratic subject, if its substantive political claims are discomfittingly indeterminate, neither is there any doubt about its skeptical resistance to governmental and disciplinary institutions in the name of its rights. In effect, however embroiled in the historical equivocality of the language of rights, Malthus, Owen, and Hazlitt each generated significantly different articulations of the contestatory possibilities of the subject of rights at the opening conjuncture of discipline, "governmentality," and the democratic revolution.

None of this, I hasten to add, is sufficient to settle the political meaning of that conjuncture. Indeed, as intimated by the oddly discordant counterpoint between Foucault's and Haskell's estimations of the ruliness of the subject of rights, continuing discursive elaborations of that moment defy any attempt to relegate its problematic to the archives, however broadly construed. But this might be taken to suggest further lines of inquiry, at once historical and theoretical, for the project of reposing the question of rights in these late days of the twentieth century. To say, for instance, that the subject of rights is a variegated and protean creature, open to contingent rearticulation, is by no means to posit the democratic revolution as a sovereign "solution" to the "problems" of governmentality and discipline. Quite to the contrary. Although the early nineteenth-century chronology, and perhaps even the geography, of Foucault's genealogy might bear adjustment, its critical and theoretical purchase remains pertinent precisely to the extent that subsequent articulations of democratic politics evidence more proximate or hegemonic alignments between sovereignty, discipline, governmentality, and the historicity of the subject of rights. And this, in turn, suggests the far more difficult task of interrogating further the vicissitudes of such historical alignments, up to and including the present.

One particularly provocative area of investigation might be suggested by returning to Laclau and Mouffe's account of the democratic revolution, in particular their rendering of its political moment as the extension of its egalitarian imaginary across a range of social relations and practices. If, as they argue, the contemporary resurgence of rights claims is to be seen not in terms of "the encroachment on the private by a unified public space," if it is distinctive for its "proliferation of radically new and different political spaces,"[93] perhaps this offers the glimpse of an answer to Foucault's call for a form of right liberated from the principle of sovereignty. The possibility is intriguing, to say the least. Hesitating at the threshold of that suggestion, however, we would do well to mark the echoes of political meaning that resonate through the space between "encroachment" and "proliferation," for they sound a cautionary note of alternative possibilities. And yet, we might resist the temptation to restrict this caution to a question of antidemocratic intrusions upon rights, in either their positive or negative liberty formulations. In the United States, in any case, seventy-odd years of antifascist and anticommunist political discourse has condensed that temptation into the common sense of liberal democracy, effectively figuring the latter as "the free world" and displacing threats to that freedom onto the totalizing social logics of both left and right. But if we take Foucault's theorization of governmentality and discipline seriously, we might scrutinize the capacities of that common sense to mask domestic complicities between state sovereignty, however modified by the adjective *democratic*, and the technologies of modern power devoted to the management of population and the orderly disposition of people and things.

Arguably, for instance, however democratically mandated, the provision of managed and measurable entitlements disbursed by a sovereign center has proven a fertile site for the elaboration of regulation and discipline as well as for the differential deployment of technologies of surveillance and social control across various sectors of national populations. If we are interested in the contestatory possibilities of the language of rights, the question that arises in this context is distant from the classic dilemma of democratic or majoritarian tyranny. Rather, because it pertains not to what the many do to the few but to the generalized if heterogeneous effects of a hegemonic alignment, it has

---

93. Laclau and Mouffe, *Hegemony and Socialist Strategy*, 181.

to do with the ways in which the various regimes and rationalities of modern power demand a rethinking of the problem of "encroachment." To the extent, for instance, that various apparatuses of discipline and governmentality have been historically articulated through one or another element of the language of rights, the political problem this presents may indeed be, as Foucault argued, irreducible to the violation of juridical liberties. At the same time, and here we might momentarily recall Hazlitt, since hegemonic articulations preclude neither skepticism nor resistant assertions of subjective right, their political meaning would appear equally irreducible to the seamless production of modern individuals as "subjected sovereignties." Here, the dilemma is more complex, for it entails the question of the ways in which, in various times and places, such hegemonic conjunctures have managed contingently to evade or constrain the historical equivocality of the language of rights—the extent to which, in short, they have hegemonized a particular distribution of emphases within the language of rights by marginalizing, disciplining, or otherwise disposing of the more troublesome of its enunciations. To put the point differently, if the triangulation of "sovereignty-discipline-governmentality" in democratic polities requires the articulation of "subjects of rights" more congenial than their excessive cousins to the ministrations of governance, perhaps we might think "encroachment" itself as something excessive to its conventional connotation of sovereign intrusions on private liberties.

This is not to urge the abandonment of the conventional view, but it is to suggest the necessity of its elaboration and augmentation to engage the intertwined dilemmas of governmentality and discipline. To this end, however, we might extend our critical energies beyond identifying the institutional sites and discursive practices through which more docile, more disciplined and dependent subjects are produced. Such analyses are significant but not sufficient preliminaries to the project of reposing the problem of rights. If, at the fluid boundary of Foucault's triangle and the democratic revolution, the problem of "taking liberties" itself resounds with the equivocality of the language of rights, if it signifies a continuing tension between invention and constraint, those analyses might profitably be pushed further. In addition to accounting for the historical production of subjects more tractable to governance, for instance, we might devote more specific attention both to the mechanisms legitimating the displacement of their

more excessive and less ruly relations and to the political insights and
provocations articulated by the latter's counterhegemonic contestations. Besides the merit of providing a more robust sense of the
polyform historicity of the subject of rights, such explorations might
hold political promise as well, for they might underwrite the extension of "encroachment" to include consideration of the operations by
which the historical equivocality of the language of rights has been
not only contingently accommodated to the discourse of sovereignty,
but subordinated as well to the discursive practices peculiar to the
regimes of discipline and governmentality. It is, of course, impossible
to say with certainty what might lie on the far side of such investigations. But I wouldn't be surprised to find the dilemma of "taking
liberties in Foucault's triangle" entangled less in the ancient webs of
sovereign right than in the subtler and more supple mediations of a
scientized sovereignty that dare not speak its name. To the extent that
such suspicions are plausible, what appeared early on as a rhetorical
question may take on a more substantive edge: what sense, after all,
could it make to contest the truths of science in the name of one's
rights?

The Discourse of Rights in Colonial South Africa: Subjectivity, Sovereignty, Modernity

John Comaroff

The Law is the greatest thing imaginable.
That's true because it's absurd.

[Without] equality . . . all rights are chimeras.
　　　　　　　　　　　　　—Carlos Fuentes, *The Campaign*

Introduction

It has become commonplace to note the centrality of law in the colonization of the non-European world; commonplace to assert

Mindie Lazarus-Black and Richard Werbner read earlier drafts of this chapter; I am grateful to both for their generous, insightful comments. As always, I am deeply indebted to Jean Comaroff for her critical acuity and creative eye. The errors of fact and judgment are, of course, mine alone.

In annotating unpublished archival sources, I refer to the London Missionary Society as the LMS; its records are part of the Council of World Mission [CWM] papers held at the School of Oriental and African Studies [SOAS], University of London. Housed there too are the archives of the Wesleyan Methodist Missionary Society [WMMS], to which reference is also made. Letters, journals, and reports are identified by author, place, and date of writing; also given, in each case, is the archival category, box, folder, and jacket in which the document is housed at SOAS.

Carlos Fuentes's novel, *The Campaign* (New York: Harper Collins, 1992), from which the epigraph is taken, is set in South America in the early nineteenth century. These lines—found on pages 202 and 211–12—are uttered by characters caught up in the independence struggle against Spain.

"its" role in the fashioning of new Eurocentric hegemonies, in the creation of colonial subjects, in the rise of various forms of resistance[1]—vide, lately, Mann and Roberts's excellent *Law in Colonial Africa*.[2] In all this, the discourse of rights has been a recurrent theme, albeit sometimes a submerged, secondary one. Historically speaking, the manner in which legal sensibilities and practices entered into colonizing processes, into their dramatic gestures and prosaic theaters, turns out to have been more subtle, less audible, murkier, than is often suggested. But, no matter, the general point has been made many times. Is there anything new to say? Anything other than confirmatory detail to add?

Perhaps the most coherent statement of received wisdom on the role of rights in colonial southern and central Africa is to be found in Martin Chanock's consistently insightful writings on the invention of customary law.[3] Treating property, after Bentham,[4] as the quintessential context in which rights are constituted, conjured with, and called into question—and, simultaneously, stressing "the power of discourses to shape reality"[5]—he argues that European colonizers took

---

1. I place *it* in quotation marks to note the fact that several disparate things are often lumped together under the term *law* in the anthropology of colonialism—among them, (European) legal institutions and sensibilities; constitutional and administrative processes; dispute management of diverse kinds; and the workings of "customary" law; cf. Francis G. Snyder, *Capitalism and Legal Change: An African Transformation* (New York: Academic Press, 1981), 6.

2. Kristin Mann and Richard Roberts, eds., *Law in Colonial Africa* (London: James Currey, 1991). Mann and Roberts introduce their volume with a comprehensive overview of recent scholarship on law and colonialism in Africa; they also include a large bibliography. For two other review essays on law, colonialism, power, and resistance—both thoughtful and cogently argued—see Sally Engle Merry, "Law and Colonialism: Review Essay," *Law and Society Review* 25 (1991): 889–992 and Susan F. Hirsch and Mindie Lazarus-Black, "Introduction," in *Contested States: Law, Hegemony, and Resistance,* ed. M. Lazarus-Black and S. F. Hirsch (New York: Routledge, 1994).

3. See Martin Chanock, *Law, Custom, and Social Order: The Colonial Experience in Malawi and Zambia* (Cambridge: Cambridge University Press, 1985) and "Paradigms, Policies, and Property: A Review of the Customary Law of Land Tenure," in *Law in Colonial Africa,* ed. K. Mann and R. Roberts (London: James Currey, 1991).

4. Chanock quotes Jeremy Bentham's statement that "property and law are born together, and die together"; Chanock, "Paradigms, Policies, and Property," 62. The citation he gives, though, is not to the original (J. Bentham, *Principles of the Civil Code* [Edinburgh: W. Tait, 1838], chap. 8, "Of Property"), but to the excerpted version in *Property: Mainstream and Critical Positions,* ed. Crawford Brough Macpherson (Oxford: Blackwell, 1987), 52.

5. Chanock, "Paradigms, Policies, and Property," 62.

possessive individualism[6] to be the axiomatic basis of civilized society, the corollary being that private property was unknown in "savage" Africa. Early administrators encouraged the "natives" to embrace the idea of individual rights in the name of modernity, in the cause of effecting the "evolution of human societies from status to contract."[7] But in due course, Chanock goes on, colonial governments did a volte-face, claiming that communalism and customary law, not individualism and a law of contract, were more "naturally" African. The reasons for this change of heart? If individual Tswana or Zulu or Ngoni or whomever had no idea of rights, only premodern "customs," it was easier to dispossess them of their land, easier to extract their labor power, easier to legitimize their subordination to a "superior" European law.[8] In short, the practical stress on communalism and custom, and the concomitant erasure of rights, was "hugely convenient" for the colonial state.[9]

The general argument, it seems, has struck a resonant chord with many anthropologists and historians,[10] echoing a persistent tendency to regard colonialism as, first and foremost, a matter of political economy; to identify its prime agents as states and statesmen, capitalists and corporations; to view other players on the imperial stage as members of its supporting cast(e), important perhaps but always secondary; to treat the colonial encounter itself as a linear, coherent, coercive process involving two clearly defined protagonists, an expansive metropolitan society and a subordinate local population; to locate its essence in the technologies by which the former imposed its axioms, ideologies, and aesthetics on the latter through a series of (relatively)

---

6. This is not Chanock's choice of term. I am, of course, aware of its complex provenance in the history of Western ideas (see, e.g., C. B. Macpherson, *The Political Theory of Possessive Individualism: Hobbes to Locke* [Oxford: Oxford University Press, 1962]), not to mention the debates sparked by it (see, e.g., Ian Shapiro, *The Evolution of Rights in Liberal Theory* [Cambridge: Cambridge University Press, 1986], 274f). Nonetheless, I use it to evoke the multifaceted construction of the self that arose with what Taylor glosses as "the culture of modernity"; Charles Taylor, *Sources of the Self: The Making of Modern Identity* (Cambridge: Harvard University Press, 1989), 285f.

7. Chanock, "Paradigms, Policies, and Property," 63.

8. Snyder, *Capitalism and Legal Change*, 298, passim.

9. Chanock, "Paradigms, Policies, and Property," 66. See also Sally Falk Moore, *Social Facts and Fabrications: "Customary" Law on Kilimanjaro* (Cambridge: Cambridge University Press, 1986).

10. See, for example, Merry, "Law and Colonialism," 890f; Moore, *Social Facts and Fabrications*.

calculated, never more than partially resisted, actions; and, once more, to hold that law, broadly conceived, was a vital part of this process. As Stamp summarily asserts:[11]

> Customary law, as distinct from precolonial jurisprudence, was introduced . . . as a tool for pacifying and governing the colonized peoples. While elements of precolonial jurisprudence survive in customary law, they have been made to serve the needs of the capitalist colonial and postcolonial states.

These generalities have been amended and modulated, of course.[12] But they have seldom been questioned tout court. And I do not mean to do so here, although what I have to say will have revisionist implications for the historical anthropology of colonialism. I seek, rather, to explore how modernist legal sensibilities and the discourse of rights figured in the colonization of the South African interior. In particular, I shall focus on the frontier at which the earliest emissaries of empire engaged the people who would become known as "the" Tswana (or "Bechuana"), there to interrogate the forms of identity and imagining to which the encounter gave rise. For reasons of space, my account is dramatically truncated.[13] Still, it turns out to be far more than a mere empirical embellishment to an already familiar story.

Let me offer a foretaste of my concerns by observing a rupture in the received narrative of the connection between colonialism and law in Africa. On one hand, we are told how, over the long run, colonial administrations denied Africans the very (individual) rights they themselves essayed as the sine qua non of modernization—enforcing, instead, a custom custom-built for the purposes of political control; we are shown, too, how "the" state contrived discourses of modernity, and invented tradition, in order to shape reality to its material advan-

---

11. Patricia Stamp, "Burying Otieno: The Politics of Gender and Ethnicity in Kenya," *Signs* 16 (1991): 808–45; cf. Snyder, *Capitalism and Legal Change*, 291 ff.

12. See, for example, the essays in the *American Ethnologist* 16 (1989): 609–65 under the title "Tensions of Empire."

13. I must perforce rely here on parts of the story documented elsewhere. See Jean and John L. Comaroff, *Of Revelation and Revolution*, vol. 1 (Chicago: University of Chicago Press, 1991); John L. and Jean Comaroff, *Ethnography and the Historical Imagination* (Boulder: Westview Press, 1992), part 3.

tage. And yet some, Chanock among them,[14] have observed how other agents of imperialism—most notably, but not only, missionaries—inculcated ideas about private property and possessive individualism; how colonial evangelists, concerned with "cultural conversion," introduced new notions of ownership, citizenship, and testamentary and civil rights.[15]

Surely there is a paradox in all this: in the fact that, while colonial officials perpetuated the "premodern" by eschewing individual rights for Africans, colonial evangelists sought to do the exact opposite in the name of civilization? This paradox, I shall argue, was not a trivial hiccup in the imperial project, a superficial tear in its otherwise seamless fabric. To the contrary: it reveals many of the contradictions of colonialism, many of the dissonances and disjunctures that were to play into the (re)construction of Africa, its structures of ethnicity and class, gender and generation. As we have said before,[16] the colonial encounter did not simply set in motion processes of domination and resistance between colonizer and colonized. It also sparked struggles among the colonizers themselves—among missionaries and merchants and mining magnates, administrators and agriculturalists and army men—as each sought to realize their own visions of the African present and future. In the course of these struggles, colonial regimes were, for all their materialities and brutalities, shaped as much by cultural forces as by the facts of political economy; as much by those seen now as bit players as by the heroes inscribed in history books. For the colonial process was never monolithic, never merely a matter of states and politics. And, far from being an encounter between two clearly defined "sides," *all* the parties involved were as much remade by it as it was by them. In all this, moreover, in the building of new identities, of newly imagined worlds of possibility and political reality, the discourse of rights, rightlessness, even righteousness, loomed increasingly large—albeit within complex cultural fields and power relations.

But I am running ahead of myself. As I said, I mean here to explore the colonization of nineteenth-century South Africa; to show how its civilizing mission, conveyed in a language of universalizing modernity, sought to instill new forms of subjectivity, sovereignty,

---

14. Chanock, *Law, Custom, and Social Order*.
15. Mann and Roberts, *Law in Colonial Africa*, 14–15.
16. J. L. and J. Comaroff, *Ethnography and the Historical Imagination*, 181 f.

and identity among Africans. In this, the discourse of rights was not only to feature centrally; it was also to feature contradictorily, playing itself out simultaneously, polyrythmically, in two registers: one may be dubbed the register of *radical individualism*, the other, the register of *primal sovereignty*. The first was to express itself in the internal stratification of black South Africa, in the rise of its new elites; the second, in the historical genesis of such "primordial" ethnic groups—yes, the irony is intended—as "the" Tswana and "the" Zulu. The *co*existence of these two registers within the colonial discourse of rights had some less-than-obvious consequences. For one thing, it laid a practical basis for cultural and material subordination, establishing a repertoire of signs and instruments by means of which it was possible for colonizers to divide and dominate others within a racinated world. But it also created the various spaces and the diverse terms in which the impaired could strike back. As this implies, it is to the cracks, crevices, and contradictions of the colonial discourse of rights—and the struggles to which it gave rise—that we may look for the seeds of modern South Africa's troubled identity politics.

Rights Stuff: Colonizing African Subjects, Subjectivities

[T]he Imperialist is not what he thinks or seems. He is a destroyer. He prepares the way for cosmopolitanism, and though his ambitions may be fulfilled the earth that he inherits will be grey.

—E. M. Forster, *Howards End*

The Nonconformist evangelists of the London Missionary Society (LMS) and the Wesleyan Methodist Missionary Society (WMMS) first settled permanently among the Tswana (Bechuana)[17] in the 1820s. The vanguard of the British presence in the South African interior— overrule by the colonial state was only to occur in 1885—they bore with them the cultural messages of the so-called "age of revolution" in Europe.[18] As Bohannan has suggested,[19] of all colonizers they were the

---

17. As we shall see, and as I hinted earlier, the term *Tswana* (Bechuana) did not exist before the colonial encounter; nor did the ethnicity to which it would later refer. For convenience, however, I use the label here in advance of describing its genesis.

18. See Eric J. Hobsbawm, *The Age of Revolution, 1789–1848* (New York: New American Library [Mentor Book], 1962).

19. Paul Bohannan, *Africa and Africans* (New York: Natural History Press, 1964), 22.

most far-reaching in their imperial vision, seeking not to rule Africans but to reconstruct their very being. For Southern Tswana, in fact, colonialism appeared, in the first instance, actually to be evangelism; when some of their number first ventured south in 1820, we are told, they "expected to find every white man in the colony a Missionary."[20]

I cannot, in this context, say much about the contemporary Southern Tswana world, save for two things. The first is that it was caught up in what historians have come to call *difaqane* (or *mfecane*), a period of subcontinental turmoil allegedly sparked by the rise of the Zulu state. This upheaval destabilized many communities in the interior and gave evangelists access to Tswana chiefdoms, whose rulers saw advantage in whites with guns, commodities, and the capacity to protect them by diplomatic means.[21] The second striking feature of this local world was its openness to novel forms of knowing and doing—*pace* those who have portrayed "traditional" African thought as inimical to the challenge of the new, as encapsulated in a "closed predicament"[22] or entrapped in "cold" cultures.[23] There is plenty of evidence that southern Tswana, and especially their chiefs and ritual experts, actively sought out fresh techniques and practices, experimenting with them and absorbing them into existing cultural repertoires.[24]

Nor shall I say much here about the background of the Nonconformists. Their civilizing mission was an epic quest cast in the fervent images of a rising bourgeoisie—in spite of the fact that they were themselves from its underbelly, from a "dominated fraction of the dominant class."[25] These images spoke in an optimistic, democratizing voice of the values of universal truth and rational knowledge; of

---

20. John Campbell, *Travels in South Africa . . . Being a Narrative of a Second Journey . . .* , 2 vols. (London: Westley, 1822), 2:139.

21. See, for example, S. Broadbent, Matlwasse, 8 June 1823 [WMMS, South Africa Correspondence, 300]; Jean and John L. Comaroff, "Christianity and Colonialism in Africa," *American Ethnologist* 13 (1986): 1–20. Chiefs spoke explicitly about the diplomatic advantages of a mission presence. They also believed that no settlement with a resident evangelist would be attacked by enemies, white or black.

22. Robin Horton, "African Traditional Thought and Western Science," *Africa* 37 (1967): 50–71, 155–87.

23. Claude Lévi-Strauss, *The Savage Mind* (London: Weidenfeld & Nicholson, 1966), 233–34.

24. See, for example, Campbell, *Travels in South Africa*, 1:307f; J. and J. L. Comaroff, *Of Revelation and Revolution*, vol. 1, 160f, passim.

25. Pierre Bourdieu, *Distinction: A Social Critique of the Judgement of Taste* (Cambridge: Harvard University Press, 1984), 421.

the capacity of man—as we all know, it was a deeply gendered fantasy—to bend History to His own Heroic will, to make himself and his world.[26] The terms of this vision are familiar. They are, to be sure, part of our own cultural heritage; though, at the time, they were less unanimously accepted, more contested, less firmly rooted in everyday practice than our collective "memory" tends to allow. Among them, three themes—tropes, really—featured with special clarity in the imaginings of colonial evangelists at the frontiers of empire.

The first was the modernist figure of the civilized, radically free individual. An autonomous citizen, this person was—or, rather, ought ideally to have been—possessed not only of private property, but, as important, of a divided, hyphenated self; one that could be, among other things and in different measure, self-conscious, self-indulgent, self-righteous, self-made, and, as Foucault would have us remember, self-disciplined.[27] Much has been written on the nature of modern personhood; much of it suggesting, as Taylor puts it,[28] that the "moral order of moderns is significantly different from that of previous civilizations." Adds Taylor, "What is peculiar to the modern West" in this regard—and, especially, to the "bourgeois ethic"[29]—is that the respect accorded to human beings came "to be [formulated] in terms of rights"; specifically, of *universal* "subjective right[s],"[30] a form of "legal privilege" enjoyed by "disengaged subjects."[31] Even the "wanderer in the desert," wrote John Philip,[32] longtime superin-

---

26. The allusion here, patently, is to Thomas Carlyle, *On Heroes, Hero-Worship, and the Heroic in History* (New York: D. Appleton, 1842).

27. See, for example, Nancy Fraser, *Unruly Practices: Power, Discourse, and Gender in Contemporary Social Theory* (Minneapolis: University of Minnesota Press, 1989), 44 f.

28. Taylor, *Sources of the Self*, 11.

29. Taylor, *Sources of the Self*, 214.

30. For discussion from a Marxist perspective of the relationship between the modern "legal" subject and bourgeois ideology—interesting for both its similarities to and differences from Taylor's account—see Snyder, *Capitalism and Legal Change*, 8 ff.

31. Taylor, *Sources of the Self*, 11–12. There is, of course, much more to the archaeology of "modern" personhood and subjectivity than these summary sentences suggest. Especially significant, perhaps, are the connections among (1) the rise of capitalism, (2) Lockean possessive individualism, (3) bourgeois notions of civility, of "public" and "private" spheres, and of the discrete, gendered family, (4) personal sobriety, labor discipline, and social order, and (5) linear conceptions of time and biography, progress and history. This chapter, however, is not the context in which to address such general issues. My concern is limited to the tropes borne by the civilizing mission to southern Africa.

32. John Philip, *Researches in South Africa; Illustrating the Civil, Moral, and Religious Condition of the Native Tribes*, 2 vols. (London: James Duncan, 1828), 1:26.

tendent of the London Missionary Society in the Cape Colony, ought
to have

> a right to his life, his liberty, his wife, his children, and his prop-
> erty . . . to a fair price for his labour; to choose the place of his
> abode, and to enjoy the society of his children; and no one can
> deprive him of those rights without violating the laws of nature
> and of nations.

Note the patriarchal, familial character of the fantasy.[33] Note, too, that
the larger this universalist image of right-bearing Man loomed in the
discourses of English modernity[34]—and in the utopian dreams of colonial evangelists—the more it was assumed to be absent from savage
sensibility. Almost all the early missionaries told tales of people dispossessed or put to death at the summary command of an African
"king";[35] the premodern monarch, it seems, had a whim of iron. This
picture of an Africa lacking all civility, citizenship, and civil rights was
to persist for a very long time in most quarters of white South African
society. In 1925, a century after evangelists arrived among the
Tswana, a parliamentary committee set up to consider "Masters and
Servants" legislation challenged Selope Thema, a highly respected
black journalist and political figure:[36]

> Of course, you have read the history of . . . Chaka and Dingaan.
> Did the natives have any right to life or property under these
> [nineteenth-century Zulu] chiefs? . . . These people [living under
> "tribal" conditions] would have had no rights except the chief's
> will.

33. Cf. Diana L. Barker, "Regulation of Marriage," in *Power and the State*, ed.
G. Littlejohn et al. (New York: St. Martin's Press, 1978), 256.

34. Philip Corrigan and Derek Sayer, *The Great Arch: English State Formation as
Cultural Revolution* (Oxford: Basil Blackwell, 1985), 183, passim.

35. See, for example, Campbell, *Travels in South Africa*, 1:211–12.

36. I am grateful to Martin Chanock for drawing my attention to this inquiry. He
discusses it in his forthcoming study of law and the state in early twentieth-century
South Africa, *Fear, Favour and Defection: Law, State and Society in South Africa, 1902–1936*.
For the full text of the report, see Union of South Africa, *Report of the Select Committee on
Subject-Matter of Masters and Servants Law (Transvaal) Amendment Bill* (Cape Town: Cape
Times Limited, Government Printers, 1925 [S.C.12-'25; Printed by Order of the House
of Assembly]); the quoted passages are to be found on p. 119.

Thema replied that Zululand had indeed once been "democratic"—
until Tshaka "learned . . . militarism" from white colonizers. "And
then," said he, "the history was written by Europeans."

The historical ideal of the modern propertied, right-bearing, autonomous individual—the model subject of the civilizing mission—
was securely founded on the principle of "reason." Writing in a philosophical key more than a hundred years later, Margaret MacDonald[37]
echoed a view shared by early nineteenth-century missionaries:
"[O]nly at a certain level of intellectual development do men claim
natural rights. Savages do not dream of life, liberty, and the pursuit of
happiness. For they do not question what is customary."[38] It followed
that only self-interested, reasoning human beings might be, in both
senses of the term, right-minded. Benighted premoderns, by contrast, were thought to live in unreflective "thralldom." Imprisoned,
even possessed, by "uncanny" forces, they could be neither disengaged nor self-possessed.[39] None of this would bear even the passing
scrutiny of a critical historical anthropology. And it ought not to pass
as modern anthropological philosophy. But it *did* provide a charter for
colonial evangelism.[40]

The second trope of salience to the colonial mission was the emerging European nation-state. Conceived as a secular universe of persons
who were free and equal before the law, it was held to share language
and culture, territory and history, values, sentiments, and interests.
This, of course, is the "imagined community"[41]—is any community *not*
imagined?—of which so much has been (re)written lately: the modernist polity that, as ideological formation, came to maturity in the age of
revolution, 1789–1848. This kind of community, indifferent to (or intol-

37. Margaret MacDonald, "Natural Rights," *Proceedings of the Aristotelian Society*
1947–48 (1949): 35–55. [Reprinted in *Theories of Rights*, ed. J. Waldron (Oxford: Oxford
University Press, 1984).]

38. Note, again, the taken-for-granted antimony between right and custom—and
its association with the opposition between civility and savagery. For insightful comment on the relegation of custom to a "peripheral, contained and decadent category" in
the British legal imagination, see Peter Fitzpatrick, " 'The Desperate Vacuum': Imperialism and Law in the Experience of Enlightenment," in *Post-Modern Law: Enlightenment,
Revolution and the Death of Man*, ed. A. Carter (Edinburgh: Edinburgh University Press,
1990), 92, passim.

39. Taylor, *Sources of the Self*, 192.

40. See, for example, Philip, *Researches in South Africa*, 2:118.

41. Benedict Anderson, *Imagined Communities: Reflections on the Origin and Spread of
Nationalism* (London: Verso, 1983).

erant of) internal difference, was itself the product of a "cultural revolution," as Corrigan and Sayer remind us.[42] And it was constituted as a state in the double sense of a political order *and* a condition of mind and being.[43] As such, it had become the taken-for-granted social context in which the right-bearing citizen was implanted.

Indeed, the state was seen as the ultimate guarantor of individual rights, the protector of propertied personhood, the space in which modern subjectivities paraded as political subjects. Founded on a social contract and codified law, rather than on status and custom, it was the model against which other, more "primitive" modes of government were to be measured.[44] After all, declared the Reverend John Philip,[45] "the character of a people depends on the influence of the laws and government under which they live." By this criterion, unsurprisingly, the Tswana were found lacking: Edward Solomon, in specifying what was particular to their "government" in the mid-nineteenth century, offered sadly, "They have no regular code of laws, . . . [but] customs . . . to [which] they rigidly adhere."[46] Some colonial evangelists, it is true, understood that the Africans *did* have a "law" which was "[far from] ridiculous or oppressive."[47] But, once remarked, such things were ignored or forgotten.

The third trope in the ideological armory of the Nonconformist mission was a positive, antirelativist conception of knowledge.[48] Expressed less in abstract statements than in everyday action and utterance, this conception relied on a number of familiar axioms: that the word and the world, fact and theory, the concept and the concrete were quite separate from one another and ought never to be confused or confounded; that truth, like civilization itself, was subject to absolutist standards; that wisdom was cumulative and irreversible; that, by extension, no two *systems* of knowledge could coexist.[49] Taken

---

42. Corrigan and Sayer, *The Great Arch*.

43. J. and J. L. Comaroff, *Of Revelation and Revolution*, 5.

44. See, for example, Robert Moffat, *Missionary Labours and Scenes in Southern Africa* (London: Snow, 1842), 248; Philip, *Researches in South Africa*, 2:132f.

45. Philip, *Researches in South Africa*, 2:317.

46. Edward S. Solomon, *Two Lectures on the Native Tribes of the Interior* (Cape Town: Saul Solomon, 1855), 46.

47. See, for example, J. Campbell, *Travels in South Africa*, 1:197f.

48. See, for instance, Philip, *Researches in South Africa*, 1:viif.

49. See, for example, David Livingstone, *Missionary Travels and Researches in South Africa* . . . (London: Murray, 1857), 19ff.

together, these axioms composed the canonical, confident bases of a universalist epistemology.

These, then, were some of the more significant tropes borne to the tropics and beyond by evangelists and other Europeans. They were to figure with special force in the colonial process—and in the dialectic of rights set in motion by it.

The onslaught of the colonial mission on the Southern Tswana occurred on many planes and in many places at once. In particular, it sought to release "the African" from a "simple socialistic life," in which "his [sic] individuality [was subordinated] to the necessities of the tribe."[50] The Reverend John Philip once wrote that "the elevation of a people from a state of barbarism to a high pitch of civilization supposes a revolution in the habits of that people, which it requires much time, and the operation of many causes to effect."[51] This evangelical first principle lay behind the Nonconformist campaign to remake Tswana subjectivity; to implant, that is, the modernist idea of the right-bearing, free citizen.[52] It is here that the first register of the discourse of rights, the register of radical individualism, was to play itself out.

The Politics of Personhood

To the extent that no practice was too petty, no "tradition" too trifling to escape evangelical attention, the struggle to refashion African individuality saturated the daily routines of the mission;[53] so much so, that it is difficult to offer summary illustration of the process without diminishing it. Nor was the concern of the colonial evangelists with "ordinary life" itself coincidental. The "affirmation of the everyday,"

---

50. William C. Willoughby, *Letter from Africa* (London: London Missionary Society for the Manchester and Salford Young Men's Missionary Band, n.d.).

51. Philip, *Researches in South Africa*, 2:355. Cf. John Mackenzie, *Papers of John Mackenzie*, ed. A. J. Dachs (Johannesburg: Witwatersrand University Press, 1975), 72.

52. That the mission had the sacred task of implanting this form of modern subjectivity was assumed by the evangelists from the first. Said Philip, quoting an unnamed source, "Religious institutions are the channels . . . by which the ideas of order, of duty, of humanity, and of justice, flow through the different ranks of the [human] community"; Philip, *Researches in South Africa*, 2:361.

53. See Jean and John L. Comaroff, "The Colonization of Consciousness in South Africa," *Economy and Society* 18 (1989): 267–96.

Taylor stresses,[54] was integral to the modernist idea of the new civility, especially in its bourgeois form. And so the lessons of the civilizing mission were taught not merely in the church and the classroom, by means of formal orations and ritual gestures. On the assumption that Africans learned by mimesis and habituation, they were conveyed as much through living example and "kind conversation."[55]

The Christian campaign to recast African personhood and subjectivity began with the "Bechuana" body. The Nonconformists were quick to grasp the salience, for colonizing purposes, of the management of the gendered human physique; all this long before Foucault opened to new scrutiny the connection between embodiment and power/knowledge, long before anthropologists wrote that the body is everywhere "the 'raw' material . . . upon which collective social categories and values are engraved."[56] These evangelists also sensed the link, analogical and substantive, between bodily politics and the body politic: it was Philip,[57] not Emile Durkheim, who first commented that the "different members of a state [are] beautifully represented by members of the human body."[58]

Tswana bodily practices were seen by the evangelists as nakedly promiscuous. Both men and (even more so) women were thought to lack physical closure, a vital characteristic of "civilized" individuals. Their clothing was "scanty," their skins "greasy," their habits "dirty,"

---

54. Taylor, *Sources of the Self*, 214–15.

55. The phrase was Livingstone's; see Livingstone, *Missionary Travels*, 21. In this connection, too, as Mackenzie wrote some years later, the mission-house was supposed to provide a model "such as can be copied . . . by the heathen"; John Mackenzie, *Ten Years North of the Orange River: A Story of Everyday Life and Work among the South African Tribes* (Edinburgh: Edmonston & Douglas, 1871), 466–67. A metonym of the European division of labor—in which "the husband [was] a jack-of-all-trades without doors, and the wife a maid-of-all-work within" (Livingstone, *Missionary Travels*, 22)—it was a model that had to be "attainable, and . . . desirable" to the Tswana (MacKenzie, 467). Cf. also Nancy Rose Hunt, "Colonial Fairy Tales and the Knife and Fork Doctrine in the Heart of Africa," in *African Encounters with Domesticity*, ed. K. T. Hansen (New Brunswick: Rutgers University Press, 1992), 143 f.

56. Jean Comaroff, "Bodily Reform as Historical Practice: The Semantics of Resistance in Modern South Africa," *International Journal of Psychology* 19 (1985): 541–67, 541 (after Arnold van Gennep, *The Rites of Passage* [Chicago: University of Chicago Press, 1960]). See also Mary Douglas, *Natural Symbols: Explorations in Cosmology* (New York: Vintage Books, 1970); Marcel Mauss, "Techniques of the Body," *Economy and Society* 2 (1973): 70–88; Terence Turner, "The Social Skin," in *Not Work Alone*, ed. J. Cherfas and R. Lewin (Beverly Hills: Sage, 1980); P. Bourdieu, *Distinction*.

57. Philip, *Researches in South Africa*, 1:386.

58. Cf. Emile Durkheim, *The Division of Labor in Society*, . . . passim.

and their sexuality uncontrolled. What is more, these Africans appeared to share magical ideas about the interconnections among persons, spirits, and things. As a result, the Nonconformists expended great effort on clothing them in European garb, all the better to close off their bodies from one another; on disseminating "modern" notions of hygiene, all the better to control their bodily extrusions; on seducing them away from local healers, all the better to have them put aside their charms and superstitions; on speaking to them of the Godly virtues of monogamy, all the better to contain their sexuality; on having them live in nuclear families, all the better to confine females to hearth and home and put men to honest work in the field.

Where better to address all these things at once than in the context of marriage?[59] The documentary record shows not just that the missionaries tried especially hard to reform Tswana conjugal relations, but that, in doing so, they relied heavily on the language of legality and rights. Thus, in a letter to London on the topic of wedlock in 1884, Roger Price, long a missionary in central Bechuanaland, wrote that "it will be some time yet before we can dispense with law as a schoolmaster for our Bechuana."[60] The point was to do more than simply convince men to marry monogamously, in church, and without "buying" their wives. It was to persuade them to treat the conjugal bond as a contract, an ensemble of enforceable rights and duties, and to disseminate a legalistic view of selfhood sui generis. To the Christians, moreover, matrimony and the family—being the core of the social division of labor at large—were also the key to those most vital sites in the struggle for modern personhood: property relations and material life.

It was here, in fact, that the lessons of radical individualism were most avidly taught and the "communal" tendencies of the savage, his enchantment and enslavement, most fiercely fought. Once the principles of private ownership and rights to property were properly inculcated, believed the evangelists, all the other bases of modern right-bearing citizenship—the right to life, liberty, wife, children[61]—might

---

59. Cf. Snyder, *Capitalism and Legal Change.*

60. Quoted in Edwin William Smith, *Great Lion of Bechuanaland: The Life and Times of Roger Price, Missionary* (London: Independent Press for the London Missionary Society, 1957), 276–78.

61. Philip, *Researches in South Africa,* 1:xxvi.

take root.[62] But first the heathen antipathy to "healthy, individualistic competition," to the maximization of time and effort, and to self-possessed industry had to be overcome.[63] Tswana might have been crafty and self-interested: "under the influence," Hodgson put it,[64] "of [the] selfish principle." But this was a far cry from the kind of refined, *rational* individualism that the Nonconformists had in mind.

In order to teach the principles of possessive individualism and private property, the Christians set out first to purchase the land on which to plant themselves, their churches, and their gardens. They insisted on ownership: their rights had to be clearly given, clearly gained, clearly grasped by the Africans, so that they might learn to do the same. Wrote Mary Moffat,[65] wife of Robert and mother-in-law of David Livingstone: "each [Tswana] individual is to purchase his own ground, the missionaries having set the example." And so, in 1820, Robert Hamilton "bought" ground from a local man, "the first . . . ever purchased in the Matchappee [Tlhaping] country."[66] A few years later, Robert Moffat could himself report that the "ground belonging to the Mission . . . was purchased . . . for 40 lbs. of beads."[67] All the evidence suggests that the Africans found these gestures, and the missionaries' explanations for them, utterly incomprehensible. The very idea of sale, Livingstone confessed,[68] "sounded strangely in [their] ears."

Once they had their land, the evangelists went about enclosing and planting gardens. Here they enacted their everyday theater of Protestant industry: Act I, the forceful conversion of nature into

---

62. Mackenzie, *Papers of John Mackenzie*, 72; note that, although published in 1975, Mackenzie wrote this in 1858.

63. Mackenzie, quoted in Anthony J. Dachs, "Missionary Imperialism: The Case of Bechuanaland," *Journal of African History* 13 (1972): 647–58, 652.

64. Thomas L. Hodgson, *The Journals of the Rev. T. L. Hodgson: Missionary to the Seleka-Rolong and the Griquas, 1821–1831*, ed. R. L. Cope (Johannesburg: Witwatersrand University Press for the African Studies Institute, 1977), 157.

65. In Robert and Mary Moffat, *Apprenticeship at Kuruman: Being the Journals and Letters of Robert and Mary Moffat, 1820–1828*, ed. I. Schapera (London: Chatto & Windus, 1951), 111.

66. See Campbell, *Travels in South Africa*, 2:149–50. Note that, at the time, the Tlhaping formed a large Southern Tswana chiefdom. It was at Kuruman, among them, that the first major LMS station was established deep in the South African interior. The Tlhaping polity was to divide later in the century.

67. R. and M. Moffat, *Apprenticeship at Kuruman*, 189.

68. Livingstone, *Missionary Travels*, 21; cf. Mackenzie, *Ten Years North of the Orange River*, 369.

private property; Act II, the cultivation of a fruitful field by self-possessed labor; Act III, the harvesting of individual wealth and value to be enjoyed as just reward for virtuous toil. Hear Samuel Broadbent, WMMS missionary, in the 1820s:[69]

> I and my colleague had each enclosed a plot of ground, which we had, of course, in English fashion, broken up and cleared of the roots of weeds, and then sown . . . [V]egetables grew much more luxuriantly, and were more productive, in our grounds than theirs. One day a number of respectable natives came to ask the reason of this difference . . .
>
> My first answer was, "Your idleness." "How so?" they inquired. I said, "You have seen that we have dug the ground ourselves; you leave it to your women . . . I added "Work yourselves, as you see we do, and dig the ground properly, and your seed will flourish as well as ours."

Here, then, were the lessons of the sacred garden: possession, enclosure, a properly gendered division of labor, hard work. Immediately around the mission stations, we are told, some southern Tswana took these lessons to heart. By 1842, at one settlement, "numerous gardens . . . [had] lately been walled in," and were being brought under cultivation; at another, "sixty large gardens [had] been enclosed, and upward of two thousand trees planted."[70] The dawn of African modernity, it seemed to the optimistic evangelists, lay just over the horizon.

As it turned out, their optimism proved premature. Beyond the compass of the mission and its well-watered stations, neither the privatization of commonage nor rights of ownership made much sense to southern Tswana. Neither agricultural nor pastoral land was scarce here. It had no exchange value, was held and distributed by chiefly favor, and was given to social groups as the basis of their membership of a political community. Many decades later, once colonial evangelism had worked its effects much further, there *would* be a

---

69. Samuel Broadbent, *A Narrative of the First Introduction of Christianity amongst the Barolong Tribe of Bechuanas, South Africa* (London: Wesleyan Mission House, 1865), 104–5.

70. J. Cameron, Platberg, 26 September 1842 [WMMS, South Africa Correspondence (Bechuana), 315–121]; J. Allison, Lishuani, 1 August 1843 [WMMS, South Africa Correspondence (Bechuana), 315–123].

move in some local quarters to introduce individual title and rights of private ownership (as will be discussed). But this was only after settler expansion had transformed the worth of real estate in the interior, after an industrial revolution had reconstructed the regional economy, after overrule by a colonial state had made the Tswana vulnerable to dispossession. But by then, as we shall see, the very idea of rights to landed property for Africans had become a hotly contested issue.

All this notwithstanding, the missionaries did not give up their efforts to inculcate the practices of "healthy" individualism. The most tenacious among them, in this respect, was undoubtedly John Mackenzie, a "humanitarian imperialist" with ambitious plans to make Bechuanaland into a Wordsworthian[71] paradise of enlightened, landowning yeomen;[72] Mackenzie, who eventually joined the colonial government in order to further his schemes, even dreamed of bringing English farmers to settle in this idyll.[73] His views were repeatedly stated in letters to colonial officials; one, condensed here to emphasize the general point, is fairly representative:[74]

If . . . people would quietly settle down [on land with long leases] and pay an annual rent for their farms . . . the "native question" would be for ever settled . . . A class of native yeomen would arise, which in some cases might merge into that of landowners, for it would be well to put it in their power to buy their farms after they had occupied them and improved them for some years. The less thrifty and capable . . . [would be allowed to] sink to [their] own level among the inferior labouring class.

71. I refer here to Wordsworth's "perfect Republic of Shepherds and agriculturalists" described in his ethnographic sketch of the Lake District; William Wordsworth, *A Guide through the District of the Lakes in the North of England, with a Description of the Scenery, &c. for the Use of Tourists and Residents* (Malvern: The Tantivy Press, 1948; facsimile of the fifth edition, 1835), 54.

72. John Mackenzie, *Austral Africa: Losing It or Ruling It,* 2 vols. (London: Sampson Low, Marston, Searle & Rivington, 1887); Anthony Sillery, *John Mackenzie of Bechuanaland, 1835–1899: A Study in Humanitarian Imperialism* (Cape Town: A. A. Balkema, 1971).

73. Mackenzie's plan, which would have alienated Tswana land for white settlement, was criticized both within and outside the mission. See J. and J. L. Comaroff, *Of Revelation and Revolution,* 291 f; Sillery, *John Mackenzie,* passim. However, his wish to create a new world of landowning, independent Tswana peasants was widely shared among his brethren.

74. Mackenzie, *Papers of John Mackenzie,* 111–12; originally written in 1878.

In *Austral Africa*, a political treatise aimed at the British parliament and public, Mackenzie went on to argue that every African "ought to feel that his house and his cornfield are his own, and not mere 'Government-land' . . . which can be sold at any time over his head."[75] Many Tswana, he said, more optimistically than accurately, now saw the disadvantages of living in concentrated "traditional" villages, far from their fields and cattle posts; they would prefer to stay, like European farmers, at their smallholdings, where they could exert "personal oversight" in "cultivating their lands," could keep their livestock with them, and might escape the irksome demands made by their rulers.[76] Already there were cases "where Bechuana industry [had] turned [a] mere cattle or hunting station into a civilised man's farm." Given the introduction of private property— and freedom from chiefly command—might not Bechuanaland become a haven of African modernity?

The tireless evangelist was convinced that, by the 1880s, Southern Tswana had *already* developed a nice understanding of private property in the European sense of the term. Even if they had not all absorbed the lessons of the mission, a colonial commission[77]— established in 1871 after the discovery of diamonds had led to conflicting land claims—had "taught . . . [them] the meaning of land-titles, and the laws and customs of the white men as to buying and selling land."[78] But, just in case they were not yet persuaded of the benefits of adopting these laws and customs, Mackenzie seized every opportunity to browbeat them. Take this fragment of a reported conversation between himself and a Southern Tswana ruler:[79]

> "You should fully face the change that has come and is coming. In the olden time you had all your gardens and cattle stations, and no one interfered with the one or the other. Now you see the coming wave of white men . . . Where they find open country they will build and put in the plough, and will tell you that the unoccupied country is God's and not yours. But white men re-

---

75. Mackenzie, *Austral Africa*, 1:30.
76. Mackenzie, *Austral Africa*, 1:76.
77. The Bloemhof Arbitration Commission, which ended with the controversial Keate Award of 1871, is discussed in every major work on nineteenth-century South African history. Hence there is no need to annotate it here.
78. Mackenzie, *Papers of John Mackenzie*, 20.
79. Mackenzie, *Austral Africa*, 1:77–78.

spect hard work, and if you improve your houses and your lands you may depend on it no English officer would dispossess you . . . Why not meet together once more as a tribe . . . and introduce a better custom as to land? Every fountain or farm should be apportioned to him who cultivates it, and he should have a title to it acknowledged by the tribe."

"But would he not sell it?" I was asked at once.

"Fools might sell," I answered, "but the men of the tribe would not . . ."

For "men of the tribe," read "socially responsible individuals," those whose private interest might be equated with the public good.

"But there is great deception about papers,—the agents deceive stupid people," said one of the men.

Here, over the issue of dispossession, is where the liberal idealism of the mission ran up against the raw realities of the colonial frontier. And where the evangelists found it necessary to modify the kind of propertied personhood of which they dreamed—or leave their would-be converts open to the rapacity of other colonizers.[80] And so:

"I have thought of all that," [Mackenzie] replied. "You ought to have individual rights and title-deeds, but it ought to be printed on every one of them, 'Not saleable—not transferable.'"

This was a new idea—individual titles, but unsaleable. It was declared on all hands that this would exactly meet their case . . . [the] idea of individual right to land beyond the power of the clever agent.

How this form of title differed from existing tenurial arrangements—other than being committed to paper—is not obvious. It may have served the evangelists by sustaining the fiction of private property. But it is unclear what the Africans had to gain from it: without the intervention of the colonial state, dispossession would go on, as indeed it did, with or without title deeds. Many Tswana seem to have

---

80. See John L. Comaroff, "Images of Empire, Contests of Conscience: Models of Colonial Domination in South Africa," *American Ethnologist* 16 (1989): 661–85.

been quick to appreciate this. As Mackenzie's own account shows,[81] it was the very language of "papers," of title and rights, that was being used by whites to expropriate African land. Somewhat less triumphantly, the evangelist reports another conversation:[82]

> ". . . why don't the white men stay in their own country?" said some intelligent natives to me one day . . . "Perhaps it is [the Queen] who sends them. Some say this is the English mode of warfare—by 'papers' and agents and courts." This was said with contempt.

In short, Mackenzie's scheme, like his text, discloses the emerging contradictions of the colonial frontier. It was, patently, a world in which the worldview of the mission stood little chance against white avarice and overrule. But more of that later. Another thing is also evident: despite the fact that propertied individualism had gained little practical purchase among Tswana, talk of rights had begun to resound in the African interior.

I reiterate that the domain of landed property was not the only one in which the lessons of radical individualism were conveyed. There were many others: the effort to construct a domestic sphere, hedged about by the right to "privacy" and enclosed in a residential architecture founded on the British idea of "home";[83] the treatment of the church as a rule-governed, voluntary association made up of spiritually autonomous individuals, each with an inalienable right to freedom of belief; the establishment of schools in which everyone might exercise their right to self-improvement, and in which pupils were subjected to individualistic disciplinary regimes; the practical dissemination of modernist notions of time and money, of free wage labor and the private estate, of refined consumption as a reward for virtue; and so on and on. Sometimes these lessons had their dramatic moments, as when missionaries and "native" Christians confronted chiefs, publicly, to demand that converts be allowed to act in accordance with their consciences—rather than be made to follow "blind custom."[84] The

81. Mackenzie, *Austral Africa*, 1:78–80.
82. Mackenzie, *Austral Africa*, 1:80.
83. J. L. and J. Comaroff, *Ethnography and the Historical Imagination*, 279f.
84. There are many well-known cases of such confrontations in the documentary record. Perhaps the most illuminating, for our purposes, occurred in the 1860s among

assertion of this right resonated closely with European ideas of citizenship: as loyal subjects of their rulers and members of their communities, church people would obey the law in all things, would pay all taxes, and would give customary tribute to their sovereigns. But they wished to pursue their own spiritual activities unopposed and to be excused from participating in "heathen" rituals. In a culture that did not echo the European distinction between church and state, religion and politics, this demand often led to bitter conflict—which merely underscored the lessons of radical individualism and universal rights that the colonial evangelists had tried so hard to teach.[85]

In what measure, then, did the Nonconformists succeed in implanting "modern" personhood on African soil? This question is not simply answered. For now, however, it is enough to note that one of the effects of colonialism, of its unresolved dialectic, was to set in motion complex processes of class formation. While joining the church did not itself correlate with social status—by the early twentieth century most Tswana were members—local communities began to spawn small but active Christian elites. Among them, identity with the ideology of the civilizing mission grew increasingly strong; members of "traditional" (non-Christian) ruling families, even those who enjoyed wealth and prestige in their chiefdoms, were more reluctant to identify. But the colonial economy impoverished the majority, leaving Southern Tswana divided into a mass of poor peasant-proletarians, an embryonic bourgeoisie, and a population of "middle" peasants situated precariously in between.[86] For those trapped, at the behest of colonial capitalism, in a promiscuous cycle of underpaid migrant labor and

the Tshidi Rolong. See Mackenzie, *Ten Years North of the Orange River*, 231; also Silas Modiri Molema, *Montshiwa, 1815–1896: Barolong Chief and Patriot* (Cape Town: Struik, 1966) and Emile Holub, *Seven Years in South Africa: Travels, Researches, and Hunting Adventures, between the Diamond-Fields and the Zambesi (1872–79)*, 2 vols. (Boston: Houghton Mifflin, 1881).

85. My use of terms like *lesson* and *teaching* is intended to capture the rhetoric of the evangelists. In Mackenzie's account of the conversations excerpted here, he refers to his interlocutors, chiefs among them, as "my students"; Mackenzie, *Austral Africa*, 1:79.

86. We have traced these processes of class formation elsewhere. See J. and J. L. Comaroff, "The Colonization of Consciousness"; J. L. and J. Comaroff, *Of Revelation and Revolution*, vol. 2, chap. 3 (in preparation). The emergence of a fragmented peasantry here was reminiscent, interestingly, of that described by Lenin for Russia; see Vladimir Illich Lenin, "Selections from *The Development of Capitalism in Russia*," in *Essential Works of Lenin*, ed. H. Christman (New York: Bantam, 1971).

unproductive agriculture, the Christian message made little sense: these people had no prospect of being propertied and found themselves with ever diminishing rights. For middle peasants, both the Protestant ethic and the promise of capitalism held greater attraction; material pressures, though, tended to push them toward the abyss of poverty. But everyone, whatever their ideological orientation or social status, now lived in a colonial world dominated by the authoritative rhetoric of rights—even if, for most black South Africans, those rights were experienced either by their absence or, worse yet, as instruments of dispossession.

But the evangelical discourse of rights, as I said, was not restricted purely to the register of radical individualism, nor just to the politics of modernist personhood. It was also to resonate in the language and the practices of primal sovereignty.

The Politics of Primal Sovereignty

Before the arrival of the colonial evangelists, it seems, there were no Bechuana in Bechuanaland, merely *batho*, "human beings." Solomon,[87] among others, tells us that these people lived in a number of chiefdoms, each named for its ruling descent group, without remarking any common cultural or political identity. Adds Mackenzie:[88]

> The name Bechuana is a word used at an early period by white men to denote the tribes of Batlaping and Barolong, with which they first came into contact. These people do not use the word of themselves, or of one another; nevertheless, they accept of it as the white man's name for them, and now begin to use it themselves . . . The Bechuana belong to the large Bantu family of people.

The Europeans did more than just name "the Bechuana." They contrived for them an entire ethnology, dividing them into "tribes" and ascribing to them a primordial identity based on common ancestors and origins, language and lore, culture and customs, sentiments and

---

87. Solomon, *Two Lectures on the Native Tribes*, 41.
88. Mackenzie, *Austral Africa*, 1:22.

interests.[89] So much so, that most nineteenth-century evangelical volumes came to include an elementary classification of tribal groups and clusters, a word list, and material on economy, society, religion, government, and "natural" characteristics. This material later found its way into mission ethnographies, the earliest anthropological writings on the Tswana;[90] into dictionaries,[91] grammars,[92] maps,[93] and typologies of languages and "dialects";[94] and, perhaps most significant for the formation of ethnic consciousness, into vernacular school texts.[95] It was also to prepare the ground for the cultural and political geography of southern Africa, the ethnoscape on which colonial rule (and later apartheid) was to be built. The organization of the evangelical field itself gave living cartographic expression to Nonconformist ethnology: divided into "Griqua," "Hottentot," "Bechuana," and other missions, its districts and stations paralleled the ethnic and tribal categories it had constructed.

Ethnic consciousness, I would argue, always has its roots in encounters between peoples who mark their differences—in power, in historical imaginings, in political ambitions and economic ends—by cultural means. As this suggests, collective identity is everywhere a relation, nowhere a thing.[96] Regarded thus, the construction of "*the*

---

89. See, for example, J. Campbell, *Travels in South Africa*, 2:193f; Philip, *Researches in South Africa*, 2:107–43; Moffat, *Missionary Labours*, chaps. 1, 15, 17; Solomon, *Two Lectures on the Native Tribes*, 4f; Livingstone, *Missionary Travels*, 9f, 122f; Mackenzie, *Ten Years North of the Orange River*, 483ff, Austral Africa, 1:21f.

90. See, for example, J. Tom Brown, "Circumcision Rites of the Becwana Tribes," *Journal of the Royal Anthropological Institute* 51 (1921): 419–27, *Among the Bantu Nomads: A Record of Forty Years Spent among the Bechuana . . .* (London: Seeley Service, 1926); William C. Willoughby, "Notes on the Totemism of the Becwana," *Journal of the Royal Anthropological Institute* 35 (1905): 295–314, *Race Problems in the New Africa* (Oxford: Clarendon Press, 1923), *The Soul of the Bantu* (New York: Student Christian Movement, 1928), *Nature-Worship and Taboo* (Hartford: Hartford Seminary Press, 1932).

91. See, for instance, John Brown, *Secwana Dictionary*, revised and enlarged by J. Tom Brown (Tiger Kloof: London Missionary Society, 1931).

92. See, for example, William Crisp, *Notes towards a Secoana Grammar*, 4th ed. (London: S.P.C.K., 1905); Alexander Sandilands, *Introduction to Tswana* (Tiger Kloof: London Missionary Society, 1953).

93. See, for example, Campbell, *Travels in South Africa*.

94. See, for instance, Mackenzie, *Austral Africa*, vol. 1; Broadbent, *A Narrative of the First Introduction of Christianity*.

95. See, for example, Moffat, *Missionary Labours*, 570f; J. L. and J. Comaroff, *Of Revelation and Revolution*, vol. 2, chaps. 9–11.

96. See John L. Comaroff, "Of Totemism and Ethnicity: Consciousness, Practice and the Signs of Inequality," *Ethnos* 52 (1987): 301–23.

Bechuana" as "*a* people"[97]—their transition, that is, from humanity to ethnicity—occurred initially in response to the terms in which they were challenged by colonial evangelists. This challenge took the form of an unremitting insistence that the Africans give coherent account of their own practices—and hear, from clerics schooled in the universalist sureties of enlightenment knowledge, why European ways were the more rational, the more advanced, the more advantageous; and why, therefore, things local ought to be forever put aside. The great teleology of modernist bourgeois thought, as I noted before, did not allow for the possibility that two systems of knowledge, each with its own ontology, might coexist or be spliced together. Consequently, Southern Tswana found themselves being asked to objectify their own culture, now dubbed *setswana*, by contrast to *sekgoa* ("European ways").

The documentary record is replete with conversations, transcribed by missionaries, about the differences between *setswana* and *sekgoa*. These accounts, unwittingly perhaps, are decidedly equivocal. And revealing. On the one hand, the evangelists often claimed that Tswana had pronounced the ways of the whites clearly superior.[98] On the other, we are told that they "could not see . . . anything in [European] customs more agreeable . . . than in their own." Worse yet, they "would, with little ceremony"—sometimes "laughing extravagantly"—"pronounce our customs clumsy, awkward, and troublesome."[99] In truth, the Africans seem to have been more bemused than amused. Given their openness to the exchange of knowledge and techniques, they found it hard to understand why *setswana* and *sekgoa* should not coexist; to wit, as the colonial encounter took its course, many would cull new cultural practices from the fusion of the two worlds. Meanwhile, however, they responded to the European demand to choose between customs, knowledges, deities by recourse to a bland, baffling relativism: "the God of the Whites," said a rainmaker to the insistent Robert Moffat, "dwells in the south . . . the Bootshuana God dwells in the north."[100] Neither should covet the terrain of the other, he implied. And neither was about to take himself off.

---

97. See, for example, Moffat, *Missionary Labours*, 236.
98. See, for example, Moffat, *Missionary Labours*, 247.
99. Ibid., 247–48.
100. R. Moffat, Kuruman, 17 May–26 November 1821 [CWM, LMS South Africa Journals, 3].

It goes without saying that the *content* of any ethnic identity is a product of complex, drawn out historical processes; being itself a heterogeneous, fluid ensemble of (variously empowered) signs and practices, a living culture is forged not merely in conversations, but also in the minutiae of everyday action, in the inscription of linguistic forms and material relations, in the course of struggle and contestation. Here, however, I wish to highlight four things about the manner in which Tswana identity was re-presented by the evangelists back to the Tswana themselves (in their schools, courts, churches, and other contexts)—and, then, to the whites of colonial South Africa.

First and foremost, "the Bechuana" were portrayed as a people governed by the primal sovereignty of their "custom" (*mekgwa*, the word now had vernacular denotation). No matter that they followed different chiefs and lived in different "tribes." No matter that they lacked any collective identity nor even, until now, shared a proper noun. Every last one of them was, allegedly, bound together by a common, ineluctable attachment to the ways of their ancestors; by their very "nature," moreover, they obeyed the command of custom without question.[101] Which is why, said the clerics, it had been so difficult to sow the seeds of "healthy individualism" among them; so difficult to make all but few of them into citizens fit for the Kingdom of God and Great Britain. Even when it was proved to these Africans that their "superstitions" served them ill—as in, say, following the futile directives of rain doctors[102]—they did not easily put aside their old ways. Even when they took on the trappings of civilization, they still "prefer[red] the customs in which they [had] been brought up."[103] Declared Moffat:[104]

> *the national council* [is] the stronghold or shield of the native customs, in which speakers have, in masterly style, inveighed against any aggression on their ancient ceremonies, threatening confiscation and death to those who would arraign the wisdom of their forefathers.

101. See, for example, Philip, *Researches in South Africa*, 2:118.
102. See Moffat, *Missionary Labours*, 305; Broadbent, *A Narrative of the First Introduction of Christianity*, 99f; Livingstone, *Missionary Travels*, 25f.
103. Mackenzie, *Ten Years North of the Orange River*, 397.
104. Moffat, *Missionary Labours*, 249–50.

Evangelists continued to report the stubborn hold of *mekgwa* well into this century, long after most Southern Tswana had joined the church; several noted the persistence of, among other things, initiation rites,[105] bride-wealth,[106] and "taboos."[107] Many of these reports—like the notion that "the Bechuana" were unreflectively submissive to ancestral usage—were based on a misreading of subtle processes of cultural exchange and transformation.[108] But that is beside the historical point: for the Europeans, the primal force that bound these people together, the sovereignty of *setswana*, was inherently and self-evidently conservative, communal, antimodern. By very virtue of being ethnic Bechuana, in sum, these Africans were benighted subjects in a prehistoric kingdom of custom. Shades here of an idea which, until recently, enjoyed wide currency in Anglo-American social science: that ethnicity, especially in the guise of "tribalism" and/or "traditionalism," is inimical to modernity. Also its corollary: that the removal of difference is a sine qua non of the worldly progress toward universal civilization.[109]

Moffat's reference to "the *national* council" is also telling—particularly since, strictly speaking, no such thing existed.[110] It presaged the vision, which spread largely unremarked among colonial evangelists, of a (supratribal) Tswana ethnonation. The germ of the idea, of course, was implicit both in the invention of the term

---

105. See Native Conference of the South African District Circuit of 1907 [W. C. Willoughby Papers, Selly Oak, Box 14: General Files on Children, Education and Puberty].

106. See, for example, A. E. Jennings, *Bogadi: A Study of the Marriage Laws and Customs of the Bechuana Tribes of South Africa* (Tiger Kloof: London Missionary Society, 1933).

107. See, for example, W. C. Willoughby, *The Soul of the Bantu, Nature-Worship and Taboo*.

108. J. L. and J. Comaroff, *Of Revelation and Revolution*, 2: passim; cf. Mackenzie, *Ten Years North of the Orange River*, 396 f.

109. See Clifford Geertz, "The Integrative Revolution: Primordial Sentiments and Civil Politics in the New States," in *Old Societies and New States*, ed. C. Geertz (New York: The Free Press, 1963); Ernest Gellner, *Nations and Nationalism* (Ithaca: Cornell University Press, 1983), *Culture, Identity, and Politics* (New York: Cambridge University Press, 1987).

110. Each chief had his own advisors and a council of headmen. Each also called meetings of various kinds; see Isaac Schapera, *A Handbook of Tswana Law and Custom* (London: Oxford University Press for the International African Institute, 1938). Chiefdoms were largely autonomous and not part of a larger "Bechuana" confederation with its own ruler, councils, or assemblies.

"Bechuana" and in the imputation of a shared allegiance to the primal sovereignty of *mekgwa*. Here lies the second of my four points: that, increasingly, "*the* Bechuana,*" in the singular, were represented as a grouping with common concerns above and beyond those of the "tribes" (i.e., chiefdoms) that formed their everyday political communities. At times, in fact, this entity was depicted as something akin to a primitive European nation. This becomes clear from a novel about a scientific expedition to South Africa written by Jules Verne in 1872. Taking its ethnographic background from early mission texts, it tells of the arrival of the scientists at a Tswana capital and of a ceremony in which they and the local ruler pulled each other's noses "according to African custom." All of which, wrote Verne, made the Europeans into "naturalized Bechuanas."[111]

It was a short step from the conclusion that Tswana shared a collective identity to the assumption that they "naturally" shared rights and interests. And so, from the 1830s onward, the missionaries allude repeatedly to what might harm or advance the commonweal of "*the* Bechuana people.*" Here, as elsewhere, the road from primal sovereignty to the "rightful" claims of an ethnic group was tarred with chimeras, myths, mirages. But it was also paved with good intentions. Many of the Nonconformists saw themselves as "protectors of the natives" against the predations of other colonizers.[112] Take just one striking instance: at the Bloemhof Commission of 1871, set up to hear the territorial disputes that had arisen upon the discovery of diamonds along the frontier, the Southern Tswana were represented by Joseph Ludorf, a WMMS evangelist.[113] Although they were given a portion of the land, Ludorf feared that it would nonetheless be seized by the white settler republics. Hence, just after the award was made, at the very moment when the republics were angrily denouncing it, the missionary drafted a manifesto for a "United Barolong, Batlhaping and

---

111. Jules Verne, *The Adventures of Three Englishmen and Three Russians in South Africa* (London: Sampson Low, Marston, Searle, & Rivington, 1876), 47.

112. See, for example, J. Freeman, Mabotsa, 25 December 1849 [CWM, LMS Home Odds (Freeman Deputation 1849–50), 2–4–D]. For further discussion, see J. L. Comaroff, "Images of Empire"; J. and J. L. Comaroff, *Of Revelation and Revolution*, chap. 7.

113. See Zachariah K. Matthews, "A Short History of the Tshidi Barolong," *Fort Hare Papers* 1 (1945): 9–28, esp. 9; cf. Eric A. Walker, *A History of South Africa* (London: Longmans, Green, 1928), 344.

Bangwaketse Nation,"[114] these being the various Southern Tswana "tribes." He wrote to their chiefs:[115]

> And now chiefs: rulers of the land, I appeal to you. Awake: arise and unite soon before your trophy is torn asunder by wolves; come ye together, make protective laws; stop all breaches and gaps and close your ranks. Safeguard the heritage of Tau your ancestor. Hear ye chiefs: Come together and unite.

Ludorf went on to propose the founding of an ethnic nation-state with a representative parliament, a charted territory, an army, a judiciary, an independent economy, and a constitution that fused *setswana* and European statecraft.[116] The plan came to naught, however; its author died just a few weeks later. Significantly, though, he was *not* dismissed as frivolous or misguided either by Tswana or by his brethren.[117] Indeed, some years on, two "Bechuana" polities were established, albeit as colonies of the United Kingdom: British Bechuanaland (later absorbed into South Africa to become, under apartheid, Bophuthatswana) and the Bechuanaland Protectorate (after 1966, Botswana). The role of the clerics in their formal creation is a complicated issue.[118] But there is no denying that colonial evangelism made these ethnonational polities thinkable in the first place—and so prepared the ground for the colonial state to sow its own special brand of

114. See George M. Theal, *History of South Africa: The Republics and Native Territories From 1854 to 1872* (London: Swan Sonnenschein, 1900), 368–69.

115. Quoted in Molema, *Montshiwa*, 66–67.

116. See Silas Modiri Molema, *Chief Moroka: His Life, His Times, His Country and His People* (Cape Town: Methodist Publishing House, 1951), 136; Theal, *History of South Africa*, 369.

117. See J. Whiteside, *History of the Wesleyan Methodist Church of South Africa* (London: Elliot Stock, 1906), 339; George G. Findlay and William W. Holdsworth, *The History of the Wesleyan Methodist Missionary Society* (London: The Epworth Press, 1922), 4:328. Ludorf's exertions, as we might expect, were ignored by the Crown and derided by the Boers; see Theal, *History of South Africa*, 368f. A politically autonomous Bechuanaland carved out along this highly contested frontier would hardly have served the interests of either.

118. See, for example, Anthony Sillery, *The Bechuanaland Protectorate* (Cape Town and New York: Oxford University Press, 1952); Sillery, *John Mackenzie*; Kevin Shillington, *The Colonisation of the Southern Tswana, 1870–1900* (Johannesburg: Ravan Press, 1985); J. and J. L. Comaroff, *Of Revelation and Revolution*, chap. 7; and, from the specific perspective of the Kwena (now of central Botswana), Frederick Jeffress Ramsay, *The Rise and Fall of the Bakwena Dynasty of South-Central Botswana, 1820–1940* (Ann Arbor: University Microfilms International, 1991).

tribal politics. It also shaped the kind of collective consciousness that persuaded Southern Tswana themselves to respond in ethnic terms. It is not coincidental, for instance, that the first local newspaper owned and published among these people—by prominent mission school alumni—was called *Koranta ea Becoana*, "The Newspaper of the Tswana." Nor that it should give voice, in the vernacular, to a "national" culture and to "national" interests and concerns.[119] In time, such Tswana voices would come to speak easily in terms of collective rights and entitlements.

But—and this leads to my third point—there was an anomaly here. On one hand, "the Bechuana" (singular) were being conjured up as an ethnic group with common political cause. On the other, these peoples (plural) inhabited a world in which everyday political processes occurred within and among autonomous chiefdoms, each ruled by its own authorities. (*Morafe*, Setswana for "polity," was rendered in mission dictionaries as "tribe" *and* "nation," and was used to describe both a chiefdom and "the Bechuana" at large.) In acting on behalf of "the natives," furthermore, evangelists usually represented specific rulers and their subjects, not "the Bechuana"; it was mainly at this local level that their day-to-day engagement in frontier politics actually occurred.[120] It was also in this context that Southern Tswana were instructed in the language of constitutionality and legality. To wit, they were encouraged to see their "tribes" as precursors, in miniature, of the European nation-state: bounded polities in which rightful potentates enjoyed territorial jurisdiction over their followers and exerted command over courts, armies, administrative arrangements,

---

119. It was not the only voice. Willan, among others, shows that the South African Tswana elite at the turn of this century became a vital source of cultural production and the assertion of collective interest; Brian Willan, *Sol Plaatje: South African Nationalist, 1876–1932* (Berkeley and Los Angeles: University of California Press, 1984). This elite eschewed tribal differences in favor of broader ethnic identities—although even the latter were regarded ambivalently (especially by those who joined the South African Native National Congress, an organization that cut across ethnic divisions). In the Bechuanaland Protectorate, indigenous invocations of "Bechuana" identity became more frequent after overrule in 1885 and often had an undisguised political character. Thus, for example, Chirenje tells how Chief Sebele of the Kwena tried to persuade another local ruler "to adopt a pan-Tswana and anti-British attitude . . . to colonial rule"; J. Mutero Chirenje, *Chief Kgama and his Times c.1835–1923: The Story of a Southern African Ruler* (London: Rex Collings, 1978), 27–28 (quoted by F. J. Ramsay, *The Rise and Fall of the Bakwena Dynasty*, 189).

120. See J. and J. L. Comaroff, *Of Revelation and Revolution*, chap. 7.

legislative procedures, and "foreign" affairs. The Africans turned out to be quick studies. In 1884, for instance, the ruler of the Tshidi Rolong, a large Southern Tswana grouping, agreed to a draft a treaty with the Crown written thus:[121]

> I give the Queen to rule in my country . . . I give her to publish laws and to change them when necessary, and to make known the modes of procedure of the courts, and to appoint judges and magistrates, and police, and other officers of government as may be necessary, and to regulate their duties and authority . . . [Also] to collect money (taxes) . . . which will go to defray the expenses of the work done in this country by the Queen; and to levy court-fees, to impose fines, and to employ the money thus obtained according to the laws of the Queen.

In 1903, his heir would ask the Colonial Secretary, on behalf of the "Barolong *Nation*,"[122] to recognize "our rights and privileges as loyal citizens." This kind of rhetoric, which became the common tender of colonial diplomacy, was often penned by evangelists. But it was uttered with growing fluency—if not always with great conviction[123]— by local leaders. And once its terms were internalized, in the parole of "tribal" politics, they were duly extended to ethnonational imaginings. That is how Tswana came to speak in the modernist argot of entitlements and legalities about a political community that did not exist, a community that was imagined for them long before it was imagined by them.

Fourth and finally, parallel to the construction of Tswana ethnicity went the progressive erosion of chiefly authority. Most evangelists, especially early on, treated local rulers with respect, abetted them in their dealings, and promised not to interfere in affairs of state;[124] some, by contrast, subverted those leaders who opposed the

---

121. [Draft] Treaty between Paramount Chief Montsioa, his Sons and Councillors and the Imperial Government, Mafikeng, 22 May 1884 [Molema-Plaatje Papers (University of the Witwatersrand), Chief Montshiwa Correspondence, Ba 9].

122. Paramount Chief, Headmen and Councillors [Tshidi-Rolong], Mafikeng, January 1903 [Molema-Plaatje Papers (University of the Witwatersrand), Chief Wessels Papers, Bb 3].

123. Cf. Ramsay, *The Rise and Fall of the Bakwena Dynasty*.

124. Some asserted openly that strong sovereigns and stable polities facilitated their work; see J. and J. L. Comaroff, *Of Revelation and Revolution*, chap. 7.

gospel; one or two came to see the chief*ship* per se as an obstacle to the civilizing mission and urged its disestablishment.[125] Over the long run, however, these differences were inconsequential: by forcing a wedge between secular and sacred authority, and by introducing alternative bases of power and legitimacy, the presence of the church itself wrought wide-ranging changes in vernacular politics. In this it was exacerbated by a colonial state that narrowed "native" legal jurisdiction, made indigenous sovereigns into tax collectors and civil servants, enforced Pax Britannica, and redefined the scope of tribal administration. And so, ironically, the more Tswana discovered and asserted a collective identity based on "traditional" affinities, the less any "traditional" political figures—singular or plural—had the wherewithal to represent them or their concerns.[126] A number of royals, it is true, remained quite influential into this century; a few, on occasion, took it upon themselves to act on behalf of "the Bechuana"—most famously when three chiefs traveled to London in 1895, accompanied by Rev. W. C. Willoughby, to protest the transfer of Bechuanaland to the British South Africa Company.[127] But such things occurred less

---

125. See, for example, Dachs, "Missionary Imperialism." Mackenzie was the most avid opponent of the chiefship. His plans for introducing a "territorial government" into "Austral Africa" would have removed all indigenous political and legal institutions. See Mackenzie, *Austral Africa*; Sillery, *John Mackenzie*.

126. When Botswana gained independence, Seretse Khama, heir to the Ngwato chiefship—the most powerful of all "traditional" Tswana offices—emerged as leader of the Botswana Democratic Party and became President. In the country itself, his prominence was widely attributed to his place in the cartography of customary politics. But this explanation is too simple: Khama's rise was occasioned by processes and forces characteristic of late colonialism.

127. See, for example, Paul R. Maylam, *Rhodes, the Tswana, and the British: Colonialism, Collaboration, and Conflict in the Bechuanaland Protectorate, 1885–1899* (Westport and London: Greenwood Press, 1980); Ramsay, *The Rise and Fall of the Bakwena Dynasty*. In the Bechuanaland Protectorate, chiefs (and other notables) formed an African Advisory Council from 1920 onwards; in South Africa, a few Tswana rulers found their way onto a Natives' Representative Council (1936–1951). See Isaac Schapera, *The Tswana* (London: International African Institute, 1953), 49–50; Isaac Schapera and John L. Comaroff, *The Tswana*, rev. ed. (London: Kegan Paul International/International African Institute, 1991), 44. These councils were ostensibly created to allow for "native leadership" to influence policy. But, official rhetoric aside, it is clear that they had little impact. The Bechuanaland diaries of Sir Charles Rey give revealing glimpses of the manner in which Tswana chiefs were regarded by the administration. Although Rey's writings are not an especially reliable historical source, his often unguarded comments provide fascinating material for an ethnographer of the archives; Charles F. Rey, *Monarch of All I Survey: Bechuanaland Diaries, 1929–1937*, ed. N. Parsons and M. Crowder (Gaborone: The Botswana Society; New York: Lilian Barber Press; London: James Currey, 1988).

and less as the colonial state in South Africa undermined local authority and divided as it ruled: the objectification of "the Bechuana," as an
ethnic group with an awareness of its own objectives, unfolded
amidst a deepening legitimation crisis—or, more properly, in a deepening political void. It was a void that would only be substantially
filled when new bases of political association, action, and representation began to emerge during the twentieth century.[128]

Drawing all this together, then, the discourse of primal sovereignty led to the construction of "the Bechuana" as an ethnic group
with inalienable rights: the right to exist, to speak its own language, to
occupy its own territory, to follow its own leaders and customs, to
husband its own interests, and so on. At the same time, however,
setswana, the primal "stuff" that made these people what they were,
was taken to be inescapably primitive; the kind of thing that had to be
erased if Africans were to be remade into moderns. The fact that the
precolonial Tswana world had had its own elaborate repertoire of
rights, its own theories of sovereignty and representation, its own
practices of personhood and property, simply went unrecognized.[129]
Further, because everyday vernacular politics were "tribal"—they
were translated into the refined language of European civics only to
be ceded to the Crown—the capacity of "the Bechuana" for political
self-representation was negated prior even to their genesis as an imagined community.

In the colonial discourse of rights, in sum, the attribution of primal sovereignty had a paradoxical quality. Apart from all else, it was
erected, to use the language of critical postmodernism, on an impossibility: in order to make "the Bechuana" into civilized moderns, it was
necessary to unmake what it was that made them Bechuana in the
first place, to remove the differences that made them different—

---

128. In this respect, as Richard Werbner has reminded me (personal communication), the situation in South Africa differed—by being much more extreme—from that
in the Bechuanaland Protectorate. In the latter case, chiefly jurisdiction was rather less
constrained; the legitimation crisis did not run nearly as deep as it did across the
border.

129. Cf. Simon A. Roberts, "The Tswana Polity and 'Tswana Law and Custom'
Reconsidered," *Journal of Southern African Studies* 12 (1985): 75–87. Due to limitations of
space, I cannot discuss precolonial (indigenous) theories of rights, sovereignty, representation, property, and so on—even though they figured centrally in the dialectical
process through which Tswana personhood was remade during the colonial encounter.
It is a topic, however, that is taken up in J. L. and J. Comaroff, *Of Revelation and
Revolution*, vol. 2.

notwithstanding that it was the civilizing mission that had conjured "them" up to start with. But this is only where the paradoxes begin. Colonialism invented groupings, with no previous existence, that were said to have rights, which were only made palpable by virtue either of their absence or of their being given up. It was only because "Bechuana" land was being seized by Europeans that "Bechuanaland" was said to exist by right and to require protection (if only so that it might be "voluntarily" alienated to European control); only because indigenous authority was being superseded by the state that a right to sovereign autonomy was articulated (if only so that local rulers might formally "petition" for European overrule); only because the language of command had become English that the right of self-expression in Setswana was essayed (if only so that Tswana might submit to the Crown in their own tongue). Here, in short, was a world of virtual realities, a world in which things were reified primarily by the recognition of their nonbeing. But there was also something more sinister at issue. Since people were held to have rights as a consequence of their membership in an ethnic group, it was also possible to remove those (or other) rights on the same basis. As we shall see, because of its putatively "premodern" infrastructure, primal sovereignty was to be used to limit, dispossess, and disenfranchise Tswana from the time of colonial overrule onward. But more of that in a moment.

Contradiction, Consciousness, Contestation

Contradictions, Recognized and Unrecognized

Most of the evangelists saw no contradiction, no disjuncture in the discourse of rights, between the register of radical individualism and that of primal sovereignty; indeed, they did not explicitly distinguish them at all. The effort to implant modern, right-bearing individualism might have pointed toward a society of free *universal citizens*, while the conjuring up of a primordial Bechuana identity gestured toward the creation of *ethnic subjects*. From their perspective, however, the two things were part of a seamless campaign to rework the indigenous world, one describing that world as it was, the other as it ought to be. The former, in short, was a narrative of being, of congealed "tradition"; the latter, a narrative of becoming, of revealed "modernity."

In fact, for the mission, the universal citizen and the ethnic subject, liberal individualism and primal sovereignty, were conditions of each other's possibility—if for reasons not readily appreciated by the Europeans. British colonialism, and colonial evangelism, was everywhere two-faced, everywhere a double gesture. On the one hand, it justified itself in terms of difference and inequality: the greater enlightenment of the colonizer legitimized his right to rule and to civilize. On the other hand, that legitimacy was founded, ostensibly, on a commitment to the eventual erasure of difference in the name of a common humanity and modernity. Of course, had the difference actually been removed, the bases of overrule would themselves have disappeared. It was not; they did not. Colonialism, in short, promised equality but sustained inequality; promised universal rights but kept the ruled in a state of relative rightlessness; promised individual advancement but produced ethnic subjection. In South Africa as elsewhere, the discourse of radical individualism and modern personhood bore the promise; the discourse of primal sovereignty and ethnic subjection, the realpolitik. It was by virtue of the latter, too, that "the Bechuana" were engrossed within a larger, more inclusive form of marking, of coloration and devaluation: that of race, in which all shades of non-European ethnicity, all kinds of colonial otherness, were finally submerged. The evangelists might have seen themselves as "friends of the natives." But like other Europeans, they viewed Africans as generic and genetic inferiors, primitive beings still a long way back on the great evolutionary road of universal history. Had they not, the civilizing mission would have had no reason to be.

I said that *most* evangelists did not see the disjuncture. One or two did. John Mackenzie's dreams for "Austral Africa" came to envisage a colorless citizenry in which "natives" would eventually be indistinguishable from anyone else. There ought to be no reservations, he argued, no tribal protectorates, no special entitlements for ethnic or racial groups,[130] just imperial subjects with equal rights. For Mackenzie, this was the only way to deal with the antinomy between universal citizenship and tribal attachments, between the perpetuation

---

130. See Ake Holmberg, *African Tribes and European Agencies: Colonialism and Humanitarianism in British South and East Africa, 1870–1895* (Göteborg: Scandinavian University Books, 1966), 55f; Kenneth O. Hall, "Humanitarianism and Racial Subordination: John Mackenzie and the Transformation of Tswana Society," *The International Journal of African Historical Studies* 8 (1975): 97–110, esp. 102; Reginald I. Lovell, *The Struggle for South Africa, 1875–1899: A Study in Economic Imperialism* (New York: Macmillan, 1934), 48f.

and removal of difference—though, obviously, he would not have put it quite this way. There is an instructive lesson in his exceptionalism. Of all the clerics, Mackenzie was the most vociferous imperialist—and *anti*-colonialist. He seems to have realized that the rhetoric of primal sovereignty would be used against the Tswana by white colonials as long as their rights depended on their ethnic and racial identity. Said he:[131]

> There is nothing in the superstition or the customs of these tribes to disqualify them from exercising their rights as subjects of the Queen, when education enables them to do so . . . There is nothing whatever in the character of the South African native to deter us from trusting him with the exercise of . . . 'rights' after the manner of the English constitution . . .

To withhold these "inherent rights" on the basis of color or race, tribe or nation, he added,[132] "is a deadly delusion."

Double Consciousness, Double Standards, and the Denial of Rights

As I have already intimated, the chimera of primal sovereignty was to be used to disenfranchise and disable black South Africans, thwarting their efforts to become free, right-bearing, propertied citizens. In this respect, recall my earlier point that Southern Tswana, one and all, had been familiarized with the authoritative rhetoric of rights by the realpolitik of the frontier; that some discerned in it the "English mode of warfare"; that others, most notably the rising elite, had internalized the Protestant ethic and the spirit of liberal individualism. It was predictable, then, that "the Bechuana," both as incipient ethnonation and as a congeries of chiefdoms, should fight the implications of overrule in the language of individual and collective entitlement, invoking it to protest against their loss of autonomy, the seizure of their territory, the imposition of taxes, the conditions of wage labor, and so on. It was also to be expected that colonizers—statesmen, settlers, manufacturers, mine managers—would speak back in the same language, often wielding it as a blunt instrument.

---

131. Mackenzie, *Austral Africa*, 2:456.
132. Ibid., 2:461.

Let me give just one example in lieu of a history of the struggle over rights in this colonial theater. It concerns a Land Commission set up by the British authorities in 1886, soon after the establishment of the Bechuanaland Protectorate and British Bechuanaland, but before the latter was absorbed by South Africa.[133]

Like many such commissions, the brief of this one was to clear up conflicting territorial claims among local "tribes," and between them and white settlers, thus paving the way for Pax Britannica. Its more self-interested aim, arguably, was to gather intelligence and to lay the geopolitical foundations for an effective administration.[134] Among the disputes heard by the Land Commission was a minor wrangle between two neighboring chiefdoms, the Tshidi Rolong and the Ngwaketse, over some 432 square miles of remote pasture that lay in their mutual borderland. Montshiwa, the Tshidi chief to whom it was awarded, used the occasion to press for the introduction of individual land ownership, registered by title deed. A canny ruler, he had learned well the language of liberal individualism; in particular, he was aware of the salience of private property to British notions of civility and modernity. Among other things, Montshiwa held that, if freehold were granted and deeds lodged with the government, the latter would have to protect Tswana owners from settler expropriation. According to Tshidi informants many years on, he also thought that the creation of heritable individual property rights might prepare the ground for other kinds of rights as well; but there is no documentary trace of any of this. What we do know, however, is that Montshiwa, strongly backed by his advisers, argued the case in a manner that would have done John Stuart Mill proud: those who had occupied the land, he said, deserved to own it

---

133. The Land Commission report is to be found in Great Britain (Colonial Office), *Report of the Commissioners Appointed to Determine Land Claims . . . in British Bechuanaland* (London: H.M.S.O., C.4889, 1886). For accounts of the events described here, see Isaac Schapera, *Report on the System of Land-Tenure on the Barolong Farms in the Bechuanaland Protectorate* (Report submitted to the Bechuanaland Protectorate government, 1943; abridged and reprinted, *Botswana Notes and Records*, 15 (1983): 15–38); John L. Comaroff, *The Structure of Agricultural Transformation in Barolong* (Gaborone: Botswana Government Printer, 1977). Mackenzie, who became involved after the event, also wrote a commentary; Mackenzie, *Austral Africa*, 2:336ff.

134. For an excellent analysis of the impact of government inquiries and official discourse on the (re)construction of indigenous populations, see Adam Ashforth, *The Politics of Official Discourse in Twentieth-Century South Africa* (Oxford: Clarendon Press, 1990). Although based in South Africa, this study has important comparative implications.

because they had "improved" it. And they would do so even more if they had secure, permanent, heritable possession.[135]

The Land Commission rejected the argument on the ground that "the Bechuana" were "not ready" for individual ownership; governed still by primal custom and primitive communalism, they were still insufficiently civilized. The old "tradition," whereby the chief was the owner of land as custodian for the tribe, ought yet to prevail. As a subsequent commission, the highly influential South African Native Affairs Commission of 1903–5,[136] was to say in its *Report*, "the Native population as a whole *instinctively* cling to and cherish the communal system."[137] What is more, the *Report* went on:[138]

> [While] it is largely held to-day, that individualism is ultimately conducive to greater industry, enterprise and production,...our limited experience has not in all cases furnished proof of this.

Having been told for almost a century that "healthy individualism" was both the means and the measure of their move toward modernity, black South Africans were to be informed that, even if they no longer "cherished" their communal ways, *their* kind of individualism was somehow different, lesser. More immediately, however, in dismissing the Tshidi case for private tenure, the Bechuanaland Land Commission simply ignored the fact that most of the intended recipients of titles

---

135. I refer here to Mill's arguments for the moral and material value of private property—in particular, to his famous popularization of Arthur Young's statement: "The magic of property turns sand into gold . . . Give a man the secure possession of a bleak rock, and he will turn it into a garden; give him nine years' lease of a garden, and he will convert it into a desert." See Arthur Young, *Travels in France During the Years 1787, 1788, & 1789; undertaken more particularly with a view of ascertaining the cultivation, wealth, resources, and national prosperity of the Kingdom of France*, 2 vols. (London: Richardson, 1794), 1:50; John Stuart Mill, *Collected Works of John Stuart Mill*, vols. 2 and 3: *Principles of Political Economy with Some of Their Applications to Social Philosophy* (Toronto: University of Toronto Press, 1965), 2:274.

136. This Commission was set up, before the establishment of the Union of South Africa, to prepare the way for a future "native administration"; see South Africa (Native Affairs Commission), *Report of the South African Native Affairs Commission, 1903–5* (Cape Town: Cape Times Ltd, 1905), 5. While recommending that most blacks continue to live under "the communal system," it suggested that individual leasehold of "arable plots" should be permitted in very limited circumstances and under highly restricted conditions (28).

137. Ibid., 26; italics mine.

138. Ibid., 27.

were highly educated mission school alumni and members of a propertied new middle class. To wit, the commissioners never deigned to
ask *who* the landowners would actually be. Their rationale for rejecting
the request—the tacit appeal to the sovereignty of custom—did not
admit a discourse of individuation. Even more, it actively denied it.
After all, the nub of primal sovereignty is the specious notion that, in
their "natural" (instinctive?) attachment to their ways, ethnic subjects
are all alike.

Montshiwa fought the decision and, in the end, gained a compromise: the territory—which was to fall into the Bechuanaland Protectorate (not British Bechuanaland, thence South Africa)—could be divided up into farms and leased, on an annually renewable basis, to
individuals. But its ownership had to remain, "according to native
custom," with the ruler and the tribe. Interestingly, after these farms
were distributed, the terms of their leases were never enforced. They
were treated by everyone concerned as if they were freehold. The
nature of their tenure was to remain ambiguous until Botswana became independent, whereupon its government declared the matter
finally resolved: the Barolong Farms, as the territory was called, was
"tribal" land.

The Land Commission of 1886, like innumerable others to follow
it, did not just deny the possibility of individual property (and other)
rights in the face of indigenous demand. Nor did it merely abort a
move in the direction of liberal individualism. It also negated the
collective capacity of a community and its leaders to remake their own
world by due process. Until overrule, Tswana chiefs regularly legislated changes in social policy, often transforming institutional, residential, and material arrangements in response to historical contingencies and shifts in popular opinion.[139] Prior to the British presence,
there was no reason why Chief Montshiwa should not have introduced some form of individual tenure through internal legislative
procedures, provided that there was sufficient support for the measure. Certainly, other sovereigns had made laws (*melao*) in the spirit of
liberal modernity. But official administrative practice effectively closed
off that possibility by asserting the primal sovereignty of custom

---

139. See Isaac Schapera, *Tribal Legislation among the Tswana of the Bechuanaland
Protectorate* (London: London School of Economics, 1943), *Tribal Innovators: Tswana
Chiefs and Social Change, 1795–1940* (London: Athlone Press, 1970).

above all else. At a stroke, the historical dynamics of Tswana politics were severely debilitated.

This, I stress, is just one example. There are many more. From the notorious Land Act of 1913[140] through a series of laws, proclamations, and other measures, "non-Europeans" were cumulatively denied individual rights or prospects of citizenship. The process began when the Commission of 1903–5 recommended that blacks should only have limited, indirect franchise.[141] And it culminated in the thoroughly racinated culture of apartheid, which was legitimized by direct appeal to primal sovereignty: to the notion, first, that "natives" naturally preferred their own traditions to the alien practices of European modernity, and ought therefore to live by them; and second, that they lacked the enlightenment, as individuals, to determine their own being-in-the-world. But that is a well-known story, a narrative that runs right up to the present.

Colonialism in South Africa, then, from its genesis in the civilizing mission to the age of apartheid, inculcated in Southern Tswana a double-consciousness to match the two-faced character of the discourse of rights itself.[142] One and all, they were encouraged to embark on the road to modernity, to fashion themselves into citizens of the civilized world. At the same time, as black Africans, they were made into ethnic subjects, ineluctably tied to their fellows, to their primal origins, and to *setswana*, a body of custom that marked them as premodern—and was invoked to deny them the kind of personhood to which they were exhorted to aspire. Precisely because of the paradoxical, polymorphous nature of the discourse of rights, as I said before, Tswana came to know themselves, and their objectified "tradition," at once by attribution and erasure; by virtue of a positive construction of identity and by its negation. *Setswana*, to those who shared it, was a highly valued possession, the cultural product of a proud history. Yet, through much of the colonial epoch, "the Bechuana" had to hear that it was better set aside. Is it any wonder that resistance to overrule should have taken root in the crevices and contradictions of their colonial experience, on the terrain between its promise and its reality? Or that

---

140. Solomon T. Plaatje, *Native Life in South Africa* (New York: The Crisis, n.d.).
141. South Africa, *Commission, 1903–5*, 97.
142. The allusion to W. E. B. Du Bois, and to the African American experience, is, of course, deliberate.

they should have contested European domination sometimes by asserting their universal rights as citizens of empire, sometimes through
carnivals of violence, rites of rebellion, and uprisings that bore the
distinctive stamp of *setswana*? These forms of protest—which came to
give voice to the double-consciousness of the colonized, racialized,
ethnic subject—have hardly been confined to South Africa, of course.
Ethnicity everywhere at once constructs people, placing them definitively in the world, and effaces them, submerging their individuality
and opening them up to the stigmatization of otherness. In some circumstances, it also affords them a basis to protest the contours of the
world as they find it. Clearly, the discourse of rights is one of the
terrains on which all this occurs, especially under colonialism. For
Tswana, it was central in shaping their identity, past and present.
  And future.

Contestation: Back to the Future

In the contemporary struggle for South Africa, the two dominant
styles of formal black political engagement—represented by the African National Congress (ANC) and the Inkatha Freedom Party (IFP)—
are each heir to one of the registers in the colonial discourse of rights.
A sizable communist membership notwithstanding, the ANC has always stuck close to the ideology of liberal modernism implanted by
Protestant evangelism; it grew out of the South African Native National Congress (*SANNC*), formed in 1912 to protest the Land Act,
and was led primarily by mission products, many of them Tswana.
The SANNC spoke the language of civil and constitutional rights,
relying heavily on rhetorical styles learned in church. In its dealings
with successive governments, moreover, it took a line more notable
for its liberal individualism than for its populism. While it envisaged a
nonracial democratic South Africa, its spokesmen (they *were* all males)
argued insistently that blacks who had improved themselves ought to
enjoy all the rights attendant on their achievements. Ethnicity was
deliberately ignored: the SANNC was steadfastly supratribal, even
pan-African, in its composition and its horizons, and avoided any
hint of identity politics. It was also emphatically British in orientation
and nonviolent in its technologies of protest. As we all know, its
efforts were not rewarded. While there are some important differ-

ences,[143] the ANC, which has a large Tswana following, retains much of the style and political ideology of its predecessor. It continues to talk the language of rights and universal citizenship; as Hobsbawm recently intimated,[144] it sustains a continuing commitment to a classically European form of nationalism.[145] Significantly, in negotiating the future, its leaders have paid painstaking attention to the promulgation of a liberal democratic constitution—although they have been pushed to concede collective rights and protections along ethnic and racial lines.

By contrast, the assertively Zulu-centric IFP owes its origins to the politics of primal sovereignty; in particular, to the creation, under apartheid, of "homelands" for tribal groupings constructed during the colonial era. The ideology and political style of Inkatha has always been ethnonationalist in tenor: since cultural identities run deeper than any other kind of attachment, goes the familiar argument, their bearers have a natural right to determine their own affairs and to be ruled by their own ("traditional") authorities. If a South African nation is to exist at all, then, it ought to give ethnic communities a high degree of autonomy, reserving to the state only those functions that cannot be devolved downward. The objective here is to secure collective entitlements—rather than unencumbered universal suffrage or individual rights—in a federated, pluralistic polity. The kind of politics that pursues this objective is typically fought along lines of ethnic cleavage, often with so-called "cultural weapons" both rhetorical and military. It is also contradictory: the IFP leadership is ardently pro-capitalist and, when it is expedient, will resort readily to the idiom of modernist politics. Inkatha, of course, is a Zulu phenomenon. But similar claims were heard until recently in Bophuthatswana, the "homeland" created for Tswana in the early 1970s. And they continue to reverberate in

---

143. Among the differences are (1) an engagement in armed struggle (after a long, futile commitment to nonviolence); and (2) talk, dating back to the Freedom Charter of the 1950s, of the possible nationalization of some public resources.

144. Eric J. Hobsbawm, "Ethnicity and Nationalism in Europe Today," *Anthropology Today* 8 (1992): 3–8.

145. See John L. Comaroff, "Ethnicity, Nationalism and the Politics of Difference in an Age of Revolution," forthcoming in *Ethnicity, Identity and Nationalism in South Africa*, ed. E. Wilmsen and P. McAllister; in *Postcoloniality and Nationalism*, ed. M. Roth and E. Barkan; and in *Perspectives on Nationalism and War*, ed. J. L. Comaroff and P. C. Stern (New York: Gordon and Breach).

white conservative circles. The colonial discourse of rights—its contradictions, paradoxes, and perversities intact—continues to make
itself felt as a new dawn rises on the South African postcolony.[146]

Conclusion

It goes without saying that colonizing processes did not work out in
exactly the same way throughout Africa. In British Tanganyika[147] and
French West Africa,[148] for example, the state seems to have encouraged individual landholding and private property more than it did in
South Africa. Nonetheless, the colonial encounter *does* appear everywhere to have involved a discourse of rights—a discourse in which
local peoples were made into ethnic subjects, racinated, and recast in
an often agonistic dialectic of construction and negation.

This is not to say that colonization was a monolithic movement
through which an expansive Europe imposed itself, systematically
and inexorably, on the peripheral populations of the planet. It may
have been a world-historical process. But it played itself out in multiple registers and in disconcertingly ambiguous ways. Never just, nor
even mainly, an affair of states and governments, an epic orchestrated
by heroic figures, it was carried on in thousands of contexts, both
mundane and magisterial, by castes of characters with different

---

146. So much so, in fact, that a "Freedom Alliance" was formed in 1993 between
the leaders of KwaZulu and Bophuthatswana on one side and conservative whites on
the other. Underlying this coalition was a shared belief in primal sovereignty and the
"natural" rights of ethnic groups. For those accustomed to reading South African history as a narrative of racial struggle, the establishment of this Freedom Alliance must
have been an irony of cosmic proportions. After all, it brought together long-standing
racial enemies in common commitment to an ideology of race. Another point here: as I
argue elsewhere, most of the recent violence in South Africa—and in other places torn
by similar ethnic struggles—has not been perpetrated between "tribes" or ethnic
groups. *Pace* the popular media, it has occurred across the line, the epistemic political
abyss, that divides primal sovereignty from liberal individualism; between, that is, two
contrasting ontologies and images of personhood, polity, subjectivity, modernity. See
John L. Comaroff, "Ethnicity, Violence, and the Politics of Identity," in *Etnicidad y
Violencia*, ed. J. Antonio Fernandez de Rota (La Coruna: Universidade da Coruna,
1995).

147. See C. Louise Sweet, "Inventing Crime: British Colonial Land Policy in Tanganyika," in *Crime, Justice and Underdevelopment*, ed. C. Sumner (London: Heinemann,
1982).

148. See Francis G. Snyder, "Colonialism and Legal Form: The Creation of 'Customary Law' in Senegal," in *Crime, Justice and Underdevelopment*, ed. C. Sumner (London: Heinemann, 1982).

means and ends. As we have seen, moreover, it was often a very messy business, wherein Europeans—settlers, evangelists, capitalists, administrators, army colonels—fought among themselves to impress their wills on the bodies, the being, the terrain of *in*significant others. These differences among the colonizers, to be sure, did not do much to ease the experience of the colonized. Still, they did create an awareness of fissures in the seams of European domination; fissures at which local resistance was directed as the impact of overrule made itself felt.

Note, too, that many of the "civilized" practices exported from Britain to the colonies were anything but uncontested at home—not least rights to property, to fair labor conditions, to the franchise. As even a cursory reading of J. S. Mill makes clear,[149] peasant proprietorship and private smallholding were not deeply entrenched in the English countryside, despite efforts to essay their virtues by, among others, Mill himself. Some contemporary "condition of England" novels, like Disraeli's *Sybil*, actually rehearse the arguments for and against individual tenure;[150] this text, itself a strident polemic for the "rights of labour," also suggests that struggles over civil and constitutional rights in the colonies were implicated in debates about the situation of the British working class.[151] Patently, the imperial frontier was not a place where a mature ideology of rights was presented, fully tried and tested, to premodern Africans. It was a space in which the unfolding sociolegal and political histories of Britain and Africa met—there to be made, reciprocally, in relation to each other. Indeed, colonialism, in the nineteenth century, was as much about reconstructing metropolitan England in the image of a triumphant bourgeoisie as it was about enlightening blacks abroad.[152]

An important qualification here: for all its association with legalities, the introduction of a modernist discourse of rights to "the Bechuana" and other African peoples was not merely a matter of law. It involved, as some of the missionaries themselves understood,[153] a cultural revolution. For this discourse bore with it an elaborate ideology of

---

149. J. S. Mill, *Collected Works*, vols. 2 and 3: *Principles of Political Economy.*
150. Benjamin Disraeli, *Sybil, or The Two Nations*, ed. T. Braun (Harmondsworth: Penguin, 1980; first edition, 1855), 91–94.
151. Ibid., 343.
152. J. L. and J. Comaroff, *Ethnography and the Historical Imagination*, chap. 10.
153. Philip, *Researches in South Africa*, 2:355; Mackenzie, *The Papers of John Mackenzie*, 72.

personhood, of social contract, of material relations. The fetishization of rights, in short, was itself part of an embracing worldview—a worldview in which, self-evidently, the language of entitlement appeared liberatory; which is why colonial evangelists saw liberal individualism as an emancipation from the enchantment of custom and communalism, from the tyranny of tradition and the chiefship. For Tswana, things seemed somewhat different, somewhat less sanguine. They always do from the perspective of the colonized. Endowed with a culture whose faiths and fetishes were not the same, the Africans—like Fuentes's fictional revolutionaries—were quick to learn that "[without] equality . . . all rights are chimeras," that the law may indeed have been the greatest, most absurd thing imaginable. On the one hand, it *was* a devastating instrument of warfare, like no other in its capacity to annihilate and dispossess without being seen to do anything at all. And yet, on the other hand, the appeal to rights was a means that, over the long run, came to be used by black South Africans in self-protection—not always successfully, but not always in vain, either. More to the point, it often seemed to be the *only* real means to hand, since it was part of the technology of rule on which rested the inequalities and disablements from which they suffered. This is why the language of the law sui generis is reducible neither to a brute weapon of control nor simply to an instrument of resistance. The inherently contradictory character of the colonial discourse of rights—its duality of registers and the double-consciousness to which it gave rise—ensured that it would be engaged on both sides of the dialectic of domination and defiance. It still does. Everywhere.

One last point, about the general and the particular. My account has focused narrowly on a South African people at a remote edge of the British Empire; such is the anthropologist's privilege. But the larger point of this excursion has been to scrutinize some generic features of colonialism and, specifically, the discourse of rights within it. Many of the processes discussed here, I would argue, are discernible in all colonizing contexts. Among the latter I include not only the overseas "possessions" of imperial powers once great, now greatly humbled. I also have in mind contemporary colonialisms "at home," the kind suffered in the Chicano barrios of Los Angeles, the black inner city of Chicago, the West African peripheries of Paris, the Turkish streets of Berlin, the white ghettos of unwaged Liverpool. And innumerable other places both far and near.

Part 2. Rights in Political Struggles

Nothing Left but Rights: Law in the Struggle against Apartheid

Richard L. Abel

The struggle against apartheid was one of the great moral dramas of the twentieth century. Rarely have good and evil been so unambiguous, the stakes so high, and the conflict so long, bitter, and costly. Race (and gender) has dominated history since World War I almost as much as class and nation did before that watershed. The century began with an unquestioning acceptance of racism, both Jim Crow laws and colonialism. Midcentury witnessed genocide in the name of racism. Desegregation and decolonialism after World War II began the dismantling of racism. Apartheid was its last bastion for several decades.

The Setting

Law played a central role in the struggle against apartheid for several reasons. First, other arenas were effectively closed to Blacks. Whites had arrogated a monopoly of political power from the moment they settled at the Cape in 1652. The Nationalists completed the exclusion of Blacks by stripping the Cape Coloured of the franchise in 1957. Although P. W. Botha's 1983 constitutional "reform" granted Indians and "Coloureds" separate houses in a tricameral Parliament dominated by

This chapter is based on fieldwork in South Africa in 1990 and 1991. I am grateful to the University of the Witwatersrand Law School for hospitality and assistance; the lawyers, parties, and organizations involved in the struggle against apartheid for their time and access to documents; and the UCLA Academic Senate, the UCLA Law School Dean's Fund, and the Law and Social Science Program of the National Science Foundation (SES 9012250) for financial support. A full account of the ten cases briefly discussed here appears in my book *Politics by Other Means: Law in the Struggle Against Apartheid 1980–94* (New York: Routledge, 1995).

a white President's Council, Africans were relegated to subordinate political roles in urban townships and rural homelands, whose regimes the long-suffering subjects accurately repudiated as impotent and corrupt. Extraparliamentary opposition was tightly controlled through the banning of mass organizations (notably the African National Congress, or ANC), the passage of increasingly draconian security laws, and the declaration of the State of Emergency in 1985 (renewed annually through 1990). The government censored all forms of public expression, eventually barring foreign reporters from scenes of unrest. Despite the courage of individual cadres, Umkhonto we Sizwe (MK; Spear of the Nation—the armed wing of the ANC) never seriously threatened the hegemony of the South African Defense Force, which outgunned the combined armies of all the rest of black Africa. Indeed, South Africa freely wielded its military might not only within its borders but also throughout the frontline states (Namibia, Angola, Mozambique, Botswana, Zimbabwe, and Zambia).

Second, the white regime loudly proclaimed its own fidelity to the rule of law. Liberal ideals were prominent, sometimes even dominant, during the half century between the formation of the Union and the National Party's 1948 electoral victory. When the Supreme Court rebuffed the government's extension of apartheid to the franchise in 1952, the Nationalists expanded and packed the Appellate Division— exactly the legalistic strategy Franklin D. Roosevelt had threatened (for different ends) two decades earlier. Comparison of the two countries does not always show us to advantage. At about the same time that the United States was prosecuting communists under the Smith Act and House and Senate committees were persecuting them through hearings, South Africa launched a treason trial against 156 leaders, intending to destroy the opposition through legal means. Unlike American judges, however, their South African brethren acquitted all the accused. In 1968 the South African Department of Foreign Affairs responded to international criticism by publishing a book brazenly entitled *South Africa and the Rule of Law.* For more than forty years the government constructed the legal edifice of apartheid—a regulatory structure whose complexity rivaled that of the most sophisticated tax code or protective legislation.[1]

---

1. For an assessment of South Africa's pretensions, see David Dyzenhaus, *Hard Cases in Wicked Legal Systems: South African Law in the Perspective of Legal Philosophy* (Oxford: Clarendon Press, 1991).

Third, the opposition enthusiastically embraced legality as both a principle and a strategy. The African National Congress was a legal organization for half a century before it was banned. In 1952 (almost a decade earlier than the American civil rights movement) it launched the Defiance Campaign, a nonviolent strategy inspired in part by Mohandas Gandhi's practice in both South Africa and India, which challenged apartheid in public buildings and parks. The government responded with massive violence and selective prosecution. Three years later the Congress of the People adopted the Freedom Charter, a strong affirmation of the rule of law, which has remained the platform of the ANC and other "charterist" organizations ever since.

Given this history, de Tocqueville's classic description of early-nineteenth-century America is nearly as appropriate to late-twentieth-century South Africa:

> Scarcely any political question arises . . . that is not resolved, sooner or later, into a judicial question. Hence all parties are obliged to borrow, in their daily controversies, the ideas and even the language, peculiar to judicial proceedings.[2]

In the late 1980s, for instance, a township debate over a government offer to sell houses cheaply to long-term tenants was adjourned when one participant insisted on consulting the Freedom Charter and seeking expert advice on whether its egalitarian collectivist principles could be reconciled with home ownership.

If the struggle against apartheid assumed legal forms, however, it was a uniquely South African legality. Unlike the United States, there were no constitutional limits on parliamentary supremacy. Unlike Britain, there was little that could be called a traditional or unwritten constitution. All the judges had been appointed by the National Party, which enjoyed uninterrupted rule from 1948 to 1994. Associations of advocates and attorneys and virtually all their members were acquiescent in if not complicit with the regime. South African jurisprudence is strongly positivist, and few academic lawyers openly criticized the government. Those who did were jailed: Albie Sachs, Barend van Niekerk, Raymond Suttner. In the mid-1980s, the level of despair was

---

2. Alexis de Tocqueville, *Democracy in America*, ed. Phillips Bradley (New York: Vintage Books, 1958), 1:290.

revealed by a debate between Raymond Wacks and John Dugard over whether judges had an obligation to resign (Wacks emigrated to Hong Kong shortly thereafter).

For these reasons, South Africa is a perfect test case of theories about legal autonomy. If the discourse of rights could survive such a hostile environment—empowering the opposition, shaping argumentation, perhaps even swaying officials sympathetic to the regime—it might deserve the attention scholars and lawyers have lavished on it. My research explores the extent to which and the circumstances under which legality shaped domination and resistance in South Africa during the 1980s.

Let me begin by situating that period within the larger historical framework. Like other liberation struggles, the antiapartheid movement experienced cycles of activity and repression. After the 1961 acquittal in the five-year treason trial the ANC despaired of legal change and adopted a policy of armed resistance. The government's ability to penetrate underground organizations allowed it to seize most of the ANC leadership at the Rivonia farm where they were hiding and, this time, convict and sentence them to heavy prison terms—Nelson Mandela and others to life. A long period of quiescence led to the black power movements of the 1970s and student opposition to Afrikaans as the medium of instruction under the detested system of "Bantu education." This resistance ended in the torture killing of black political activist Steve Biko at the hands of his captors, the successful prosecution of black power and student leaders, the crushing of the 1976 Soweto rebellion, and the flight of thousands into political exile and military organizations.[3]

The last cycle arose from these ashes but assumed a qualitatively different form. At the urging of large capital eager to increase productivity, which was constantly interrupted by labor unrest, the government institutionalized black trade unions, which rapidly organized millions of black workers. The Congress of South African Trade Unions (COSATU) overcame some of the deep ideological differences to unify many of the principal unions, including the powerful National Union of Mineworkers (NUM) and National Union of Metal Workers of South Africa (NUMSA), in a federation sympathetic to

---

3. Michael Lobban has explored the principal cases in *White Man's Justice: South African Political Trials in the Black Consciousness Era* (Oxford: Oxford University Press, 1995).

the ANC. The United Democratic Front (UDF) did the same for more than 600 organizations of residents, youths, women, church members, sports teams, and so on. Umkhonto we Sizwe, strengthened by recruits from the "Soweto generation," demonstrated its ability to bomb targets almost at will throughout South Africa. Despite U.S. President Reagan's policy of "constructive engagement," the international boycott intensified the hardship of a chronically recessionary economy increasingly dependent on international trade because more fully integrated into world markets. In 1984 the Vaal uprising against township rent increases and the corrupt tyranny of black local government stooges initiated an escalating sequence of resistance and repression (35,000 detentions, military occupation of the townships, thousands of deaths) that led unexpectedly to F. W. de Klerk's accession in September 1989, the prompt freeing of Mandela and other leaders, legalization of all opposition groups, the return of exiles, and the difficult but ultimately successful negotiations for democratic rule.

These events were accompanied by growing use of law to challenge the apartheid regime. The tiny handful of lawyers who had been representing the opposition since the war rapidly multiplied to fifty to 100 in the 1980s. Foreign donors provided ample funds for the defense of political prisoners, much of it conducted by private lawyers. The International Defense and Aid Fund channeled £100 million into the country over a quarter century; North American and Western European trade unions, churches, and lawyers' associations supplemented this. The examples of public interest law and activist legal services as well as the experience of Black Sash inspired the creation of the Legal Resource Centres, rural legal advice centers, the Centre for Applied Legal Studies at the University of the Witwatersrand, and its associated law firm of Cheadle, Thompson & Haysom. Black trade unions supported a rapidly expanding labor law bar.

The Cases

I investigated ten cases (or campaigns), chosen to contrast situations in which opposition and government were proactive or reactive, mobilized law or avoided it, in the principal terrains of confrontation: political authority, labor, and land. Brief descriptions follow to acquaint readers with the actors and events before I present the analysis.

Political Authority

Alexandra Five Treason Trial. In the mid-1980s the government launched three major treason trials. The Pietermaritzburg trial of UDF and trade union officials collapsed when the state's expert witness conceded he could not establish treasonous intent and the judge threw out transcriptions and translations of video and audio tapes, which the defense had shown to be hopelessly inaccurate. After creating a record of some 25,000 pages, accompanied by exhibits half again as long, the two-year Delmas trial ended in convictions and heavy sentences for key UDF leaders, which were overturned on appeal because the judge had committed procedural errors in dismissing an assessor. The government had a great deal riding on the third of these trials, intended to discredit both Moses Mayekiso (general secretary of the Metal and Allied Workers Union [MAWU]) and the entire trade union movement, and the Alexandra Action Committee and all community organizations, by associating them with the ANC and the excesses of people's courts. The accused surprised the prosecution with a comprehensive set of minutes of their meetings, but they faced difficulties in reconciling the exigencies of trial strategy with political integrity. Justice van der Walt, educated by a tour of Alexandra (probably his first visit to a black township) and impressed by the accused's dedication and intelligence, not only acquitted them but also criticized the government for having brought the charges.

"New Nation" Closure. Although the government long has wielded plenary power over the media, Emergency regulations allowed it to suspend newspapers for up to three months. It threatened and closed several opposition papers, notably the *New Nation*. In challenging this action, the paper had to walk a fine line between disavowing its attacks on the government and maintaining its commitment to ending apartheid. Like most of the attacks on the Emergency, this legalistic strategy failed.[4]

Conscientious Objection. Resistance to conscription has been one of the most visible contributions by Whites to the struggle against apartheid. Before 1980, only Jehovah's Witnesses refused to serve; during the 1980s they were joined by objectors holding various ethical and

---

4. See Stephen Ellmann, *In a Time of Trouble: Law and Liberty in South Africa's State of Emergency* (Oxford: Clarendon Press, 1992).

political beliefs. Several were jailed, some sentenced to six years. The two chosen for test cases could not have been more different. Ivan Toms was a doctor who established the only clinic in one of the poorest Cape townships. Deeply religious, he was involved in church activities and the End Conscription Campaign. David Bruce, a recent university graduate, was irreligious and shunned political organizations, basing his objections on a detestation of racism, which he traced to his mother's experience as a Jew in Nazi Germany. Although every previous court had read the relevant legislation as prescribing a *mandatory* prison term, the Appellate Division construed it as a *maximum*, allowing trial judges to take ethical scruples into account and impose minimal sentences. In the aftermath of this decision (and the repeal of the Population Registration Act—a cornerstone of apartheid), the entire conscription system unraveled.

Police Torture. The security forces routinely used torture to extract information, repress populations, eliminate leaders, and take revenge. When the government first declared the Emergency in July 1985, Eastern Cape security police in Port Elizabeth and Uitenhage rounded up and systematically tortured hundreds of prisoners. Dr. Wendy Orr had been appointed to the Prisons Department at the beginning of the year, immediately after graduating from university (where her fellowship required repayment through government service). Deeply disturbed by what she saw, Dr. Orr contacted a human rights lawyer and decided to seek an injunction. Her superior, who ten years earlier had certified the tortured Steve Biko as "fit" for the 800-mile trip during which he died, feared a new scandal and instructed her to photocopy all the medical records, in case the security police sought to destroy the evidence of its culpability. Her affidavit based on these records, together with those of prisoners' relatives, secured a temporary injunction and lawyer access to the prisoners. Their own affidavits and extensive coverage by the domestic and international media temporarily suspended this wave of state terror.

Inkatha Violence. Following the ouster of MAWU from the BTR Sarmcol plant in Howick (second case cited in upcoming Labor section) and its replacement by the Inkatha-aligned United Workers Union of South Africa (UWUSA), Inkatha decided to take over the company town, Mpophomeni, and eradicate support for MAWU and the UDF. It bused in dozens of youth brigade members for a deliberately provocative rally. During the night Inkatha forces kidnapped four MAWU activists, murdering three, and murdered another resident the next day. The police arrived to protect Inkatha members from the angry populace, escorting them out of town and returning their "traditional" weapons. MAWU retained a lawyer to represent the families of the deceased at the inquest. Inkatha members openly flaunted their contempt for legality by displaying guns at the hearing in order to intimidate witnesses. Deeply angered, the magistrate accepted the survivor's testimony, castigated Inkatha witnesses for lies and deceit, and found that the deaths were homicides, naming the suspects and forwarding the file to the attorney general. No prosecution ever ensued, but the leading suspect surfaced years later as a member of an Inkatha fighting force trained by the SADF.

Labor

Challenges to Influx Control. Until their repeal in 1986, the pass laws were one of the most hated weapons in apartheid's legal arsenal. In the early 1980s the newly founded Legal Resources Centre dramatically demonstrated its worth by overturning two crucial provisions. On behalf of Tom Rikhoto, it successfully argued that a Black who had worked for the same employer for ten years or lived in the city for fifteen qualified for section 10 rights (permanent urban residence), notwithstanding annual leaves to return to the homeland. On behalf of Nonceba Mercy Meriba Komani it won similar rights for the dependents (wives, children, and unmarried daughters) of section 10 rightholders. The government resisted these decisions relentlessly through appeals, threats to pass new legislation, and obdurate refusal to comply with final judgments. The two cases materially affected hundreds of thousands of Blacks and symbolically revealed the vulnerability of the apartheid regime to legal attack. At the same time, they reconfirmed the limitations of paper victories without political organizations to implement them.

MAWU's Campaign for Recognition by BTR Sarmcol. In the early 1970s MAWU (later NUMSA), the second largest black union and one of the most aggressive, began seeking recognition from the South African Rubber Manufacturing Company Ltd. (Sarmcol, later acquired by the multinational British Tyre & Rubber). The campaign gathered intensity in the 1980s, leading to a strike, lockout, and dismissal of the entire labor force. MAWU sued in the Industrial Court, charging BTR Sarmcol with an unfair labor practice (failing to bargain in good faith) but lost after a six-month trial (the longest labor case in South African history). Justice Didcott subsequently set aside the ruling because shortly before giving judgment the Industrial Court president had delivered the keynote address at a seminar organized by Sarmcol's labor consultant, over the objection of MAWU's lawyers. The Appellate Division affirmed, setting the stage for a new trial.

Land

Brits/Oukasie. During its forty-year rule, the National Party forcibly expelled an estimated 3.5 million Blacks from their land—a crime comparable in magnitude to the worst outrages against indigenous peoples in the Americas and Australia or peasants in Europe and Asia. In the 1980s, Blacks began to resist through law. In 1985 the government attempted to remove Oukasie, the black township of Brits, to Lethlabile, adjacent to Bophuthatswana, in the hope of recapturing the constituency from the Conservative Party. Residents appealed to the Legal Resources Centre, which brought two challenges. It sought an order compelling the white superintendent to allocate vacant houses and lots to those wishing to remain. The Supreme Court judge granted the relief, outraged that the superintendent had told the black applicant to take the letter back to his lawyer and "tell him to stick it up his ass." In response, the government declared the location an emergency camp, allowing it to promulgate regulations so restrictive that life became almost unbearable. When Arthur Chaskalson argued the second challenge, he found himself before Justice van Dijkhorst, who had convicted Chaskalson's clients in the Delmas treason trial only to have the convictions reversed, and himself reprimanded, for procedural errors raised by Chaskalson on appeal. Although van Dijkhorst was politically conservative and probably resentful of Chaskalson, he invalidated the declaration, ruling that the government could not use a statute about homelessness against applicants who sought to remain in or move into existing homes.

Magopa. The Magopa were the last victims of forcible removal. At first the government lost its nerve in the glare of television cameras from domestic and foreign networks, but three months later it caught the community by surprise in the middle of the night. Although the Magopa subsequently won a legal victory in the Appellate Division, the government promptly expropriated the land. After years of wandering in the wilderness, community members began returning surreptitiously, first to clean the graves of their ancestors and then to resume farming and herding. This time the government won the lawsuit—a Supreme Court ejectment action—but was ordered by the Appellate Division to negotiate a political settlement with the Magopa. Intent on preserving its reformist image, it has allowed them to remain and gradually improve the property. This victory has inspired many other groups to reoccupy ancestral land, seeking to negotiate from a position of strength.

Moutse/KwaNdebele. When the government could no longer remove Blacks physically, it tried to incorporate them into one of the ten homelands. In pursuit of grand apartheid, it also wanted the six homelands that had not done so to accept "independence." Only the corrupt rulers of KwaNdebele could be swayed, bribed by the offer of Moutse, an adjacent territory nearly as large and endowed with good farmlands, roads, schools, and a hospital. The Moutse people, justifiably terrified of oppression by KwaNdebele, asked John Dugard to represent them. Turning the apartheid ideology of ethnic homogeneity against the regime, Dugard persuaded the Appellate Division to annul the incorporation because of linguistic and cultural differences between the people of KwaNdebele and Moutse (a success he repeated in challenging the incorporation of Botshabelo into QwaQwa). While this case was pending, many KwaNdebele residents continued to resist independence. One tactic in their struggle was to fight the disenfranchisement of women (unique to that homeland). In the only country in the world with a *racially* based franchise, the Supreme Court held that a *sexually* based franchise violated natural justice! Once women got the vote, they used it to defeat independence decisively.

The Roles of Law

Party Strategies

Although most discussions of legality and rights focus on the behavior of officials—judges, legislators, and executives—the decisions of private parties are more important. Citizens are more numerous, enjoy greater discretion, and usually must initiate the encounter with law. It is not surprising that the South African opposition generally preferred negotiation to more public confrontation—a recognition that the law favored the government or could always be changed to do so. Centuries of oppression created a colonized mentality, particularly among the older generation, a need to believe in government benevolence; this was the stimulus for the black consciousness movement of the 1970s. Weakness compelled the opposition to appear reasonable, moderate, in order to persuade officials to do what could not be demanded as of right. The opposition deployed its limited leverage to persuade the government to negotiate. After the Magopa had been removed to Bethanie and then Onderstepoort, they threatened to return home unilaterally. Although they probably could not have broken through the security cordon, the force necessary to stop them might have embarrassed the government. The government also preferred negotiation, but for different reasons. Negotiation allowed it to shape publicity—preserving secrecy when it was exerting pressure or failing to make progress, drafting and issuing press statements when the outcome was satisfactory. Negotiation allowed the government to control timing, giving it endless opportunities for delay. Like others negotiating from a position of power, officials used the good cop–bad cop ploy: negotiate with us or you will have to deal with our much less reasonable superiors/inferiors or successors (a Conservative Party government).

Next to negotiation, the government preferred executive action, where it retains considerable control over timing and publicity: the deployment of police, the use of bulldozers to remove residents, the seizure of newspapers, the promulgation of regulations. Next it resorted to legislation to achieve its ends. This much slower, more public process risked some embarrassment from the miniscule opposition. After 1983 the (infrequent) noncooperation by the Indian House of Delegates or the "Coloured" House of Representatives required the President's Council to expose their impotence by overruling them. Just as the government preferred executive action to legislation, so it preferred detention (under the Internal Security Act or Emergency Regulations) to prosecution. The wisdom of this reticence was vividly confirmed by the dismal failure of the three show trials of the 1980s—Pietermaritzburg, Delmas, and Alexandra—and the government's inability to evict the Magopa even after obtaining a civil judgment against them.

These rights-based strategies did not exhaust the government's arsenal. It possessed virtually unlimited power over Blacks and did not hesitate to use it—detaining tens of thousands during the Emergency, killing and wounding thousands, using the SADF to occupy the townships, and torturing detainees. As the hearing in Wendy Orr's application for an injunction showed, the purpose of torture was only partly to extract information; the government was equally interested in terrifying opponents into submission. But torture often had perverse consequences. Most activists were too committed to be turned this way. The political costs of killing them—intentionally or inadvertently—were high: Steve Biko, Matthew Goniwe, and Victoria Mxenge were almost as potent as dead martyrs as they had been as living leaders. Indeed, the opposition could turn physical weakness to its advantage (as Gandhi had shown at the beginning of the century): mass hunger strikes threatening death forced the government to release a thousand Emergency detainees in spring 1989. Even lengthy detention could become an embarrassment, as shown by de Klerk's release of Mandela and others. Rank and file might be incapacitated, discouraged, or killed, but there were millions to take their places. Indiscriminate state violence transformed the customary stigma of arrest, detention, and punishment into a badge of honor. This experience also educated cadres and intensified their commitment: "graduation" from Robben Island became the revolutionary equivalent of an Oxbridge or Ivy League degree. The opposition used violence, too, but with even less effect. For all the talk by both government and the ANC about Umkhonto we Sizwe, the bombings—even at their height—had little effect on white society. And though acts of intimidation were widespread, they hardly explained the massive support for boycotts of elections, schools, shops, and workplaces, or mass democratic organizations like UDF, COSATU, and the illegal ANC.

If one strategic decision is the mode of engagement, another is whether to seek it proactively or react to an adversary's moves. Proactive parties can gain strategic advantages in political arenas, both Parliament and extra-parliamentary: they control timing, content, forum, and publicity. This possibility may reflect the proactive nature of executives and legislatures. In courts, which are inherently passive, reactivity may be the stronger posture. When the opposition sought a judicial confrontation, the government tried to defuse the situation by making strategic concessions: paying damages to torture victims or the families of prisoners who died in custody, consenting to an interdict against further state violence. Law is more effective as a shield than as a sword. Once the government had removed the Magopa from Zwartrand, an Appellate Division judgment invalidating the action was virtually worthless (especially since the government unilaterally expropriated the land). Once the Magopa had reestablished a foothold by cleaning the ancestral graves, a seemingly omnipotent government found it difficult to expel them. Even a favorable Supreme Court decision in the eviction action did not help. In each instance, therefore, the party seeking a legal remedy obtained it only to find it worthless. The residents of Oukasie prevailed in their two lawsuits partly because they maintained a physical presence in the township. Many political activists accused of ordinary crimes (such as public violence) won acquittals. Indeed, the 1989 Defiance Campaign (like its 1952 predecessor) was predicated on the strategy of inviting prosecution by seeking access to public amenities: parks, beaches, hospitals, transportation. In the changed political climate of the de Klerk administration, the later campaign succeeded. Conversely, the opposition was singularly unsuccessful in securing prosecution and punishment of white racists or members of the security forces who committed ordinary crimes against Blacks, as Mpophomeni illustrates.

Even when reactive strategies succeed, however, they have serious limits. The legal shield may protect against particular acts of oppression, but it rarely changes policies. After losing a criminal prosecution, the state often charged the accused with another crime or simply resorted to detention. A massive national and international campaign saved the Sharpeville Six from the gallows, but it did not free them from prison or eliminate the death penalty (which was effectively suspended several years later, at the same time as the amnesty). Ivan Toms and David Bruce won for their fellow conscientious objectors the "right" to a sentence at the judge's discretion; only the repeal of the Population Registration Act as part of the repudiation of apartheid could fundamentally transform conscription. The affidavits of Wendy Orr and dozens of detainees temporarily halted torture by the Port Elizabeth security branch but did not secure their release or prevent torture from recurring. The Supreme Court could nullify the government's declaration that Oukasie was an Emergency Camp, but it could not compel the restoration of services. Courts invalidated the incorporation of Moutse into KwaNdebele and of Botshabelo into

QwaQwa, but the state succeeded in incorporating Braklaagte and Leeuwfontein into Bophuthatswana.

Because the government deployed overwhelming military force, monopolized formal political power, and outlawed most extraparliamentary activity, the opposition rarely enjoyed the strategic advantages of planning. Many of the most dramatic protests were spontaneous: the 1976 Soweto uprising, the 1984 Vaal rent boycott and subsequent township violence. Even strikes, work stayaways, and election and consumer boycotts often were reactions to an adversary's initiatives. The government made good strategic use of its proactive ability to achieve surprise and publicity. De Klerk was a master of such dramatic flourishes: his February 1990 speech announcing the release of Mandela and other prisoners and the legalization of the ANC and other organizations; his February 1991 speech promising to scrap the legislative foundations of apartheid: the Group Areas, Land, and Population Registration Acts; and his April 1992 white referendum. More often, however, the government used its control over timing to achieve delay, seeking to wear out the opposition and distract media attention. Officials failed to respond to letters and phone calls, postponed meetings, and endlessly passed the buck—up and down the bureaucratic hierarchy and laterally across departmental jurisdictions.

But the government's sense of timing was far from perfect, as the Magopa removal illustrates. When the government finally proclaimed the removal, it gave the Magopa ten days notice. On the eve of the last night, reporters and television cameras from South Africa and abroad were poised to record yet another outrage, leaving the government little alternative but to back down. Three months later, when the media had lost interest, supporters were dispersed, and the Magopa were demoralized from endless suspense, the government secretly conducted the forced removal. Government control over timing also can be constrained by procedural formalities, which tend to increase with the amount of power the government seeks to wield—executions being an extreme example. As Samuel Johnson said, the prospect of death concentrates the mind wonderfully—and not only that of the victim. Each time the government scheduled the execution of the Sharpeville Six, a storm of protest arose, paralyzing its will. Furthermore, the government controls timing only in the short run. For decades everyone but South African Whites saw apartheid as an anachronism, ultimately fated to collapse. The opposition had inexhaustible powers of endurance because Blacks had nowhere to go. Like other long-oppressed peoples—Irish, Poles, Armenians—South African Blacks turned defeats into collective memories whose annual celebration strengthened resistance: Sharpeville, Soweto, Langa. Indeed, the very delay that was a favorite government strategy worked against it in the long run. Liberal critics reflected this belief in their obsession with time running out; the opposition proclaimed it in the slogan: "victory is inevitable."

Just as the government chose the political arena (which it controlled) over the legal (which is more autonomous) and preferred to make the opposition brandish the legal sword rather than hide behind the shield, so it sought to define the issues in litigation as narrowly and legalistically as possible. It distinguished sharply between law and politics, seeking to portray political opposition as common criminality: the murder trials of the Sharpeville Six and Upington Twenty-five, prosecutions for "Black-on-Black violence," the Winnie Mandela trial for the death of Stompie Mokhetsi. The opposition, by contrast, insisted that under apartheid all law was political; what the government depicted as legally mandated was actually the exercise of naked power. Even the "ordinary" enforcement of criminal law was politically motivated. (American criminal law has been viewed through similar racial lenses: Tawana Brawley, the Central Park jogger, Bernard Goetz, the police beating of Rodney King and the subsequent civil disorder.) Such issue definition has obvious strategic significance, but it also is an end in itself, given the visibility of major political cases.

The opposition was strikingly effective in forcing the government to engage its own broad definition of the issues. The treason trials addressed the real goals of the UDF and the Alexandra Action Committee as well as the substantive grievances fueling black protest. The trials of conscientious objectors examined the role of the SADF in repressing township residents and committing aggression in frontline states. The Magopa educated the Appellate Division about their title to the land. Moutse persuaded the court to consider the ideological foundation of apartheid, and KwaNdebele women advanced a natural law critique of gender inequality. But the opposition was not always successful. MAWU could not make the Industrial Court see the injustice of BTR Sarmcol's refusal to recognize the union. And the

New Nation could not persuade the courts to look beyond the Emergency regulations to the arbitrariness of censorship.

Although the concept of legitimation raises difficult questions about which audience is being addressed and how to measure the impact of the message, much party strategy does seem to be directed toward the "court of public opinion" as well as the formal organs of state power. A principal tactic of human rights activists is to expose the behavior of repressive governments in the belief that daylight is a strong antiseptic for moral as well as physical infection, that exposure unmasks authority as naked coercion, reducing its power (at least temporarily). The inquest into the Mpophomeni murders revealed both Inkatha's violence and the government's indifference (and possible complicity). The documentation of police torture in Port Elizabeth halted it for the time being, while demonstrating *whose* voices counted: black complaints about torture were disregarded for years until corroborated by a white physician. The audience of Black Sash, prominent clerics, international observers, and domestic and foreign media delayed removal of the Magopa. In each instance the brute force had hidden under cover of darkness: the Mpophomeni murders at night, torture inside the Port Elizabeth police headquarters, and the Magopa removal three months later, when nobody was watching. And in each, publicity was the opposition's *only* recourse, since the legal system offered no remedy: the Mpophomeni murderers were not prosecuted, the Port Elizabeth security police were not disciplined, the Appellate Division decision in favor of the Magopa was nullified by expropriation. But the efficacy of this strategy tends to be ephemeral: Inkatha violence, police torture, and removals resumed when the spotlight shifted and audience attention waned.

If each side seeks support from both sympathizers and an uncommitted audience, it also hopes to educate its adversary. Harold Berman has described Soviet law as parental—an attempt to mold citizens into the new Soviet man. The opposition sought to educate judges: about township life, SADF atrocities in Namibia, unemployment, long-distance commuting, police violence, rural agriculture, and the nature and goals of antiapartheid organizations. Judges, in turn, lectured parties about democracy, the need for social order, and the government's good intentions. Blacks certainly were not convinced by the government line, but some officials may have broadened their horizons. All the magistrates and judges who heard Ivan

Toms and David Bruce fully accepted their bona fides. Justice van der Walt probably had not visited a black township before he toured Alexandra during the Mayekiso treason trial.

In order to get, hold, and sway the audience, the opposition characterized government actions as atrocities, highlighting the most egregious behavior, imputing the worst motives. Hanging, always difficult to justify, became indefensible if there were doubts about guilt—as there inevitably were when the government used the "common purpose" doctrine to charge as many as twenty-five people with the same murder. Prisoners dramatized and exacerbated the hardship of indefinite detention without trial by engaging in hunger strikes. The Magopa claimed that the government was stealing their diamonds and other valuable minerals, despite documentary proof that they had alienated those rights decades earlier. Oukasie residents made effective use of the white superintendent's vulgar response to a Black who asked to be allocated a vacant house. The wanderings of the homeless Magopa remained a constant embarrassment to the government. Newspapers pictured houses and churches destroyed and the untended graveyard, focused on the plight of the most vulnerable and innocent—children, women, the elderly (some of whom fought for South Africa in World War II)—and recorded illnesses and deaths (whether or not attributable to exile). Some crimes needed no exaggeration: the testimony of the Port Elizabeth torture victims, for instance. The principal problem of this strategy is the limited capacity for moral outrage. Those not suffering personally tire of hearing about others (the analogy to donor fatigue in international relief efforts). Guilt turns into indifference or even into anger at being forced to listen. New and more extreme offenses must be revealed. And the state can play the game too, pointing to necklacing, people's courts, or communist ideology. In the prosecution of Ivan Toms the state stooped to unregenerate McCarthyism by making wholly irrelevant charges of homosexuality and homosexual activism in an attempt to discomfit Toms's church supporters.

Publicity could backfire. Instead of persuading an adversary to concede for fear of seeming intransigent, it could harden resistance for fear of appearing to sell out or display weakness. The government was unwilling to acknowledge publicly the innocence of the Sharpeville Six or even the irregularity of the prosecution. The state president ultimately granted clemency as an act of grace, without any admission of error. Pressed by the government to admit their crimes and plead for mercy, many black accused refused to compromise their principles. Those tried for treason were torn by the dilemma of minimizing punishment without disavowing ideals or repudiating tactics. The Umkhonto we Sizwe cadres charged with murder in the Delmas Two prosecution displayed extraordinary commitment by refusing to participate in the trial at all.

Since publicity was the opposition's chosen battleground, the government usually beat a tactical retreat. When the opposition sought confrontation in order to embarrass, the government made strategic concessions to defuse the demands and minimize visible injustice. If David Bruce did not want to serve in the military, the government would do anything to satisfy him without legitimating his moral scruples. If the Magopa were unhappy about moving to Pachsdraai, the government would offer them numerous other sites but not Zwartrand and demand a signed statement that this last move was entirely voluntary. The government was prepared to pay compensation to detainees and their relatives as long as it did not have to admit or stop police torture and killings.

If the government could not silence or co-opt opposition voices, it used its totalitarian powers to prevent them from being heard. It excluded the media from the scene of removals, prohibited them from observing or reporting about the security forces or prison conditions, and made them engage in self-censorship under threat of suspending publication. It disseminated disinformation. It alternated between castigating the media and wooing it with trips, tips, and press conferences. It expelled foreign television cameras from the townships during the Emergency. Government officials and Inkatha leaders frequently sued critics for libel (if they rarely won).

Finally, the government sought to emulate the opposition by claiming the moral high ground. Given the universal condemnation of apartheid outside South Africa, it could do so only by dramatic announcements of reform proposals: no more forced removals, repeal of the Black Administration Act, even "the end of apartheid." Promises carry dangers, however. Just making them admits past injustice (when did you stop beating your wife—or your citizens?). Once made, they exert pressure for performance. Once fulfilled, they may escalate. If removals are ended, perhaps the 3.5 million dispossessed should be allowed to return. If conscientious objection is recognized, perhaps conscription can be abolished.

The Rule of Law

Decisions to seek or avoid legal remedies may be influenced by the party's desire to gain or avoid publicity, but the real goal is winning a legal victory or avoiding a legal defeat. This section will explore the central question: did law make a difference? The bottom line is an unambiguous yes. The opposition won victories in court they could not win elsewhere and won them at least partly because of law. I will begin with those victories before turning to the limitations of legality.

Most judges followed clear statutory language, even when doing so frustrated the government that had appointed them and might have conflicted with their own preferences. Justice van Dijkhorst, a conservative, ambitious, irascible Afrikaner, clashed repeatedly with Arthur Chaskalson, defense counsel in the Delmas treason trial, the most important of the decade. He threatened Chaskalson with contempt when the advocate persisted in objecting to van Dijkhorst's dismissal of an assessor who had signed the UDF petition campaign. Shortly after Chaskalson persuaded the Appellate Division to throw out the convictions, effectively thwarting van Dijkhorst's hope of further career advancement, Chaskalson asked the judge to hold that the Prevention of Illegal Squatting Act did not authorize the government to declare Oukasie an "Emergency Camp." This decision ended the government's effort to win Brits back from the Conservative Party while pursuing its program of grand apartheid by moving the black residents to the Bophuthatswana border. It followed a ruling by Justice Stafford that the white superintendent of Oukasie lacked discretion to deny house and site permits to residents. In another blow to grand apartheid, the Appellate Division invalidated the Magopa removal on the ground that Parliament could not give the requisite consent without being informed of the residents' destination. It had earlier invalidated the excision of Ingwavuma from KwaZulu because the latter had not consented.

Unambiguous facts, like unambiguous law, also could lead to politically unpopular decisions. The Supreme Court in Port Elizabeth saw no alternative to granting an injunction against the security police in the face of overwhelming evidence of torture. Some judges construed ambiguous facts to reach conclusions that doubtless angered the government. Justice van der Walt acquitted the accused in the Alexandra treason trial despite the visibility of the case, a vigorous prosecution effort, and evidence that two of the five had been involved in people's courts. Magistrate S. M. Nieuwoudt, a young Afrikaner woman whose office did not carry lifetime tenure, found that a crime had been committed in the deaths of the three Mpophomeni MAWU activists and named some of the Inkatha members responsible, rejecting their defense as a tissue of lies. The Natal Supreme Court dismissed the treason charges against prominent UDF officials when the defense discredited the state's expert witness and unmasked errors in the transcription and translation of videotaped meetings.

Some courts would not tolerate procedural irregularities. After the two-year-long Delmas trial had led to convictions and harsh sentences for key UDF leaders, the Appellate Division reversed because van Dijkhorst dismissed an assessor. Justice Didcott (ultimately affirmed by the Appellate Division) threw out the Industrial Court decision in MAWU's unfair labor practice action against BTR Sarmcol because the presiding judge had been the keynote speaker at a seminar organized by the defendant's labor consultant. Justice Spoelstra released activists opposing KwaNdebele independence, who had been kidnapped by South African Police and handed over to homeland authorities.

Sometimes judges went well beyond the plain meaning of statutes to address the underlying political issues. The Appellate Division invalidated the incorporation of Moutse into KwaNdebele because it violated not only the text of the National States Constitution Act of 1971 but also the grundnorm of grand apartheid—ethnic homogeneity. The normally conservative Supreme Court of the Orange Free State promptly followed this reasoning by invalidating the incorporation of Botshabelo into QwaQwa. The Transvaal Supreme Court based on natural law its decision that KwaNdebele could not deny women the right to vote in the absence of any statutory authority.

Occasionally judges even disregarded the plain meaning of statutes. For seven years after its passage everyone believed that the 1983 Defence Act compelled judges to impose a prison sentence of one-and-a-half times the outstanding military obligation on all those who refused conscription without meeting the narrow criteria for conscientious objectors. Two magistrates and two Supreme Court benches reached this conclusion with respect to Ivan Toms and David Bruce. But the Appellate Division created a loophole restoring full sentencing discretion to judges. (The court's resentment of legislation derogating judicial authority may have been a crucial factor in this case.)

For all its importance, however, legality had severe limitations as a resource in the struggle against apartheid. Since the white legislature wrote the statutes, it was hardly surprising that they favored the regime more than the opposition. Even Laurie Ackermann, one of the most liberal judges (who finally left the bench for academia), felt compelled to reject the Seleke challenge to their incorporation into Lebowa because the statute did not require their consent but only that of the jurisdiction from which they were being excised—South Africa! When the opposition was able to find statutory language justifying its position (usually because of inept drafting or executive bungling) courts disregarded it, rejecting Lebowa's challenge to the excision of Moutse (which turned on the relative meaning of parentheses and commas) and Magopa's defense to eviction from the Zwartrand cemetery (which argued that the government had used the wrong statute to expropriate the land). Justice van Dyk upheld the Magopa removal, rejecting the statutory interpretation that the Appellate Division later found persuasive. If courts reached out to engage the larger substantive issues—as when the Appellate Division invalidated the Magopa removal because legislative approval rested on inadequate disclosure—the government displayed its contempt by reiterating the discredited argument that there had been no removal because it had bribed Jacob More to lead one faction to Pachsdraai.

Courts construed ambiguous facts as well as laws against the opposition. Despite the extraordinary skill and energy of the defense team, Justice van Dijkhorst and the remaining assessor convicted some Delmas accused of treason. If Magistrate Nieuwoudt found that the deaths of the three MAWU activists were criminal and named suspects, Magistrate Scholts did neither in a companion case involving a fourth Mpophomeni death. Courts consistently favored some witnesses: Whites over Blacks, government officials over private citizens, the security forces over everyone. The opposition sometimes turned this weakness—like others—to its advantage. Witnesses for whom English was a second language (or third or fourth) took refuge in linguistic incompetence and incomprehension. They also invoked the inherent ambiguity of words and symbols and the opacity of motive. Accused who wore the black, gold, and green of the banned ANC pointed out that these also were the colors of the legal Inkatha movement. Accused who sang militant songs argued that singing was integral to African culture. The treason trials were full of inconclusive debates over the meaning of such words as *revolution, socialism, struggle, democracy,* and *people's power.*

Some government witnesses were so contemptuous of legality that they blatantly told incredible stories full of internal contradictions and inconsistent with the rest of the state's case, as in Inkatha's account of their Mpophomeni rally or the Port Elizabeth security police version of their treatment of detainees. Police—presumably selected and trained for observation and recall—were extraordinarily forgetful. Furthermore, the government saw nothing wrong with using torture or other inducements to elicit "truth."

The government was at least as effective as the opposition in its invocation of procedural niceties. Despite parliamentary supremacy, the (white) House of Assembly displayed an unusual solicitude for separation of powers in refusing to hear Moutse's petition against its incorporation into KwaNdebele because Lebowa's Supreme Court action had rendered the matter "sub judice." When the government sued to eject the Magopa from the Zwartrand cemetery, Justice van der Merwe refused to consider the defense challenge to the expropriation of the farm because the Magopa had failed to join the Minister of Community Development as a party. The KwaNdebele Legislative Assembly almost refused to discuss independence in August 1986 because it was not on the agenda—although people were dying daily in the struggle over that issue. The assembly's unanimous decision against independence was repudiated a year later—again because of its earlier omission from the agenda and the lack of a formal vote. The government also created "legal" forms that dispensed with virtually all procedural constraints—as in detentions under the Internal Security Act or the Emergency Regulations.

In South Africa, as everywhere, the degree of legality was proportional to the visibility of government action. Courts might extend section 10 rights to black workers and their dependents, but local officials still refused or simply failed to endorse passes. The scrupulous procedural regularity of the prosecutions of Ivan Toms, David Bruce, and other conscientious objectors coexisted with violent attacks on ECC activists, SADF involvement in the dirty tricks campaign, and a plan by the CCB (Civil Co-operation Bureau) to assassinate ECC director Gavin Evans. The government refused to delay the Magopa removal pending the Appellate Division decision on leave to appeal. When the AD finally addressed the merits, it may have invalidated the removal precisely because the issue had been mooted by expropriation of the land. Magistrate Scholts issued a permit for the Mpophomeni rally knowing that residents were hostile to Inkatha and likely to react violently. Magistrate S. M. Nieuwoudt named those responsible for the murders and recommended prosecution—but the Natal attorney general took no action. The police favored Inkatha members here as elsewhere: escorting them to safety after the murders and returning their "traditional" weapons; dragging out the investigation while one key witness died and others disappeared (into the security forces!). The Transvaal attorney general delayed as long as possible in charging Simon Skosana, Piet Ntuli, and George Mahlangu with kidnapping and torturing several hundred Moutse opponents of incorporation into KwaNdebele. When he could stall no longer, he charged them with simple assault, allowing them to pay R 50 admission of guilt fines without standing trial. The security forces constantly referred complaints about brutality to their internal review procedures; but these did nothing to restrain or correct the Port Elizabeth security police—or any other. Oukasie superintendent de Beer blithely disregarded Justice Stafford's ruling that he lacked discretion to refuse house and site permits. The Ventersdorp magistrate simply failed to perform his statutory obligation to pay pensions or endorse reference books for Magopa who declined to move; and he refused to protect them against the trespassing cattle of white farmers. The Klerksdorp magistrate audited the books of Magopa headman Jacob More, as ordered, but then refused to let anyone see the books or his report. When the Magopa were on the verge of purchasing the Holgat farm as a new home, the government expropriated it.

The loose coupling between top and bottom, the coexistence of rare but conspicuous legalism with pervasive covert illegality, is universal, but South Africa has refined this moral division of labor into a high art. Superiors do not know what inferiors are doing. Judges refuse to acknowledge what the police are doing. The inaptly named Justice Human, for instance, convicted the Sharpeville Six on the basis of confessions that clearly had been extracted by torture. Apartheid ensures that whites do not know what Blacks are doing. Indeed, South Africa created urban township councils and rural homeland governments partly to be able to blame Blacks for the illegality and violence indispensable to white rule. The increasing number of black police, especially kitskonstabels (instant cops), also served this function. The racial division of political responsibility not only allowed South Africa to continue proclaiming its fidelity to the rule of law but also constituted powerful evidence that Blacks were unprepared for democracy. The strategy could work, however, only if homeland leaders were granted some autonomy, creating the risk that they might act independently. It also required the more visible black leaders to maintain their distance from the dirty work. KwaNdebele Chief Minister Simon Skosana and Home Minister Piet Ntuli seriously compromised South Africa by openly directing the kidnapping and torture of hundreds of Moutse residents opposing incorporation—an embarrassment conveniently ended within the year by Ntuli's assassination (which conspiracy enthusiasts attributed to South African security forces) and Skosana's death from diabetes. The use of vigilantes, the incitement of "black-on-black" violence, and the "third force" of military, police, and right-wing civilians served the same purpose. Law is not the rule and violence the exception; rather, law is the continuation of violence by other means.

South Africa's pretensions to respect as a rechtsstaat suffer from another, more distinctive, flaw: parliamentary supremacy unconstrained by natural law. What does the rule of law mean if the government can change the law at will? If the Appellate Division invalidated the Magopa removal, the government mooted the decision by expropriating Zwartrand. If even a faithful Nationalist like Justice van Dijkhorst held that the government could not declare Oukasie an Emergency Camp, the government promptly disestablished the township. If the Appellate Division followed its Ingwavuma precedent and required Lebowa's consent for the excision of Moutse, the government passed two retrospective acts, one stating that the consent was deemed to have been given, the other that Lebowa had never contained Moutse—an Orwellian rewriting of history. Yet the government did not always use its plenary legislative and executive powers. Although it introduced bills to overturn the Appellate Division decisions invalidating the Magopa removal and the Moutse incorporation, it withdrew both of them.

The Logic of Ideology

In the previous section I explored the ways in which a government that purports to rule through law is constrained by it. This is just a special case of the universal principle that no one can govern exclusively through naked power. All forms of domination seek to transform power into authority by offering reasons for their actions. This section examines the opposition's efforts to turn those reasons against the state.

Two of the most dramatic instances were Moutse's challenge to incorporation by KwaNdebele and the KwaNdebele women's demand for the vote. Moutse resisted incorporation by invoking the grundnorm of apartheid: ethnic homogeneity. Elsewhere the government had argued that mixing ethnic groups not only robbed them of their cultural and linguistic heritage but also generated violence and disrupted production and education. The early months following incorporation amply confirmed the reality of these dangers. When the government justified homelands as a vehicle for black self-determination, Moutse responded that P. W. Botha had denied its repeated requests for a referendum and excised it from Lebowa without consulting the latter. When the government invoked geographic contiguity and administrative convenience, Moutse pointed to the government's total disregard of those factors in other homelands, such as Bophuthatswana. Indeed, the government had just incorporated Botshabelo into QwaQwa, more than 300 kilometers away. Moutse also argued that incorporation into KwaNdebele would strip its women of the vote, a right enjoyed by all South African women regardless of race. Indeed, it took the government's argument in the women's vote case—the uniqueness of Ndebele culture—and turned it into an argument against subordinating Moutse to an alien culture.

In the women's vote case, ideology played an even more important—and more surprising—role. Whereas Moutse could cite statutes and principles of administrative law, KwaNdebele women had to rely exclusively on analogy and natural law. Furthermore, they were in the anomalous position of challenging sex discrimination in the only country in the world whose official policy was race discrimination. They had to be inventive, and they were. They pointed to the internal illogic of disenfranchisement: Ndebele women living in other homelands could vote, whereas Ndebele women living in South Africa and Moutse women living in KwaNdebele could not. When the government alleged that African political tradition denied women equality, the plaintiffs responded in kind. Ndebele women played a larger role in traditional tribal councils than in the artificial KwaNdebele legislative assembly. Furthermore, the "traditional" inferiority of women did not prevent them from voting in all other homelands and all urban councils. Indeed, it was not the traditional Ndebele leaders who opposed the franchise for women but Simon Skosana, a homeland chief minister devoid of traditional legitimacy. In any case, tradition was irrelevant to homelands created out of whole cloth by the white regime. The government itself showed contempt for tradition by denying KwaNdebele men the right to vote until they reached the age of twenty-one, although tradition recognized them as adults when they were circumcised at sixteen.

When the government—with a Whitmanesque disdain for consistency—also justified the homelands as a means of introducing "modern," "Western," "democratic" political institutions, KwaNdebele women responded in the same language. African women today played a much larger political role. Apartheid tore men out of the home, either as migrant workers away eleven months at a stretch or as long-distance commuters, at work or in transit all week and exhausted on weekends. Women had to manage the farm, household, children's education, and locality.

KwaNdebele citizens could not attack the homeland's independence in court, since the decision was entrusted to the unfettered discretion of a state president able to find, or bribe, an acquiescent leader. But the successful challenges to Moutse's incorporation and the all-male franchise eliminated the essential political support. Without Moutse, KwaNdebele was uninterested in independence, as well as economically unviable. Once KwaNdebele women could vote, they decisively rejected the pro-independence slate for the Legislative Assembly. The struggle also revealed the bankruptcy of grand apartheid. "Modern" political institutions such as the homeland governments were supposed to be more democratic and enlightened than "traditional" tribal leaders. In KwaNdebele, however, the Ndzundza royal house (particularly Prince James Mahlangu) was far more progressive than the tyrannical, corrupt, and brutal homeland cabinet. Chief Minister Skosana, whose only claim to legitimacy rested in his "modernity," had almost no formal education. Once KwaNdebele decisively rejected independence, that cornerstone of grand apartheid disintegrated.

Lacking political power, legal rights, economic leverage, and military force, Blacks threatened with forcible removal had no choice but to contest the government on the terrain of ideology. One tactic was to highlight the fundamental contradiction of apartheid: whites' determination to retain political domination and social separation while exploiting black labor. Oukasie residents were able to enlist white employers in Brits to oppose the removal advocated by other white residents (workers or middle class). Blacks opposing the incorporation of Moutse into an independent KwaNdebele—the dream of Pretoria politicians— could appeal to neighboring white farmers. Even the brother of AWB leader Eugene Terre'Blanche and his fellow Boers wanted the custom and labor of the Magopa badly enough to speak against removal.

The opposition's ideological leverage was enhanced by the government's desire to appear reformist. In February 1985 it proclaimed the end of "forced removals" and subsequently repealed the Black Administration Act. Botha declared that apartheid was dead. If removals were voluntary, however, residents could refuse to leave despite the penalties (termination of services, deterioration of infrastructure, vigilante attacks, denial of compensation) and incentives (land and housing for those prompt to accede). When government sought to justify "voluntary" removal on the ground that Magopa and Oukasie were unplanned and undeveloped, residents responded that they would be happy to accept government money for improvements. When government claimed improvement was too expensive, residents commissioned a study that found it far less expensive than removal. When government voiced sudden solicitude for the health of Oukasie residents, they conducted a survey showing it was no worse than that in other black townships. When government characterized Oukasie residents as homeless, they had two retorts: the government itself had destroyed their homes, terminated their services, and refused to maintain their infrastructure; nevertheless, many of the holdouts still had perfectly good homes.

The Magopa so effectively mobilized official ideology that they persuaded the government to reply on their own terms. Like the

Boers, they had bought the land and owned it for generations. They were more than self-sufficient, selling their surplus to the local white cooperative. They had buried their ancestors on the land and had religious obligations to care for the graveyard. Their traditional leadership had not accepted the move. The government responded by offering compensatory land and urging the Magopa to adapt their farming practices—but implicitly conceded that the tribe would be worse off. It maintained that graves were a modern practice, which certainly did not justify a large encampment to clean them. But Boers could hardly criticize others for being religious and respectful of ancestors. The headmanship was not traditional—after all, the government appointed officeholders. The challenge to Jacob More's leadership was nothing more than political rivalry and internecine conflict. But this argument undermined the institution's only legitimacy.

The opposition could deploy the logic of ideology only as long as the government itself cared about the coherence and integrity of its justifications. The South African government often made do with much less, giving vague, ambiguous, internally contradictory reasons and shifting ground when one was unmasked. Like other regimes, it took refuge in newspeak. The "Department of Co-operation and Development" coerced and underdeveloped Blacks. The Civil Cooperation Bureau was responsible for bombing, torture, kidnapping, and assassination. Some arguments were directed exclusively to whites: they had suffered as much as Blacks to achieve the shared dream of apartheid; the restoration of land to any Blacks inevitably would lead to the return of all 3.5 million removed. Some government arguments bordered on the outrageous. Allowing the Onderstepoort Magopa to return to Zwartrand would endanger the rights of those who had settled at Pachsdraai—this from a government that had ruthlessly uprooted millions of Blacks over four centuries. Tired of giving reasons, government resorted to the impatient parent's ipse dixit. The Magopa removal could not be stopped because the government had ordered it; government decisions increased in value with the passage of time, like fine wines or antiques. P. W. Botha thought of himself as national patriarch. I'm a hard man, he told Moutse; you should know better than to ask me to change my mind. In the end, government acknowledged that it wielded naked power, taking refuge in its unfettered discretion to expropriate Magopa, excise Moutse from Lebowa, or disestablish Oukasie.

Conclusion

A reader looking for sweeping generalizations about the capacity of law to constrain power will be disappointed with the foregoing analysis. Most of the observations are specific to a few cases. For each, there seems to be a counterexample. Rather than apologize for the apparent lack of theoretical ambition, I want to argue that such particularity is essential and appropriate to the phenomena under examination. Major political cases do not resemble the routine microbehavior that is the grist for most sociology of law theorizing: about deviance, correction, regulation, impact, complaints, disputing, and the like. I am dealing here with large, complex events, often extending over many years, involving dozens or even hundreds of participants, with repercussions for the entire society. Each case is idiosyncratic and inherently unpredictable, peculiar not only to South Africa in the 1980s but also to the unique circumstances of time, place, and actors. Historical interpretation must complement, and often displace, sociological generalization. This conclusion reiterates the centrality of chance.

The inquest into the Inkatha murder of the three Mpophomeni MAWU activists reached its conclusions only because the hit squad bungled the job, permitting the escape of Micca Sibiya, one of the intended victims. The death of the Inkatha leader Joseph Mabaso prior to the inquest conveniently allowed the suspects to pin the blame on him without fear of rebuttal or retaliation. Although I often feel that South African commentators, like their American counterparts, place too much emphasis on judicial personality,[5] the two Mpophomeni inquests revealed profound differences: J. J. Scholts conducted a perfunctory inquiry, reaching no conclusion; S. M. Nieuwoudt reprimanded Inkatha for intimidation, demonstrated her impatience with the officious ineptitude of Inkatha's counsel, dismissed the suspects' tissue of lies, and forthrightly named those she believed to be guilty. The political spectrum among Supreme Court justices is even greater, ranging from a few liberals to a much larger number of party hacks.

The security forces tortured black detainees for decades, suffering

---

5. Hugh Corder, *Judges at Work: The Role and Attitude of the South African Judiciary, 1910–50* (Cape Town: Juta, 1984); C. F. Forsyth, *In Danger of their Talents: A Study of the South African Appellate Division of the Supreme Court of South Africa, 1950–1980* (Cape Town: Juta, 1985).

exposure only when they killed an unusually visible victim, such as Steve Biko. Otherwise the government and most of the media disregarded and discounted the thousands of complaints. The same silence would have greeted the massive repression in Port Elizabeth following the 1985 Emergency but for the presence of Wendy Orr. She was no political activist. She had not entered the Prisons Department out of any sense of mission but only to repay the government for her university scholarship and spend some time in her hometown. Nor did medical training explain her decision to publicize the systematic torture of detainees. Her superiors, who had practiced medicine for years, routinely protected the security forces. Indeed, it was the anxiety of a superior who had been responsible for Biko's death that enabled her to copy the prisoners' medical records, which became the foundation for her lawsuit. Her shock at the torture of detainees ultimately assumed a legal form because her sister in Johannesburg happened to encounter a human rights lawyer at a party. Ultimately, however, the decisive factor was Wendy Orr's character—courage, inexperience, perhaps even foolhardiness.

The ECC's contribution to supporting conscientious objectors revalidates sociological theories about collective action. But the ECC had almost nothing to do with David Bruce, a highly visible conscientious objector (CO) and one of the two defendants whose case persuaded the Appellate Division to rewrite the Defence Act. He was a loner who would not join the organization. Indeed, after his unhappy experience in Wits student politics, he did not belong to any organization. He was not a model CO, like Ivan Toms, and probably would not have been selected by the ECC as its test case. His political philosophy was far from coherent. He had no orthodox religious beliefs. He was not engaged in public service. He lacked influential friends who could attest to his character. If he had any model, it would have been Herman Melville's Bartleby the Scrivener. He just preferred not to serve—and was prepared, at the age of twenty-two, to spend the next six years in prison. For him (as for Toms and the handful of other COs), refusing complicity with the military apparatus of apartheid—and suffering the harsh consequences—was the only way to cleanse the moral taint of being a white South African.

M. B. de Beer, the white superintendent of Oukasie, was not unusually villainous, nor was he acting out of character in ordering a black applicant to take his letter back to his lawyer and "tell him to stick it up his ass." His real error was admitting to Justice Stafford that he had said this, thereby transforming the routine (and hence acceptable) oppressions of apartheid into gratuitous individual discourtesy, which could be neither justified nor ignored. Even after this reversal the government might have succeeded in forcing the residents to leave had it not made the mistake of arguing that people living in adequate houses were homeless.

The struggle over KwaNdebele independence could easily have ended differently. The Appellate Division's invalidation of the incorporation of Moutse was a serious blow—but the South African government could have overcome it through legislation (and actually introduced a bill for this purpose). The Supreme Court's extension of the franchise to women was another government defeat—but many other homeland regimes consistently disregarded the popular will. The assassination of Piet Ntuli (probably by Umkhonto we Sizwe) was a dramatic demonstration that the forces of repression were not invincible, while the death of Simon Skosana from diabetes deprived the independence movement of vital leadership.

Chance played an important role in all the criminal prosecutions. In the Sharpeville Six trial, the personal attorney for one of the key prosecution witnesses "happened" to be an associate of the attorneys defending the accused and thus was able to alert them to the fact that his client had been coerced into giving evidence, which he later recanted. The state botched the Pietermaritzburg UDF treason trial in two ways. First, its transcriptions and translations of allegedly incriminating videotapes were so hopelessly inaccurate that the court threw them out altogether. Second, the state's expert witness, whose testimony was supposed to show that the UDF followed the ANC line, instead exposed his own ignorance and eventually abandoned that position entirely. In the Alexandra Five treason trial, the defense was able to surprise the prosecution by producing minutes of the allegedly seditious Alexandra Action Committee meetings, showing that they were entirely innocent. Although the police had ransacked Alexandra township looking for evidence, the AAC secretary had given the minutes to the wife of the principal accused, who had taken them to her office to type. And in Delmas, Justice van Dijkhorst need not have dismissed the assessor who signed the UDF petition; even without his cooperation the court would have achieved a conviction, which the Appellate Division probably could not have overturned.

A similar error undermined the BTR Sarmcol victory over MAWU. Shortly before the trial ended, the Industrial Court judge accepted an invitation from Sarmcol's labor consultants to speak at a management seminar—over the objections of counsel for the union. This was such an obvious breach of judicial neutrality that Justice Didcott summarily overturned the judgment—which probably would have withstood substantive attack.

Cases do follow patterns, both legal and sociological. But they are located in a history that is constantly changing. The pace of that change has accelerated in South Africa since the early 1980s. Strategies adopted at the beginning of a case often became obsolete by its end. Influx control was abandoned after it had patently failed to limit black migration to the cities. Conscientious objection was accepted partly because the government acceded to the independence of Namibia and realized that military might could not repress township rebellion. The people of Magopa, Oukasie, and Moutse prevailed partly by simply surviving until the government was forced to abandon grand apartheid. KwaNdebele avoided independence for similar reasons. The acquittal of the Alexandra Five and the Appellate Division reversal in Delmas partly reflected the government's recognition that it could not crush the "mass democratic organizations" and ultimately would have to negotiate with them. The legal strategies were neither essential nor irrelevant to the struggle against apartheid; their intricate interconnection can only be understood within the context of the larger historical narrative.

Wife Battering and the Ambiguities of Rights

Sally Engle Merry

In 1990, George Wailea walked into the courtroom of the Family Court in Hilo, the county seat of the island of Hawai'i, feeling very alone. He felt shame and isolation, as he had earlier when a police officer handed him a form which said that his wife was accusing him of hitting her. He was told he must leave the house. No one had prepared him for what was going to happen in court. He was confused about where to sit and what to expect. The bailiff seated him alone at a table in front of the judge. Across the courtroom, his wife, Jane, felt very differently. Although she was frightened about taking her husband to court, she had a woman advocate from the violence control program beside her. The advocate stayed with her, explained what was going to happen, and comforted her whenever George complained about Jane to the judge and blamed her for his violence. After the judge heard the case and determined that there was indeed evidence of violence in the relationship (ignoring George's accusations of Jane's responsibility for his violence), the judge turned to the advocate to ask what Jane wanted the court to do. Jane whispered to the advocate that she didn't want to see George any more right now, but

Research for this chapter has been generously supported by two grants from the National Science Foundation, Anthropology and Law and Social Sciences Program, #SES-9023397 and #SBR-9320009. It originated as a paper prepared for the Amherst Conference on the Paradox of Rights. I am grateful for the help of my research assistants: Marilyn Brown, Joy Adapon, Tami Miller, and Linda Andres. The staff of the Family Court, the Alternatives to Violence program, and the people I interviewed all gave very generously of their time and insight. Martin Chanock, Jane Collier, Marlene King, Tami Miller, and Susan Reverby generously read the chapter and provided me with valuable ideas and suggestions. Portions of this chapter appeared in *Identities: Global Studies in Culture and Power*.

that she wanted him to get some help. The advocate announced to the court that Jane wanted a no-contact TRO (a temporary restraining order). The judge granted the order for 180 days, reading from a document, in formal legal language, the conditions of the restraining order: during this period, George was to stay away from Jane, make no attack on her or her property, and attend a treatment program for men who are violent. Any violation of the terms of this order earned George up to one year in jail and/or a fine of up to $2,000.

This brief drama, a typical case in family court, reveals a new mobilization of rights in cases of spousal violence. Jane is encouraged to think of herself as a person with rights as she is helped and supported through the intricacies of a legal system that, until recently, took little notice of problems like hers. George, on the other hand, finds himself isolated and stripped of some of the rights of male authority that he had in the past taken for granted. He enters alone into the foreign terrain of the courtroom, not entitled to free legal representation because this is a civil proceeding. Notions of rights are reshaping the definitions of selves in domestic relations, but for men and for women, the way their selves are being redefined by rights is quite different. Moreover, their experience of the legal system is dramatically different.

What are the consequences for gender identities in this deployment of the language of rights? A discourse of rights is essential to engineering protection and punishment from the legal system. Does this mobilization of rights empower women, as its feminist advocates hope? Does it lead to new cultural images of masculinity in which violence is no longer essential to maintaining connections with women and new cultural images of femininity that no longer require submission to male violence? Or does the reliance on the language of rights and the procedures of the law compel an individualistic interpretation of the problem of wife battering because of the "egoism" inherent in rights language, to borrow Marx's phrase?[1] Does it serve to conceal the social and economic inequalities of gender relations, papering over substantive inequality with political equality?

I argue that the new legal and educational procedures adopted to control violence against women in the town I studied are indeed disrupting the linkages between masculinity/violence and femininity/

---

1. See Wendy Brown, "Rights and Identity in Late Modernity," in this volume.

subjugation. But at the same time, the formal equality of rights has been expanded without any substantive change in the economic and social position of the women nor any diminution of their economic paralysis. Despite changes in consciousness of rights and gender, there have not been shifts in the social and economic condition of the women suffering violence in this community, nor of the men who perpetrate it. Moreover, despite the feminist commitments of the leaders of the movement against wife battering who see domestic violence as part of a larger system of oppression, the rights frame they rely on fosters the interpretation of wife battering as a problem of particular men and women rather than as a facet of larger systems of class, race, and gender inequality.

What do I mean by rights? The concept of rights takes on a different meaning for anthropologists doing close ethnography of everyday life than for scholars of the law. In this chapter, I focus on the everyday meanings of rights for people not trained in the law. I am interested in the way rights are commonly used as the basis of claims for help or definitions of self in relation to others. Rights in this sense are acquired through school, media discussions of law and rights, and encounters with law. My previous research in New England urban areas suggests that nonprofessionals hold a rich understanding of political rights that shade into legal rights, a sense of entitlement, and a working recognition that rights define the self and relations with others.[2] Thus, I am looking at "rights talk" as it appears in everyday speech rather than the formal vocabulary of rights in legal discourse.

In the past, anthropologists labeled such nonprofessional understandings folk concepts, differentiating them from the analytic concepts employed by the social scientist or the expert. While this division between local knowledge and expert, privileged knowledge no longer seems viable to me, the term *folk concept* does emphasize a kind of knowledge grounded in everyday life and practice. I have used the term *legal consciousness* to refer to the way a person's sense of self is defined by law.[3] Legal consciousness shapes the individual's conception of a problem as involving rights such that he or she feels justified in turning to the law for help or protection. Rights, in this sense, are

2. Sally Engle Merry, *Getting Justice and Getting Even: Legal Consciousness Among Working Class Americans* (Chicago: University of Chicago Press, 1990).
3. Ibid.

central to legal consciousness. And an important place where consciousness of rights is produced is in the activities of courts themselves.

Courts and Cultural Production

I argue that courts and their related social service programs provide
important arenas for the production of cultural meanings. Courts are
places where cultural images and meanings are formed, as are the
media and the arts. Of course, as with the media and the arts, they
reflect as well as produce cultural meanings. There is a critical difference between the media and the law, however: courts exercise force
behind their cultural meanings, backing their pronouncements with
threats of fines, supervision, or prison.[4] Moreover, this force is presented as the legitimate action of the state, with the accoutrements of
state seals, formal procedures, costumes, and arcane legal language. In
these ritualized settings, courts declare certain forms of behavior acceptable and others unacceptable. Courts do not simply announce new
social rules; they also apply them to the life situations of concrete
persons. Moreover, the court's influence does not end with the appearance before the judge but frequently includes ongoing supervision,
mandatory social service participation, and occasionally incarceration.

This chapter focuses on one instance of cultural production in the
courts: the management of violence between men and women in
intimate relationships. The setting is a small town in Hawai'i that,
starting in the early 1980s, has developed an increasingly activist,
feminist approach to spousal violence. There has been an astronomi-
cal increase in the number of cases coming to court in the last ten
years, both in family court as victims seek protective orders and in
criminal court as batterers are criminally prosecuted. Women are more
inclined to turn to the legal system for help and police are more
energetic in making arrests and prosecutors in pressing charges.
There also has been a significant strengthening of the laws, including
an increase in penalties for spousal violence. At the same time, feminists in the area concerned with violence against women staffed a
shelter, developed a violence control program for men, and formed a
support group for women. Many convicted batterers and men subject

---

4. This definition of law dates back at least as far as E. Adamson Hoebel, *The Law
of Primitive Man* (Cambridge: Harvard University Press, 1954).

to restraining orders are mandated by the court to attend the violence control program.

As courts handle domestic violence cases, they redefine gender roles and reconstitute the importance of law to everyday family life in gendered ways. The messages communicated to men and to women about rights, about themselves, and about their relationships to the law are very different. While men are presented with the carceral side of law, women experience it as supportive and are encouraged to use it for help. The court becomes a place for women to turn for protection rather than a place that reinforces male authority. For men, it is a place of alienation, a disruption of their sense of the social support for male authority.

Moreover, the court communicates messages about connection and violence that have very different implications for men and for women. Violence is presented as something that severs relations rather than something that maintains them. Men, who have in the past used violence to maintain relationships with women, are encouraged to see that connection is enhanced by suppressing their violence. The men's violence control program creates a therapeutic community of connectedness without violence among the male participants and teaches that connectedness with women and children will similarly be enhanced by refraining from violence. It seeks to redefine masculinity in terms of connection and negotiation rather than "toughness" and self-assertion. Women are encouraged by the court to leave their violent partners rather than remain with them and give in to them. The women's support group encourages women to rely on the law and the support of others in like situations instead of their violent spouses and extended kin networks, often sites of violence themselves.

Most significantly, the discourse of the court denaturalizes domestic violence. As judges, attorneys, and advocates talk about domestic violence, it slips from the unseen to the seen, from the natural to the cultural. Actions that were part of the "normal" order of family relationships acquire new names, such as abuse. And abuse, unlike the violence embedded in patriarchal authority, is reconstituted as crime, subject to carceral response.

This is not a study of the effectiveness of legal intervention in social life. My focus is the cultural production of the court rather than its impact on behavior. Although I interviewed about thirty men and women after their participation in court proceedings and in the violence control program, I was not trying to assess whether this participation changed their actions, their beliefs, or their patterns of violence. Instead, I was interested in what they heard in court and in the violence control program. I used interviews and observations of the court and the group discussions in the violence control program to get a sense of what was being said to them and how the participants understood it. It was impossible to track the men through the courts and the program to see if the violence recurred, but many of those I talked to, particularly those who stayed with the program to the end, said that they now think about their violence in a new way. Even those who most earnestly try to avoid violence find that, when thrust into similar situations, the violence sometimes recurs.

The most striking change I noticed was that the men started to use the new vocabulary of the violence control program to talk about their own anger—to me, to one another in group discussions, and to judges and attorneys in court. Men who had complained about "feeling pressure" and "just snapping" began to talk about "cool downs," engaging in "positive self talk" and not exercising "male privilege." I think these linguistic shifts imply that they at least heard some of the message of the program. Here I will discuss the meanings created by the courts and the violence control program as they handle spousal violence, looking at the ways these meanings are new in this social world. In order to understand the larger significance of this redefinition of gender roles, it is necessary to explore the social context of the people involved and the historical formation of the cultural categories within which they live.

Denaturalizing Domestic Violence in a Plantation Town

Hawai'i still retains vestiges of the cultural pluralism produced by its colonial past. A highly stratified Polynesian state in the eighteenth century when Captain Cook arrived in 1778, the kingdom of Hawai'i during the nineteenth century increasingly came under the domination of European and American immigrants.[5] The early years of contact were marked by mercantile trade in sandalwood, foodstuffs, and sexual services, generally controlled by Hawaiian elites. By the mid-

---

5. See, generally, Gavan Daws, *Shoal of Time: A History of the Hawaiian Islands* (New York: Macmillan, 1968).

nineteenth century, Hawaiian commoners traded foodstuffs and labor to visiting whaling ships, and the Hawaiian population became gradually more involved with the cash economy both as petty traders and as sailors. However, during the first century after contact, the Hawaiian population plummeted as the people suffered from the onslaught of diseases against which they had little resistance.[6]

During this period, the Hawaiian government became increasingly dependent on American advisors, many of whom were missionaries from New England. Under their direction, the Hawaiian monarchs adopted a constitutional monarchy and a legal system modeled after that of Massachusetts and, to a lesser extent, Louisiana. A project of land division and reallocation in 1848 broke apart the traditional chiefly estates and the linkages between chiefs and their dependents, paving the way for the acquisition of large tracts of land in fee simple ownership for the development of sugar plantations.[7] Although the early sugar plantations in the town I studied were developed by Chinese sugar masters who brought the skills of sugar making from China, by mid-nineteenth century their businesses were largely in the hands of American and British entrepreneurs.[8] As the need for labor in the expanding sugar plantations became acute, the planters imported a succession of foreign laborers. In Hilo, these laborers came from China in the 1850s to 1870s, Japan and Portugal in the 1880s to the early 1900s, Puerto Rico at the turn of the century, and the Philippines in the period from 1920 to 1960. The population of white Americans and non-Portuguese Europeans, who tended to occupy top managerial positions, remained small and socially separated from the labor force.

The plantation economy dominated Hilo until the 1970s, when profits continued to fall and plantations began to close. Since then, the number of sugar mills on the island of Hawai'i has continued to decline, with only three remaining in place in 1992 out of a maximum of twenty-six earlier in the century. The job market is now being sharply reoriented as plantation jobs give way to work in the burgeoning tourist industry, which is located on the other side of the island, a two-hour drive away. Since Hilo provides low-cost housing but few

---

6. David Stannard, *Before the Horror* (Honolulu: University of Hawaii Social Science Research Institute, 1989).

7. Marion Kelly, "Land Tenure in Hawaii," *Amerasia Journal* (1980): 57.

8. Peggy Kai, "Chinese Settlers in the Village of Hilo before 1852," *Hawaiian Journal of History* 8 (1974): 39.

jobs while the other side of the island offers much more expensive housing plus work, many of the residents of Hilo now find themselves commuting long distances to work in fairly well-paid but uncertain construction jobs or low-paid hotel work. Many of the men and women in the domestic violence program are unemployed or on welfare; a few commute to the other side for construction jobs and even fewer still work for plantations. The town, which is the county seat, offers a large number of government and service jobs as well.

The present legal system was established under the Hawaiian monarchy in the mid-1800s at a time when the beleaguered kingdom adopted many of the legal institutions and laws of the United States in a desperate attempt to preserve its independence in the face of continued threats of takeover by several major powers. This legal system played a critical role in the cultural transformation of the Hawaiian population during the nineteenth century and of the immigrant sugar workers in the twentieth. After 1876, the social order was increasingly dominated by plantation forms of discipline and order because the passage of the Reciprocity Treaty in that year guaranteed Hawaiian sugar planters privileged access to the American market and fueled the expansion of sugar plantations. In the 1800s, many judges and attorneys were also sugar planters. Many of the cases involved disciplining contract laborers who refused to work, ran away from their jobs, or resisted their supervisors. Each ethnic group (or nationality, as groups are called in Hawai'i) appears in substantial numbers in the criminal courts during the first decades after their arrival, although the offenses are various. Thus, the courts served to impose new cultural practices on colonized Hawaiians and on immigrants from Europe and Asia both during the monarchy period and after 1900 when Hawai'i was annexed as a colony of the United States.

The courts of the nineteenth century and early twentieth century were not concerned with violence in families. I have examined the court records of the Hilo District Court every decade from 1853 to 1903 as part of an ongoing effort to chart the changing caseloads of these courts. In this early period, there is a conspicuous absence of cases concerning violence within the family. Although a few cases do end up in court in which a man assaults his wife, they are rarely prosecuted and penalties are typically quite light. [9] In the nineteenth

9. Peter Nelligan, in his study of rape law, argues that in the nineteenth century, European notions of coverture and female subordination were imposed on Hawaii,

century, the courts failed to see violence in the family as a problem. In contrast, there are a large number of cases concerning adultery and fornication, particularly in the 1850s when missionary influence was relatively strong. The courts did intervene in family life, but largely to control sexuality rather than violence. In the mid-nineteenth century, the legal system supported the rights of husbands over the sexual behavior of their wives, and in the late nineteenth century, the authority of the sugar planters and their supervisors over the workers. Unfortunately, I am unable to trace the changes in the caseload of the lower courts continuously until the present since the lower court records of Hilo between 1910 and 1970 have disappeared. However, interviews with older people, an examination of police reports and other records, and ethnographic studies from earlier periods suggest that before about 1980, there was little legal attention paid to domestic violence.

My ethnographic research on law in Hawai'i focused on the management of domestic violence cases over a period of fifteen months, over the period 1991 to 1994. I made periodic trips to Hilo, spending a total of six months in the town. One research assistant, Marilyn Brown, worked in Hilo and Honolulu for a total of nine months, while a second, Joy Adapon, spent almost two months in Hilo. Two other research assistants, Tami Miller and Linda Andres, worked several weeks over the spring and summer of 1992. Together we observed thirty-three sessions of the violence control program over a period of one year, observed domestic violence proceedings at the Family Court and District Court (nineteen weekly sessions), interviewed fifteen men and fifteen women about their reactions to the court, and coded a massive amount of historical case record material not discussed here. At the same time, we talked to a wide variety of people in the community and the courts, including the leaders of the movement to deal with domestic violence.

Domestic Violence in Court

By the 1990s, there were a burgeoning number of defendants in domestic violence cases going through the courts. Spotty data as well as observations confirm that most, though not all, of the defendants are

leading to a loss of status by Hawaiian women (Peter James Nelligan, *Social Change and Rape Law in Hawaii* (Ph.D. diss., Department of Sociology, University of Hawaii, 1983).

men and victims are women.[10] As the changing caseloads and the historical material suggest, these men are going to court for behavior that 20 years ago was taken for granted as a part of male authority.

Although cases of domestic violence appear in the court records in Hilo from time to time during the nineteenth and early twentieth centuries under assault charges, in most cases they appeared only when the violence was frequent and the injuries severe. The court typically failed to prosecute these cases or imposed a fine far less than that for adultery or selling liquor without a license. By the mid-1970s, there were the beginnings of a change. The first law specifically addressed to domestic violence was passed in 1973 in Hawai'i, but based on caseload figures and interviews, seems to have had little effect. On the island of Oahu, the major urban area of the state, of 103 spouse abuse cases between 1973 and 1979, only three resulted in conviction.[11] In 1984–85, in contrast, there were 45 convictions for spouse abuse on Oahu and 41 criminal contempt convictions for violation of spouse abuse protective orders.[12]

The law first enacted specifically targeting spousal violence in 1973 was gradually strengthened during the 1980s. Before 1973, such cases had typically been handled as assault or harassment cases. In 1985 the spouse abuse law was amended to provide a mandatory forty-eight hour sentence for people convicted of abuse of a household member, with a possible jail sentence of up to one year. The cooling-off period was increased from three hours to twelve.[13] In 1986, the statute was amended to require the police to issue a written citation to abusive persons required to leave the premises for a cooling-off period.[14] The law in effect since 1991 allows the police officer to require the person to leave the premises for a twenty-four-hour cooling-off period, to give a written warning citation, and to

10. When the 151 calls for domestic trouble to the Hawaii County Police are broken down by gender, of the 130 for which information is available, 117 (90 percent) have female victims and male perpetrators, 10 (8 percent) have male victims and female perpetrators, and 3 (2 percent) have male victims and male perpetrators (Hawaii Island Spouse Abuse Task Force, "A Report on Spouse Abuse in Hawaii County and Recommendations for Change" [Hawaii County Committee on the Status of Women, 1989, typescript], Appendix A-3).

11. Oahu Spouse Abuse Task Force 1986, quoted in Hawaii Island Spouse Abuse Task Force, "A Report on Spouse Abuse," Appendix C-8.

12. Ibid.

13. Hawaii *Revised Statutes, Session Laws* (1985), act 143, 253.

14. Hawaii *Revised Statutes, Commentary* (1991), 66.

arrest a person who refuses to leave. An arrested person must post bail of $250 for pretrial release. In addition to the forty-eight-hour jail sentence, convicted persons are "required to undergo any available domestic violence treatment and counseling program as ordered by the court," a provision in effect since 1985.[15] Moreover, the law applies to household or family members: "spouses or former spouses, parents, children and persons jointly residing or formerly residing in the same dwelling unit."[16] Individuals can apply to have the record expunged if there are no further offenses after one year, changed in 1987 to five years.[17]

Thus, the legal response to domestic violence has shifted from an approach common in the 1970s of separating the parties and allowing them to cool off without further intervention to an increasingly severe penalty for the offender, both incarceration and mandatory treatment programs, and more extensive record keeping that isolates and identifies this problem in particular and labels the offender. This bureaucratic change signals not only that the problem is viewed as more serious, but also that it is separated out from the larger stream of assault cases and marked as different. Such shifts in record keeping, as the Oahu Task Force notes, increase the visibility of the action and shape consciousness about the offense and its frequency.[18]

On the island of Hawai'i, the mobilization for a stronger legal approach occurred in the late 1970s as the nascent women's center found that the demand for a shelter for battered women was strong. A shelter was founded in 1978 by a charismatic and effective woman who mobilized support, fought resistance from those who declared the shelter hostile to men, and gathered significant support from private charities to continue its operation. The founder continued to press the legislature, at the time a liberal, Democratic body, for further protections for women. Several significant changes occurred in Hilo in 1989 that altered the legal terrain for domestic violence cases. First, a new, autonomous Family Court was established in 1989 under a judge who had many years of experience as a legal aid attorney seeking to get protection for battered women. This judge had worked closely with the shelter

---

15. Hawaii *Revised Statutes* 709–906 (1991), sec. 4.

16. Hawaii *Revised Statutes* 709–906 (1985), sec 1.

17. Hawaiii *Revised Statutes Commentary* (1991), 66.

18. Oahu Spouse Abuse Task Force 1986, quoted in Hawaii Island Spouse Abuse Task Force, "A Report on Spouse Abuse," Appendix C-5.

for many years and had served on its board.[19] Second, the long-entrenched leadership of the Police Department changed with a new chief of police more concerned with family violence. In the same year, the Hawaii Island Spouse Abuse Task Force published a report urging more arrests in cases of domestic violence so that victims were not burdened with filing complaints themselves, more energetic prosecution of these cases, enhanced victim services for abused persons, and both criminal sanctions such as jail and fines as well as mandatory treatment programs for convicted spouse abusers.[20]

Since 1989, the number of cases has increased sharply. This change reflects new police arrest policies, a new willingness by women to turn to the courts, and new efforts by the Family Court and the District Court to prosecute these cases. At the same time, since 1986 the courts have supported a training program for men who abuse their partners which focuses on learning to manage anger and on retraining beliefs. The courts routinely require a significant proportion of the men accused of domestic violence to participate in this program and encourage their partners to attend a women's support group. The violence control program is part of the shelter and comes out of the same political movement dedicated to protecting women. Leaders of the program say that their main concern is with women's safety and that the training program for men is one way of increasing women's safety.

There are two distinct routes, one civil and one criminal, by which a case of domestic violence comes to the attention of the courts. They differ significantly in the amount of initiative required of the victim. Civilly, a victim can file for a temporary protective order, generally called a temporary restraining order or TRO, from the Family Court. A law providing for Ex-Parte Temporary Restraining Orders for victims of domestic violence was passed in 1979.[21] Since this is a civil action, the law does not provide an attorney for

---

19. The concern with domestic violence is a latecomer to the Family Court agenda, however. A report describing major conferences in 1972 and 1973 in which the Family Court idea was developed and promoted talks only about the needs of children and juveniles. Violence against women is never mentioned (*The Family Court: Its Goals and Role*. A Summary Report of the Project: Community and Family Courts in Program Goal Planning [An LEAA Funded Project, 1974]).

20. Hawaii Island Spouse Abuse Task Force, "A Report on Spouse Abuse," 6–9.

21. Oahu Spouse Abuse Task Force 1986, quoted in Hawaii Island Spouse Abuse Task Force, "A Report on Spouse Abuse," Appendix C-5.

the person accused. There is a hearing in Family Court one to two weeks after the application is filed at which the Family Court judge reads the written account provided by the victim, asks the accused if he or she acknowledges the charge, and takes testimony if the accused denies all violence. If the accused accepts the charge or the evidence is persuasive, the judge issues a temporary restraining order for a period of months with a series of conditions. If there are no children and a desire by both to separate, they are told to stay away from each other and have no further contact. If they have children but the victim wishes no contact, the judge will arrange visitation or custody for the children and specify no contact between the adults. If they wish to continue the relationship and to live together or to have contact, the judge will often send them to the violence control program, requiring either the accused or both to participate in the program and allow them contact without violence. The judge points out that any violation of the conditions of the protective order is a misdemeanor, punishable by a jail sentence of up to one year and/or a fine of $2000.

The judge frequently schedules a review hearing in a month or two to monitor the situation, particularly for the contact restraining orders. The victims (usually women) typically fill out the request for a TRO in the shelter or at the violence control program where workers, some of whom receive pay from the court, help them. Victims are almost always accompanied by a woman advocate from the violence control program, called Alternatives to Violence (ATV). The man appears alone, although there is always a male advocate from the ATV program present in the waiting area of the court and willing to talk to the men. The men's advocate says that the men typically are not interested in talking at that time and do not regularly talk to him until the judge tells them they must go to ATV and should make arrangements with the advocate. Thus, access to this process requires the initiative of the victim and her willingness to summon the accused to court.

The number of requests for TROs has increased dramatically since the early 1970s. Between 1971 and 1978, there were seven TROs issued in Hilo for domestic violence situations. By 1985, however, the year the new spouse abuse law went into effect, the numbers were much larger, as Table 1 indicates. These figures are only for cases from Hilo. I was unable to locate figures for the period from 1979, when the regulation providing for these protective orders in domestic situations came into effect, to 1985.

A second route by which domestic violence cases arrive in court is through the criminal process. If a victim (usually a woman) calls the police and they arrive to find her injured or a situation of abuse in progress, they can arrest the perpetrator under the statute *Abuse of a Family or Household Member*. They are also empowered to impose a temporary cooling-off period. Under the abuse statute, convicted people serve a minimum of forty-eight hours in jail. Those who cannot make the bail of $250 commence this jail time immediately. The charge is a misdemeanor with a possible jail sentence. These cases frequently result in a mandatory assignment of the defendant to the ATV program, sometimes with a suspended sentence hanging over his/her head. It is fairly common for the same incident to lead to a TRO in Family Court and an abuse charge in District Court. If the police officer does not arrest the offender, the victim can also file an application for a criminal complaint.

Prosecuting abuse cases in District Court poses significant difficulties, however. If the offender is in custody and the case can move rapidly to trial, the victim may be willing to testify. However, if he is released on bail and the process takes several months, she is frequently increasingly unwilling as the incident fades and the perpetra-

TABLE 1.   Number of TRO Cases in Family Court by Year

1985	250
1986	327
1987	355
1988	277
1989	289
1990	338
1991	320

Note: Counts based on Circuit Court case files of miscellaneous Family Court cases; these numbers were produced by going through the files of miscellaneous cases looking for those concerning domestic violence. Figures for 1991 are up until Dec. 22, 1991. After 1990, domestic violence cases were cataloged separately under the designation FC-DA.

tor appears as a needed source of support for her and her children. He is often penitent and promises to reform. She then becomes the agent of his incarceration, and he puts considerable pressure on her to withdraw the case. The prosecutor's office points out to the woman that it is no longer her case but the state's case, and that she cannot simply withdraw, although I heard frequent stories about women signing papers to take away the charges. The dilemma for the prosecutor is that without a victim willing to testify, the case is hard to prosecute. Consequently, many cases are settled by guilty pleas or by deferred prosecutions dependent on continued good behavior instead of by trials; a member of the court staff estimated that only one in fifteen or twenty cases comes to trial. Attending the violence control program is frequently one of the conditions of deferred prosecution as well as a common sentence in guilty pleas. The only cases in which an incident of abuse is likely to come to trial is when the abuse occurs in conjunction with a more serious felony, such as burglary or murder. One of the important trials in 1992, in front of a jury in the Circuit Court, concerned a man who had a long history of abusing his wife and was accused of murdering his ex-wife and a young man living with her. He was convicted.

The number of cases of domestic violence appearing in court as criminal cases has increased enormously. Indeed, the increase has been more pronounced than the increase in TRO applications. Table 2 lists the number of domestic violence cases in court for both East and West Hawaii by year.[22]

The sharp increase is in part the result of a decision by the police to arrest all perpetrators of abuse in a household relationship, not just those who resist leaving, who come back before it is over or who inflict serious injury. I was told by a public defender that this policy change occurred in 1989. In 1987 there were 151 cases of abuse of household members reported to the police, in which only 23 of the perpetrators were arrested and 126 were referred to the prosecuting attorney.[23] There has also been an expansion of the victim/witness program,

---

22. Unfortunately, these figures are not separated by the side of the island. East Hawaii has a little over half the population of the island. The total population of the island of Hawaii is 120,317, according to the 1990 Census; the area I am calling East Hawaii (roughly the catchment area for the District Court) has a population of 77,123, and the town of Hilo has a population of 39,537.

23. Hawaii Island Spouse Abuse Task Force, "A Report on Spouse Abuse," Appendix A-1. Sixty-seven of these cases came from East Hawaii, 84 from West Hawaii.

which endeavors to encourage women to press charges, particularly in the last three years. At the same time, the victim/witness program has developed a more cooperative working relationship with the shelter, which facilitates prosecutions. These changes are even more marked in more urban areas, such as Honolulu. A bill presented to the House of Representatives for the 16th Legislature, HB No. 364, S.D. 1, claims that on Oahu, arrests for domestic violence increased from 128 in 1986 to 1,400 in 1988, while restraining orders issued by Family Court on Oahu increased from 164 in 1980 to 918 in 1988.

Although it is difficult to find these cases in earlier periods when they were not classified separately but appeared as assault cases or were lumped into larger categories such as miscellaneous family problems, early police reports do include reference to family violence. Statistics kept by the County of Hawaii Police Department islandwide indicate a continuing demand for police intervention in domestic problems, as the information in Table 3 indicates. These statistics report what are described as "domestic trouble cases" and are buried in

TABLE 2.   Number of Cases
of Abuse of a Household
Member Presented in District
Court by Year

1979	31
1980	9
1981	4
1982	15
1983	14
1984	6
1985	15
1986	35
1987	63
1988	95
1989	125
1990	291
1991	551

Note: Information derived from district court case records. Numbering was sequential from 1979 to 1989, during which time there were 412 cases. Beginning in 1990, each year begins with a new number. Data on 1991 are up until Dec. 6, 1991.

TABLE 3.   Domestic Trouble
Cases Handled by Hawaii
County Police Department
Islandwide by Year

1974	520
1975	556
1976	541
1977	646
1978	703
1979	826
1980	948
1981	893
1982	830
1983	866
1984	999
1985	1,295
1986	1,282
1987	1,368
1988	1,629

Note: All information from Hawaii
County Police Department Annual Re-
ports: 1984–88 directly from Annual Re-
port, 1974–83 quoted in Hawaii Island
Spouse Abuse Task Force, "A Report on
Spouse Abuse," Appendix B-1.

police reports in a long list of "Miscellaneous Public Complaints" or "Miscellaneous Services and Reports."

Although these figures are islandwide, a breakdown for 1987 indicates that 561 of the total (41 percent) were from Hilo and 895 (or 65 percent) were from East Hawaii.[24] These numbers record calls, not cases. Some people call repeatedly, so that the actual number of cases may be fewer, offset by the number of victims who fail to call at all. Of the 78 women who filled out intake forms for the violence control program in 1989–90, 86 percent said that they had called the police for domestic violence, with an average of 14 calls per person. In 1990–91, of 73 women who did intake interviews, 67 percent said they had called the police, an average of 6 times per person. In both years, only 35 percent said that their partner was issued a warning citation by the police, despite the statutory requirement.

24. Quoted from Lieutenant William S. Silva, in Hawaii Island Spouse Abuse Task Force, "A Report on Spouse Abuse," Appendix B-1.

Although the number of calls to police has risen threefold over the last two decades, the increase is much smaller than the increase in the number of TRO cases or the number of criminal cases. This observation suggests that the largest changes have occurred in the inclination of the legal system to prosecute or to offer protective injunctions, not in the violent behavior itself.

In earlier years, the situation was quite different. I have only spotty information on past police management of domestic violence. Indeed, it is the silence about this problem rather than its noisiness that is remarkable. In 1947, the police reported 13 offenses against the family and 11 arrests of adults for these offenses for the whole island of Hawaii, although in the same year they reported 8 aggravated assaults and 241 other assaults.[25] All the aggravated assault arrests and 191 of 200 other assault arrests were men, but only 7 of the 11 offenses versus the family arrests were men.[26] Of the 200 other assaults for which information is provided, 19 percent were Hawaiian, 14 percent Caucasian/Hawaiian, 6 percent Asian/Hawaiian, 16 percent Portuguese, 12 percent Puerto Rican, 11 percent Other Caucasian, 1 percent Chinese, 9 percent Japanese, 2 percent Korean, and 12 percent Filipino.[27] Of these defendants, 64 percent were convicted, but only 11 people were jailed.[28]

It is impossible to know how many cases of domestic violence are concealed in these figures, although it seems likely that a substantial percentage of these cases did involve assaults within the family. More noteworthy, perhaps, is attention to the categories that are used and those that are not in dividing up the universe of criminal behavior. The fact that domestic violence was not differentiated in 1947 as a distinct crime suggests again the silence, the nonseeing of this as a distinctive problem that appears from other sources as well. In fact, the record-keeping procedures of the courts have only distinguished this kind of case from others since 1990, suggesting that there may be a fundamental shift occurring in the way the behavior is considered, now fully entrenched in the taken-for-granted world of bureaucratic record keeping.[29]

---

25. Police Department of County of Hawaii, Territory of Hawaii, *Annual Report* (1947), 17.

26. Ibid., 18.

27. Ibid., 19.

28. Ibid.

29. See Susan Silbey, "Case Processing: Consumer Protection in an Attorney General's Office," *Law and Society Review* 15 (1980/81): 849.

At the same time that domestic violence is not separated out for attention, other characteristics of individuals clearly are, such as age, gender, and "race" or "nationality." The designations listed in the 1947 statistics are presented as natural categories, although even then, and increasingly now, ethnic identity is extraordinarily fluid and contested in this community in which generations of marriage among peoples of different historic backgrounds has produced a genetically mixed but socially differentiated population. Nationality and class are inextricably joined together in the definition of identity, and one of the most fundamental markers of personhood is dialect or accent. Moreover, the meaning of the identity of being Hawaiian has shifted dramatically over the last fifty years from one of opprobrium by the larger society in the 1940s to one of pride and entitlement in the 1990s. Patterns of self-identification have shifted at the same time. Thus, the tabulation of crimes by nationality renders unproblematic what is problematic, fixing categories of things to be noticed, such as race and gender, and subsuming or ignoring other categories of things, such as domestic violence, which are not noticed.

The County of Hawaii police report for 1956 similarly lists 167 other assaults and 15 offenses against the family,[30] indicating that the same pattern of nonseeing continued in the 1950s. By 1988, the annual report of the Hawaii County Police Department still failed to separate out domestic violence cases but listed "domestic trouble" in a list of other miscellaneous services and reports. Other assault complaints had risen to 1,102 and arrests to 221 while offenses against the family number 27 and arrests 2, with aggravated assault complaints at 136 and arrests 53.[31] Unlike the 1940s and earlier, however, there is no break-down by ethnicity or race of defendants nor by gender and age except for juveniles. The racial and gendered categorization of adult defendants disappears, yet the system of crime categories employed, long in use throughout the United States, still fails to distinguish domestic violence. Nor does the police report catalog it elsewhere. Violence in the family is not differentiated and counted, while various forms of theft of property, arrests for drunk driving, and numbers of marijuana plants eradicated are given high profiles in the annual reports.

In sum, in the 1990s the courts have begun to take seriously and prosecute as crimes actions that in the past were taken for granted

---

30. Hawaii County Police Department, *Annual Report*, 1956.
31. Hawaii County Police Department, *Annual Report* (1988–89), 16, 20–21.

and largely overlooked. The law is denaturalizing domestic violence. What has shifted is not the behavior but the definition and meaning of the behavior as the boundary between legitimate violence and illegitimate violence is redrawn. The law plays a role in deploying and enforcing this new boundary. It is, of course, responding to the political mobilization of groups concerned with violence against women. But the example illustrates the capacity of the law to present new discourses, to shift consciousness through processes of meaning making backed by force. The next section of this chapter describes in some detail the meanings that are made, particularly in the violence control program, and analyzes how these meanings redefine gender conceptions and at the same time present a different notion of the significance of law to everyday life.

Teaching Violence Control

The Participants in ATV

A significant proportion of people convicted of abuse of a household member or who are the subject of a TRO for domestic violence are sent every year to a violence control program located in Hilo, the Alternatives to Violence (ATV) program.[32] Men are typically required to attend by the courts while women are encouraged to but not required. In 1989–90, intake figures for the program indicated that 90 percent of men who participated were mandated and only 1 percent of the women, although 68 percent of the women were referred by the courts. In 1990–91, 71 percent of men who participated were mandated and 27 percent of the women were. The program is unambiguously attached to the court process, with judges routinely advising or

32. In 1989, when 289 TROs were issued and 124 abuse cases heard, of which roughly half were probably from East Hawaii, there were 89 men and 78 women admitted to the ATV program. It is very likely that many of the abuse defendants were also subject to TROs, so that these do not represent two different groups of people. Perhaps a third of those brought to court for domestic violence problems end up having an intake interview and attending some classes. The program offers a range of services, however, and estimates that in 1987–88 it serviced 101 people referred by the judiciary and in 1988–89, 343, including men and women. In 1990–91, there were 320 TROs, 291 abuse cases (again probably half from East Hawaii), and 99 men and 73 women who completed intake interviews at ATV. There is another ATV program now operating in West Hawaii, which handles similar numbers of cases. In 1989–90, it did intake interviews on 72 men and 50 women and in 1990–91, on 98 men and 66 women.

requiring attendance, backed by threats of fines and prison for those who fail to attend when they have been mandated.

Based on statistical surveys from 1989–90 and 1990–91 filled out by 188 men and 151 women at intake, about two-thirds of the men (68 percent and 76 percent in the two respective years) and four-fifths of the women (80 percent and 85 percent, respectively) were high school graduates, but only a few (3 percent and 5 percent of the men, 6 percent and 4 percent of the women) were college graduates. In 1990, 23 percent of the men and 67 percent of the women were on public assistance. The median income of the men was about $9,500 for 1989–90 and $8,000 for 1990–91, and that of the women was about $8,000 both years. In 1990, 52 percent of the men were employed full time, 13 percent part time, and 35 percent were unemployed, although the 1990 census reported that the unemployment rate for Hilo was 4.3 percent and the median family income $35,506. Most participants had some experience with marriage but fewer than half were married at the point of entry into the program. They had already been through an average of two to three relationships and had on average between two and three children. This population thus is far younger, poorer, less educated, and less employed than the general population in Hilo. It is important to remember that this profile describes the people who turn to the court for help, are referred to ATV, and follow through with the intake. This does not mean that violence occurs only in poor families; it shows simply that poor families are more likely to end up in the legal process.

In both 1989–90 and 1990–91, about half the men claimed to be of Native Hawaiian or part Hawaiian ancestry, and about a third of the women made that claim. The population of Hilo was about 19 percent Hawaiian in 1980, the most recent census data available on ethnicity. On the other hand, very few of the participants (men 1 percent and 2 percent, women 5 percent and 6 percent) were Japanese-American, yet the population of the town was 38 percent Japanese-American in 1980. Moreover, some groups are strongly overrepresented in comparison to the population at large, such as Native Hawaiians and Portuguese-Americans, and some are underrepresented, such as the Japanese-Americans and the non-Portuguese whites, called Caucasians in official parlance and *haoles* in everyday talk. These ethnic distributions are reflections of social class differences, since the Japanese and haoles have moved most extensively into the middle class while many Hawaiians and Portuguese remain locked in the underclass, underscoring the fact that those who end up in court with domestic violence problems and are sent for mandatory treatment are disproportionately the poor.[33]

Most of the participants in the ATV program identify themselves as "local", a quasi-ethnic identity defined primarily by rearing in Hawai'i but marked most significantly by the use of pidgin, a distinctive dialect of English with a heavy sprinkling of Hawaiian words. Among the many sources of the culture and identity of "local" is the experience of subordination to educated white elites. Polynesian Hawaiians, who were displaced and marginalized by colonialism but after the 1870s no longer formed the backbone of the plantation labor force, have joined with other groups who became plantation laborers at the end of the nineteenth and early twentieth centuries in constituting this culture.

The Men's Program and the Women's Program

ATV offers very different programs for men and for women. Both men and women meet regularly with a same-sex group of about fifteen people who are in similar circumstances. Women attend a support group, which meets two hours a week. If mandated, they are required to attend ten sessions, and they receive a certificate at the end. Men attend a thirty-one-week training program, which meets for two hours every week, and they also receive a certificate at graduation. The programs are held in the same rooms, with women meeting during the day and men attending in the evening. However, in many respects the two programs are vastly different: in level of coerciveness, in the training each provides, and in the way the relationship between the participants and the law is described. The women's support group is organized around the trope of empowerment, in which women are encouraged to see the law as a source of help and support while they gather strength from others in the same position. The men's program adopts the trope of the school and the prison, requiring attendance, demanding homework, and threatening jail for failure to attend. Men who are

---

33. This group of men and women are similar in their socioeconomic position to the men and women I observed turning to courts for domestic violence situations in the very different social context of an old New England mill town (*Getting Justice and Getting Even* (Chicago: University of Chicago Press, 1990).

recalcitrant and continue to claim the right to beat their "old ladies" if they do wrong are told they may have to start the program all over again. Indeed, if a woman reports to the program that her partner has violently assaulted her, he may be forced to begin the program from the beginning and to follow the entire sequence again. The law is always present in the room as a threat, and all the men I interviewed said that they understood that if they did not attend, they would go to jail. Although it is frequently mentioned by ATV leaders and participants, men are rarely, if ever, sent to jail for failure to participate. It is much more common for them to face jail as a result of a new incident of violence against their partners.

Other differences in organization reinforce the carceral nature of the men's program and the supportive nature of the women's. The men are required to pay on a sliding scale depending on income. If they miss a class, they must take a makeup class, which costs $20. For these men, who typically have little income, this is a major cost, which sometimes leads them to drop out of the program. If a man misses three sessions, he must start the program all over again. The men must attend on time and cannot leave until the program is over. They often joke about "How long are you going to keep us tonight?" and wanting to go home early. Women, on the other hand, typically drift in and out of the support group meeting, arriving late or leaving early as they choose. Some of the men complain about the differences between the two programs, particularly when both individuals have been mandated to attend. One woman said that her partner comes home from the men's program and says, "They treat me like a criminal, like I'm real bad. Do they treat you like that?" She told him that she had an intake interview, too. Then he came home after the third week and said it was very good; he liked the program. The facilitator responded:

> When guys come in, we are careful to treat them as people, but they *are* criminals. We treat them as people who can change, but you are the victims, they are the criminals.

Thus, despite the effort to see wife battering as a collective problem and to encourage women to feel more power in themselves, there is a tendency to see women as victims as they and the staff talk about their own experiences.

The men's program, in contrast, is designed as a class, with two
leaders, a man and a woman, sitting in front of a group of ten to
fifteen men with the large loose-leaf notebooks in which the program
materials are held providing instruction on the topic of the day. Although the atmosphere is informal, with considerable joking among
the men and between the teachers and the men, there is a clear sense
of a subject to be covered, with frequent use of a blackboard or lists on
paper. The men are required to do written homework every week and
must turn this homework in when they arrive. Both men and teachers
refer to the group meetings as "class" and the project as "learning"
new beliefs about violence and how to manage their own violence.
After the first three weeks, in which the men receive lectures and fill
out forms, the chairs are arranged in a circle in the room and men
are encouraged to participate. The sessions generally begin with a
"check-in" in which each participant describes how his week has been
going. Thus, the structural analogy to a group therapy session is
clear, but the language and forms of school are much more pervasive.

One small indication of this emphasis on the disciplinary order of
the school as the organizing principle is a prohibition against the men
sitting on the sofa in each room. Instead, they are to sit on folding
metal chairs. The rule excluding them from the sofa evokes good-
natured bantering when a man does happen to sit on the sofa, but the
rule is strictly maintained. Some of the leaders are afraid the men will
fall asleep if they sit on the sofa. Fixed above the sofa is a hand-
lettered sign which reads:

> *Men's* Program Participants
> Do *Not* sit on Couch!!!
> This means YOU!

In contrast, there is no reference to school, homework, or curriculum in the women's group. Instead of being marked present by a
monitor, they are free to sign themselves in. Although those women
mandated by the court are expected to attend, they can arrange to be
absent without great difficulty. There is no payment for attendance.
They are welcome to sit on the sofas. The meetings consist of "check-
ins" in which each woman describes her week and others ask questions and make comments. The leader, a woman, provides literature
to read and offers advice about the legal system but does not give any

instruction about managing anger or rethinking marital relationships. Sometimes the leader will encourage women to use the courts for help. Most of these women have already tried the courts and have been to Family Court or District Court after a worker, called an advocate, at ATV or the shelter has helped them file a complaint or an application for a TRO. Some complain that the court is not doing more, not forcing their partners to go to ATV or punishing them for dropping out, but many feel that the courts have been helpful to them.

One of the intriguing features to me, after attending both men's and women's groups (unlike any of the trainers or the participants), was the disjunction between the image of the legal system presented to the women and to the men.[34] While men experienced the carceral side of law in the program and were "taught" new ways of thinking about violence and its price, women were offered a supportive environment, connected to and provided by the courts, in which they could learn how it operated and come to use it more effectively. While the women were being encouraged to think of themselves as people with rights and entitlements, the men were being encouraged to reconceptualize the violence they had perpetrated as a crime rather than a natural part of male prerogatives.

Ironically, although women's new consciousness of rights and willingness to seek legal help has changed their fatalistic acceptance of male violence, at the same time it has substituted the state for patriarchal authority. For example, a leader in the women's group said that sometimes women need TROs and the shelter because men will pay attention to these things. Friends and family cannot offer this help, cannot protect the women the way the courts and the shelter can. One woman, a thirty-four-year-old white woman born and raised in Minnesota who has lived in Hawaii for fifteen years, said that through the legal process, she found out that she had rights. As she told my research assistant, they were separated two and a half years, and he abused her in various ways all that time. "I felt it was an incredible shift. He really respected the judge, but he never respected me." It is the judge, not the woman, who earns respect. But another young woman, local in accent and appearance, says shyly in the

---

34. I and my research assistants attended thirteen meetings of the women's group and twenty of the men's group.

women's group, "I braver now." Although her partner, who participates in the men's program, still shows signs of violence, it is no
longer directed at her.

On the other hand, some women find the promise of rights
hollow. One twenty-two-year-old woman of Filipino/Portuguese/
Hawaiian/Chinese ancestry whose family had been in Hawaii for
four generations, was arrested along with her partner after a fight
because she had threatened him with a knife. She also expressed a
sense of rights, but in a different relationship to the law: she felt that
the system didn't protect her rights because she was arrested for
using a weapon to defend herself when her life was threatened.

Meanwhile, men experience the carceral side of law. One man
told me how, during a group meeting, a fellow participant had described "flinging" his partner across the room. The leaders told him
he would have to start the program over again for that. My inter-
viewee protested vociferously, saying that it was just a little shove and
that it wasn't fair to send him all the way back. "You guys don't
understand," he told me he said to the facilitators, "you are sitting up
there in front, not like us back here behind bars." Since the group sits
in a circle facing the two facilitators, this statement presents his own
vivid reconstruction of the room. Another man talking in a group
session wrestled with the difference between the judge's power and
his own violence. His statement, presented in a local accent and based
on my notes of what he said, puzzles over this difference:

> It seems like the judge can say anything he wants. He told me to
> shut up when I tried to talk and told me he could have me
> removed from court. It seems to me that this is a kind of violence
> too. I have been thinking about this for the last two days, and I
> keep thinking about that, that I can't say anything back. And I am
> the one who is being accused of violence. But where is the vio-
> lence, really? What about the judge who could throw me out,
> stop me from speaking?

This man is describing another kind of power, one based on class,
education, and the force of the state.

One of the most striking parts of the men's program, in fact, was
the presentation of a new vocabulary for male-female relations and
anger. Men were taught to refer to the women in their lives as "part-

ners" rather than their "old ladies," to see "just a slap" as a case of "physical abuse," and to identify "battering" as consisting of four forms: "physical battering, sexual battering, psychological battering, and destruction of property and pets." The term *lickins'* or *dirty lickins'* is replaced by *abuse*. Men learn the unfamiliar term (many ask for a definition of the word) *intimidation* to describe what they were doing when they smashed the windshield on their wife's car to prevent her from driving to town and *male privilege* to describe their taken-for-granted idea that they could decide where their wives went, if they had a job, whether or not they took drugs, and did not need to consult their wives if they bought a new truck. The men were told the problem was not their anger but their violence and taught to recognize the body signs of anger and pursue strategies to "cool down."

After a few weeks in the program, men began to use these terms in conversation with each other, with me in interviews, and to judges in court. Attorneys and other court officials also noted this new language, although they were a little skeptical about how much it signaled a change in behavior. The unreconstructed discussion in the men's group, on the other hand, tends to naturalize violence, drawing connections between physiological states (high pressure) and violence as a release of that pressure. It is sometimes described as a natural emanation of character. Violence against women is also linked to images of masculinity and power that are rooted in distinctive ethnic and class cultures. One man, who appeared to be over fifty and white and who spoke pidgin (indicating that he was born and raised in Hawaii), said (here I quote as much as possible from my notes, but in standard English, since I am unable to reproduce the pidgin):

> I lived a violent life. It is a natural thing for me. I just go into a situation and it happens. My philosophy is, you mess with me, I warn you. Next time, I just do it. She knew this in Honolulu. I was as surprised as she was that I kicked her. [The woman he kicked in the head died ten hours later of a blood clot in the brain.]

One of the other men in the group objects to this account, saying:

> In every person I ever hit, I chose where I hit 'em. I do little punches. People pick their shots.

The other man continues:

> But it just happened. Neither of us realized how serious it was. The lawyer said I had a good chance to get off. My son says, I want to be just like you when I grow up, only thing is, I don't want to kill my wife. I sure miss my mom.

An older man, proud of his ethnic Hawaiian identity, links his violence to sexual attractiveness and to "local" images of power and to the burgeoning sense of entitlement of Native Hawaiians. This man has eight children aged ten to twenty-two. The haole wife is his second wife. The family lives on ancestral Hawaiian lands on a beach in a makeshift shelter. A significant number of families live this way on land designated as Hawaiian Homelands. After commenting that a slap is "Hawaiian love" (a phrase I heard from others as well), he said (and again, I am not able to reproduce his pidgin):

> Who's not afraid of one Hawaiian who act like an asshole? I'm born here, raised here, on my own land. I'm *kama'aina*.[35]

The female facilitator queries, What about her rights? He replies,

> She doesn't have any. She's a haole, I took her away from a haole husband, so she likes me better. She has no right to be at my sister's place, to leave my kids there [one point about which they were fighting]. That's why they call us Hawaiians. We don't steal wives, they come to us. Don't even have to play slack key. [36]

On the other hand, when recounting the fight that ensued, he continues:

I felt like an asshole, mad at myself when the cops came.

Facilitator:

How did your son [ten years old] feel?

---

35. This term means "native, person born in Hawaii."
36. "Slack key" refers to a style of music played on the guitar that is unique to Hawaii.

He replies:

He said, you are a fucker.

Facilitator:

As long as you tell yourself you didn't do anything wrong, you won't change.

Refiguring Violence and Connection

One of the most significant messages offered to the men in this program is a new understanding of the linkage between violence and connection. One exercise, repeated in various forms throughout the training session, is to take a man's account of his experience of violence, usually something that has happened in the past, and break it down into the feelings, the actions, the underlying beliefs, and the consequences to him, to his partner, to their children of this action. The man presents the situation, and the group collectively analyzes it. The conclusion drawn from the exercise is that the incidence of violence provided him with control and power in the short run but in the long run undermined his relationship with his partner and his children, who became fearful and suspicious of him. He also risks other forms of separation in the form of prison. Many of the men discuss how they use their violence to hold their women, either by preventing their leaving by attacking their car or threatening violence or by using violence when there is the possibility of another man. The men are constantly afraid that their women will leave them for other men, and quite often jealousy or even suspicion that the woman is trying to make contact with other men leads to efforts to isolate her and to eruptions of violence. Men have historically used violence to maintain their connections with women.

Here, the program reverses the link, arguing that violence breaks the connection, and that only by living without violence will they be able to maintain it. This discussion takes place in a therapeutic group situation in which each man is surrounded by other men in like circumstances, thus enacting the possibilities of connection if violence is not used. The legal system is a central actor in reconstituting

connection and violence in its threat that if the violence recurs, the
man will go to jail—the ultimate separation.

For women also, connection and violence are linked, but their
position is clearly different. In order to escape the violence, they must
also end the connection, but they may end up replacing it with a new
dependence on the state in the form of the courts and the welfare
system. For many women, the violent partner is also someone they
love and someone on whom they depend for sex and for economic
support. One woman talking in the support group, for example, be-
wailed the "hormones" that pulled her back to her abusive man and
regretted that there was no way she could see him just for her sexual
needs. Men are typically penitent after incidents of violence and promise not to do it again. Women want to believe these promises. The
dilemma the woman faces as she turns to the legal system for help is
that she is encouraged to leave the man. As one woman put it, "There
is an emotional side to this situation that the courts don't understand." The women also want connection, but without the violence,
and the courts encourage women to leave men who are violent. Of
course, if a woman does leave, she reinforces the aforementioned
message that violence leads to loss of connection. Thus, women are
encouraged to break the connection with their partners and turn to
the courts and to support groups provided by the courts where they
form connection with other women in similar situations.

If a woman repeatedly calls the police and presses charges, then
withdraws and refuses to prosecute, the courts and police become
frustrated and ignore her complaints. In other words, if the woman is
to mobilize the help offered by the legal system, she must be willing
to go through with the process of penalizing the husband, of sending
him to jail or to ATV, and consequently, with severing her relationship
with him. She is offered, instead of subordination to patriarchal authority in a violent relationship, the promise of liberal legalism: a self
protected by legal rights, able to make autonomous decisions, as long
as she is willing to sever the relationship with the man or, at the least,
risk making him very angry by filing charges against him or testifying
against him. Not only is this a difficult decision, but it is also a dangerous one. Men are most likely to be violent to women after the women
have left them. The men rely on the old strategy of achieving connection through violence, putting the woman in considerable danger,
which the law can do little to mitigate. Indeed, the staff of the violence

control program told me that after a highly publicized event of male violence occurs, women quietly slip back to the violent men they may have left out of fear that something like that will happen to them. There are frequent stories about rejected men hanging around the shelter, setting it on fire, going to their partner's houses, and other forms of harassment.

ATV deals with this period of risk by monitoring the relationship, calling the women at home to see if they have been attacked in a process called "safety checks," and confronting the men in group classes with incidents in which they have been violent or sexually abusive toward their partners if the women wish them to. A woman can fill out a violence report against the man with the program and choose whether or not she wishes to have the man confronted by the leaders in group sessions with this accusation. I observed a few confrontations of this kind, and the other men typically rallied around the confronted man in support, but the accused generally reacted with considerable anger and defensiveness.

The pressure to separate from the man in order to receive the protection of the legal system often poses severe financial and emotional difficulties for these women. Since they are typically poor, young, relatively uneducated, and caring for small children, they are dependent on their husbands as well as welfare for support. Moreover, many wish to hold on to the man. One woman who is local, Hawaiian, and in her forties with teenage children, complained in the women's support group:

> I didn't ask for a no-contact TRO, my dumb lawyer did. I'm angry at him. Now I can't ask for money for bills. Now I got to go to the kids for money, and they ask him. The kids are getting in the middle. He comes by every day, but he is not supposed to. This is an order that lasts until November [meeting is in July]. There is no chance of my marriage getting back together now since I can't see him until then. He's living with another girl now; I've lost him. Jane [pseudonym for one of the women advocates at ATV] forgot about that appointment in court, so I had to handle it the best I could alone. I said in court I wanted contact, but the judge told me to be quiet. I didn't know what else to do. I don't know if he's coming to ATV because I can't talk to him. So I can't keep him.

This statement encapsulates the dilemma for women: protection requires ending a relationship that involves love and financial support. Yet, the legal system recognizes that violent men very often hit their wives again, and returning women to the same situation poses a substantial risk of further violence to them.

There is a further twist to the connection/violence relationship. Women who are violent, or even who remain in violent homes, risk having their children removed by the child protective services. This is a constant source of discussion among the women in the support group. One woman, for example, stabbed her husband as he attacked her, and she is warned by the other women to be careful, that others who were railroaded into pleading guilty to such charges in the past lost their children. Thus, acknowledging the violence by asking the legal system for help or by fighting back risks another loss of connection, that with the children. Here, the message is that maintaining connections requires accepting violence.

Thus, I argue that the courts and ATV convey messages about violence and connection that have quite different implications for men and women. While men are told that violence earns them separation, a message emphasized when they first walk into Family Court completely alone while their partners are accompanied by a woman advocate, the women are encouraged in the support group to form other kinds of connections besides those premised on violence. One of the new connections proffered is with the legal system. The law expects women to leave the violent partner in order to earn its full support. Thus, women are encouraged to reconstitute themselves not as selves defined by relationships but as selves connected to the law, with rights defined by the legal system.

Not only does this situation represent a significant departure from the gender roles of earlier decades, but it also represents a new stance for the legal system. In the past, law supported the interests of the dominant groups against the subordinated groups: the planters against the workers, the missionaries against the allegedly sexually licentious Hawaiians, the moral order of the elite against bachelor workers who engaged in sex with young girls or immigrants who grew marijuana and held cockfights. Violence against subjugated groups was not counted, not noticed, not punished, by and large. The plantation system was an extremely hierarchical one that joined a system of racial supremacy with patriarchal authority: plantations

were run by white men, and jobs, housing, and access to management positions were all allocated on the basis of race and gender
identities. As the plantations are breaking down, so also are the structures of authority that underlie them. In the new, late capitalist service
economy, perhaps there is space for connections to be forged without
the violence.

Why can the courts now challenge the use of violence to maintain
structures of authority? Linda Gordon, in her historical study of family violence, suggests that spousal violence acquires visibility during
periods when feminism is relatively strong and loses public interest
during periods of conservatism when family unity becomes paramount.[37] The present moment is one in which feminism is politically
relatively powerful, although clearly it could lose this power in the
future. But I think that the assault on spousal violence is also related
to the demise of the plantation system and the shift to a service-based
economy reliant on new forms of authority less dependent on physical violence. Plantations depended on a gendered and raced division
of labor that a challenge to those categories would undermine. It
seems unlikely that the substantial court intervention and the ATV
program could have developed while plantations, with their incred-
ibly hierarchical forms of organization, both patriarchal and racial,
were still in full swing. The cultural space to mount this challenge to
gender identities opened at a time when the legal system was no
longer so closely tied to maintaining plantation discipline, colonial
authority, and white privilege.

Conclusions

What is the meaning of the extension of rights for gender relations in
this context? Clearly, ATV and the courts are engaged in producing a
new consciousness, a new definition of gender, in which rights, as
popularly understood, are a key ingredient. Women are promised a
more autonomous self and experience the law as help, albeit not always reliable help. Men, on the other hand, learn the carceral side of
law, its penalties, and discover that the authority of court is, this time,
at least, exercised on side of women. Their "natural" behaviors are

---

37. Linda Gordon, *Heroes of Their Own Lives: The Politics and History of Family
Violence, Boston 1810–1960* (New York: Viking, 1988).

penalized. This situation seems to reverse the traditional stance of law as the supporter of existing authority. Women, of course, are receiving the classic message of liberal legalism about the autonomous self defined by rights enforced by the legal system, while men are hearing the therapeutic language of connection, of needing to get along, of the losses suffered by asserting patriarchal authority through violence. They are confronted in group discussions focused on their own lives with the short-term gains of violence and the long-term losses in their relationships with women and children. Women are encouraged to trust the legal system, men to fear it. Women go to court with advocates, victim-witness helpers. Men go alone. And the ultimate threat for men is always jail, an extreme form of isolation and separation.

But the price the woman pays for going to court against her spouse is also separation, isolation. She, too, must play a part in the game that says that the reward for violence is isolation. Yet, women often desire to preserve connections with these men. Thus, there is a paradox for women to this mobilization of rights. The underlying cultural meaning of rights in the Western legal tradition is premised on an autonomous, choice-making self. In situations of spousal violence, women are expected to sever connections with violent men. Yet, separation from men who are frequently providers and often loved seems economically impossible or emotionally undesirable to many women. As poor women generally dependent on welfare for support, they lack the economic basis for autonomy. Moreover, separation is frequently dangerous, inspiring the more intense violence Mahoney labels "separation assault." [38] Yet, as Mahoney observes, if a woman fails to leave her violent spouse, the law asks why she failed to do so. In the town I studied, women who repeatedly failed to prosecute cases or who returned to violent men were considered difficult and less deserving of help. Thus, if a woman mobilizes rights as a mode of protection yet fails to conform fully to the conception of the autonomous, rights-bearing individual by leaving and prosecuting the batterer, she loses some of her entitlement to help from the legal system. She glimpses the possibility of a more autonomous and alienated but safer world in which femininity no longer means acquiescing to battering.

---

38. Martha R. Mahoney, "Legal Images of Battered Women: Redefining the Issue of Separation," *Michigan Law Review* 90 (1991): 1.

Are rights, in this situation, simply an empty promise, since they cannot guarantee protection nor replace the love and financial support of men? If this is the case, then the discussion of rights obscures women's continuing subjection to violence under the ascription of rights and the illusion of equality it produces. Beginning from Marx's critique of rights, Wendy Brown argues that the problem of rights for emancipation is not their inadequacy to accomplish these goals, but the creation of a promise "which they never fulfill but to which their aspirants remain in thrall. In this case, the 'magic' of rights may inhere in the fact that while they formally mark personhood, they cannot confer it; while they promise protection from humiliating exposure, they do not deliver it."[39] She continues, with reference to rights, "Their abstract and ahistoricizing discourse mystifies the conditions and power which delimits the possibility of achieving personhood, while their decontextualizing force deprives political consciousness of recognition of the histories, relations, and modalities of power which produce and situate us as human."[40]

Moreover, since the new gender consciousness is founded on rights, it is inevitably individualizing, reinforcing the idea that the woman alone is responsible, that the assault she suffers is the result of her actions, not because she belongs to a class of permitted objects of violence. She is the individual plaintiff and receives individual remedies from the law. ATV struggles against this construction of self and is aware of its disempowering implications, yet the nature of the law and its individualist construction of rights continue to construct the battered woman as an individual subject, enduring an individual injury rather than a collective wrong. Support group discussions with the sharing of experiences encourage women to reconceptualize their injuries as shared, but their encounters with the courts continue to individuate the experience. Perhaps this is the consequence of using the same system for resistance as the one that has discursively created the subject in the first place. [41]

Moreover, despite the political commitment of ATV and the

---

39. Wendy Brown, "Rights and Identity in Late Modernity," in this volume.
40. Ibid.
41. Judith Butler, *Gender Trouble: Feminism and the Subversion of Identity* (New York: Routledge, 1990), 2. But, as McClure points out, the language of rights has long functioned as a vibrant source of disruption and opposition to the discourse of sovereignty in the English context ("Taking Liberties in Foucault's Triangle: Sovereignty, Discipline, Governmentality, and the Subject of Rights," in this volume).

shelter to a social analysis of wife battering, a rights-oriented intervention of the legal system obscures the analysis of larger structures of power that impinge on both men and women. Neither ATV nor the court offers a class analysis by which the men and women could reinterpret their own subordination in a class system that valorizes violence, along with property and education, as symbols of power.

The legal redefinition of wife battering disrupts images of masculinity that have emerged in response to particular historical conditions of class power and racial stratification. Men acquire more negotiative and connected selves capable of managing their own anger. Will these men be welcomed into the new economic relations and positions of power in the postplantation economy, or will the traditional class and racial exclusions propel them back to older images of self-respect and efficacy premised on violence? Without changes in the material relations that created a violent patriarchy, it is possible that, despite the valiant efforts of ATV and the courts, masculinity will resist this redefinition.

The First Amendment and the Meaning of America

Steven Shiffrin

Political pundits often proclaim the view that conservatives know how to tap into American values in a way that progressives do not. Consider this tiny masterpiece from Patrick Buchanan: "The arts crowd is after more than our money, more than an end to the congressional ban on funding obscene and blasphemous art. It is engaged in a cultural struggle to root out the old America of family, faith, and flag, and recreate society in a pagan image."[1]

Buchanan's value-packed epithets have much to teach American progressives, and the lessons are ultimately quite somber. But let us begin with the obvious, albeit the underappreciated obvious. Everyone understands that the "arts crowd" is engaged in a cultural struggle. From the perspective of the arts community, that struggle is ordinarily seen as one in which the country's cultural standards are improved or "elevated." Moreover, the arts community has a well-developed sense that the denial of funding to blasphemous art is contrary to the art community's understanding of the first amendment. Indeed, the art community's sense of the First Amendment sometimes runs to the more demanding notion that the First Amendment requires funding for the arts in general—though how much funding is not too clear.

I owe thanks for helpful comments to Kathy Abrams, Gregory Alexander, Cynthia Farina, Tracey Maclin, Seana Shiffrin, Gary Simson, Steve Thel, and David Williams. I also owe thanks to participants in workshops at Boston University, Cornell University, and the University of Washington, and, of course, to the participants at the Amherst conference.

1. Patrick Buchanan, "This is the Battle for America's Soul," *L.A. Times* (March 25, 1990), M5.

What is less well appreciated is that the First Amendment itself is at the heart of America's cultural struggle and that cases involving the arts are perhaps the easiest illustrations of a more general phenomenon. Although I will discuss the First Amendment ramifications of the selective denials of funding to controversial artists, I will focus on what may appear to be a digression from the arts, namely the flag-burning cases.

But the flag-burning cases are no digression. After all, the flag is art, a national art form designed to bring the nation together. Moreover, like those who sponsored the flag, those who fund the arts frequently seek to produce works that can induce a sense of national pride and accomplishment.

In a way, this issue makes sense of what might be otherwise inexplicable. The nation has spent considerable sums on art and on museums to house art. It invites citizens to come and appreciate that art. Yet, without substantial artistic education, education that the overwhelming majority of citizens do not have, much of the art housed in museums cannot be appreciated for its place in (or departure from) the tradition that precedes it. Museums, then, are designed in substantial part to show that the nation has a great culture. Like the flag, they represent the Nation.

In part because they are "our" museums, in even greater part because "we" fund what goes into those museums, the public exhibits an interest, even occasional outrage, when museums house materials that offend deeply held values. Citizens ask why the public should have to pay for materials they regard as offensive.

But public displays of some art exhibits would attract public outrage even in the absence of public funding. Take, for example, the artistic representation of Christ—dipped in the artist's urine. So too, when someone burns a flag, the public response is outrage whether or not public funds have been used to support the "performance." Here many members of the public (including Patrick Buchanan) argue that such expressive actions so deeply offend cherished traditions that they should not be tolerated.

But the law is not on Patrick Buchanan's side—at least, not yet. The public must tolerate most offensive speech, including flag burning, and the public is constitutionally required to pay for offensive art in some circumstances. Of course, the latter conclusion is more controversial and more difficult to reach than the first. Nonetheless, the path to the second conclusion follows from the first. In approaching the flag cases, therefore, we do not digress. Indeed, we enter the forest from a spot where we can see it for more than a collection of trees.

In approaching questions such as flag burning and subsidies of the arts, however, we have more to learn than lessons in First Amendment geography. These disputes give us more than basic insight about free speech theory—important as that may be; in the end, they become an appropriate vehicle for considering important aspects of the relationships among liberalism, radicalism, and national identity.

The First Amendment and the Flag

In 1988, during the Republican National Convention, Gregory Lee Johnson doused an American flag with kerosene and set it on fire. While the flag burned, his fellow protestors shouted, "America the red, white, and blue, we spit on you." Johnson was convicted for violating a Texas statute that outlawed the knowing or intentional damaging of a state or national flag in a way that the perpetrator "knows will seriously offend one or more persons likely to observe or discover his action."[2] In *Texas v. Johnson*,[3] the United States Supreme Court held that Johnson's conviction violated his First Amendment rights.

On October 30, 1989, Gregory Lee Johnson appeared on the east steps of the United States Capitol in Washington D.C. In protest against the Flag Protection Act of 1989 (an act passed to circumvent the *Johnson* decision), Johnson sought to burn another flag. As luck would have it, however, Johnson's flag failed to ignite. But several of his compatriots, including Shawn D. Eichman, succeeded in burning their flags, and the government proceeded to prosecute Eichman for violation of the very act she sought to protest. In *United States v. Eichman*,[4] the United States Supreme Court rebuffed the prosecutions and held once again that the First Amendment protects the right to burn a flag.

The Rehnquist Court has decided countless cases the wrong way, but this time the Court got it right. The flag-burning cases were not

---

2. Texas *Penal Code, Annotated* (Vernon 1989), sec. 42.09.
3. Texas v. Johnson, 491 U.S. 397 (1989).
4. United States v. Eichman, 110 S. Ct. 2404 (1990).

only rightly decided, but also should stand as a fixed point in any reckoning of what the First Amendment is all about. Easy cases make good law. They can also open a window into the weaknesses of theory, and weakness of theory has pervaded the commentary surrounding the flag-burning dispute. Much of that theory is insufficiently rich. Its defense of free speech is excessively mechanical, and it possesses insufficient resources to explain why the flag-burning cases and the arts subsidy cases are as important as they are.

Ideas and the "Bedrock Principle"

Proponents of flag desecration statutes argue that the expressive conduct associated with the burning of a flag should be recognized as an exception to the general principle that freedom of expression is ordinarily protected. In both *Texas v. Johnson* and in *United States v. Eichman*, Justice Brennan invoked the "bedrock principle . . . that the Government may not prohibit the expression of an idea simply because society finds the idea offensive or disagreeable."[5] Moreover, he found

> no indication—either in the text of the Constitution or in our cases interpreting it—that a separate juridical category exists for the flag alone. [The] First Amendment does not guarantee that other concepts virtually sacred to our Nation as a whole— such as the principle that discrimination on the basis of race is odious and destructive—will go unquestioned in the marketplace of ideas. . . . We decline, therefore, to create for the flag an exception to the joust of principles protected by the First Amendment.[6]

Bye-bye to the proposed flag exception.

An air of inevitability punctuates Justice Brennan's line of reasoning. "We've never done it before; we would be inconsistent if we did; we won't do it." But the rush to judgment is a bit fast. Consider, first, the bedrock principle. It is carefully phrased: "[T]he Government may not prohibit the expression of an idea simply because

---

5. *Texas v. Johnson*, 414; *United States v. Eichman*, 2410.
6. *Texas v. Johnson*, 417–18.

society finds the idea offensive or disagreeable." Only by resort to literalism does the bedrock principle pass First Amendment inspection. Candor dictates the recognition, for example, that obscenity is subject to restriction because people find it offensive. How does that recognition square with the bedrock principle? The conventional response is buried in Justice Brennan's formulation of the bedrock principle: "[T]he Government may not prohibit the expression of an *idea* simply because society finds the idea offensive or disagreeable." In other words, by prohibiting obscenity, the argument goes, no idea is suppressed. People are free to express whatever ideas they choose; they are simply barred from using obscenity as a method of expressing their ideas.

But now the hole is big enough for a truck, and Justice Stevens knows how to drive:[7]

> The [flag-burning] prohibition does not entail any interference with the speaker's freedom to express his or her ideas by other means. It may well be true that other means of expression may be less effective in drawing attention to those ideas, but that is not itself a sufficient reason for immunizing flagburning. Presumably a gigantic fireworks display or a parade of nude models in a public park might draw even more attention to a controversial message, but such methods of expression are nevertheless subject to regulation."[8]

This line of argument leads to an obvious question: Why would the protection of speech depend upon judicial assessments of whether the speech contains an idea? My answer comes down to this: Justice Holmes was too eloquent for the First Amendment's long-term good.

In *Abrams v. United States*,[9] the Supreme Court upheld the conviction of Jacob Abrams for charges arising out of the printing of a leaflet that strongly opposed the "capitalist" invasion of Russia during World War I. In a ringing dissent, Justice Holmes stated:

---

7. In fact, he has driven this truck before. See FCC v. Pacifica Foundation, 438 U.S. 726 (1978) (Stevens, J., joined by Burger, C.J., and Rehnquist, J.).

8. *United States v. Eichman*, 2411 (Stevens, J., joined by Rehnquist, C.J., White and O'Connor, JJ.).

9. Abrams v. United States, 250 U.S. 616, 624 (1919).

[W]hen men have realized that time has upset many fighting faiths, they may come to believe even more than they believe the very foundations of their own conduct that the ultimate good desired is better reached by free trade in ideas—that the best test of truth is the power of the thought to get accepted in the competition of the market, and that truth is the only ground upon which their wishes safely can be carried out. That at any rate is the theory of our Constitution.[10]

The marketplace analogy was an elegant turn employed in a good cause, but there is no excuse for elevating it into a guiding framework. Free speech is an important principle, but there is no reason to assume that what emerges in the "market" is usually right or that the "market" is the best test of truth. If the marketplace metaphor encourages the view that an invisible hand or voluntaristic arrangements have guided us patiently, but slowly, to Burkean harmony, we might be better encouraged to believe that the cozy arrangements of the status quo have settled on something less than the true or the just. If the marketplace metaphor encourages the view that conventions, habits, and traditions have emerged as our best sense of the truth from the rigorous testing ground of the marketplace of ideas, we might be better encouraged to believe that conventions, habits, and traditions are compromises open to challenge. If the marketplace metaphor counsels us that the market's version of truth is more worthy of trust than any that the government might dictate, we might be better advised to be suspicious of both the government and the market. Societal pressures to conform are strong, and incentives to keep quiet about the corruptions of power are often great. The truth cannot emerge in the marketplace if it cannot be displayed in a marketfront. Except for frightened politicians with their fingers in the air, it is simply ludicrous to imply that truth is best found by taking a public opinion poll.

Nonetheless, owing primarily to the rhetorical power of a single paragraph, generations of students have been told that the major purpose of the First Amendment has been to protect the now proverbial marketplace of ideas. Thus, when the Court sought to explain how the First Amendment and the prohibition of obscenity were com-

---

10. Ibid., 630.

patible, it resorted to the suggestion that the prohibition did not exclude ideas from the marketplace. *Eo instanto*, we were supposed to imagine that Justice Holmes would have nodded in agreement.

Ironically, the same Justice Brennan who used marketplace theory to suppress speech in the obscenity context ultimately came to renounce his prior views.[11] But the technique lives on. It has been used to limit profane speech, and it rests at the heart of the dissents in the flag-burning cases.

Once the bedrock principle is shaken, it becomes less persuasive to insist that there is no possible room in the First Amendment for a flag exception. There is the stopping place problem ("if we create an exception today, the world will tumble tomorrow"), but exceptions to free speech protection are abundant (consider, e.g., libel, obscenity, perjury, and espionage). To be sure, as Justice Brennan suggests: "[The] First Amendment does not guarantee that other concepts virtually sacred to our Nation—as a whole—such as the principle that discrimination on the basis of race is odious and destructive—will go unquestioned in the marketplace of ideas."[12] But the creation of a flag-burning exception would not prevent any concept associated with the flag from being questioned "in the marketplace of ideas"; it would only prevent flags from being destroyed.

All this leads back to the bedrock principle. All is saved if it can be applied to the flag-burning dispute. Perhaps flag burning is like poetry in that the idea and the expression run together.[13]

But what an odd debate. Absent the power of Holmes's rhetoric and the perceived desire to justify the exclusion of particular categories of speech from First Amendment protection, who would have thought to suggest that the First Amendment was limited to ideas?[14] Imagine telling Walt Whitman: "If there are any ideas in *Leaves of*

---

11. See Paris Adult Theatre I v. Slaton, 413 U.S. 49 (1973) (Brennan, J., joined by Stewart and Marshall, JJ., dissenting).

12. *Texas v. Johnson*, 418.

13. It is also possible to argue that foreclosing the method of expression in the flag-burning cases is not justified by a sufficiently substantial interest. But once the idea is separated from the method, the outcome is not obvious, particularly in light of the many other possible modes of communication.

14. According to standard legal doctrine, the First Amendment is not confined to the protection of ideas. In certain circumstances, it protects the publication of drug prices, the names of rape victims, true factual statements that harm the character of individuals and in some cases false factual statements that damage the character of individuals.

Grass, go ahead and express them, but stop writing this offensive poetry." Of course, you may believe that expression and ideas run together in poetry, but how would you distinguish obscenity?

Perhaps your answer is that the obscenity exception should be overruled rather than distinguished. But if you are an advocate trying to persuade a majority of the Supreme Court, or a justice trying to put together a majority, you are trying to persuade people who are not about to dispense with the obscenity exception. Placed in that situation, of course, you could invoke the bedrock principle and proceed to duck. But the principle used in the flag-burning dispute does little to capture the free speech position. Who among us really thinks that protection for flag burning should depend upon its relationship to poetry? Who among us believes that the heart of the issue can be reached by philosophical contemplation about what the word *idea* really means? Far from capturing the essence of the dispute, the marketplace of ideas metaphor defines the dispute in a way that puts the free speech proponents on the defensive. If we need a metaphor, we could use a better one.

Content Neutrality and "Exacting Scrutiny"

The image of a content neutral government has played an important role in First Amendment discussions in general and in the flag-burning dispute in particular. That image is related to the marketplace metaphor, but it is not the same. Consider, for example, the statute at issue in *Johnson*. The statute made it an offense to "deface, damage or otherwise physically mistreat [a flag] in a way that the actor knows will seriously offend one or more persons likely to observe or discover his action."[15] Respected commentators have suggested that the Texas statute "restricted the use of the flag as a means of expression *only* when it was used to convey *ideas* that are offensive to others."[16] But the dissenters in *Johnson* could give the statute quite a different gloss.

Johnson allegedly[17] burned the flag as part of a demonstration to

---

15. *Texas v. Johnson*, 400.

16. Geoffrey R. Stone, "Flag Burning and the Constitution," *Iowa Law Review* 75 (1989): 116 (first emphasis in original; second emphasis added).

17. There is substantial room both to doubt that he did and to doubt that he was convicted for any such act. See Steven H. Shiffrin and Jesse H. Choper, *The First Amendment* (St. Paul, Minn.: West, 1991), 232.

protest the policies of the Reagan administration and of certain Dallas corporations.[18] Certainly he knew that the flag burning would seriously offend one or more persons in the crowd witnessing the event, but nothing in the statute seems to require that his opinions be offensive. Many people might agree with Johnson's ideas about the Reagan administration and the Dallas corporations while still being offended by the method of communicating or drawing attention to those ideas.

On the other hand, it is hard to disagree with the Supreme Court when it says that violation of the Texas law "depended on the likely communicative impact of his expressive conduct."[19] Johnson can be taken to know that people would be offended by his flag burning precisely because it communicated an attitude of disrespect toward the flag. And, whether or not one calls the communication of that attitude the communication of an idea, it is the communication of a message[20] that offends most Americans, including Texans.

The stage was thus set in *Johnson* for the model of a content-neutral government. As Justice Brennan put it: "[Johnson's] political expression was restricted because of the content of the message he conveyed. We must therefore subject the State's asserted interest in preserving the special symbolic character of the flag to 'the most exacting scrutiny.'"[21]

Getting to that stage was a touch more complicated in *Eichman*. Indeed, the legislation had been crafted with the hope that it might appear to be unconcerned with the content of any message. The Flag Protection Act of 1989 provided that whoever "knowingly mutilates, defaces, physically defiles, burns, maintains on the floor or ground, or tramples upon any flag of the United States shall be"[22] fined or imprisoned. Notice that the act prohibited the burning of a flag whether or not the actor intended to communicate anything by doing so and whether or not one or more persons were offended or were likely to be offended by the burning.

Thus, in defending the statute, the federal government maintained that its interest was in " 'protect[ing] the physical integrity of

18. *Texas v. Johnson*, 399.
19. Ibid., 411.
20. I assume that the communication of an *attitude* is the communication of a *message*.
21. *Texas v. Johnson*, 412.
22. 18 U.S.C.A. sec. 700 (a)(1) (Supp. 1990).

the flag under all circumstances' in order to safeguard the flag's identity ' "as the unique and unalloyed symbol of the nation." ' "[23] So, to take Kent Greenawalt's example, if a tired hiker burned a flag to light a campfire without any intent to communicate a message, and even without an audience to witness the destruction, the statute would apply.[24]

But from the Court's perspective in *Eichman*, the invocation of this interest counted against the statute, not for it. As Justice Brennan stated:

> [T]he mere destruction or disfigurement of a particular physical manifestation of the symbol, without more, does not diminish or otherwise affect the symbol itself in any way. For example, the secret destruction of a flag in one's own basement would not threaten the flag's recognized meaning.[25] Rather, the Government's desire to preserve the flag as a symbol for certain national ideals is "implicated only when a person's treatment of the flag communicates [a] message" to others that is inconsistent with those ideals.[26]

Thus, Justice Brennan was back to asserting that "exacting scrutiny" was called for.

But we must now confront the shell game of First Amendment doctrine. The rule in those cases where government restricts speech because of the content of the message is this: "Exacting scrutiny is called for—except when it's not."

Take the example of obscenity again. "Exacting scrutiny" was certainly *not* used in determining that obscenity was beneath First Amendment protection. In *Paris Adult Theatre I v. Slaton*, the Court recognized that "although there was no conclusive proof of a connection between antisocial behavior and obscene material, the legislature

---

23. *United States v. Eichman*, 2408, quoting Brief for United States 28, 29.

24. Kent Greenawalt, "O'er the Land of the Free: Flag Burning as Speech," *UCLA Law Review* 37 (1990): 932.

25. It might. If people know that they cannot legally destroy a flag, even in their own basement, the message communicated by the legislation is all the stronger. To break the law in your basement could be a cathartic release of disrespect for the symbol. The government could care about the actor's views even if there were no audience.

26. *United States v. Eichman*, 2408.

of Georgia could quite reasonably determine that such a connection does or *might* exist."[27] This is the language of deference, not the language of exacting scrutiny. Even more telling, the Court explained that obscenity is beneath the protection of the First Amendment because it " 'intrudes upon us all.' "[28] It invades our privacy.[29] But why doesn't the burning of a flag invade our privacy? Quite obviously, if there is a distinction to be made here, it cannot be derived from the model of a content-neutral government. Nothing in the idea of content neutrality can distinguish the flag example from the obscenity example. The interesting question is to determine what accounts for the selective use of exacting scrutiny.

Geoffrey Stone has suggested that the Court employs exacting scrutiny for content-based restrictions except when low-value speech is at issue.[30] My own view is that Stone's account of the doctrine is brilliant and heroic, but seriously flawed.[31] Even if one accepted Stone's view of the doctrine, one would need an explanation of what distinguishes low value from high value. Whatever the character of that explanation might be, except in rare cases,[32] it would not be a content-neutral explanation.

Finally, suppose that the First Amendment were said to bar any assessment of the value of speech and that First Amendment doctrine were revised accordingly. One might presume, for example, that obscenity doctrine and commercial speech doctrine would look quite different since both areas have been influenced by judicial assessments of the value of the speech involved. But the leveling effect of content neutrality exposes its rhetorical poverty. Even if one wanted to protect commercial speech, the model of content neutrality would give us no explanation of why we might regard the flag-burning cases as somehow special. The books are filled with cases that violate the

---

27. *Paris Adult Theatre I v. Slaton*, 60–61 (emphasis added).

28. Ibid., 59, quoting Alexander Bickel, *The Public Interest* 22 (Winter 1971): 25–26.

29. Ibid., 59.

30. Geoffrey R. Stone, "Content Regulation and the First Amendment," *William & Mary Law Review* 25 (1983): 189.

31. To take just one example, the advocacy of illegal action is restricted in certain circumstances not because it has little value but, rather, because its value is outweighed by the harm it is feared might be caused in those circumstances. See generally Steven H. Shiffrin, *The First Amendment, Democracy, and Romance* (Cambridge: Harvard University Press, 1990), 35–44.

32. Subliminal speech might be considered of low value because of its insidious method of persuasion.

principle of content neutrality, and some of those cases have aroused more furor than others. If the Court had ruled that flag burning was not protected, I submit that First Amendment progressives would have been wounded by such a development far more than if a hawker of commercial goods or services were denied First Amendment protection. The question is: Why?

The First Amendment, Dissent, and Political Speech

Perhaps the flag-burning question touches a special chord within us because the government was attempting to suppress political speech. Undoubtedly, the suppression of political speech is revolting, but I do not think the concept of political speech gets at the heart of the matter. That is a point we can only appreciate, however, when we examine the alternative of dissent as a First Amendment value.

The flag-burning prohibition is uniquely troubling not because it interferes with the metaphorical marketplace of ideas, not because it topples our image of a content-neutral government (*that* has fallen many times), and not merely because it suppresses political speech. The flag-burning prohibition is a naked attempt to smother dissent. If we must have a "central meaning" of the First Amendment, we should recognize that the dissenters—those who attack existing customs, habits, traditions, and authorities—stand at the center of the First Amendment and not at its periphery. Gregory Johnson was attacking a symbol that the vast majority of Americans regard with reverence. But that is *exactly* why he deserved First Amendment protection. The First Amendment has a special regard for those who swim against the current, for those who would shake us to our foundations, for those who reject prevailing authority. In burning the flag, Gregory Johnson rejected, opposed, even blasphemed the nation's most important political, social, and cultural icon. Clearly Gregory Johnson's alleged act of burning the flag was a quintessential act of dissent. A dissent-centered conception of the First Amendment would make it clear that *Johnson* was an easy case—rightly decided.

If dissent were thought to be at the heart of the First Amendment, there could be no evasion of the First Amendment issue. Any justice who looked at the case to find out whether Johnson had communicated an "idea" that might emerge in the metaphorical marketplace would clearly be in pursuit of the irrelevant. So too, if dissent, as opposed to content neutrality, were thought to be at the heart of the First Amendment, our primary focus would be on dissent as a First Amendment value, not on the methodological niceties associated with the determination of whether the government's action was or was not content neutral. To elevate content neutrality to a central place in First Amendment methodology—even as a guiding metaphor—would take too benign a view of content-neutral regulations.[33] The metaphor tempts us to forget that dissent smothered by government action is dissent smothered even when the government's action is regarded as content neutral.

A politically centered conception of the First Amendment—one that relies on the metaphor of the citizen-critic in an American democracy—might seem a more promising base from which to confront flag-burning statutes. And in many ways, it is. After all, the flag-burning prohibition comes uncomfortably close to a seditious libel law,[34] and in the eyes of many the notion of seditious libel "has become a symbol—a symbol of the first amendment's ultimate opposite, what the amendment is today above all understood to have banished from the land."[35]

Perhaps one reason that flag-burning statutes arouse such strong feelings in American progressives is that they grievously affront *both* the dissent model and the political speech model. The two models come together in finding the concept of seditious libel repulsive. From the political speech perspective, flag burning is protected political—dare I use the word—*dissent*. It is an attack on the political establishment, and if the political speech model protects anything, it is attacks on the political establishment. From the dissent perspective, flag-burning statutes are a particularly naked display of the

---

33. As a decision-making methodology, this problem is importantly mitigated if the question of content neutrality is looked at from the perspective of the speaker and the audience. See Susan H. Williams, "Content Neutrality and the First Amendment," *University of Pennsylvania Law Review* (1991). Our methodology for decision making, however, will ordinarily range beyond the metaphors that capture our strongest sense of First Amendment meaning.

34. See Frank I. Michelman, "Saving Old Glory: On Constitutional Iconography," *Stanford Law Review* 42 (1990): 1337, 1348.

35. Ibid. See also Harry Kalven, Jr., *A Worthy Tradition* (New York: Harper & Row, 1988), 63 "A society may or may not treat obscenity or contempt by publication as legal offenses without altering its basic nature. If, however, it makes seditious libel an offense, it is not a free society, no matter what its other characteristics."

conviction that government can suppress those who attack societal customs and traditions *just because* society holds its beliefs and symbols dear.

The political focus has its weaknesses, however. The flag is not just a symbol of government. Those who see a flag burned often feel that they have been personally assaulted. To burn a flag is perceived by them as an attack not merely of the existing government, but of the society and the country of which they feel themselves a part. In short, flag burning has social and cultural dimensions that range beyond the political. Thus, the dissent focus is superior to the political focus because it encourages the view that people should be free to attack not merely politicians and government, but deeply held customs, attitudes, and traditions that range beyond the political.[36]

The Value of Dissent

A significant advantage of a focus on dissent is that it serves to consolidate the values ordinarily associated with the First Amendment. A focus on dissent does not liquidate liberty, freedom, equality, justice, tolerance, respect, dignity, self-government, truth, marketplace values, the checking value, associational values, cathartic values, or any other value that has been tied to freedom of speech or press.[37] But the advantage of the dissent perspective runs even deeper: it implicates important cultural and communitarian values.

The aftermath of the *Johnson* decision and the debate surrounding

36. In addition, as has frequently been noted, a politically centered conception of the First Amendment is either too narrow or too broad. Either it excludes speech that ought to be considered important—consider Shakespeare, Aristotle, Einstein—or includes such speech by principles that magnify the work's political importance and offers no obvious stopping point. Notice that the politically centered conceptions of speech ordinarily offered are focused on democracy and government. The feminist conception of the political, as I understand it, focuses on power. That starting point has more in common with a dissent model.

37. First Amendment values look different, however, through a dissent lens than in the form in which they are ordinarily presented. Protection for commercial speech, for example, is more difficult to defend under a dissent model than it would be, for example, under a marketplace model or a diversity model. (Consider a prohibition on the use of the flag for commercial purposes.) Nonetheless, the dissent model is partially justified by truth values and diversity values. I do not believe, however, that First Amendment issues should be looked at exclusively through a dissent lens. For discussion, see Shiffrin, *The First Amendment, Democracy, and Romance*, chap. 3.

it sheds substantial light on this important point. In response to *Johnson*, Congress passed the Flag Protection Act of 1989, which attached criminal penalties to the knowing mutilation, defacement, burning, maintaining on the floor or ground, or trampling upon any flag of the United States. Prior to adopting the Flag Protection Act, the Senate by a vote of 97–3 had passed a resolution expressing "profound disappointment with the [*Johnson*] decision." The House had approved a similar resolution by a vote of 411–5, and President Bush had proposed a constitutional amendment to overrule *Johnson*. Opponents of the amendment argued that a carefully drawn statute might (or would) be upheld by the Court. Most liberal legislators supported such legislation. Although some feigned genuine appreciation for the action, the liberal's motivation is best captured in this exchange during hearings of the House Subcommittee on Civil and Constitutional Rights on *Statutory and Constitutional Responses to the Supreme Court Decision in Texas v. Johnson* (1989).

Former Solicitor General Charles Fried: My good friends and colleagues, Rex Lee and Laurence Tribe, have testified that a statute might be drawn that would pass constitutional muster. [I] hope and urge and pray that we will not act—that no statute be passed and of course that the Constitution not be amended. In short, I believe the *Johnson* [decision] is right [in] principle. . . .

Representative Schroeder: I thought your testimony was eloquent. I think in a purist world, that is where we should go. But [we] are not talking about a purist world. We are talking about a very political world. . . .

Mr. Fried: There are times when you earn your rather inadequate salary by just doing the right thing, and where you seem to agree with me is that the right thing to do is to do neither one of these. . . . It is called leadership.

Representative Schroeder: It is called leadership. . . . But I guess what I am saying is if we can't stop a stampede on an amendment without something, isn't it better to try to save the Bill of Rights and the Constitution?[38]

---

38. House Committee on the Judiciary, *Statutory and Constitutional Responses to the Supreme Court Decision in Texas v. Johnson: Hearings Before the Subcommittee on Civil and Constitutional Rights of the House Committee on the Judiciary*, 101st Cong., 1st sess., 1989, 225, 231–32.

I suppose that progressives would be divided on this exchange. Many would side with Fried.[39] Many would support Schroeder. But few progressives were suggesting that a congressional statute (upheld by the Supreme Court) might be *worse* for the progressive cause than an amendment of the First Amendment.

Frank Michelman is one such progressive, and his argument is well worth considering. First, Michelman for many years has been attracted to and influenced by a communitarian perspective. For conservative communitarians, the flag-burning issue is easy. A minimum conservative communitarian requirement might be that Americans not physically degrade the one symbol that stands for the country.[40] Michelman, however, is no conservative; and no progressive, whatever his or her communitarian leanings might be, is likely to uphold a flag-burning statute. Michelman's communitarian inclinations show up both in his discussion of the flag-burning issue per se and in his arguments for the proposition that a congressional statute (upheld by the Supreme Court) might be worse for the progressive cause than an amendment of the First Amendment. As I shall explain, those arguments will lead us to an appreciation of some of the differences between a communitarian approach and a dissent perspective—at the same time it reveals the communitarian dimensions of the dissent model.

In exploring Michelman's position, I should hasten to observe that he does not claim that a statute upheld by the Supreme Court *is* a worse alternative than an amendment. He suggests only that it *might* be worse,[41] and, in the end, concludes that both alternatives are equally bad: "[I]n the respects that ought finally to dominate our judgment the two come very much to the same thing."[42]

In support of the view that a statute upheld by the Supreme Court is just as bad as a constitutional amendment, Michelman first asks us to consider the situation from the perspective of "constitutional law" rather than that of the "scriptural Constitution." Constitutional law is the "body of normative material that the Supreme Court both creates

---

39. Fried, of course, is a strange bedfellow for a progressive.

40. See, for example, Senate Committee on the Judiciary, *Measures to Protect the Physical Integrity of the American Flag: Hearings Before the Senate Committee on the Judiciary*, 101st Cong., 1st sess., 1989, 100 (testimony of Robert H. Bork).

41. See generally Michelman, "Saving Old Glory."

42. Ibid., 1359.

and consults when it resolves questions about the legal validity of governmental actions challenged as unconstitutional."[43] This body of law includes principles, precedents, and doctrines and is thus different from the "scriptural text we know as the Constitution."[44] As between the scriptural text and constitutional law, Michelman argues:

> [I]t must be *constitutional law* that is the immediate concern of the practical-minded. . . . One could even ask why anyone ever cares at all what the scriptural Constitution says. Why is the prospect of constitutional amendment *ever* an occasion for practical concern? One answer, again obvious, is that while constitutional law is not identical with the scriptural Constitution, neither is it independent of it. To the practical-minded, constitutional amendments matter—perhaps among other reasons—because of their anticipated effects on constitutional law.[45]

From the perspective of "constitutional law," as he has set it out, Michelman maintains that any opinion upholding a flag protection statute in the wake of *Johnson* would create dangerous doctrine.[46] Even if the Court were to uphold the statute as a "flag exception" to ordinary First Amendment principles, Michelman argues that there could be no assurance that the opinion would stay confined.[47] By contrast, an amendment could be carefully drafted to prevent a radiating effect. Indeed, the amendment could state explicitly that it "shall not be in any way relied upon in any case to which its terms are not directly applicable."[48]

As Michelman recognizes, there are other practical effects of amending the Bill of Rights that might concern progressives. It might be legitimately feared that " 'the appetites of many for quick ways to leap over constitutional barriers will be whetted. . . . With each amendment [curtailing the rights of dissidents], resistance would be lessened for the next amendment affecting an unpopular group.' "[49]

43. Ibid., 1339.
44. Ibid., 1340.
45. Ibid.
46. Ibid., 1351, 1353.
47. Ibid., 1355.
48. Ibid., 1343.
49. Ibid., 1357, quoting House Committee, *Measures to Protect the Physical Integrity of the American Flag*, 553 (testimony of Walter Dellinger).

Nonetheless, Michelman has little patience for this line of argument:

> This all seems dangerously close to declaring that the People cannot be trusted with self-government under this Constitution, at least not if the ring of fire around the Bill of Rights should ever be broken. . . . To speak as sharply as I can, I don't see how to distinguish our own resort to sacralization of the Bill of Rights from the kind of aversion and squeamishness towards open political conflict displayed by our adversaries who want to cast a special pall of sanctity over the stars-and-stripes. It seems to me that idolatry is idolatry, sacrosanction is sacrosanction, whether poured over the flag or over the Bill of Rights.[50]

In short, we should place more trust in democracy and be prepared to compete by argument "on the merits ungirded by mystique."[51] This does not mean we must shun "any nonmystical arguments we have that there ought to be a strong presumption against messing with the Bill of Rights."[52] It does seem to foreclose resort to an argument that would invoke those "mystic chords of memory that have kept the Bill of Rights, to date, an object of civil awe that mustn't be disturbed, upon pain of tempting a great Wrath."[53]

Finally, Michelman states that the best reason for preferring an amendment over a statute may "lie beyond a concern about constitutional *law*, in some other kind of care, some other sort of regard, that people feel for *the Constitution*."[54] I can only puzzle why this argument does not get more weight. One possibility is that Michelman ultimately finds the argument too mystical, insufficiently practical minded, but, judging from his other writings, I doubt it. Michelman understands that symbols matter. Another stronger possibility is that it reaches beyond one of Michelman's principal purposes in the article, namely, to use the flag-burning controversy to explore the conventional wisdom that judge making is principled and guided by an external source and that amendments to the Constitution need not be principled.

---

50. Ibid., 1358–59.
51. Ibid., 1357.
52. Ibid., 1358.
53. Ibid., 1357.
54. Ibid., 1354.

What he says in connection with *"the Constitution"* is that a constitutional flag amendment would " 'graft a permanent blemish onto our most fundamental constitutional principle,' and would 'mak[e] us a little silly, and a little less free, and a little less brave.' "[55] Michelman regards this "aesthetic and psychological" argument as particularly attractive because of its recognition that the Constitution assumes and pictures an "us," a political and moral community, a community that includes the majority, its opposition, and its dissenters.[56] Of course, our community falls short of what it ought to be, and he suggests that if our conceptions of community govern our " 'aesthetic' "[57] response to proposed alterations of the Constitution,

> then one would have to consider, on behalf of a flag amendment this argument: that some speech acts are so antithetical to any serious profession of aspiration toward political community, and so destructive of movement toward it, that a Constitution depicting that aspiration cannot shelter such acts against the community's prohibition, and at the same time retain the force of apparent moral seriousness.[58]

But flag burning, Michelman argues, is not paradigmatically at odds with political community:

> Rather the flag burner charges the nation with betraying its ideals as the flag burner understands them and would have them (and herself) understood.[59] . . . Among modes of political expression, flag burning is not paradigmatically antithetical to American communitarian aspiration."[60]

---

55. Ibid., 1361, quoting Dellinger in House Committee, *Measures to Protect the Physical Integrity of the American Flag*, 557.

56. Ibid., 1362.

57. Ibid.

58. Ibid.

59. Of course, a flag burner might not believe that the country has ideals to betray. The flag burner might affirmatively hate the political community. A dissent model would protect the speech. Michelman's formulation suggests that a communitarian model might not. Of course, a communitarian might be reluctant to formulate a standard requiring ad hoc exploration of the speaker's stance toward the political community. This same division in philosophy (if not the result) between the dissent model and the communitarian model suggested by Michelman's brief remarks also has implications for the contexts in which speakers advocate overthrow of the government.

60. Michelman, "Saving Old Glory," 1362–63.

In response to Michelman, I want to suggest first that his own premises lead, albeit not inexorably, to the conclusion that a flag-burning constitutional amendment would be a more serious loss for progressives[61] than a flag-burning statute upheld by the Supreme Court. As Michelman recognizes, a citizen's relationship to the Constitution is an important psychological connection. Indeed, the Constitution plays a special role in *constituting* who we are and who we aspire to be.[62] The flag amendment was uniquely threatening to progressives because it struck a *symbolic* dagger at the notion that the First Amendment is an important reflection of our "profound national commitment" to protect dissent. No doubt, the symbolic effect of a flag-burning statute upheld by the Supreme Court would be disheartening, but the relative rhetorical and constituting power of statutes, decisions, and the Constitution are not the same. The scriptural Constitution is a more important cultural symbol, and it constitutes us in ways that statutes upheld by the Supreme Court do not.

Moreover, from the perspective of encouraging a sense of belonging to a moral and political community (however aspirational), we should applaud the divide between constitutional law and the scriptural Constitution. If the Court had upheld the Flag Protection Act, liberals could say that what the Court says is not what *the Constitution* says. But if the Constitution were amended, it would be hard for them to avoid profound alienation. To experience the Supreme Court as a morally bankrupt institution can be an important psychological event in a person's political development; to experience the Constitution itself as embodying repugnant principles is a much more profound psychological moment. It encourages estrangement from a sense of moral and political community.

That estrangement might be somewhat less if one is a Michelman-type progressive (a "democratic progressive"). If I read him correctly, Michelman would prefer to risk the Bill of Rights rather than settle for distrust of the People over democracy.[63] For some democratic

---

61. Perhaps not for some radicals, however.

62. See Michelman, "Saving Old Glory," 1364, citing Hanna Fenichel Pitkin, "The Idea of the Constitution," *Journal of Legal Education* 37 (1987): 167, 168; Charles R. Lawrence, "Promises to Keep: We are the Constitution's Framers," *Howard Law Journal* 30 (1987): 937, 942–43.

63. See Michelman, "Saving Old Glory," 1358–59. Compare Bruce A. Ackerman, *We The People: Foundations* (Cambridge: Harvard University Press, Belknap Press, 1991) 16, 320–21 ("would be a good idea to entrench the Bill of Rights against subsequent

progressives—I do not claim that Michelman is one of them—a flag-burning amendment, albeit "ugly and dispiriting," is still a part of a Constitution in which the People rule, and if the People get it wrong in one amendment, they may well be persuaded to change. A flag-burning amendment would be no occasion for dancing in the streets, but it would not necessarily be an occasion for feeling a sense of estrangement from the moral and political community. Those democratic progressives could believe that a flag-burning statute upheld by the Supreme Court and a constitutional amendment "come very much to the same thing."[64] In either case, the dominant feature of the Constitution—rule of the People—would be undisturbed.

I doubt Michelman himself would go so far. In his other writings Michelman exhibits no tendency to equate the people with the People. In "Law's Republic," for example, the People is an aspirational concept and the constitutional community is an aspirational community.[65] Michelman is obviously offended by a political community that is not inclusive or is not open to dialogic questioning of its traditions and ideals. Nonetheless, the value he places on being a part of a political community makes him a more likely candidate to stay the course than for some other progressives (the "Bill of Rights progressives").

The Bill of Rights progressives emphasize that some rights are sacrosanct, and the majority—even a supermajority—has no right to interfere. Of course, Article V of the Constitution gives the People the *power* to outlaw seditious libel, for example, criticism of the government in wartime, but more than a few progressives believe that the People have no *right* to do any such thing. Moreover, *if* the People enshrine their violation of rights in the Constitution, the Bill of Rights progressives are more likely than the democratic progressives to be estranged. For them, the "mystic chords of memory that have kept the Bill of Rights, to date, an object of civil awe that mustn't be disturbed" have been an important psychological and aesthetic component of what the Constitution means and what the country means.

---

revision by some future American majority") with Mary E. Becker, "The Politics of Women's Wrongs and the Bill of 'Rights': A Bicentennial Perspective," *University of Chicago Law Review* 59 (1992): 453 (suggesting that changes to the Bill of Rights could make it more "responsive to the needs of women and other outsider groups and should produce a more democratic structure").

64. Michelman, "Saving Old Glory," 1359.
65. Frank I. Michelman, "Law's Republic," *Yale Law Journal* 97 (1988): 1493.

Moreover, the Bill of Rights progressives are at ease in distinguishing between their "own resort to sacralization of the Bill of Rights from the kind of aversion and squeamishness towards open political conflict displayed by our adversaries who want to cast a special pall of sanctity over the stars-and-stripes."[66] First, the Bill of Rights progressives themselves are unabashedly squeamish about certain forms of political conflict. For example, they do not want the polity to debate which church should be established as the national church; they do not want the polity to debate whether the slave trade should be reinstituted; they do not want the polity to debate whether the institutional press should be abolished, or whether citizens should be prohibited from criticizing existing habits, traditions, institutions, and authorities. By placing prohibitions on action in areas such as these, the Constitution with the full support of these progressives discourages political conflict over these issues. Whether it is fair to say that the Bill of Rights progressives engage in "idolatry" or "sacrosanction" when they invoke the Bill of Rights as the centerpiece of the Constitution and the country, their "mystical" appeals can easily be distinguished from those who would "sacralize" the flag. As Michelman recognizes throughout his article, the attempt to use legal penalties against flag burners is a pure exercise in repression. But Michelman's objection goes more to the use of emotional appeals than to the object of those appeals. What is missing from that argument (other than its privileging of the People over the Bill of Rights) is an explanation of how the invocation of the People is any less a piece of mysticism than the symbolic use of the Bill of Rights. Further missing is a delineation of the line between building an attractive psychological picture of the Constitution and engaging in unacceptable mysticism. Without further explanation, it seems that one person's unacceptable mysticism is another person's attractive psychological and aesthetic ground.

In fact, the democratic progressives and the Bill of Rights progressives share mystical ideals that are not far apart. The democratic progressives long for informed democratic dialogue. Flag burning is seen as an important component of democratic dialogue because it and other acts of dissent like it call attention to the failure of the country to live up to its ideals.

The Bill of Rights progressives seek to encourage and protect the

---

66. Ibid., 1359.

Emersonian dissenter,[67] and flag burners squarely fit that model. But the dissent model is not premised exclusively on notions that individuals thrive when they feel free to speak out.

It Is Not Just a Self-Expression Model

The dissent model assumes that in large-scale societies powerful interest groups, self-seeking politicians, and bureaucrats are unavoidable. Injustice will always be present (although the severity can vary). Dissenters and the dialogue that follows will always be necessary. On this premise, dissent has important instrumental value. So, of course, does democratic dialogue. Indeed, the dissent model would hope that dialogue would ultimately be spurred by the presence of dissent. In this respect the dialogue model and the dissent model run together.

But instrumental value is also *not* the point of the flag-burning dispute. From an instrumental perspective one might wonder why anyone should care if people are free to burn flags. After a flag-burning amendment, dissenters would still be free to burn copies of the Constitution or to melt down images of the Washington Memorial, the Lincoln Memorial, or the Statue of Liberty.[68] Dissent would not be smothered by a flag-burning amendment.

No, the contest is about ideals. For the majority of Americans, flag burners were contemptuous of the community, and congressional response was necessary to affirm the community's values. For these Americans, the flag stands for the country; for them, free speech is one thing but disrespect for the symbol that binds the Nation together is quite another.

Opponents of flag-burning prohibitions also sought to affirm the community's values. But the values were different. For the opponents, particularly the Bill of Rights progressives, the American community is committed to the notion that dissent should be protected, and the First Amendment is the legal manifestation of that cultural commitment. For such progressives, the point of the flag-burning dispute was not about the self-realization of the Gregory Johnsons of the world. Nor did such progressives lose sleep fearing that Gregory Johnson's truth would not emerge in the marketplace of ideas. (Few

---

67. See generally Shiffrin, *The First Amendment, Democracy, and Romance.*

68. See Yale Kamisar, "Keeping Up With the Gregory Johnsons," *Baltimore Sun* 22 July 1989, 9(A).

people had even the slightest idea of what Johnson was trying to say.) Rather, such progressives forge their identity in a country that, in their mind, is (or ought to be) committed to protecting dissenters. To prevent people from burning the flag is to violate the First Amendment principles for which the flag ought to stand. It is to transform the very meaning of the country and thus to threaten the political identity of American liberals. The value of dissent, then, is not merely that it fosters individual development or self-realization or even that it is of instrumental value in exposing injustice and bringing about change. The commitment to dissent and the First Amendment is of national symbolic value: it is a form of cultural glue that binds citizens to the political community.

The First Amendment and the Arts

It should now be clear that the cases involving the refusal to subsidize controversial artists are flag-burning cases with a doctrinal twist. Once again the conservatives believe that the First Amendment is one thing, but that our "public morality" is quite another. Again, whatever the progressives say, I do not believe that the issue involves a worry over the question of whether Robert Mapplethorpe's truth will or will not emerge in the marketplace of ideas, nor is this a contest about Mapplethorpe's self-expression. Again, this struggle is all about cultural ideals. For the conservative, the point is that our Constitution does not and should provide protection for those who flout our customs and our morality. To the contrary, for the progressive, the point is that our Constitution has a special place for those who reject or leap beyond our prior understandings of tradition, order, and morality.

So understood, the doctrinal twist is of no constitutional moment. Money simply has no pride of place in this constitutional battlefield. To be sure, the conservative claim is readily understood. The Mapplethorpes of the world may have a constitutional right to produce and display their work, but surely taxpayers incur no constitutional obligation to subsidize that work. The failure to fund art is not its prohibition. Nor can it plausibly be argued that artists have a First Amendment right to government funds.

These observations, however, are quite beside the constitutional point and skirt the cultural heart of the dispute. The failure to fund art may well not involve its prohibition.[69] Nor is there any general right of artists to government funds. The progressives make neither of these claims. What the progressives do claim is that an artist cannot be denied funds for unconstitutional reasons.

Let us sneak up on the First Amendment point. Suppose a government funding agency as a matter of policy denies artistic subsidies to all black applicants. No doubt, everyone agrees that policy is unconstitutional, and no one would think it important to observe in that context that the failure to fund art does not involve its prohibition or that there is no general right of artists to government funds. Similarly, suppose a government funding agency as a matter of policy denies artistic subsidies to all Republicans. Here, there is no constitutional distinction between racial and political discrimination: both policies are unconstitutional.

Now suppose the government denies an artistic subsidy to a piece of blasphemous art or to a person who has produced blasphemous art. On the argument we have been following, that denial may or may not have been unconstitutional. If the denial is based on the belief that the work in question or the work to be produced is unlikely to meet artistic standards, the denial is not open to constitutional question. On the other hand, if the work or the probable work is deemed to be *otherwise deserving* of artistic support, a subsidy cannot constitutionally be denied on the ground that the work is offensive. Under the First Amendment, dissenters have no right to be subsidized, but dissenters cannot be denied subsidies just because they are dissenters.

Of course, these principles can be evaded in practice. If concealing a purpose to discriminate on the basis of race or gender has been relatively easy in a wide variety of contexts, discriminating against artistic material on the basis of its controversial character should not be difficult.

To some extent, the possibility of evasions can be minimized by structural mechanisms. For example, in order to assure that political appointees do not intervene on an ad hoc basis to block subsidies for material that might be politically embarrassing, it might seem

---

69. But see Donald W. Hawthorne, "Subversive Subsidization: How NEA Art Funding Abridges Private Speech," *Kansas Law Review* 40 (1992): 437 (NEA plays pervasive role in the art world and its intervention dries up or controls sources of private support).

appropriate to assure that the artistic community, rather than politicians, determines which applications are deserving of support and which are not.

But this kind of step also muffles dissent, albeit more subtly. Built into the conception of what counts as artistically valuable are a set of conventions and expectations. Those who break with those conventions may meet a chilly reception precisely because they broke with the conventions. In other words, artistic professionals (or the arts community) police the boundaries between art and mass culture and between good and bad art. They, like academic bureaucrats at large, are masters of channeling conceptions of merit in self-serving ways. Just as power participates in the construction of knowledge, power participates in the construction of beauty, the sublime, and the artistic. In the politics of aesthetics, dissent is frequently praised in the abstract and besmirched in the concrete.[70]

Nonetheless, the reliance on artists to make decisions about artists has some advantages from a dissent perspective. Artists as a subgroup of the population are particularly likely to run against the current; they are more likely than others to appreciate the avant garde.[71] Thus, the crisis over subsidies to controversial artists would never have arisen if artists had not first declared the works in question to be of substantial artistic value.

The First Amendment, Cultural Struggle, and National Identity

All of which returns us to Patrick Buchanan: "The arts crowd is after more than our money, more than an end to the congressional ban on funding obscene and blasphemous art. It is engaged in a cultural struggle to root out the old America of family, faith, and flag, and recreate society in a pagan image." From a legal perspective, part of this statement is pure gobbledygook. If work has serious artistic value, it is not obscene by definition. From a conservative perspective, the notion of

---

70. The situation should get worse before it gets better—if it ever does. Consider: "What we have seen in the last several years is the virtual takeover of art by big corporate interests. . . . Corporations have become the major patrons of art in every respect." David Harvey, *The Condition of Postmodernity* (Oxford: Basil Blackwell, 1989), 62, quoting Crimp, "Art in the 1980's: The Myth of Autonomy," *PRECIS* 6 (1987): 83, 85.

71. See, for example, James Davison Hunter, *Culture Wars* (New York: Basic Books, 1991), 237.

obscene art is oxymoronic. From that perspective, work that is blasphemous or obscene can not be sublime and, *therefore,* cannot be art.[72] But this is nit-picking. Buchanan is on to something even if his statement reeks of overwrought conspiratorial designs. The artistic community is more likely to question the conventions Americans hold dear. And despite America's professed commitment to the First Amendment, few Americans want their values mocked in public.

The failure of liberals to command a majority of the American public, then, should not be surprising. The best liberal theory almost guarantees that liberals will occupy a minority. One need not read far in John Stuart Mill's *On Liberty* to find him writing "against the tyranny of the prevailing opinion and feeling; against the tendency of the society to impose, by other means than civil penalties, its own ideas and practices as rules of conduct on those who dissent from them . . ."[73] That tyranny is with us now, and it always will be. If liberals seek to protect and promote[74] dissent, they will ride against the current. The only way for liberals to become a part of the majority on this kind of issue is to stop being liberals.

Nonetheless, it would be simplistic to regard the liberals as carriers of the torch of dissent in American society and not just because dissent is a multifaceted aspect of daily power relationships at every level of human existence. Liberals are often said to value freedom and dissent over community, but I think this characterization ignores political psychology and the liberals' characteristic attitudes toward change.

Consider another characterization of liberals that is just as frequently heard. Liberals are pragmatic realists who are prepared to compromise with the system in order to get something accomplished. Radicals believe that liberals "sell out" for prices that are far too low.

Why would liberals sell at too low a price (assuming they do and surely they sometimes do)? First, there is the possibility that they miscalculate the possibilities for change. Second, and more interesting from the perspective of political psychology, liberals may want

---

72. Ibid., at 238–39.

73. John Stuart Mill, *On Liberty,* ed. David Spitz (Indianapolis: Hacket Publishing Company, 1975), 6.

74. Many liberals would protect dissent but would not necessarily seek to promote it. I will not explore here the relationships between toleration, dissent, and diversity, but they deserve to be explored.

personal influence. Less frequently observed, however, and most interesting of all is the possibility that liberals crave community. It is one thing not to be a member of the majority; it is quite another to be a psychological outcast from the political community. By moving too far from the center, liberals risk marginalization and alienation. This is the posture of the true dissenter, and it involves difficult psychological burdens. My claim is that liberals are loathe to accept these burdens. Indeed, my suggestion is that in this sense, despite the common stereotypes, American liberals typically value community over freedom and dissent.[75]

From the same perspective, radicals defy the conventional stereotypes. They are often believed to value community over freedom, but this too ignores political psychology. Radicals are the political individualists of American society. They have the integrity to speak out against the dominant structure of the society even though most Americans have been socialized to deplore their views. They dissent more thoroughly than the liberals. This is not to say that radicals do not value community. Indeed, they may be more self-conscious about the need for community and their own personal needs than liberals. Instead of embracing a form of national identity, many radicals forge an identity with the workers of the world, the oppressed of the world, or the "arts crowd." But they also work hard at building a local community of like-minded individuals. Of course, this community building fits with the radical's political perspective, but it also fits important psychological needs. To be at the political margin almost necessitates the building of networks that nurture the continuing capacity to dissent. Even these radicals forge a national identity of a sort. They criticize America more frequently than other countries and perhaps more bitterly because they feel attached[76] and responsible. As Henry Louis Gates Jr. puts it, "[C]ritique can also be a form of commitment, a means of laying a claim. It's the ultimate

---

75. Liberals in dictatorships either stick with their principles and exalt freedom over community—at the risk of their lives—or they adjust to the existing community and attempt to compromise from within. My claims, therefore, do not apply to all liberals, nor do they make claims about what those who compromise in this context might do in a different context.

76. For an insightful development of this point, see Charles Taylor, "Cross-Purposes: The Liberal Communitarian Debate," in Liberalism And The Moral Life, ed. Nancy L. Rosenblum (Cambridge: Harvard University Press, 1989), 174–75.

gesture of citizenship. A way of saying: I'm not just passing through, I *live* here."[77]

Nonetheless, the liberals ordinarily forge a stronger connection to the community than the radicals in that liberals are more uncomfortable with and more resistant to feelings of alienation. Moreover, if I am right that liberals were more concerned about the cultural meaning of the First Amendment than the self-expression of Gregory Johnson, the notion of liberal individualism needs substantial revision. The connection of liberals (and many radicals) to the country is not just a Hobbesian bargain, it is a form of nationalism,[78] a matter of cultural and political identity. It may be thought that this is a benign form of nationalism, and to a large extent it is. If political identity is bound up with the protection of dissent, nationalism would seem to strengthen, not to threaten, free speech.[79] Nonetheless, the liberal position on free speech rights has political costs. Some of the subtle political costs are intrinsically bound up with the flag-burning controversy or the controversy over funding of the arts. In order to uphold their position, liberals[80] have championed the view that this country values and prizes dissent, freedom, liberty, the marketplace of ideas, democratic dialogue, and/or controversy. This is what the country *stands* for, or so goes the argument.

This line of argument is part of the standard stock of the practicing liberal. The ideals of the country are X, but we've fallen short; therefore, we must do Y. In so doing, we will reconcile our theory with our practice. This stock argument has the force of exposing contradiction. Moreover, it takes a moral and political high ground, and it has a communitarian appeal urging its auditors to reaffirm their commitment to the ideals of the polity.

But the argument is mined with conservative aspects. "Ideals" are easily manufactured from pious statements by political, including judicial, leaders. To take those stated ideals seriously as a statement of what the country *in fact* stands for is to lose critical edge.[81] It is an

---

77. Henry Louis Gates Jr., "Patriotism," *The Nation* (July 15/22, 1991), 91.

78. See generally Bernard Yack, "Nationalism and Individualism: Odd or Happy Couple?" (paper delivered at the annual meeting of the American Political Science Association, September 1992).

79. See Taylor, "Cross Purposes," 280–81.

80. Many radicals have championed this view as well. See note 84.

81. The need to operate within such frames exposes social movement organizations to the threat that they will be "outbid" by more radical groups. See Sidney G.

argumentative strategy that functions to make the country look better than it is—even as it is used to condemn a particular practice.[82] Moreover, the style of argument promotes self-deception. To habitually use such arguments is to risk seeing the country through a distorted lens.

Nonetheless, in the legal world of constitutional interpretation, it would be a nonstarter to say that this country does not now value and never has valued dissent *even if it were true*. To defend flag burning or blasphemous art as protected speech under the First Amendment, it is crucial to paint an argumentative picture that frames some ideal like dissent or its toleration as a vital ideal in the American culture.[83]

Necessary as the stock argument may be, the existence of the First Amendment as a cultural symbol masks the extent to which dissent is discouraged and subordinated.[84] Therein lies the paradox: the First Amendment serves to undermine dissent even as it protects it. Of course, the First Amendment protects dissent. It offers a legal claim for dissenters, and it functions as a cultural symbol encouraging dis-

---

Tarrow, "Mentalities, Political Cultures, and Collective Action Frames," in *Frontiers In Social Movement Theory*, ed. Aldon D. Morris and Carol McLurg Mueller (New Haven: Yale, 1992), 174, 190, 196.

82. In addition, to succeed in opposing a particular practice frequently takes the energy out of a broader movement. See, for example, Kimberle Crenshaw, "Race, Reform, and Retrenchment: Transformation and Legitimation in Antidiscrimination Law," *Harvard Law Review* 101 (1988): 1331, 1385: "As long as race consciousness thrives, Blacks will often have to rely on rights rhetoric when it is necessary to protect Black interests. The very reforms brought about by appeals to legal ideology, however, seem to undermine the ability to move forward toward a broader vision of racial equality. In the quest for racial justice, winning and losing have been part of the same experience." James MacGregor Burns and Stewart Burns argue that this phenomenon is generally true in rights movements, in their *A People's Charter: The Pursuit Of Rights In America* (New York: A. A. Knopf, 1991).

83. Substantial evidence supports the view that some such framing is a necessary, but not sufficient, feature of successful social movements in the United States. See, for example, Tarrow, "Mentalities," (suggesting, among other things, that McCarthyism and other political activity have largely destroyed oppositional subcultures as an effective force in the United States while resort to oppositional subcultures is a livelier option in many European countries). For the suggestion that the use of the metaphor of America has served to co-opt oppositional forces, see Myra Jehlen, "The Novel and the American Middle Class," in *Ideology and Classic American Literature*, ed. Sacon Bercovitch and Myra Jehlen (New York: Cambridge, 1986), 127–28.

84. See, for example, Sacon Bercovitch, "Afterword," in *Ideology and Classic American Literature*, ed. Sacon Bercovitch and Myra Jehlen, 434 (emphasis in original): "Having adopted their country's *controlling* metaphor—'America' as synonym for human possibility—and having made this the ground of radical dissent, they effectively redefine radicalism as an affirmation of cultural values."

senters to speak out. Nonetheless, the symbolism of the First Amendment perpetuates a cultural myth. It functions as a form of cultural ideology through which the society secures allegiance. It leads us to believe that America is the land of free speech, but it blinks at the "tyranny of the prevailing opinion and feeling," and it masks the extent to which free speech is marginalized, discouraged, and repressed. Even as it promotes dissent, it falsifies the willingness of the society to receive it, and it tolerates rules of place and property that make it difficult for people of modest means to address a mass audience.[85]

To get beyond the First Amendment paradox, one needs to take a broader look at the conditions of cultural struggle in America. One needs to ask how the political consciousness of the American majority is developed and why it is different in the United States than in other developed countries. To what extent does commercial art—that is, advertising—play a role in molding the values of this culture? Does an advertiser-dominated medium adversely stack the deck against progressive politics? To what extent does the role of corporate money undermine the possibility of even incremental liberal reform? To what extent would access by powerless groups to the mass media have an impact in affecting the terms of cultural struggle? Is more thorough restructuring necessary? Desirable? Possible?

Issues such as flag-burning and subsidies for the arts raise important questions about the character of our culture. To fight about these questions is to reinforce the legitimizing myths of the society. Not to fight about them is a formula for political suicide. They are battles that need to be fought, but they should be placed in perspective: They are warm-ups for a larger war.

If the First Amendment paradox poses a challenge, some postmodernists pose a related but somewhat different First Amendment challenge. Their argument is not that First Amendment practice is a better description of the First Amendment values of the culture than its ideals. The argument is that the purportedly timeless ideals of the culture are utterly constructed, that they bear no relationship to any

---

85. See, for example, Perry Educators' Association v. Perry Local Educators' Association, 460 U.S. 37 (1983) (Court adopts set of rules making it extremely difficult for dissenters to gain access to property controlled by government except for streets and parks); Clark v. Community For Creative Non-Violence, 468 U.S. 288 (1984) (demonstration in Lafayette Park and the Mall concerning homelessness stifled by Park Service's time, place, and manner regulations); Hudgens v. NLRB, 424 U.S. 507 (1976) (dissenters have no constitutional right of access to shopping centers).

prepolitical reality, that the very idea of rights is suspect. Of course, the argument often goes deeper—to an interrogation of truth and of the very possibility of human subjectivity.[86] Postmodernists see themselves as well situated to question the foundations of scientific, moral, and political discourse and regard that undertaking as a politically powerful means of attacking hierarchy. Their perspective is valuable in showing the many ways in which power has constructed knowledge to the disadvantage of oppressed people.

Although I delight in the energy and ferocity of postmodernism and I believe that much work produced by postmodernists has contributed to our understanding of power and its abuse, I do not endorse postmodernism in any of its usual versions. I do not think it is necessary to be a postmodernist in order to attack and expose unjust concentrations of power, unjust hierarchy, the failures of grand theory or grand narratives, the pretensions of neutrality, or any of the authoritarian ways in which power constructs knowledge.[87] Indeed, a nonpostmodernist can launch such attacks without having to fend off conversations about relativism, skepticism, or nihilism. I do not see an attack on truth[88] or morals as an important part of a fruitful political strategy,[89] particularly not one that has democratic aspirations and hopes to involve any large sector of the public.[90] More important,

---

86. See, for example, James Boyle, "Is Subjectivity Possible: The Postmodern Subject in Legal Theory," *University of Colorado Law Review* 62 (1991): 489.

87. As Kobena Mercer puts it in a related context,"no one has a monopoly on oppositional identity." "'1968': Periodizing Politics and Identity," in *Cultural Studies*, ed. Lawrence Grossberg, Cary Nelson, and Paula A. Treichler (New York: Routledge, 1992), 424, 426.

88. I believe, however, that truth is vastly overrated as a political weapon. See Jane Flax, "The End of Innocence," in *Feminists Theorize The Political* ed. Judith Butler and Joan Wallach Scott (New York: Routledge, 1992), 445, 458 (articulate and appreciative discussion of postmodernism as a political strategy).

89. Indeed, in some respects the strategy is counterproductive. Postmodernism in many of its forms tends to form an alliance with the crassest forms of commercialism. See Harvey, *Condition of Postmodernity*, 59–65; Frederic Jameson, "Postmodernism and Consumer Society," in *Postmodernism And Its Discontents*, ed. E. Ann Kaplan (New York: Verso, 1988). By making "truth" an enemy rather than an ally, many postmodernists have no ground for criticizing the status quo and foreclose possibilities for a constructive politics. See generally David McGowan, *Postmodernism and Its Critics* (Ithaca, N.Y.: Cornell University Press, 1991).

90. At the same time, however, those who adhere to a postmodern perspective have produced much significant political commentary, and the postmodern perspective may have been vital in producing that commentary. Moreover, many of the same writers are political activists. Ironically, grassroots political culture frequently induces postmod-

although postmodernism tends to focus our attention on some important issues, it distracts us from others. Among other things, postmodernism is a reaction to the failure of Marxism to speak to issues of difference. As Linda J. Nicholson writes,

> Twentieth-century Marxism has used the generalizing categories of production and class to delegitimize demands of women, black people, gays, lesbians, and others whose oppression cannot be reduced to economics. Thus, to raise questions now about the necessary liberatory consequences of universalizing categories is to open spaces for movements otherwise shut out by them.[91]

To be sure, this is important work, and postmodernists, among others, have done it well. But the focus of postmodernism toward the local and the particular tilts against all grand narratives, including narratives about the destructive impact of uncontrolled capitalism with its international conglomerates, together with their flights to exploitable labor and their political influence in national governments. As David Harvey writes:

> [Postmodernism denies] that kind of meta-theory which can grasp the political-economic processes (money flows, international divisions of labour, financial markets, and the like) that are becoming ever more universalizing in their depth, intensity,

---

ernists to use the language of the culture, and that language assumes the existence of truth, morals, and—to a lesser extent—rights. Indeed, many postmodernists engage in a form of "strategic essentialism" (see generally Gayatri Chavkravorty Spivak, *In Other Worlds: Essays In Cultural Politics* [New York: Routledge, 1988], 197–221) in which rights and humanism are denied in theory but adopted in practice. This move is sometimes described as the "double gesture": Amanda Anderson, "Cryptonormativism and Double Gestures: The Politics of Post-Structuralism," *Cultural Critique* 21 (1992): 63, 65 (criticizing the practice and turning to a revision of Habermas as a way out of the problems posed by poststructuralism).

William E. Connolly uses different terminology in his brilliant book *Identity\Difference* (Ithaca, N.Y.: Cornell University Press, 1991):

> While modernists univocally apply the code of interrogation and coherence to discourse on the implicit faith that only this code can save us, the postmodernist thinks within the code of paradox, because only attentiveness to ambiguity can loosen the hold monotonic standards of identity have over life in the late-modern age. (60)

But Connolly is careful to observe that *the postmodernists do not and cannot avoid the code of coherence.* That is why self-irony permeates much postmodern discourse.

91. Linda J. Nicholson, "Introduction," in *Feminism/Postmodernism*, ed. Linda J. Nicholson (New York: Routledge, 1990), 1, 11.

reach and power over daily life. . . . The rhetoric of postmodernism is dangerous for it avoids confronting the realities of political
economy and the circumstances of global power.[92]

Beyond truth, morals, and political economy, I believe in some
prepolitical rights.[93] For example, I believe people have rights not to
be gratuitously tortured[94] or held in slavery, and I believe that some
free speech rights are prepolitical. I do not claim that I can *prove* there
is a right not to be gratuitously tortured or that there is a right of free
speech, but I am prepared to trust my reflective intuitions, even recognizing that my reflective intuitions are socially constructed and even
though my reflective intuitions are often wrong. Socially constructed
intuitions need not be wrong. Moreover, our inability to *prove* we are
right does not mean we are wrong, nor does it mean we are disabled
from believing we are right.

Finally, it is not clear that the stance taken by many postmodernists[95] toward rights is politically progressive. Critical race theorists[96]
among others[97] have argued that reliance on the rhetoric of rights has

92. Harvey, *Condition of Postmodernity*, 117. On the other hand, postmodernists
come in many varieties. See Judith Butler, "Contingent Foundations: Feminism and the
Question of 'Postmodernism,' " in *Feminists Theorize The Political*, ed. Judith Butler and
Joan Wallace Scott (New York: Routledge, 1992); Jennifer Wicke, "Postmodern Identity
and the Legal Subject," *University of Colorado Law Review* 62 (1991): 455, 456–57. Although others read him differently, I think the kind of analysis Harvey would press for
is not inconsistent with Foucault's recommendations for studying power. See Michel
Foucault, *The History of Sexuality*, vol. 1 (1978), chap. 5. Nonetheless, the emphasis on
starting with the local is there, and, as Anthony E. Cook observes, that followers of
Foucault emphasize thick descriptions of power relations in local situations frequently
leads to an insularity that discourages more general theory. See Anthony E. Cook,
"Reflections on Postmodernism," *New England Law Review* 26 (1992): 751, 759.

93. Although I believe that some rights are prepolitical, I do not deny that my
belief has been socially constructed. I mean that those rights do not depend upon
political arrangements.

94. I leave to the side whether torture can be justified in some rare and usually
quite hypothetical circumstances.

95. Postmodernists can and do divide over this issue. The question of whether
rights exist in an abstract way is separate from the question of whether it is strategically
desirable to invoke the language of rights discourse.

96. See, for example, Patricia J. Williams, *The Alchemy Of Race And Rights* (Cambridge: Harvard University Press, 1991), 148–61; Crenshaw, "Race, Reform, and
Retrenchment."

97. See, for example, James T. Kloppenberg, *Uncertain Victory: Social Democracy
And Progressives In European And American Thought, 1870–1920* (New York: Oxford University Press, 1986).

been historically valuable. Perhaps they are wrong, but I do not think so. Few could deny that the rhetoric of rights has been a valuable tool in organizing grassroots emancipatory movements. Thus, James Mac-Gregor Burns and Stuart Burns have chronicled the populist and broad-based character of "historic rights movements in which all participants are engaged in forging a dynamic, evolving people's charter of rights."[98] As the Burnses well understand and as some in critical legal studies[99] and critical race theory[100] have argued (influencing the Burnses as well as others), rights rhetoric has its costs. But which political strategy has the best overall chances is a matter of context. To rule out rights rhetoric altogether sweeps too broadly, too fast.

Nonetheless, the postmodernist claim about rights has substantial value in the First Amendment context. Many, if not most, First Amendment claims involve issues of balancing and social engineering. They often depend upon complex empirical and policy judgments. To what extent would a particular state interest be advanced by the state regulation in question? To what extent would speech be chilled by the regulation? Is the particular state interest as weighty as the particular free speech values imperiled by the regulation? What would be the consequences associated with other regulations that might impact on free speech values less severely?

Conceding that a legal right may be at stake, is it not a bit much for a First Amendment proponent to claim that his or her "rights" in any stronger sense have been violated in such a complex context? At least much of the time, I would agree that the existence of any such strong prelegal right cannot plausibly be defended.

Too easily, the rhetoric of First Amendment discourse projects a halo around the claim of the First Amendment claimant. To argue that the First Amendment dictates an outcome is to insist not merely on a legal right, but also on a constitutional right with a Bill of Rights pedigree. Indeed, the invocation of rights smells of *rights*. It suggests that the proponents have a natural law right, an absolute right to what they claim.[101]

---

98. Burns and Burns, *People's Charter*, 12–13.

99. See, for example, Mark Tushnet, "An Essay on Rights," *Texas Law Review* 62 (1984): 1363.

100. See, for example, Crenshaw, "Race, Reform, and Retrenchment."

101. See generally Mary Ann Glendon, *Rights Talk: The Impoverishment Of Political Discourse* (New York: Free Press, 1991), chap. 2.

And that is where the point of postmodernism has much to rec-
ommend it in First Amendment discourse. As William Connolly puts
it, "The point is to refuse to curtail thinking in the name of guarding
the faith."[102] Yet invocations of faith abound in First Amendment
discourse. Perhaps the First Amendment faith does little harm when
it applies to flag burning and the arts. But it is out of place when it
comes to issues such as pornography and hate speech. What is
needed to address these problems is not faith, but analysis. Whatever
the role of the First Amendment in these circumstances, it should not
be dictated by the fiat of faith. If the First Amendment is to nurture
dissent, it must be open to dissent about its own role as well.[103]

Nonetheless, a postmodernist trap lies down this trail as well. If
the First Amendment is no longer an absolute faith, its capacity to
ground a political identity seems concomitantly diminished. Thus,
the resort to dismissive conclusory assertions by many liberals in First
Amendment contexts is understandable. If the First Amendment is an
important part of a liberal's political identity, new challenges to free
speech are psychologically threatening. If the First Amendment *faith*
is dead, can the First Amendment be far behind?

But progressives cannot cling to a world of innocence. The innocent believe it possible to discover "some sort of truth which can tell
us how to act in the world in ways that benefit or are for the (at least
ultimate) good of all."[104] But the world of innocence was always a
dream world in First Amendment law. Too many values interact in too
many complicated ways to be able to hope or expect that something
important need not be sacrificed. Many have blinked at this reality
before, but issues such as hate speech have opened more eyes.

Prior to the hate-speech issue, progressives could comfortably
sponsor a nation that treasures free speech *and* equality. Proponents
of hate-speech regulation argue, however, that historically disadvantaged groups are "silenced" by hate speech. In a sense this is an
imperfect formulation. To be sure, many members of disadvantaged
groups are silenced by such speech in the straightforward sense that
their speech is chilled in many different ways. But the disadvantaged
class as a class is "silenced" in a different sense, in the sense that its

---

102. Connolly, *Identity\Difference*, 61.
103. Shiffrin, *The First Amendment, Democracy, and Romance,* 128; Lee C. Bollinger,
The Tolerant Society (New York: Oxford, 1986), chap. 3.
104. Flax, "The End of Innocence," 447.

members are not *heard* except through the distorting lens of hate speech. If truth emerges in the marketplace on issues of racism and sexism, perhaps it should be observed that it's a long wait. Thus, Cornel West can still speak of the ways in which black intellectuals are plagued by a "very deep racist legacy in which [they] are guilty before being proven innocent, in terms of perceiving them capable of intellectual partnership, capable of being part of a serious conversation."[105] And women are frequently heard as sex objects before they are recognized as citizens.[106] Proponents of hate-speech regulation argue, therefore, that values of free speech and equality collide in the hate-speech context and that equality is more important.

If dissent is at the heart of the First Amendment, the equality claim not only deserves a fair hearing, but also the collision may not be as substantial as it first appears. To be sure, racist speech has dissenting values. It attacks mainstream views of the society,[107] and it is ordinarily important to encourage those who would attack existing norms and conventions to do so.

Nonetheless, there are arguably deeper concerns associated with the dissent model which suggest that the ordinary presumption in favor of free speech should be displaced in the hate-speech context. A dissent-centered conception of the First Amendment assumes that wielders of power have advantages in defending their position and that their use of power is often abusive.[108] People of color are disadvantaged in this society, and race has been and continues to be used as a means of perpetuating disadvantages. The initiator of hate speech further aggravates the position of disadvantage. The dissent model is designed to assure that those who are out of power or lower in a hierarchy have means of combating the inevitable abuses of power.[109] A regime that is blind to the importance of assuring that

---

105. Cornel West, "The Postmodern Crisis of Black Intellectuals," in *Cultural Studies*, ed. Lawrence Grossberg, Cary Nelson, and Paula A. Treichler (New York: Routledge, 1992), 699.

106. See, for example, Catharine MacKinnon, *Feminism Unmodified* (Cambridge: Harvard University Press, 1987), 164.

107. On the other hand, it could be argued that the speech reflects the deeper racist impulses of the society. Both perspectives seem correct.

108. In this sense the dissent model is ahistorical. On the other hand, the question of what counts as dissent in a particular society is necessarily contingent. Indeed, the ability of a regime to define *dissent* might rob the term of its liberating potential.

109. Of course, it would also protect dissenting speech by powerful politicians or by a powerful press.

disadvantaged groups are not intimidated will favor substantial corruption and abuses in the status quo. On this understanding, the
dissent model is fueled by the ideal[110] of substantive equality.

Thus, the claim that a measure is designed to combat inequality
and to further the equality of disadvantaged groups would seem to
have a special claim to be heard under a dissent model of free
speech. In this respect, the claim is akin to that of affirmative action
in the racial context. Most progressives see racial discrimination as a
violation of equal protection except when it is a reasonable means of
compensating for discrimination, preventing discrimination, or including a disadvantaged minority in an underrepresented sphere.
Even if affirmative action were nonexistent, the equal protection
clause has long been understood to afford legal protection to members of disadvantaged groups. Thus, the First Amendment and the
equal protection clause can be read together as functioning to combat injustice.[111]

But we should not blink the tension between these amendments.
As David Cole writes, "Proponents of racist speech—Klan members,
Nazis and the like—are also a minority, and a particularly unpopular
one at that."[112] In the end, no matter what we do, I think we must
give up something of value and that even more thought needs to be
given to the relationship between morality, law, and political strategy.

This is not to argue, therefore, that regulations of hate speech

---

110. At the same time, the model recognizes that the goal will always remain
out of reach. In large-scale societies, hierarchies and injustice in those hierarchies are
inevitable.

111. Compare Charles R. Lawrence, "If He Hollers Let Him Go: Regulating Racist
Speech on Campus," *Duke Law Journal* (1990): 431, 474: "If one asks why we always
begin by asking whether we can afford to fight racism rather than asking whether we
can afford not to, or if one asks why my colleagues who oppose all regulation of racist
speech do not feel the burden is theirs (to justify a reading of the first amendment that
requires sacrificing rights guaranteed under the equal protection clause), then one sees
an example of how unconscious racism operates in the marketplace of ideas. . . . [O]ur
unconscious racism causes us (even those of us who are the direct victims of racism) to
view the first amendment as the 'regular' amendment—an amendment that works for
all people—and the equal protection clause and racial equality as a special interest-
amendment important to groups that are less valued."

112. David Cole, "Neutral Standards and Racist Speech," *Reconstruction* 2 (1992):
65, 67. On the other hand, a cross burning directed at the home of a particular black
family is quite unlike a cross burning at a public political rally. Whether or not the latter
should be protected, the former is a threatening act of power against a victim, not
dissent against a powerful status quo. See R.A.V. v. St. Paul, 112 S. Ct. 2538, 2541 n.1
(1992) (suggesting that some cross burning could be prosecuted under a threat theory).

should be upheld.[113] It is not even easy to determine whether hate-speech regulation would help disadvantaged groups or harm them.[114] My own view is that such regulations would do some of both, and that some hate-speech regulations should be upheld. But to some extent this is beside the point. Much of this debate is about symbols and not about important threats to free speech or about effective attacks on racism. And that places the hate-speech issue in the picture I have been trying to paint in this chapter: From the flag to the arts, from racist speech to pornography, we ought not to underestimate the extent to which First Amendment debates implicate cultural struggles over the meaning of America.

---

113. Certainly all racially stigmatizing speech should not be forbidden. See Frank I. Michelman, "Universities, Racist Speech and Democracy In America: An Essay For the ACLU," *Harvard Civil Rights-Civil Liberties Law Review* 27 (1992): 339, 344. Nonetheless, there is a strong case for a fairly broad prohibition of hate speech directed against historically oppressed groups. See Mari J. Matsuda, "Public Response to Racist Speech: Considering the Victim's Story," *Michigan Law Review* 87 (1989): 2320.

114. The claim that stigma is created by affirmative action programs is a legitimate concern even though I believe it is outweighed by the advantages of such programs. Beliefs that members of oppressed groups are being specially favored and the anger triggered by that belief could aggravate the very racism that hate-speech statutes are designed to combat.

Rights and Cultural Difference

Martha Minow

Political pundits and scholars alike call the end of this turbulent century a period of renewed tribalism. It would be hard to deny the salience of conflicts among ethnic and religious groups around the globe, including the fight between French- and English-speaking Canadians, the ethnic conflicts in eastern Europe, and the cross-tribal violence in South Africa. Patterns in the United States may not be entirely analogous, but many people describe the 1980s and 1990s in this country as a period of identity politics in both electoral and college settings.[1] Other related developments include the surge in membership of fundamentalist brands of religion[2] and land claims pursued by people asserting wrongful displacement by other groups, whether due to twentieth-century wars or sixteenth-century conquests. Each of these developments shares with the ethnic conflict claims of historic and genealogical group membership. What identity politics adds to the mix are claims of authority, harm, or interest by dint of memberships in groups that may cut across ethnic, religious, or traditional ties, such as status as female, gay or lesbian, or a person with a disability. Taken together, these trends threaten both the ideal and reality of "unity," whether pitched at the level of nation, society, or

---

This chapter was prepared for the Amherst College conference, "Paradoxes of Rights," Nov. 6–8, 1992.

1. The debates between men and women, blacks and whites, and others over the appointment of Clarence Thomas to the United States Supreme Court reveal how even the judiciary has been touched by identity politics.

2. See Martin Marty et al., *The Fundamentalism Project* (Chicago: University of Chicago Press, 1991).

even subcommunity.[3] Recognizing the many, then, seems to threaten "the one."

This formulation of the problem depends upon an unstated point of view. That is the point of view that treats unity as more important than recognition of diversity; that is a view that neglects how "the one" may threaten "the many." I will examine here how shifts in point of view affect evaluations of problems clustered under the phrase "the one and the many." I will also suggest that couching claims for the many in the language of rights should trouble those committed to the interests of the many more than those preoccupied with the demands of unity. I will begin, however, with a brief discussion of the problematic nature of "unity" as a goal.

Unity as a Controversial Goal

Iris Young, among others, has argued that appeals to unity in politics can be unrealistic, oppressive, and unresponsive to historic patterns of domination.[4] One need not agree with this position in order to acknowledge that past campaigns for political or social unity endangered the autonomy and at times the very existence of individuals identified with one or another minority group. The fiction of marital unity according to legal writers such as William Blackstone merged separate people into one by submerging the wife into the legal identity of the husband;[5] the banner of national unity similarly often stands for the victory of one group over others in defining the shape of national identity. Such calls to unity often reflect a dominant group's fears about other groups. A president of Amherst College voiced the concerns of many of his times and status when in 1899 he called upon teachers to protect the standards and aims of old New England's civilization against the rival standards of immigrant

---

3. See discussion in subsequent text regarding the diversity within each "culture." See also Iris Marion Young, *Justice and the Politics of Difference* (Princeton: Princeton University Press, 1990), 162–63 (each social movement asserting positive group identity has group differences within).

4. See Young, *Justice*, 179–81 (arguing against the appeal to the unity of a single harmonious polity because the goal is unrealistic, oppressive, and unresponsive to larger patterns of domination and oppression).

5. See Martha Minow, "'Forming Underneath Everything that Grows': Toward a History of Family Law," *Wisconsin Law Review* (1985): 828–30.

groups.[6] Progressive reformers at that time urged the "Americaniza-tion" of the immigrants, newly arrived from Europe. Assimilating these people into the mores and traditions of the white Anglo-Saxon middle class took on the status of a "national" mission.[7]

Perhaps paradoxically, those who pushed to retain the suprem-acy of Anglo-Saxon culture in the United States shared a fundamental assumption with many they sought to dominate: neither side believed that all human beings underneath are basically alike. Instead, each believed that ancestry determined destiny, that tribal status conferred immutable identity.[8] Thus, the inventor and defender of the term, *cultural pluralism*, Horace Kallen, meant to defend new immigrant groups against Anglo-Saxon supremacy by asserting that genealogy immutably determines[9] religious and ethnic identity.[10] Kallen also maintained that a strength of the United States had long been its federation of diverse cultures, heralded in the phrase *E pluribus unum*.[11] Yet even the tolerant vision promoted by Kallen foundered. Congress adopted and enforced immigration restrictions. Eugenics infected United States scholarship and politics between the world wars.

6. John M. Tyler, in 1899 speech, "The Teacher and the State," *Association Review* 1 (October 1899): 12–13. He asserted his faith in teachers who could protect New England's values against the lawlessness and anarchy threatened by immigrant groups: "Waterloo was won at Rugby [and] it was the German schoolmaster who triumphed at Sedan."

7. The sentiment applied to blacks as well as recent immigrants; for example, Edward A. Freeman, an Oxford University professor, told an American audience in 1881, "The best remedy for whatever is amiss in America would be if every Irishman should kill a negro and be hanged for it" (Arthur Mann, *The One and the Many: Reflec-tions on the American Identity* [Chicago: University of Chicago Press, 1979], 129). The Americanization drive, seeking assimilation of immigrants, motivated such social think-ers as Jane Addams and John Dewey. On similar motives as in the English-only move-ment, see Note, " 'Official English': Federal Limits on Efforts to Curtail Bilingual Ser-vices in the State," *Harvard Law Review* 100 (1987): 1345. The Francophone effort to ban English from commercial signs reflects a different kind of fear—here the worry is that the language (and culture) that dominates the rest of Canada would come to displace the minority enclave.

8. See Mann, *The One and the Many*, 125.

9. Note how this resembles contemporary claims that biology determines sexual orientation.

10. Kallen's fullest statement did not appear until 1959; see Horace Kallen, *Cul-tural Pluralism and the American Idea* (Philadelphia: University of Pennsylvania, 1959), 24, 52–55; but he started expressing the idea of cultural pluralism in 1915. See Mann, *The One and the Many*, 137–41.

11. Mann, *The One and the Many*, 141.

More generally, when unity is the asserted goal, a subcommunity may fall vulnerable to the projected fears and hopes of others, with little or no reference to the needs and desires of members of the subcommunity itself. This danger arises not because of the recognition of the subcommunity's difference. The danger arises when representatives of the larger (or dominant) society conceive of that difference based on ignorance or prejudices.

A striking example appears in the educational practices for deaf people controlled by hearing individuals in the United States over the course of the nineteenth century. During the early part of the century, U.S. educators promoted sign language, while in the latter half of the century, they forbade the use of signing. Educators in both periods called for unity, but the reference points for this unity changed.[12] In the first period, the vision of unity stemmed from Christianity; the educators approved sign language because they wanted to promote access to the gospel by whatever method was necessary. Later, in contrast, the educators worried about national unity and viewed sign language as part of a dangerous separatism, a foreign culture, and a threat much like that of contemporaneous immigrant groups clustering in their own clubs and neighborhoods.[13] Aspiring to a form of unity in both eras, the educators neglected the views and desires of deaf people themselves and projected upon them their own goals.[14]

A very different way that deaf people could learn and live emerged on the island of Martha's Vineyard. Isolated from the main-

---

12. Douglas C. Baynton, " 'A Silent Exile on this Earth': The Metaphorical Construction of Deafness in the Nineteenth Century," American Quarterly 44 (June 1992): 216.

13. Besides analogizing deaf people to foreign immigrants, the educators also drew on views about Native Americans and workers—other groups the educators believed needed to assimilate into the mores of the dominant culture.

14. Cultural and ethnic analogies dominated debates over deaf education in the 1890s, and it is hard to unpack entirely the argument of one angry deaf member at the Convention of American Instructors of the Deaf in 1890, who said, "Chinese women bind their babies' feet to make them small; the Flathead Indians bind their babies' heads to make them flat" and those who prohibit sign langauge in the schools "are denying the deaf their free mental growth . . . and are in the same class of criminals." Baynton, "A Silent Exile," 219 (citing quotation from Harlan Lane, When the Mind Hears [New York: Random House, 1984], 371). Implicitly, this individual seemed to be urging intervention to halt the cultural practices of Chinese women and Flathead Indians but arguing against interference with the cultural practice of sign language developed by deaf people themselves.

land, a large number of deaf people lived on the island during the nineteenth century, and the population of deaf people grew due to an inherited condition producing deafness. The deaf residents used sign language. In fact, so did the hearing community; sign language was simply one of the ways to communicate. A scholar who studied that community concluded that deafness just did not mean a disability there as it did elsewhere in the United States.[15] No one talked of unity in Martha's Vineyard; the community members simply created it by treating sign language as a shared language.

The problems of "the one and the many" would disappear if there were no reasons to preserve or enhance multiple communities. But such reasons are abundant. As Robert Cover wrote about the value of redundancy in the existence of both state and federal courts, the preservation of multiple communities promotes correction of errors in one community, permits challenges to the ideology of dominant elites, and provides space against oppression.[16] More fundamentally, of course, protection for multiple communities literally means survival for those minority cultures that dominant groups otherwise would conquer. And, in the terms advanced recently by Charles Taylor, the recent identity politics movements make eloquent arguments for including in the guarantee of fundamental rights not only liberty and equality, but also recognition of identity.[17]

Invoking the language of rights to claim recognition, members of historically excluded or subordinated groups frame their struggles for survival and equality in terms that may seem to challenge the unity of the larger polity. The drafters of the materials for the conference soliciting the article that became this chapter are worried about just such a challenge; they ask, "How should we think about rights in light of the politics of difference in the United States and abroad? Can a coherent notion of rights reconcile strivings for unity with respect for separate ethnic, racial, and cultural traditions?" Implicit here is a view that the very coherence of rights may be jeopardized if used to straddle strivings for unity with respect for difference. My sympathies for

15. Nora Ellen Groce, *Everyone Here Spoke Sign Language* (Cambridge: Harvard University Press, 1985).

16. Robert Cover, "The Uses of Jurisdictional Redundancy: Interest, Ideology, and Innovation," William & Mary Law Review 22 (1981): 639.

17. Charles Taylor, *Multiculturalism: Examining the Politics of Recognition* (Princeton: Princeton University Press, 1994).

historically excluded groups lead me to ask how their perspectives are, and are not, reflected in this very concern. The concern with coherence, and indeed with unity, may well express the vantage point of dominant groups, or at least those with enough stake in the current structure of governance and the current distribution of rights to fear the extension of respect for separate ethnic, racial, and cultural traditions. This issue of vantage point can be highlighted by a contrasting question: What jeopardy, and what opportunities, does the language of rights afford those who currently advance respect for separate ethnic, racial, and cultural traditions?

Let's try for a spell to pay attention to the effect of perspective on potential evaluations of the challenge to unity posed by the politics of difference. In so doing, I will argue that for majority or dominant groups concerned with unity, rights arguments pursued in the name of difference should be less worrisome than other tactics those groups could adopt. At the same time, I will suggest some genuine concerns of certain ethnic, racial, or cultural groups that cannot be expressed adequately through the rhetoric of rights. Finally, I will consider special problems faced by individuals who identify with certain ethnic, racial, or cultural groups but also object to some of their practices. The language of rights presents particular dilemmas for those individuals. By urging attention to these different perspectives, I hope to suggest not only their inherent value, but also their critical contribution to a serious analysis of the problems of pluralism, labeled at least since the time of Horace Kallen as "the one and the many."

Unity and the Concerns of the Dominant Group

If we focus on those who worry about coherent conceptions of rights to reconcile strivings for unity with claims of difference, one worry seems misplaced: the fear that claims of respect for separate ethnic, racial, or cultural traditions could render rights incoherent. That fear could arise from the view that the concept of rights presupposes and depends upon the universal applicability of norms and claims. Or it could arise from the view that rights become incoherent if claimed by groups rather than individuals. But most, if not all, claims of respect for ethnic, racial, or cultural traditions can be couched in terms of universal applicability, rendering them applicable to anyone who satisfies their terms. Similarly, the intended agent for such rights can remain individuals, rather than groups. After explaining these assertions, I will suggest how the very willingness of historically excluded groups to use rights language actually draws them into the process designed by the dominant group and thereby advances the unity that group seeks.

Formulating Rights

Let us assume for now[18] that a coherent concept of rights calls for universal applicability, that is, the right should apply to anyone who satisfies its terms; rights should not be trump cards for the special uses of only a subset of potentially eligible people. It is this dimension of universal applicability that may make some people queasy at the call for "special treatment" rights, or rights to accommodate some people's special needs given their membership in particular subcommunities.

Certainly, the notion of universal applicability—and neutrality in application—has supported denials of rights claims proffered by members of subcommunities. Telling, I think, is a claim made before the American Revolution by an individual who refused to swear by the particular version of the Protestant Bible required by the local courts before a person could give sworn testimony. Although the colony in question subscribed to a free exercise of religion guarantee, the interpreting court found no problem in the Bible-swearing requirement, although it failed to accommodate the individual claimant and in effect excluded him from the role of testifying witness. The court reasoned that he remained free to practice his religion; he just could not give sworn testimony without complying with the requirement.

This conclusion gives no support, however, to a view of rights that precludes "special treatment" or accommodation. Instead, this conclusion betrays the faulty assumption of neutrality in the selection of the particular Protestant Bible for the swearing-in requirement. This background norm itself was exclusionary. Therefore, a right to testify that would accommodate the claimant could be crafted to

---

18. I will save for another day a discussion about whether a coherent concept of rights could be forged that does not aspire to universal form and applicability. Universal does not mean general. Universal calls for the application of the norm to all to whom it applies according to its own scope, meaning the span of cases to which it intends reference. General refers to a broad scope of application as compared with a narrow scope, again, as defined in the norm itself. See Martha Minow and Elizabeth V. Spelman, "In Context," *Southern California Law Review* 63 (1990): 1597.

recognize a Bible he would swear upon, or to substitute another instrument for assuring his truthfulness. These alternatives would seem
to lack universal applicability only if the exclusionary quality of the
initial rule is left veiled. Once revealed, the exclusionary effects of the
rule can be remedied. And the ensuing right can still be couched in
universal terms, such as: anyone who swears before this particular
Protestant Bible or a substitute means for securing truth telling can
give sworn testimony in the Court. If the objection to this rule is that
its content is changed, this is a very different kind of charge than the
charge of incoherence.

Similarly, a more contemporary example concerns claims for pregnancy or maternity leaves advanced by women employees. Opposed
by many employers and some women's groups on the grounds that
such claims call for special rather than equal treatment, pregnancy or
maternity leaves might seem to violate bans against sex discrimination. Yet Justice Thurgood Marshall refuted such an argument in his
opinion for the Court in *California Federal Savings & Loan Association v.
Guerra*.[19] Justice Marshall reasoned that the employer should ensure
both women and men the same opportunities to combine work and
family. Thus, state-mandated maternity leaves do not violate the federal ban against sex discrimination in employment. Moreover, any
tension between the two could be resolved through the provision of
parental leaves to men as well as to women.[20] Once again, the right
need not seem incoherent nor nonuniversal. Instead, it can be formulated to bypass special treatment and instead encompass seemingly
disparate groups. And again, if the content of the right changes in this
reformulation, the change unearths the exclusionary assumptions
(here, assumptions about the typical worker) that rendered the initial
claim to appear to call for special treatment.

Let's take one more example. Claims to receive public school instruction in Spanish, Chinese, or some other non-English language
may seem nonuniversal in a school system that ordinarily uses English.
But there is nothing departing from universal applicability in a right to
receive instruction in the language the child speaks at home. Or, as the
Supreme Court concluded in *Lau v. Nichols*,[21] the public schools must

19. California Federal Savings & Loan Association v. Guerra, 107 S. Ct. 683 (1987).
20. Ibid.
21. Lau v. Nichols, 414 U.S. S63 (1974).

not deny the students who do not speak English at home a meaningful opportunity to participate in the educational program.[22]

Note how each of these examples reflects the efforts by a group to recast basic entitlements to include their needs. Nonetheless, each of the rights can be, and has been, formulated to assure and require exercise by individuals rather than by groups. This should also quell worries that claims based on difference may render rights incoherent by hinging them to group identity or exercise.

Even when a group, *as a group*, claims a right, as with an asserted entitlement to self-determination, the norm at issue can be articulated in universal terms. For example, land claims expressed by Indian tribes may reflect the particular dimensions of tribal history and specific treaties or agreements, but the principles invoked to interpret such history and agreements are applicable to all such contexts. The sheer group aspect of a kind of claim does not undermine unity where the principles it triggers stem from the larger polity and where the recognition of the group is itself a commitment endorsed by the larger polity.

Rights as Words in the Language of Unity

Most fundamentally, however, rights claims deployed to ensure respect for ethnic, racial, or cultural differences (couched in individual or group terms) do not jeopardize unity because they channel dissent and opposition into a communal language and secure participation and respect for the dominant structures of law. The willingness of a minority group to use the language of rights thus constitutes in a profound sense a willingness to join the dominant community. Linguistically, conceptually, and politically, rights claims draw the claimants into the community that prescribes the terms for claiming and obtaining rights. Framing their assertions in rights terms, the claimants at least gesture toward obedience to the dominant legal system and the state that maintains it.

I do not mean to imply that rights claims proffered in arenas beyond law—such as claims presented in political terms—secure quite this degree of obedience or respect for prevailing mores. Claims of ethnic self-determination accompany secession and at times conquest. Yet

---

22. Ibid. (interpreting section 601 of the Civil Rights Act of 1964, *U.S. Code*, vol. 42 sec. 2000d).

even in these instances, sadly often instances of violent conflict, the problem stems not from the language of rights but instead from the impatience with legal institutions to adjudicate them. Rights talk itself betokens a culture that makes rights the medium of exchange, and participation in rights talk may be one of the few mechanisms for symbolizing and securing unity in multicultural, polyglot communities.

A similar point should reassure those who fear claims for greater respect for distinctive ethnic, religious, and cultural traditions within the elementary, secondary, and postsecondary education in this country. By seeking to include texts about women, Native Americans, African Americans, Italian Americans, and other historically excluded groups, the claimants may seem to undermine the image of unity in the curriculum and the conception of American culture, literary canons, and what every educated person should know. Yet the very focus for the claims—inclusion in the teaching materials in mainstream institutions—reveals the claimants' respect for those institutions, shared faith in education, and acknowledgment of the value of cultural transmission. More serious threats to unity would come from movements that disrespected schools, teaching, texts, and the transmission of culture.

Yet even claims for separate education, or exemption from universal educational requirements, bolster national unity when couched in terms of national, constitutional rights. The classic example for students of American pluralism is the Amish schooling case *Wisconsin v. Yoder*.[23] There, adult members of a secluded religious and ethnic community faced fines if they failed to deliver their children to high school, and yet they claimed that the compulsory schooling law threatened their simple way of life by exposing their children to abrasive ideas and values. The Supreme Court accepted the challenge and excused the Amish adults on several grounds. The court reasoned that not only would the compulsory schooling fines undermine their free exercise of religion, but also the Amish achieved through their own methods the very goals of the compulsory schooling requirement: they assured that their children would grow into independent, self-sufficient adults. Although this decision accords a degree of self-determination to a minority group and marks a victory for pluralism, the Amish parents did couch their claims in the terms prescribed by

---

23. Wisconsin v. Yoder, 406 U.S. 205 (1972).

the United States Constitution. They used the language of constitutional rights to express their desires for autonomy and exemption from the universally applicable compulsory schooling law.

In this respect, *Wisconsin v. Yoder* supports an image of Russian nesting dolls in which each subcommunity fits comfortably within the larger enclosure of the dominant state. The very claim to autonomy and separateness asserted by the Amish parents fits inside the language of the United States Constitution, and the interpretation and approval of the United States Supreme Court. This model is quite different from one in which various subcommunities vie with the state for authority as contestants for moral and political turf. This second alternative model could be illustrated by an image of spinning tops, each pursuing its own orbit but occasionally running into another, with such collisions setting each off balance. Colliding, spinning tops would indeed depart from a vision of unity, unless the organizing legal framework itself specifies the spaces for each subcommunity's distinct orbit. But from the vantage point of the dominant group that adopts the compulsory schooling law, and elects presidents and senators who in turn select Supreme Court justices, *Yoder* is a testimony to unity and the order secured by the system of rights. Even though the decision creates the high-water mark for religious and ethnic pluralism under American constitutional law, it does so as a testament to the national constitutional commitment to tolerance, conditioned on assuring that the tolerated also comport with goals approved by the majority. Asserting rights to exercise difference would itself support the community of the whole. This is one of the paradoxes of rights.

Why Some Minority Groups May Find Rights Claims Unacceptable

If we shift gears and ask how members of minority groups might view the use of rights language to secure respect for their distinctive traditions, we may see greater grounds for discomfort or fear.

Rights Claims Subordinate the Subcommunity to the Power of the Dominant Society

To the very degree that dominant groups should feel reassured when subordinate groups use rights claims to secure respect for their own terrain, those subordinate groups may feel undermined or hamstrung by those same claims of rights. Again, *Yoder* provides an example. In approving an exemption from the compulsory schooling law on the ground that the Amish fulfilled the goals of the secular school system, the Supreme Court offered far less than the ideal of recognition for the Amish. That ideal would entail affirmation to their distinctive values, way of life, and dissent from the larger society and a genuine scope of autonomy and self-determination. Perhaps more profoundly, it may disserve the Amish parents to assume that submitting their case to the Supreme Court amounted to submitting themselves to that court as final adjudicator. Given their willingness in the past to move to another nation to practice their way of life, the Amish probably would leave the country rather than submit to a Supreme Court rejection of their argument. If this is the case, then the image of nesting dolls is also faulty for describing the Amish community's relationship to the larger society. Other groups, such as Native Americans, may also resist and resent such a conception, and may seek to use rights only to translate their claims before a foreign tribunal as a peaceful—or instrumental—effort to secure space for their self-governance.

In the field of international human rights, many nations routinely refuse to sign conventions or reserve their noncompliance with certain features precisely because they understand how the rights rhetoric would undermine their self-governance. Many nations expressed reservations with article 16 of CEDAW, the Convention on the Elimination of All Forms of Discrimination Against Women, specifically for this reason. Perhaps paradoxically, they also cited their rights to religious freedom and family integrity as reasons for refusing to abide by the protections for women; perhaps this simply illustrates the ambiguity of rights given crosscutting claims of difference.

When rights claims aim solely to obtain autonomous self-governance, the subcommunity signals its rejection of at least some aspects of the dominant culture. A poignant example appears in the facts of *Santa Clara Pueblo v. Martinez*.[24] There, a woman who was a member of a Native American tribe objected to the tribe's rule that denied membership to her children because their father was not a tribal member. The children of a male tribal member and a female outside of the tribe would, however, obtain membership under the tribe's rule.

---

24. Santa Clara Pueblo v. Martinez, 436 U.S. 49 (1978).

The claimant asserted that the tribe's membership restrictions violated a federal statute, the Indian Civil Rights Act, which ostensibly applied fundamental individual rights to tribe members. The tribe argued that matters of tribal membership belong properly within the tribe's exclusive jurisdiction; the Supreme Court essentially agreed by refusing to find an implied right of action allowing any individual to sue under the Indian Civil Rights Act.[25] The Court thereby rejected the view that rights—whether directed to Native Americans or rights secured more generally by the United States Constitution—adhere to individuals regardless of their tribal membership.

This case could be viewed as simply the sacrifice of individual rights in the face of strong pluralism. But the larger pattern of domination and control of tribes throughout United States history must also be part of the analysis. The case reflects a history in which Native American tribal sovereignty has been more often suppressed than respected. Native American tribal sovereignty endures entirely subject to approval by the United States government and the points of autonomy granted to tribes reflect the dominant society's ordering of priorities. Perhaps, then, it reflects the larger society's overall values that the tribe is allowed discretion over how much to protect its women from discriminatory treatment; or perhaps the larger society's values are served by allowing the tribe to exclude some candidates from tribal membership. The tribe itself has no genuine autonomy to sort out its own values and preferences in a system in which control over their own affairs has been so often undermined.

A similar issue in Canada arose, and those who have examined it point out that rules denying First Nation status to offspring of women who are members of bands and men were not rules that originated with the bands. Instead, Jesuit and state officials forced these rules on the bands in the course of pressuring for change of the communal and egalitarian practices of the native peoples.[26] Given a history of colonialism, determining what the meanings of rights to autonomy and respect

---

25. See generally Judith Resnik, "Dependent Sovereigns: Indian Tribes, States, and the Federal Courts," *University of Chicago Law Review* (1989): 671.

26. See Lisa Fishbayn, " 'A People Are Not Conquered Until the Hearts of the Women are On the Ground' ": First Nations Women and *The Indian Act*," (L.L.M. thesis, Harvard Law School), Dec. 8, 1989; Peter Kirby, "Marrying Out and Loss of Status: The Charter and New Indian Act Legislation," *Journal of Law and Social Policy* 1 (1985): 77; Kathleen Jamieson, *Indian Women and the Indian Act* (Toronto, Minister of Supply and Services Canada, 1978).

for community practices are quite difficult. Paradoxically, rights produced within a system of colonial control may not signal the respect for the individuals within the colonized communities that the language of rights implies precisely because the rights entrench colonial power.

Conflicts between colonized groups and the individuals within them do pose special problems. Such conflicts arise for labor unions, which under federal labor law obtain some degree of power vis à vis employers by controlling which individual claims and grievances from workers should be pursued. That power of self-determination for the group allows the union to target its bargaining strategy and challenges to the employer as well as to obtain governing power over employee members. Obviously, that power also could be abused and interfere with the rights an individual worker otherwise would have to object to an employer's conduct or treatment. To recognize this risk to the individual, the courts created an exception to the usual rule according unions power over worker grievances. The exception arises where the individual shows that the union breached its duty to assure fair representation in either collective bargaining or enforcement of a labor contract secured through collective bargaining.[27] Workers have successfully invoked the doctrine to challenge union practices segregating men and women[28] and union failures to communicate with workers who lack English proficiency.[29]

However important the duty of fair representation may be to individual workers, and to classes of workers who may experience discriminatory or arbitrary treatment by unions, the doctrine reveals the dilemma for groups seeking to preserve group power while operating within the larger legal framework. For the doctrine is the device by which the federal government, via the courts and the public officials on the labor board, monitors union decisions and strategies. However powerful the claim and deserving the individual worker, the language of individual rights may undermine the viability of the union itself. Subordinating the union to the power of the dominant

---

27. See Vaca v. Sipes, 386 U.S. 171 (1967) (union's duty is to serve the interests of all members without discrimination or hostility or arbitrary conduct); Steele v. Louisville & Nashville, Railroad, 323 U.S. 192 (1944) (union breached duty of fair representation when it secured an agreement that excluded all black workers).

28. NLRB v. Local 106, Glass Bottle Blowers, 520 F.2d 693 (6th Cir. 1975).

29. Retana v. Apartment and Elevator Operators Local 14, 453 F.2d 1018 (9th Cir. 1972).

society may actually subordinate workers to the power of employers by loosening the foundation for union authority.

Rights Claims Invite the State to Act as a Competing Culture

Thus far, I have suggested that some subcommunities may find rights frameworks troubling because they place those communities under the authority of the larger society even while assuring rights to its members. Even this concern seems modest compared with the risk that the larger society may itself be controlled by another subgroup. This risk arises from the fact that a minority group can seize control of the instruments of the state and impose its will on other subgroups.[30]

The problem can be put more starkly as a question: how is the state ever to respond to the presence of multiple ethnic, racial, or cultural communities in its midst—as a neutral arbiter or as another competing community seeking to impose its values on the others?[31] The likelihood of the second alternative led Robert Cover to coin the term *jurispathic* to describe how state officials, notably judges, destroy norms developed in enclaves away from the state. Rather than serving as a neutral arbiter, then, the state can appear to be a voracious competitor, fighting to displace the values and mores of a subculture. Relatively transparent statements by state officials occasionally reveal this behavior; consider the Supreme Court's opinion approving the prosecution of a polygamous Mormon for bigamy.[32] There, the Supreme Court wrote, "Polygamy has always been odious among the northern and western nations of Europe," obviously unconcerned about contrary views elsewhere in the world.[33] Yet when phrased in terms of rights, state norms veil their competition with the norms of other communities behind a guise of neutrality and universality. Some subcommunities may find this veil

---

30. It may well be important to distinguish the concerns and needs of groups into which people are born and cannot leave compared with groups in which one's membership is to some important degree voluntary, but this too must be treated elsewhere.

31. See Robert Cover, "Nomos and Narrative," *Harvard Law Review* 97 (1983): 4.

32. Reynolds v. United States, 98 U.S. 145 (1879).

33. The fact that polygamous marriages were commonplace among biblical patriarchs apparently did not matter to the drafters of that opinion. But biblical authority is invoked by judges and justices, often with no acknowledgment of its status as one competitor among many possible sources for moral authority. See, for example, Bowers v. Hardwick, 478 U.S. 186, 197 (1986) (opinion of Burger, C.J.).

itself problematic, especially when they seek an acknowledgment that the state's views are not neutral.

Rights and Individuals within Ethnic, Racial, or Cultural Communities

Individuals within ethnic, racial, or cultural communities who criticize some practice of their own communities may nonetheless want to defend their subcommunities against the assimilative demands of the larger polity. But those individuals may also face a dilemma when offered the language of rights to express their interests. If that language is offered to protect the subcommunity from state regulation, it risks treating the community as homogeneous and suppressing its diversity. If rights rhetoric in contrast is framed to protect individuals within community that differs from the majority society, those individuals may face the unhappy realization that asserting those rights means exiting from the subcommunity.

Individuals versus Groups? Groups versus the Larger Polity?

As demonstrated by the case of *Santa Clara Pueblo v. Martinez*, deference to a subgroup can come at the expense of an individual member's access to the central legal system. Besides the disappointment for that individual, a decision affirming a subcommunity's rights to self-determination may pretend that the subcommunity is like a self, rather than itself a heterogeneous, diverse community. If the subcommunity's own methods of governance do not allow for full participation by all members—or do not provide the kinds of protections for minority members that the larger society would provide—group membership will interfere with individual rights.

Yet the avenue afforded by rights arguments may force the dissenting individual to leave the subcommunity. If the rights asserted are framed to bypass the subcommunity and indeed address the centralized government, members of the subcommunity may formally or informally reject any member who asserts those rights. The language of rights may not help individuals who disagree with a practice of their own subgroup if invoking rights before the larger polity means opting out of their subgroup, risking excommunication, electing individual identity over group identity, or losing the chance to change the subgroup from within.

Perhaps we need a third image to line up beside the picture of Russian dolls, nesting inside one another, and spinning tops, occasionally bumping into one another. For individuals who experience tensions between their membership in a subgroup that is not predicated upon individual rights and membership in a larger polity that advances the language of individual rights, consider the image of a Walkman that produces different voices or different languages in each side of the earphones. The individual wearing those earphones experiences conflicting messages. It is not obvious to me how my conception of rights will help such an individual sort out the music or avoid a headache.

At the same time, posing the conflict as if it pits individuals against "the culture" or the subgroup neglects the very diversity and mutable norms and practices of each cultural, ethnic, or racial group.[34] Such groups inevitably include people with different views and roles. The language of rights risks assigning an individual who disagrees with a standard practice of the group to the kind of position held by an individual who challenges a state or federal practice, for standard rights rhetoric contemplates two positions, that of the individual and that of the state. More complex intragroup and intergroup relationships are not well expressed through the language of rights.

Robert Paul Wolff has registered a similar concern, though perhaps in more emphatic terms, in a recent paper criticizing the entire concept of culture as incoherent.[35] He specifically points to the example of South Africa, in which defenders of apartheid emphasized culture as a way of seeking protection for the White minority; they even used a notion of group rights "to rationalize the continued rule of the many by the few."[36] Wolff asks: "how shall we evaluate the

---

34. See Mann, *The One and the Many*, 157. See also James Clifford, The Predicament of Culture (1988). The diversity within a culture includes divisions according to other group-based identities, such as gender and religion; it may also include differences due to parentage, as when children have one parent who is a member of a particular culture and one who is not. Cf. *Santa Clara Pueblo v. Martinez.*

35. Robert Paul Wolff, "A Critique of the Concept of Culture," presented at University of Durban, South Africa, 1992.

36. Ibid., 34.

recent calls for a *national* culture, a culture of liberation, to replace the divisive culture of the Apartheid system?"[37]

Here Wolff distinguishes one unobjectionable possible meaning of national culture as a celebration of the arts from a worrisome movement "that, in the process of overthrowing the tyranny of a small, powerful minority, too easily loses sight of the conflicts of interest within the Black majority. I see a highly publicized circle of newly visible, increasingly powerful men—and, I might say, very few women indeed—who manifestly represent the interests of only a segment of the total Black population, but who speak in the name of all, and make decisions for all."[38]

Not only does the trend strike Wolff as contrary to the diverse history and experiences of South Africans, it also would "obscure the competing projects, plans, aspirations and needs of the many segments of South Africa, and hegemonically impose one collective vision to the detriment of all others."[39] Although Wolff does not—nor should he—blame this possibility on the presence of rights rhetoric, that rhetoric exacerbates the difficulty by calling for singularity in the previously oppressed groups as they seek to assert their rights.

Deeper Problems Still

Perhaps the difficulties lie deeper than the language of rights and its paradoxes. My discussion reflects histories of inclusion and exclusion, domination and conflict experienced by individuals and their subgroups, between subgroups, and between subgroups and the nation. The same tensions I have discussed recur recently in a deliberate effort to bypass rights rhetoric and use the alternative language and process of mediation.

The *New York Times* recently reported about an interfaith mediation program developed at the DePaul Law School to respond to conflicts over child custody when the parents subscribe to different religions.[40] The mediation program invites parties to forgo a contested court battle and instead bring their chosen clergy and work through a

---

37. Ibid., 34–35.
38. Ibid., 35.
39. Ibid.
40. Lawrence I. Shulruff, "When a Child-Custody Tug-of-War Is on Religion," *New York Times*, 13 October 1992, sec. B16, col. 3.

process that focuses on what the children need. A rabbi who participated in one mediation explained how it overcomes the all-or-nothing approach of parents who want to raise their children in incompatible religious traditions: "'Even a rabbi or priest may have to say there is more than one true path to God. If God is looking, he wants people to get to the top. Maybe he's not concerned about what path they take.'"[41] In other words, the religious leaders are able to indicate to the parents a more generous, open-minded, and tolerant approach to other religions than the parents themselves may show. Certainly, this attitude departs from the implications of a rights framework that would encourage each parent to claim his or her own right to free exercise of religion.[42]

Yet, even this world of mediation is marked by the fissures and tensions posed by deep lines of group identity. The seemingly intense divisions between Jews and Christians and between different sects within each of these religions apparently pale in contrast to the gulf between such parents and parents who are atheists or members of "cults." A founder of the program thus acknowledged doubts about whether the program is equipped to handle such cases: "a marriage in which one parent is an atheist or a cult member may be ill-suited for the program because it may be more difficult to find a clergy member willing to assist these parents" and "because [such] parents are more inclined to disagree about the role religion should play in their child's [sic] lives."[43]

It is not by accident that so many of my examples concern parental decisions about children and schooling, for there lie often the most vigorous attachments to group identity and indeed the future course of groups themselves. Perhaps if we could understand the resolutions of tensions between "the one and the many" within families, we would make some headway on the analogous issues for cultures and societies.

---

41. Ibid.

42. See Martha Minow, "In All Families: Loving and Owing," *Western Virginia Law Review* 95 (1992–93): 275 (discussing divorce visitation cases posing conflicts over religious upbringing of children).

43. Shulruff, supra n.40 (quoting Katheryn M. Dutenhaver).

Is Nationalism Compatible with Human Rights? Reflections on East-Central Europe

Elizabeth Kiss

Introduction

A specter is haunting the new world order: the specter of violent and exclusionary nationalism. It alarms and discomfits those on both sides of recent debates over the validity of universal norms of justice and rights. Universalists who saw the collapse of communism and the rise to power of human rights champions such as Vaclav Havel as a re-sounding vindication of their convictions are now shaken by the breakup of Czechoslovakia, the bloodbaths in Vukovar and Sarajevo, rising ethnic conflict in the former Soviet Republics, and the growth of xenophobic groups both at home and abroad. But advocates of a "politics of difference"[1]—a diverse collection of communitarians,

This chapter was written while I was a fellow of the Program in Ethics and Professions, Harvard University. I am grateful to the program for its generous support. Versions of this chapter were presented at Amherst College and at Yale, Northwestern, and Prince-ton universities, and I learned a great deal from all of these audiences, especially from Austin Sarat, Ian Shapiro, and John Waterbury. My special thanks to Larry Blum and Jeff Holzgrefe for their detailed comments on earlier drafts.

1. The recent literature on the "politics of difference" is vast and diverse. Among its proponents are communitarians such as Michael Sandel (*Liberalism and the Limits of Justice* [Cambridge: Cambridge University Press, 1982]), social democrats such as Michael Walzer (*Spheres of Justice* [Oxford: Blackwell, 1983]), and radical democrats such as Iris Marion Young (*Justice and the Politics of Difference* [Princeton: Princeton University Press, 1990]). Liberals who have argued for greater sensitivity to groups and cultural difference include Will Kymlicka (*Liberalism, Community, and Culture* [Oxford: Claren-don, 1989]) and Charles Taylor (*Multiculturalism and the Politics of Recognition*, ed. Amy Gutmann [Princeton: Princeton University Press, 1992]). Many feminist theorists have

postmodernists, proponents of multiculturalism, and radical democrats who have criticized universalistic norms for being too rationalistic and individualistic and insufficiently sensitive to differences of
culture, race, gender, and social power—also derive little comfort
from recent events in Eastern and Central Europe. Having argued for
the need to give different group identities a more prominent place
within moral reasoning and political institutions and strategies, they
now have to confront the dangers posed by the preeminent politics of
difference in the modern world, nationalism.

With the collapse of communism, nationalism's ambiguities
have come vividly into view.[2] The contrasting images are searingly
familiar: on the one hand, we see a crowd of unarmed Lithuanians,
carrying national flags, demanding democracy and the right to free
speech and assembly as they confront heavily armed Soviet black
berets in the streets of Vilnius. On the other hand, we have a crowd
of Bulgarians using their newly won right to freedom of assembly to
demonstrate in favor of forcing their fellow citizens of Turkish descent to change their names to Bulgarian ones. Such scenes, repeated all over the region with rotating antagonists, demonstrate the
aptness of Hugh Seton-Watson's famous comparison of nationalism
to the two-faced Roman god Janus. As Arthur Schlesinger noted,
nationalism has assisted "democracy here and despotism there, revolution in one decade and reaction in the next."[3] And in the swagger-
ing warriors of "ethnic cleansing" in Bosnia-Hercegovina we confront a revival of the most horrifying specters of nationalism and of
modern European history.

What lessons should we draw from these images? Should we

---

criticized universalistic theorizing about gender and focused on the importance of
cultural difference. See, for instance, Maria Lugones and Elizabeth Spelman, "Have We
Got a Theory for You!" *Women's Studies International Forum* 6, no. 6 (1983): 573–81. For an
example of the dispute between modernists and postmodernists over universalistic
theorizing, see the debate between Noam Chomsky and Michel Foucault in *Reflexive
Water* (Toronto: J. M. Dent, 1974).

2. This essay focuses on East-Central Europe. But nationalist and ethnicist political movements and events can be found around the world, from Quebecois seces-
sionism to Hindu-Muslim violence in India to the recent violent tension between Ha-
sidic Jews and blacks in New York City.

3. Arthur Schlesinger, Jr., "Nationalism in the Modern World," in *Nationalism:
Essays in Honor of Louis L. Snyder,* ed. Michael Palumbo and William Shanahan (Westport, Conn.: Greenwood, 1981), ix–x.

despair of human nature's primordial attachments to kinships of blood and culture and our fearful hatred of those we view as different from ourselves? Should we resign ourselves to the inescapable backwardness and brutality of certain peoples and look back with nostalgia to the *pax Sovietica,* lamenting, under our breaths, the passing of imperial enforcement of a repressive but universalistic communist ideal? Should we conclude that all politics that grants any moral weight to an ethnic or national community leads by some inescapable logic to intolerance and chauvinism? I believe that all these conclusions, though partly instructive, are ultimately seriously mistaken.

This chapter is an attempt to evaluate the moral and political status of ethnic nationalism and to consider the challenges it poses to those committed to ideals of democracy and human rights. The central question I consider is whether ethnic nationalism is intrinsically incompatible with human rights, the preeminent universalistic ideal within contemporary moral discourse. It is all too obvious that nationalism can be grossly incompatible with human rights and democracy. But the judgment that nationalism is necessarily incompatible with human rights is both incorrect and politically unhelpful. I shall argue that the charge of incompatibility is incorrect because nationalism can be compatible with human rights. Indeed, the links between the two can go beyond mere compatibility: a commitment to respecting human rights can be a constitutive element of some forms of nationalism, and, conversely, the contemporary human rights ideal seeks to guarantee respect for many of the demands voiced by nationalists. Each, in other words, encompasses elements of the other. Moreover, since repression has often been directed against national and ethnic groups, and since membership in such groups is often the basis for profound social inequalities, it is both understandable and justifiable that national or ethnic mobilization play a part in struggles for human rights and democracy. All in all, the relationship between universal norms and particular allegiances is far more complex than any simple opposition between nationalism and human rights would suggest.

These are all arguments about possible ideal forms of nationalism. But it may be objected that such ideal theorizing about nationalism is at best unhelpful, and at worst dangerously misleading. For even if these arguments demonstrate that there is no necessary incompatibility between nationalism and human rights, they fail to grasp the fact that nationalism in practice usually does not take such benign forms. Beyond ideal theory lies the real world of nationalisms that are morally ambiguous or worse; how should we evaluate and respond to these?[4] I shall argue that, even in the real world of actually or potentially dangerous nationalisms, it is unhelpful to analyze the situation as one of a necessary incompatibility between nationalism and human rights. The political strategies for taming such nationalisms are complex and difficult. But in designing these approaches we will not get far if we think our task is to overcome or get rid of nationalism as such.

First, however, I must explain what I mean by nationalism and by human rights. I offer definitions in the following two sections and then examine, in the next three sections, various ways in which nationalism and human rights construct *individual and collective identity, moral community,* and *political community.* While identity, moral community, and political community are obviously closely intertwined, analyzing them separately will help isolate elements or strains of nationalism and human rights that are complementary and those that are in fundamental conflict.

Defining Nationalism

Nationalism is a fundamentally contested concept; no one seems to agree on what it is, much less on how to evaluate it. Ernst Haas has compared the definitions of nationalism to the proverbial descriptions of an elephant offered by a group of blind people who had each touched the beast in a different part of its anatomy.[5] For example, nationalism has been variously defined as an *ideology* that makes national self-government the criterion of political legitimacy,[6] an *organizational principle* for world politics requiring congruence between

---

4. I would like to thank John Waterbury and Larry Blum, whose comments on different versions of this chapter helped me clarify this distinction.

5. Ernst Haas, "What is Nationalism and Why Should We Study It?" *International Organization* 40, no. 3 (Summer 1986): 707.

6. Elie Kedourie, *Nationalism* (London: Hutchinson, 1960), 9. Bernard Yack has argued that a weaker and more plausible version of this idea of legitimacy is that nations should not be governed by foreigners. Yack, "Nationalism and Liberal Individualism: Odd or Happy Couple?" (paper presented to the annual convention of the American Political Science Association, Chicago, Ill., 1992), 9.

national and political boundaries,[7] a *political movement* seeking to establish this congruence through the creation of a sovereign nation-state,[8] a distinctly modern form of collective *identity*, which has supplanted earlier identities based on religion, dynastic kinship, or hierarchical status groups,[9] and as a *moral code* or *secular religion* that elevates chauvinistic loyalty to one's nation above all other duties.[10]

Even such a partial list clearly demonstrates the perversely polymorphic nature of nationalism. Rather than a concept with a clear essential meaning, nationalism refers to a range of related phenomena. Any particular definition will be unsatisfactory in some respects, since it will blur some distinctions even as it highlights others, and hence will prove useful for pursuing some questions while impeding the pursuit of others. My own definition is as follows: *nationalism is a form of political consciousness that revolves around identification with and allegiance to a nation. A nation, in turn, is a group whose members consider themselves to have a shared culture and history and who in fact typically share one or more objective characteristics, such as language, ethnicity, race, religion, or political history.*

Nations are distinct from families and communities because they are too large for their members to know one another; they are, in Benedict Anderson's evocative phrase, "imagined communities."[11] While common ancestry is an important element in many nationalists' conception of their nation, most nations are quite distinct from kinship groups, since most are in fact ethnographically complex and mixed.[12] The term *nation* refers to a general population, cutting across

---

7. Ernest Gellner, *Nations and Nationalism* (Oxford: Blackwell, 1983), 1; E. J. Hobsbawm, *Nations and Nationalism since 1780* (Cambridge: Cambridge University Press, 1990), 9.

8. Oscar Jászi, *The Dissolution of the Habsburg Monarchy* (Chicago: University of Chicago Press, 1966), 26.

9. Benedict Anderson, *Imagined Communities* (London: Verso, 1991); Liah Greenfeld, *Nationalism: Five Roads to Modernity* (Cambridge: Harvard University Press, 1992), 3–4, 20; Ernest Renan, "What is a Nation?" in Homi Bhabha, *Nation and Narration* (New York: Routledge, 1990), 9, 19–20.

10. Hans Kohn, *Nationalism: Its Meaning and History* (New York and Cincinnati: Van Nostrand, 1965), 9; Tom Nairn, *The Break-Up of Britain* (London: New Left Books, 1977), 359; George Orwell, "Notes on Nationalism," in Orwell, *As I Please*, vol. 3 of *Collected Essays, Journalism and Letters* (New York: Harcourt, Brace and World, 1968), 362.

11. Anderson, *Imagined Communities*.

12. For a reference to nationalists' ethnographic illusions, see Ernest Renan, "What is a Nation?" 13–16. For a more complex discussion of the "family resemblance" between kinship and ethnicity, see Donald Horowitz, *Ethnic Groups in Conflict* (Berke-

boundaries of class, status, or caste, in contrast to earlier understandings of the word, which referred to a community of opinion or a
generic collectivity,[13] as in Montesquieu's reference to monks as "the
pietistic nation,"[14] or which limited membership in the "nation" to the
aristocracy. In Poland and Hungary, for instance, a feudal-aristocratic
understanding of "nation" lasted into the nineteenth century. According to this understanding, the "Hungarian nation" consisted of all the
nobles of Hungary, including those who were not ethnic Hungarians
and spoke no Hungarian, and excluding serfs and peasants who
spoke a Hungarian dialect.[15]

My understanding of nationalism is rather broad. So, for instance, while nationalism by my definition requires a degree of political mobilization, it can take a variety of forms and pursue a variety of
ends. The political aims of nationalists can range from self-protection
and advancement within a larger polity, through demands for some
form of autonomy (legal or territorial) within a multinational state, to
the classical nationalist demand for political sovereignty, to various
forms of imperialism, in which nationalists seek to forcibly assimilate,
conquer, dominate, or expel nonnationals. As a result of my broad
construal of the political manifestations of nationalism, I draw no
distinction between ethnic nationalism and ethnic politics. While
some nations do not conceive themselves in ethnic terms (for instance, the Swiss, Australians, Canadians, and Americans are non-
ethnic groups whose sense of shared history, culture, and political
traditions constitute them as nations), most nations are at least partly
defined by ethnicity. Such nations, in my view, are politically conscious or politically mobilized ethnic groups. While this blurring of
the line between nation and ethnic group goes against ordinary usage
in some respects, I think it is a helpful way to think about nationalism,
for it stresses that there is no sharp distinction between "ethnic" and
"national" political aims. For instance, in the postcommunist period,

---

ley: University of California, 1985), chap. 2. I return to this point in the later section
titled Visions of Moral Community.

13. See the discussion in Greenfeld, *Nationalism: Five Roads to Modernity*, 4 ff.

14. Kedourie, *Nationalism*, 14.

15. See George Barany, "Hungary: From Aristocratic to Proletarian Nationalism,"
in Peter Sugar and Ivo Lederer, *Nationalism in Eastern Europe* (Seattle: University of
Washington Press, 1969); and Emil Niederhauser, *The Rise of Nationality in Eastern Europe*
(Budapest: Corvina, 1981), 154 ff, 195 ff.

Slovak nationalists have sought special legal protections, a federal devolution of power, and, finally, secession from Czechoslovakia and the creation of a sovereign Slovakia. My definition focuses attention on the underlying connection between this range of political aims, all of which were demands motivated by nationalism.[16]

My definition of nationalism does, however, draw a sharp distinction between nations and states. Anyone focusing on East-Central Europe needs to be able to draw this distinction, since it is people's perceptions of a lack of fit between state and national boundaries that has been so crucial to the dynamic of nationalism in the region. Yet states and nations are often treated as synonyms in the literature on nationalism, and this blurring is reinforced by common expressions such as the "United Nations" or by use of the term *nation-state* to refer to all modern states, or of the term *national* to refer to a citizen of any state. General use of the term *nation-state* also suggests that the principle that the boundaries of nations and states should be congruent is largely met in the global political system. But if we distinguish between nations and states, we discover that there are, strictly speaking, very few homogeneous nation-states, with Portugal, Iceland, and Norway being the most commonly cited examples; all other states are multinational to a significant degree.[17]

Finally, my definition shuns the "demonizing" characterizations of nationalism, those that define it as inherently intolerant and chauvinistic. Such definitions, which rule out by definition the possibility of tolerant forms of nationalism, often contrast "bad" nationalism with "good" patriotism.[18] But since patriotism tends to be conceived as allegiance to a state rather than to a nation, this usage ends up asserting, usually without argument, that allegiance to a nation as

16. This point is also stressed by Paul Brass, *Ethnicity and Nationalism* (Newbury Park, Calif.: Sage, 1991), 20, note 8.

17. Uri Ra'anan, "Nation and State: Order Out of Chaos," in *State and Nation in Muti-ethnic Societies*, ed. Uri Ra'anan et al. (New York: Manchester University Press, 1991), 4.

18. A recent article on Eastern European nationalism had a section titled "Patriotism Good, Nationalism Bad." Paul Lendvai, "Eastern Europe: Liberalism vs. Nationalism," *The World Today* 46, no. 7 (July 1990): 133. See also István Bibó, "The Principle of Self-Determination," in Bibó, *Democracy, Revolution, Self-Determination*, trans. András Boros-Kazai (New York: Columbia University Press; Highland Lakes, N.J.: Atlantic Research and Publications, 1991), 372–74; and Orwell, "Notes on Nationalism."

distinct from a state can never be morally acceptable. In my view, then, nationalism is allegiance to one's nation and patriotism is allegiance to one's state. Like nationalism, patriotism can be chauvinistic and intolerant;[19] the distinction between the two is a distinction between the object, rather than the moral quality, of one's allegiances. One can also be a nationalist while being a patriot of a multinational state. So, for instance, there were no doubt some Slovak nationalists (people with a special identification with and allegiance to the Slovak nation) who were also Czechoslovak patriots (people who identified with and gave their allegiance to a multinational Czechoslovak state), who therefore regretted the recent secession of Slovakia.

Defining Human Rights

While nationalism involves identification with and allegiance to a particular group of human beings, the language of human rights asserts that all human beings have (or should have guaranteed to them) certain rights simply by virtue of their humanity. The moral core of the human rights ideal is the claim that all human beings have the same basic moral status. While there is a great deal of disagreement over the range of rights that should be considered human rights, and over the way in which these rights can be justified, there is considerable agreement on a core of rights whose violation is deemed to deprive people of the possibility of leading fully human lives. Hence, for example, torture, arbitrary arrest, and interference with basic forms of personal freedom are considered violations of fundamental liberties and immunities, and being deprived of the basic means of life is considered a violation of fundamental human claims.

To be sure, the conviction that all human beings have an equal moral status is older than the idea of human rights and can be found within a number of religious and moral traditions. But it has been articulated with particular clarity and precision, and with considerable global influence, by the contemporary human rights movement. What distinguishes human rights from other moral views that also

---

19. In fact, patriotism is often associated with militarism and blind allegiance. For a defense of moderate patriotism that explicitly contrasts it with its immoderate forms, see Stephen Nathanson, "In Defense of 'Moderate Patriotism,' " *Ethics* 99 (April 1989): 535–52.

grant equal moral status to all human beings is that it expresses these norms as *rights*. Inherent in the language of rights is the idea that rightholders can make claims on others, can exercise or appeal to their rights in the public realm, thus giving voice to their vital interests, fundamental needs, and basic aspirations.

Human rights norms have evolved through a process of contestation and struggle. Rather than regarding them as a fixed set of norms logically derived from human nature, we should, I think, conceive them as representing a vision of the basic relationships that must be created and sustained among human beings in order to enable them to lead human lives. This vision is itself a terrain of moral and political contestation. It is through contestation that human rights have been extended (in principle if not in practice) to previously excluded and disenfranchised groups and categories of persons, giving them "lifeblood," as Martin Luther King put it,[20] and that conceptions of human rights have been broadened from the "life, liberty, and property" championed by eighteenth-century gentlemen in powdered wigs to the richer range of civil, political, economic, social, and cultural rights to which people commonly make appeal today. In Kantian terms, the human rights ideal envisions human beings as legislators engaged in a continuous process of defining the institutional requirements for human dignity.

Rights are a terrain of contestation in another sense as well. A commitment to human rights—unlike, say, a commitment to humanitarianism or to the view that we are all children of God—is connected to a vision of human beings mobilized, if necessary, in their own defense—ready to articulate the injustice of their suffering and deprivation.

Finally, human rights are conceived as having overriding moral priority; they should operate as normative side constraints[21] on our actions. While they are usually conceived as rights that give rise to corresponding obligations on the part of governments, more generally they are supposed to oblige everyone to respect them.

How does a commitment to nationalism relate to a commitment to human rights? In the next three sections I will examine this

---

20. James Cone, *Martin and Malcolm and America* (Mary Knoll, N.Y.: Orbis, 1991), 70.
21. For a discussion of side constraints, see Robert Nozick, *Anarchy, State, and Utopia* (New York: Basic Books, 1974), chap. 3.

question from three perspectives, that of identity, moral community, and political community.

Constructing "I" and "We": Identity and Solidarity

Perhaps the most obvious difference between nationalism and human rights is the different answers they offer to the question of who we are. By asserting that all human beings have the same rights, the human rights ideal encourages me to see myself as "essentially" human. At the same time, it points to a vision of collective identity that encompasses the human species as a whole. By contrast, nationalism fosters solidarity with other members of my nation, focusing attention on my nation's cultural and historical particularity. It encourages me to see myself as "essentially" Polish, or Hungarian, or Greek. Human rights constructs a universal "we" embracing, without internal moral differentiation, the entire human species, while nationalism constructs a particular "we" embracing a community of human beings with a shared culture, history, or tradition that sets them apart. The particularity of nationalism seems to be fundamentally at odds with the universality[22] of human rights.

But does the vision of human identity inherent in human rights require us to reject the particular identities inherent in nationalism? Rights have sometimes been associated with a vision of human beings as innately autonomous, rational, and competitive individuals. This conception of human identity, which may be called the apotheosis of the free individual, informs some classical formulations of rights theory and their contemporary descendants.[23] It is also the image to which critics of rights frequently appeal. As Karl Marx put it in the classic formulation of this critique, "none of the so-called rights of man goes beyond egoistic man, man as he is in civil society, namely an individual withdrawn behind his private interests and whims and

---

22. Of course the "universality" of human rights is viewed as simply a broader form of particularism by those who support extending rights to animals and other nonhuman beings.

23. The best-known contemporary version of such a view is Robert Nozick's libertarian defense of rights in Nozick, *Anarchy, State, and Utopia*. While Nozick advocates the creation of and participation in voluntary associations, he does not devote much discussion to group identities like nations.

separated from the community."[24] Such a conception of human identity does seem to reject fundamental allegiances to any community, including a nation. As Ernest Renan noted in his classic 1882 lecture, "What is a Nation?" private interests do not suffice to make a nation: "community of interest brings about trade agreements, but nationality has a sentimental side to it; it is both soul and body at once."[25]

However, nothing inherent in rights talk entails this conception of human identity. Indeed, there is another, rather different conception of human identity that is much more closely associated with the contemporary human rights movement. It was eloquently expressed recently by Rigoberta Menchú, a Quiché woman from Guatemala and prominent activist for indigenous people's rights who was awarded the Nobel Peace Prize. Her words on hearing of the award were:

"I hope this is a contribution so that we Indian peoples of America can . . . demonstrate that the wound we feel is a wound of all humanity."[26]

In her reference to humanity's wounds, Menchú expressed a vision of human identity centered on shared vulnerability and on an empathetic solidarity arising from shared vulnerability. It is this vision, I believe, that informs the contemporary human rights movement's conception of human identity. This conception declares that we are all the same, not because we are all selfish and competitive individualists, but because we are all needy, fragile beings, vulnerable to ill fortune and to the brutalities and cruel indifference of the powerful in our midst.

To be sure, the recognition that all human beings are equally vulnerable does not necessarily entail a commitment to human rights. On the contrary, it may encourage aggressive domination of others as a form of preemptive strike, or a withdrawal into the protection of a small and exclusive moral community. The connection between acknowledgement of a shared human vulnerability and human rights is not one

---

24. Karl Marx, "On the Jewish Question," in *Karl Marx: Selected Writings,* ed. David McLellan (Oxford: Oxford University Press, 1977), 54.

25. Renan, "What is a Nation?" 18.

26. Rigoberta Menchú cited in Tim Golden, "Guatemala Indian Wins the Nobel Peace Prize," *New York Times,* 17 October 1992, A5.

of logical or psychological entailment.[27] Nor does an emphasis on shared vulnerability come at the expense of an emphasis on human autonomy. Rather, I am suggesting that conceiving other human beings as bearers of rights is commonly informed and motivated by a recognition of shared vulnerabilities as well as potentialities and aspirations such as a desire for more autonomy and control over our lives. Human rights evoke a response to others' wounds by getting us to reach across the differences that divide us and assert a solidarity in the aspirations and vulnerabilities we have in common as human beings.

While this vision of human identity focuses on individual wounds and aspirations, it is no longer the apotheosis of free individuality. Moreover, it can acknowledge, among shared human aspirations, the creation and preservation of communities, including nations. Hence, human rights is not incompatible with identification with a nation.

Just as human rights can, but need not, be based on an apotheosis of the free individual, so nationalism can, but need not, be based on an apotheosis of the nation. Nationalism has been associated with a number of quite different conceptions of individual and collective identity. Some of these are *organicist* or *collectivist*, holding that a nation is a primordial supraindividual entity that has an absolute existential priority over individuals and that acts almost like an autonomous historical agent. The early-twentieth-century Polish nationalist Roman Dmowski referred to Poland as "a living social organism."[28] This conception of the nation as organic subject can be found in its most extreme form within fascism. For fascists, the nation is an enduring entity through which, Mussolini wrote, an individual "may be freed from the limitations of time and space" and may achieve a "purely spiritual existence" in which his "worth as a man consists, by self-sacrifice, in the renunciation of self interest, by death itself."[29] Those who apotheosize the nation tend to disassociate the nation's well-being from that of its individual members and to treat the nation as a collective subject with its own interests independent of the interests of individual members. When

27. I thank Austin Sarat for criticisms that helped me correct and clarify this point.

28. Dmowski cited in Peter Brock, "Polish Nationalism," in Peter Sugar and Ivo Lederer, *Nationalism in Eastern Europe* (Seattle: University of Washington Press, 1969), 342.

29. Benito Mussolini, *The Doctrine of Fascism*, cited in Hans Kohn, *Nationalism: Its Meaning and History* (New York and Cincinnati: Van Nostrand, 1965), 170.

self-proclaimed President of the Serbian Republic of Bosnia Radovan Karadzic, one of the architects of the policy of "ethnic cleansing," says that "terrible" actions are "the price that a great people has to pay"[30] for their nation's glory, he demonstrates an indifference to his own people, giving us a tragic contemporary example of the effects of conceiving the nation as a reified subject.

Nations may also be conceived in *racial* or *genetic* terms. Ernest Renan's prophetic 1882 lecture on nationalism warned Europeans against racial and genetic illusions about their identity, pointing out that all the peoples of the continent were genetically intermingled. But, half a century after the debacle of Nazism, some East-Central Europeans are embracing such racial identities. Romania's extreme nationalist movement Vatra Romaneasca, whose political arm, the Party of Romanian National Unity, won the mayoralty of the Transylvanian city of Cluj in 1992, embraces a racial conception of the nation. Vatra's Vice President Ion Coja once remarked in an interview that Romanians must not shy away from using any means necessary to protect their "race."[31] In a recent journal article the controversial Hungarian nationalist István Csurka referred to "genetic reasons" for the "deterioration" of the Hungarian nation and argued, "Society must now support the strong families that are fit for life."[32] And a pamphlet distributed in Slovakia claimed that God had given Slovaks white skin and Hungarians yellow skin and urged that all Hungarians be rounded up and sent back to Mongolia to "guard horses." In a chilling example of the way racism can even turn against its own, the pamphlet urges Slovaks to look carefully in the mirror to see whether their own facial coloring is "Asiatic or Slovak."[33]

A concern with national purity is typical of such genetic or racial conceptions of national identity. The imagery of foreigners as sources of impure blood and genetic pollution and the rhetoric of "ethnic cleansing" appear to evoke this racial or biological conception of the nation.[34]

---

30. Karadzic cited in Robert Sam Anson, "Letter from Yugoslavia," *Esquire*, October 1992, 125.

31. Interview, *Beszélö* (Budapest), 30 March 1991.

32. István Csurka, "Thoughts on the Two-year History of Political Change," *East European Reporter* 5, no. 5 (September–October 1992): 47.

33. "A pamphlet from Slovakia," a Hungarian translation of an anonymous Slovak pamphlet. English translation by the author.

34. Although "purity" can also be a concern for cultural forms of nationalism.

Nationalisms that divide the world into reified national subjects are metaphysically incompatible with a commitment to human rights, and nationalisms that divide the world into races that have different moral statuses thereby reject the fundamental conviction of human rights that all human beings have the same basic moral status. However, nations may also be conceived as groups united by common culture, history, or ancestry, without a belief in the genetic superiority of one nation over another. I shall call such forms of nationalism *cultural* or *historical* nationalism. Cultural nationalism can acknowledge a shared human identity across national boundaries and hence is in principle compatible with a commitment to human rights. To be sure, cultural nationalism may still be concerned, in exclusionary ways, with cultural "purity" or "authenticity." For instance, one powerful strand of East-Central European nationalism associates the authentic nation with a romanticized vision of simple rural folk whose lives are untarnished by the foreign decadence and cosmopolitan ideas of the city. These conceptions of populist nationalism are typically anti-intellectual, antitechnocratic, and anti-Semitic.

Identities and the meanings we ascribe to them are shaped by historical processes. There seems, however, to be a crucial distinction between nationalism and human rights: for while there is a genuine biological basis for identifying the species as a natural category, nations are historical constructs. Yet all nationalisms, including cultural nationalism, tend to regard nations as natural, or at least very ancient, collectivities.[35] Yet this is an illusion. As Ernest Gellner put it, "nationalism is not what it seems, and above all not what it seems to itself."[36] Or, as Louis Snyder once remarked, rather more colorfully, nationalism is "as artificial as the Panama Canal."[37]

Identification with groups is an enduring part of human life, but there is nothing natural or inevitable about identification with na-

---

35. This tendency for nationalists to insist that nations are natural collectivities led one scholar to define a nation as "a people united by a common dislike of its neighbors and by a common mistake about its origins." George Brock, cited in Alfred Pfagiban, "The Political Feasibility of Austro-Marxist proposals for the Solution of the Nationality Problem of the Danubian Monarchy," in *State and Nation in Multi-ethnic Societies*, ed. Uri Ra'anan et al. (New York: Manchester University Press, 1991), 54.

36. Ernest Gellner, *Nations and Nationalism* (Oxford: Basil Blackwell, 1983), 56.

37. Louis Snyder, *Varieties of Nationalism* (New York: Holt, Rinehart and Winston, 1976), 3.

tions. The tendency to treat nations as "primordial givens"[38] is an example of the more general human propensity to naturalize historical outcomes.[39] Before the rise of modern nations, the identity of Europeans was shaped by ideas of "Christendom," by various (often territorially discontinuous) dynastic kingdoms and empires, and, for the vast majority of the population, by localized identities centered around family, village, market town, and dialect.[40] It took a combination of contingent historical factors, including the centralizing force of modern state bureaucracies, technological innovations such as the printing press, the breakdown of Catholicism's cohesive force as a result of the Reformation, and what Benedict Anderson vividly called "the revolutionary vernacularizing thrust of capitalism"[41] to lead to the standardized national languages and cultures that are the defining features of the region's nations and the basis for its nationalisms. Nations are the effect of historical change, political struggle, and intentional artifice.

The artificial aspect of nation building is especially clear in the case of East-Central Europe. Many of the nations of the region arose as a result of the work of the so-called "awakeners"—philologists, writers, and other intellectuals who consciously set about during the nineteenth century to create national languages and identities.[42] The language reforms the awakeners created required, in some cases, the standardization and modernization of languages that already had a literary tradition, while in others it was necessary to create a written language out of a particular vernacular dialect. The awakeners invented new words, wrote dictionaries and grammars, and founded newspapers and journals. The linguistic ferment in nineteenth-century Europe is shown by the fact that the number of "standard" written languages grew from 16 in 1800 to 30 in 1900 to 52 in 1937.[43]

---

38. Anderson, *Imagined Communities*, 89.

39. Benedict Anderson remarks on the "wonderful" aptness of the legal expression "naturalization" to describe the acquisition of citizenship. Anderson, *Imagined Communities*, 145.

40. Ibid., chap. 2; Claude Karnoouh, "National Unity in Central Europe: The State, Peasant Folklore and Mono-Ethnism," *Telos* 53 (Fall 1982): 95–105.

41. Anderson, *Imagined Communities*, chap. 3, esp. 39.

42. For a detailed account of the Eastern European awakeners, see Emil Niederhauser, *The Rise of Nationality in Eastern Europe* (Budapest: Corvina, 1981).

43. Brass, *Ethnicity and Nationalism*, 24.

The awakeners' motives were not, of course, purely philological—they were driven by visions of progress and modernity, by political dreams of reproducing the glory of the French Revolution, or by the desire to resist the hegemony of the Austro-Hungarian, Russian, or Ottoman empires. Some were radical democrats who wanted to emancipate the serfs and to fashion, out of a population of disenfranchised peasants, a nation of citizens. Others were champions of the nascent Eastern European bourgeoisie and wanted to modernize and enrich the region. National awakening had a sort of domino effect, with action provoking reaction. So, for instance, the Hungarian awakening during and after the 1848 revolution served as a catalyst for Romanian, Croatian, and Slovakian awakeners who organized to resist coercive Magyarization and Hungarian political control.

The awakeners made a big difference politically. This impact is particularly clear in the case of numerically small groups with no history of political independence. A philologist invented the name "Slovene" in 1809 and became the architect of Slovenian national identity; the movement he helped start led eventually to Slovenia attaining republic status within Yugoslavia, then, in 1991, becoming a sovereign state. At the same time, members of other dialect groups, like the Sorbs, never attained a self-conscious collective identity and as a result have no distinctive political or cultural presence in contemporary Europe.

Although the awakeners built on earlier cultural traditions, the term *awakener* is somewhat misleading, since what was occurring was as much invention as awakening. While the new standard languages were constructed on the basis of existing, often ancient, dialects, the path of linguistic, and hence national, development was by no means always self-evident. Thus, there were struggles among awakeners over national self-definitions. For instance, throughout the nineteenth century, there were disputes over whether Serbs and Croats formed two separate nations or comprised a single South Slav nation. An influential movement favored the latter national identity, calling it "Illyrian."[44] One of the most important Czech awakeners, Jan Kollar, came from a family that spoke a Slovak dialect and refused to accept the separate Slovak language championed by the Slovak awakener L'udovit Stur, advocating instead a united Czechoslovak language

---

44. For an account of the Illyrian movement, see Niederhauser, *Rise of Nationality*, 112.

and national identity. The history of the awakeners also abounds with linguistic ironies. Many of the awakeners did not at first speak the languages they championed, and many continued to use more established languages in their written work. The delegates to the first Pan-Slav Congress spoke German, and Czech awakener Jan Kollar continued to write in German throughout his life, just as many Bulgarian awakeners continued to write in Greek. Janez Bleiweis, the publisher of an influential Slovenian newspaper aimed at peasants and craftworkers, accepted the editorship before he himself had learned how to speak Slovenian.[45]

An important aspect of national awakening was the rewriting of history to project national identity and consciousness back into the dim past. Just as every English schoolchild is convinced that William the Conqueror spoke English, although the language did not yet exist, and just as French children grow up with the exploits of the semifictional Vercingétorix, so every Hungarian schoolchild is convinced that Mihály Zrinyi is a great Hungarian hero of impeccable ethnic Hungarian credentials, whereas he was of Croatian ethnicity. The search for a glorious past also led to outright frauds, such as the tenth-century Czech epics that the archivist Vaclav Hanka forged on fake parchment.[46]

False beliefs about national identity pervade nationalism, especially organic and genetic nationalisms. Nationalisms that conceive the nation as a reified subject or as a pure blood group cannot stand up to demystification because there are no such subjects and because no modern nation is racially or genetically "pure." Europe is such an ethnic and genetic melting pot that it is nonsense to think one could find a "pure" genetic strain of Romanianness, Polishness, or Hungarianness,[47] even independently of questions about why such genetic purity, if it existed, should have any moral or political significance. Cultural nationalisms also often rest on irrational beliefs. The claim that has been made, both explicitly and in veiled form, by politicians in postcommunist East-Central Europe that Jews are culturally "alien"

---

45. Ibid., 222.

46. Ibid., 59. See also Eric Hobsbawm, *The Invention of Tradition* (Cambridge: Cambridge University Press, 1983), 7.

47. Many common East-Central surnames reveal people's ancestral connection to other ethnicities or nations. For instance, among the most common Hungarian surnames are Horvath, which means "Croat," and Toth, which is an old (now considered derogatory) term for "Slovak."

and cannot be "authentic" Poles or Hungarians[48] is a disturbing example of such an irrational belief. The Jewish communities in Poland and Hungary are culturally assimilated and have played an important role in the shaping of Polish and Hungarian culture, economics, and history. The vague cosmopolitan "ideology" attributed to Jews is not universally shared by them and at the same time is shared by many non-Jews. The elaborate casuistry that many East-Central Europeans engage in to determine who is Jewish reveals, in the expenditure of energy it requires and in its frequency of error, the absurdity of the enterprise.[49]

Obviously, irrational convictions can remain psychologically and politically potent, and attempts to rationalize or demystify nationalism have no guarantee of success. But some forms of nationalism can also survive demystification while retaining their legitimacy and power. People can still feel French, or Polish, or Slovenian, and identify with these national cultures, even when they recognize that they are artificial creations of relatively recent historical vintage. For all their artifice, national "awakenings" made themselves true—they made possible achievements about which nationalists can justly be proud, such as great works of literature. Nationalism can also provide people with a sense of dignity and belonging that fulfills perennial human aspirations.[50]

Nevertheless, this demystification of the origins of nationalism has some important consequences. First, it points to a flaw in the despairing view of those who see, in the recent upsurge of nationalism in East-Central Europe, evidence of primordial collectivities and hatreds that four, or seven, decades of communist rule left untouched. Hatred as such is no doubt primordial, though its expressions can be tamed. But nations are not primordial, and this view

---

48. Hungarian writer and then-parliamentarian Sándor Csoóri set off a storm of protest with his 1990 article claiming that it was no longer possible for Jews to assimilate into Hungarian society: "Nappali Hold," *Hitel* 19 (September 1990). More recently, another Hungarian parliamentarian wrote that the term *Jewish Hungarian* made no sense unless it referred to a bilingual dictionary. See George Soros's account of recent Hungarian anti-Semitism in "Termites are Devouring Hungary," *New York Times*, 5 October 1992, A21.

49. For an insightful discussion of Jewish identity in Eastern Europe, see János Kis, "On Ways of Being a Jew," *Politics in Hungary* (New York: Columbia University Press; Highland Lakes, N.J.: Atlantic Research and Publications, 1989), 233–43.

50. This point is stressed by Liah Greenfeld (*Nationalism: Five Roads to Modernity*) and Donald Horowitz (*Ethnic Groups in Conflict*).

ignores the ways in which nationalisms were manipulated by communist leaders during the Soviet era[51] and, more generally, the ways in which Soviet modernization, combined with Soviet federalism and the experience of aggressive Russification, helped constitute and "awaken" some of the nations that are now demanding sovereignty.[52] Demystification also helps us recognize the permeable and fluid nature of identities. Global telecommunications, the world market, the large movements of population that have occurred in the aftermath of colonialism and war, and the rise of new "nations of immigrants," such as the United States, Canada, Australia, and Israel, have all loosened old identities and shaped new ones. Ernest Renan famously described national identity as the result of a "daily plebiscite,"[53] and historical changes have made the constructed nature of national identities more obvious. Immigrants, refugees, postcolonial peoples, and many others experience multiple national identities and identities that are open to individual choice to a significant degree.[54] When people wholeheartedly experience and acknowledge multiple identities, they help demystify national identities without delegitimating them. Consider again the words of Nobel laureate Rigoberta Menchú:

> I hope this is a contribution so that we Indian peoples of America can live forever, and so that we demonstrate that the wound we feel is a wound of all humanity.[55]

In one breath, these words affirm three identities: an identity as a human being, as a Quiché Indian, and as a member of a preeminently "imagined community," the community of the "Indians of the

---

51. This point was stressed by Gail Kligman in a roundtable on "Nationalism and Ethnic Particularism," *Tikkun* 7, no. 6 (November–December 1992): 49.

52. This point is argued in Philip Goldman, Gail Lapidus, and Victor Zaslavsky's introduction to *From Union to Commonwealth* (Cambridge: Cambridge University Press, 1992).

53. Renan, "What is a Nation?" in Kohn, *Nationalism: Its Meaning and History*, 139.

54. For instance, I consider myself a Hungarian-American but recognize the contingency of both these identities. My parents ended up in the United States after fleeing Hungary as refugees in 1956 but could have settled in France or Austria instead. And my Hungarianness is a chosen identity: it is something I consciously embrace, which I could also ignore, and its meaning is constantly contested within emigré communities and tested by my mixed feelings of being at home and a stranger when I am in Hungary or among Hungarians.

55. Rigoberta Menchú cited in Golden, "Guatemala Indian Wins Nobel," A5.

Americas," a pan-Indian identity born out of Menchú's political work as an activist for indigenous people's rights and out of the shared history of colonization and oppression experienced by indigenous people.[56]

Nationalism is more than a way of describing ourselves; it is a moral allegiance. I turn now to examine how nationalism and human rights construct moral identity.

Visions of Moral Community

What moral visions do nationalism and human rights construct, and to what extent are these moral visions compatible? Once again, an apparently stark contrast between the two turns out to be more fine-grained and complex on closer examination. If all conceptions of human rights simply proclaimed that the only thing that matters morally is our status as human beings, and if all conceptions of nationalism simply proclaimed that the only thing that matters morally is the nation, then the two would be in fundamental moral conflict. But these are not the only moral visions possible for either human rights or nationalism.

According to the ideal of human rights, the species boundary has paramount moral importance. Yet this idea is by no means self-evident. As a moral boundary the species line is constructed, even if as a descriptive boundary it is natural. Champions of animal rights, for instance, urge us to recognize the moral arbitrariness of "speciest" thinking and to redraw the boundaries of the moral community on the basis of some other criterion, such as the capacity to suffer.

Questioning the moral significance of the species boundary points to two questions included within the vision of moral community associated with human rights: (1) why does humanity have moral value? and (2) what are our moral obligations to this community?

To the first of these questions, human rights theories usually respond by appealing to certain features, actual or potential, of human beings. This appeal to shared characteristics supports, although

---

56. No doubt there are other identities important to Menchú, such as her identity as a woman—and, as a writer and activist, by no means a traditional Quiché woman. Smaranda Enache, a Romanian who has attained notoriety by virtue of her public support for minority rights, commented: "[I]n my opinion another nationality exists, called the intelligentsia, and I would like to think that I belong to this as well." "Complicity and Ethnicity," *East European Reporter* 4, no. 4 (Spring–Summer 1991): 89.

it does not prove, the idea that all human beings have an equal moral status. But the practical moral implications of our shared humanity are conceived rather differently by different understandings of human rights. They may range from a comparatively minimalist view that we are obliged to refrain from interfering with the basic freedoms of other human beings to more robust positive duties to ensure equal protection from deprivation and harm. At its most demanding, the human rights movement holds that as members of a global human community we must strive to transform institutions so that all human beings can enjoy a broad range of human rights. But all forms of human rights demand that we be concerned, to a greater or lesser extent, about the security and well-being of individuals who are strangers to us, even those who live in alien countries and cultures on the other side of the globe. Thus, human rights views conceive moral obligations as crossing boundaries of state, race, and class.

Given its cosmopolitan scope, the moral vision of human rights can appear to evoke a view of moral progress that is hostile to nationalist commitments. Moral progress, in this view, consists in the gradual withering away of the barriers of caste, class, race, nation, tribe, and religion, and in an increasingly robust sense of common humanity. In the vernacular of rights, this progress consists in the withering away of the special rights of class, race, and tribe and the gradual extension of equal rights to all human beings. (Those who argue that using the species as the line of demarcation for rights is morally arbitrary would project this progressive narrative beyond human rights.) Such a view may justify nationalism when it serves as a means toward the extension of rights to broader categories of persons. But to see nationalism as a permanent moral ideal is to fall into a kind of arrested moral development.[57]

But the moral vision of human rights is not necessarily linked to this cosmopolitan conception of moral progress. Such a vision can encompass particular moral claims and obligations to others that are not based solely on their humanity. These claims may include obligations or commitments to loved ones, to a cause or a vocation, or those arising out of contracts and promises. These obligations are not envisioned as withering away through moral progress but, rather, are

---

57. This point is eloquently argued by Lord Acton in *Essays on Freedom and Power* (Glencoe, Ill.: The Free Press, 1948), 166–95.

generally conceived as ongoing constitutive elements of moral life. Like families and vocations, national communities can be seen as an example of the sort of special obligations and allegiances that are constitutive elements of moral life.[58]

Certainly, international human rights law grants protection to many of the cultural, linguistic, and religious activities in which people engage as members of national communities. The International Covenant on Civil and Political Rights is quite explicit for instance on the rights of minorities. Article 27 states: "In those States in which ethnic, religious or linguistic minorities exist, persons belonging to such minorities shall not be denied the right, in community with the other members of their group, to enjoy their own culture, to profess and practice their own religion, or to use their own language."[59] Respecting people's allegiance to a national community and culture is certainly recognized, in texts like these, as part of the moral vision of human rights.

How does nationalism conceive the moral community? Some forms of nationalism make the nation into the sole arbiter of value and deny the possibility of moral obligations that extend beyond it. Not surprisingly, it is conceptions that conceive the nation in organic or racial terms that tend to yield moral visions most hostile to affirmation of the equal moral status of human beings. According to such views, the nation is a Destiny whose welfare and glory become the sole criterion of value.[60] It is typical of such forms of nationalism to conceive members of the nation as mere means or instruments to national glory, which fundamentally violates the moral vision of human rights. Moreover, since moral obligations do not, in this view, extend beyond the boundaries of the nation, this form of nationalism

---

58. Will Kymlicka argues for the value of cultural membership in *Liberalism, Community, and Culture* (Oxford: Clarendon, 1989). I have also benefited from Larry Blum's interesting discussion of what he calls "morally significant group identities" in "Gilligan's 'Two Voices' and the Moral Status of Group Identity," in Lawrence Blum, *Moral Perception and Particularity* (Cambridge: Cambridge University Press, 1994), 237–65.

59. United Nations International Covenant on Civil and Political Rights (1966), Article 27, in *Basic Documents on Human Rights*, 3d ed., ed. Ian Brownlie (Oxford: Clarendon, 1992), 134.

60. A recent pamphlet by Hungarian writer and parliamentarian István Csurka struck a note in this vein when he wrote, "the only thing that is sacred is the national interest." The pamphlet set off a storm of protest in Hungary. Csurka, "Thoughts," 47.

cannot be conceived as a special moral community within a more expansive one.

Organic forms of nationalism may also conceive national self-determination as an intrinsic and basic moral good, in the way that moral autonomy is for individuals.[61] This conception is in tension, however, with the moral vision of human rights, for it is insensitive to the human rights concerns that can be raised about self-governing nations. National self-determination does not guarantee respect for human rights, and for that reason it cannot be seen as a fundamental moral good from a human rights perspective.

If the nation is not an exclusive arbiter of value, its value must be measured in ways that are intelligible beyond national boundaries. Nationalists may appeal to some moral or cultural value they perceive in their nation's history or culture, or they may value their national culture and community simply because it is their own.[62] People will of course tend to overvalue what is their own; this phenomenon is by no means exclusive to nationalism. But these understandings of nationalism contain a possibility of reciprocity, of acknowledging that others also value what is theirs or that other nations also have a valuable heritage. Diverse national cultures, and the experience of having a culture with which you identify, are both viewed as human values.

What moral commitments do these forms of nationalism ask of members? They tend to center on a commitment to relieve the suffering and foster the well-being of other members and a commitment to preserve "my" community's culture. These commitments can be nested within a moral vision that also encompasses people outside the nation. Thus, while nationalism may be in tension with the most robustly cosmopolitan forms of obligation to a human community, some forms of it are compatible with the basic moral vision of human rights.

One of the most distinctive aspects of nationalism is its commitment to the survival of a national culture. Rigoberta Menchú affirmed such a commitment when she expressed her hope that "we Indian

---

61. I owe this formulation to Donald Horowitz, "Irredentas, Secessions and Self-Determination" (Paper presented to the Joint Harvard–M.I.T. Seminar on Political Development, Cambridge, Mass., November 18, 1992).

62. For a discussion of the distinction between these two modes of valuation, see Susan Wolf's comment on Charles Taylor's essay in Taylor, *Multiculturalism and the Politics of Recognition*, 79 ff.

peoples of the Americas can live forever." Her words articulate a
dream of a historical future in which the Indians of the Americas have
a place as self-conscious cultural communities. However, given the
historical contingency and fluidity of national identities, is the goal of
cultural survival a realistic and legitimate one? Much depends on how
"survival" is interpreted. For instance, images of purity pervade
many nationalist discussions of culture. But attempts to preserve the
"purity" of a culture can reproduce at the cultural level the exclusionary paranoia that racial nationalism exhibits at the biological level,
leading to the exaggerated fears of foreign influence that constitute
one of the hallmarks of xenophobic nationalism. Like their racialist
counterparts, cultural purists can base their views on false beliefs
about the past, believing that the culture they celebrate is the product
of a pristine community. More important, making a fetish out of cultural purity tends to encourage moral exclusion. Placing moral value
on cultural survival legitimates repression if it is combined with an
irrational inflation of what constitutes a danger to cultural survival. In
1991, for instance, a riot broke out in the Romanian city of Tirgu
Mures after a Hungarian-language sign was placed in a pharmacy
window. Thus, while making and maintaining culture is an important
part of our shared human experience, and while concerns to protect
indigenous national cultural production against the onslaught of the
international mass media are understandable, an uncritical stress on
the overriding value of cultural survival can justify jeopardizing the
basic commitment to the equal moral status of human beings.[63] Like
national self-determination, cultural survival is a controversial value
from a human rights perspective because cultural practices can violate
human rights. While the moral vision of human rights can respect the
value of cultural survival because of its value to members of the culture, it cannot ascribe fundamental or overriding moral value to cultural survival.

Constructing the Political Community

These concerns about the political implications of nationalist commitments bring me to my third topic, which is an examination of the

---

63. Charles Taylor does not, in my view, treat the category of cultural survival
critically enough in his essay on the politics of recognition. See ibid.

ways in which nationalism and human rights construct political community. The core political ideals associated with human rights are equal citizenship and equal protection under the law.[64] But the ideal of human rights is more or less silent on two crucial political questions: where the borders of the political community should lie and what forms of political mobilization are required to achieve recognition and enforcement of rights. Nationalism offers a possible answer to each of these questions.

While the human rights ideal insists that the moral community must encompass all of humanity, it has little or nothing to say about the proper boundaries of political community. So, for instance, while the post–World War II human rights movement has sought to create global or regional legal tribunals to which individuals can appeal for redress of rights violations, human rights is not explicitly connected with a commitment to the ideal of world government. It appears that nationalism can fill this lacuna in the human rights ideal by mandating that national boundaries determine political borders. Indeed, the "right to national self-determination" is often, inaccurately, considered a human right. However, nations simply are not distributed in discrete territorial units. In East-Central Europe, as John Stuart Mill observed, national groups are geographically "so mixed up as to be incapable of local separation," posing an insuperable practical obstacle to the principle "that the boundaries of governments should coincide . . . with those of nationalities."[65] The concept of national self-determination achieved prominence as a way of justifying the independence struggles of former colonies, and it continues to have relevance in colonial and quasi-colonial contexts today, such as those of the former Soviet republics. But dogmatic adherence to the principle of national self-determination in a mottled multinational context can become a recipe for coercive policies, ranging from forced assimilation to expulsion ("ethnic cleansing") and genocide. Even with nations that live in homogeneous territories, the "right to national self-determination" offers no guidance concerning when a national group should

---

64. Henry Steiner notes that equal protection is "perhaps the preeminent human rights norm." Steiner, "Ideals and Counter-Ideals in the Struggle over Autonomy Regimes for Minorities," *Notre Dame Law Review* 66, no. 5 (1991): 1548.

65. J. S. Mill, "Considerations on Representative Government," in *Utilitarianism, On Liberty, and Representative Government*, ed. H. B. Acton (London: J. M. Dent, 1972), 394.

seek sovereignty and when it should seek protection for its interests as a minority within a larger state. Pragmatic factors regarding material and human resources, economic prospects, infrastructure, and security concerns are also crucial in determining the desirability of national self-determination. Most important of all, however, are the actual wishes of members of a nation, and indeed of all persons living in the territory to be affected. Often self-determination may conflict with basic nationalist commitments to the well-being of members of the nation. Hence, the political slogan of national self-determination can be dangerous to human rights in practice.

Human rights are not self-enforcing, and yet the human rights movement has also tended to be silent on questions concerning the kind of political mobilization required for achieving respect for and enforcement of rights. Thus, human rights offers a detailed moral standard by which to judge political arrangements, but not a detailed political strategy for securing respect for human rights. In practice, group mobilization (by or on behalf of slaves, workers, women, nations, and others) has played a crucial role in the successful institutionalization of rights and in extending rights to previously disadvantaged groups.

Nationalist politics involves the political mobilization of a national community in its own interest. For disenfranchised and disadvantaged nations, nationalist politics offers a partial answer to the second lacuna of the politics of human rights. Instead of, or in addition to, moral exhortation to the international community, it advocates political mobilization to gain the power and resources to effectively articulate and protect the community's members. Nations, in this view, especially weak and disadvantaged nations, have to mobilize to protect themselves and to survive. As Bernice Johnson Reagon put it, "At a certain stage nationalism is crucial to a people if you are going to ever impact as a group in your own interest."[66] Nationalist politics may be the best means available to ensure that an oppressed group is empowered to seek respect for the rights of its own members.[67]

66. Johnson Reagon is using the term *nationalism* more loosely than I do, since she is referring to the feminist movement. Bernice Johnson Reagon, "Coalition Politics: Turning the Century," in *Home Girls: A Black Feminist Anthology*, ed. Barbara Smith (New York: Kitchen Table: Women of Color Press, 1983), 358.

67. See Steiner, "Ideals and Counter-Ideals," for an excellent discussion of the advantages and disadvantages of autonomy regimes from the perspective of human rights.

However, like the political slogan of national self-determination, political mobilization around the nation also has its dangers, as the postcommunist evolution of East-Central Europe demonstrates. It clearly has dangers for the human rights of strangers. But it also has dangers for the nation's own members. As Johnson Reagon put it, "Nationalism at another point becomes reactionary because it is totally inadequate for surviving in the world with many peoples."[68] Nationalist politics may encourage wildly impractical political preoccupations, such as a fixation on symbolic politics at the expense of facing up to economic and social crises. Many of the new parliaments of East-Central Europe, for instance, spent hundreds of hours in acrimonious debate over new national flags, seals, and coats of arms. Nationalist politics may seek in authoritarian fashion to create a false national unity by declaring that the Nation has one voice, making it difficult for members to articulate where their interests and values differ or to forge coalitions with members of other nations. Such a focus on national unity has a tendency to be exclusionary; for instance, nationalist political parties in postcommunist Poland, Hungary, and Slovakia have attempted to arrogate "true national identity" to themselves, with corrosive effects on these countries' political culture. Of course, such claims to represent the nation all too often hide brazenly opportunistic partisan purposes and fuel the megalomania of authoritarian politicians.[69]

Nationalist politics can also lead to destructive polarization. Among the most poignant stories coming out of what used to be Yugoslavia are those of young people who were unaware of the national differences over which a brutal war is now being fought. One young woman who was interviewed noted, "Now everyone hates Tito, because he was a Croat. I didn't even know he was a Croat until this began. If I had known, I wouldn't have cared. Until this began, no one would have cared." She added, "I have no Serbian identity at all. I am forced to be a Serb by events over which I have no control . . . I am a Yugoslav."[70] Indeed, one of the ironies of

---

68. Johnson Reagon, "Coalition Politics: Turning the Century."

69. Naomi Chazan, "Irredentism, Separatism, and Nationalism," in *Irredentism and International Politics*, ed. Naomi Chazan (Boulder, Col.: Lynne Rienner, 1991), 141.

70. Robert Sam Anson, "Letter from Yugoslavia," *Esquire* 118, 4 (October 1992), 116.

the war in Bosnia is that Serbian fear of Muslim fundamentalism is beginning to conjure up its enemy. Under pressure from the war, Bosnian Muslims are beginning to be attracted by Islamic fundamentalism, a development that may well encourage further tension and instability in the future.[71] Serbia is a powerful example of how nationalist politics can not only wreak havoc on one's neighbors but also on oneself. These dangers of nationalist politics all have a political flaw in common: they substitute concern about national authenticity for pragmatic institution building to protect national interests in the long run. As we saw earlier, the way in which some forms of nationalism conceive national interests is intrinsically incompatible with human rights. But even forms of nationalism that are compatible with human rights may lead to a politics that fails to pursue its own goals pragmatically, bringing destructive instability to its neighbors and its own members.

Nationalism and Human Rights: Compatibilities

I can now return to the question I posed at the outset. Is nationalism incompatible with human rights? Assertions of its necessary incompatibility are incorrect, for three reasons. First, and most straightforwardly, it is incorrect because some forms of ethnic nationalism are compatible with a commitment to human rights. In East-Central Europe as elsewhere, there are men and women who strongly identify with their nation as a cultural group and who feel special allegiances and responsibilities toward its members, but who are also committed to respecting human rights. The two commitments may at times pull in different directions—I may devote more energy and resources to working on behalf of my co-nationals, for instance, than I do to supporting Amnesty International's work on behalf of people who are in more urgent need of help—but these are tensions rather than incompatibilities, in the same way that I can be committed to respecting human rights while strongly identifying with and committing myself to my family or my vocation.

Second, there are also some deeper ways in which nationalism and human rights can be compatible. Nationalists may consider efforts to foster a tolerant and democratic political culture and to create

71. Ibid., 125.

a political and legal system that guarantees the rights of all citizens, including members of minority groups, to be a constitutive element of their nationalism.[72] Their allegiance to their nation is at the same time a critical commitment to fostering their nation's political virtue, with respect for human rights occupying a central place among these virtues. Hence, a commitment to human rights can be encompassed within some conceptions of nationalism. Conversely, some of the central concerns of nationalism can be encompassed within a conception of human rights. Loyalty toward particular cultural communities, and commitment to their survival and well-being, is not only permissible under broadly accepted definitions of human rights, but the free and secure pursuit of such commitments is arguably an integral part of the human rights ideal. Many of what are considered to be the most basic human rights, such as the right to free exercise of religion or to freedom of expression and association, are frequently exercised in the interests of preserving a particular cultural community. While human rights cannot elevate cultural survival or national self-determination to the status of overriding moral or political principles, it can encompass many of the concerns that motivate nationalist politics—the right to speak one's language, to worship in one's own way, to educate one's children in one's own tradition, to maintain a flourishing national culture.

The third reason why it is incorrect to assert a necessary incompatibility between nationalism and human rights is because nationalist politics may play a crucial role in securing respect for the human rights of members of a nation. Violations of human rights often take the form of systematic efforts to prevent people from freely organizing themselves to maintain their culture; such cultural repression frequently accompanies "political" repression more narrowly defined, such as the denial of voting rights or of rights to due process of law. Thus, the judgment of incompatibility ignores historical patterns of rights violations as well as the political processes necessary to redress them. Political mobilization by groups, including national groups, has been essential to securing equal protection of the law for such groups.

---

72. For a recent defense of tolerant, liberal nationalism, see Yael Tamir, "The Right to National Self-Determination," *Social Research* 58 (1981): 564–90, and *Liberal Nationalism* (Princeton: Princeton University Press, 1993).

Ethnic Politics and Political Process: Nationalism in Multiethnic Societies

Nationalism can be compatible with human rights. But often, it is not. How, then, should we approach actually existing nationalisms, with all their potential dangers? I want to argue that asserting the intrinsic incompatibility of nationalism and human rights is unhelpful in the task of devising political strategies to tame nationalism. It is particularly unhelpful in the East-Central European context because of people's vivid memories of the political and cultural oppression, justified by appeal to a universal socialist ideal, that they experienced under Soviet domination. For instance, in the years following his break with Tito, Stalin used the pretext of rooting out "nationalist aberrations" in Eastern Europe to crush even the most tentative efforts by communists to democratize the party or to deviate from Stalinist blueprints for industrialization in order to raise the population's standard of living. Appeals to the universal ideal of socialism were used to veil Soviet imperialism and, in some cases, aggressive efforts at Russification. Thus, blanket denunciations of nationalism and exhortations to embrace universal and international ideals can evoke bad memories. Such exhortations may even prove counterproductive by playing into the hands of antidemocratic forces—either authoritarian communists who, while invoking internationalism, seek to preserve the ancien régime, or authoritarian nationalists who welcome arguments that suggest that civil liberties threaten the nation as a pretext for curtailing civil liberties and as an opportunity to galvanize public support and seek national unity in the face of hostile foreign public opinion.[73]

More generally, in situations in which people have deep nationalist commitments in multiethnic societies, it is unhelpful to conceive the task as one of overcoming nationalism and replacing nationalist politics with a civic democratic culture in which national allegiances play no political role. This is so for two reasons. First, it is unhelpful because it encourages the view that politics is polarized between civic democrats and nationalists. To be sure, such polarization may occur unavoidably if nationalists violate the rights of nonnationals. But if

---

73. Serbian leader Slobodan Milosevic, who presented himself as the savior of multinational Yugoslavia before proclaiming himself the savior of the Serb Nation may, ironically, fit both of these descriptions.

possible, such polarization should be avoided, since it encourages a dynamic of increasing extremism in nationalist politics. Much more desirable is a politics that encourages moderate nationalists who are committed to protecting national interests but who are also willing to compromise in the interest of creating stable democratic institutions.

Second, pitting civic democracy against nationalism is unhelpful in nationally divided societies because it tends to obscure the ways in which pure civic democratic institutions untempered by concern for ethnic accommodation can be destabilizing or even unjust. So, for example, majoritarian democracy can be severely destabilizing and unjust in multiethnic societies where it creates a permanently disenfranchised national minority.[74] Free elections are likely to be extremely destabilizing if they are boycotted by a national group, as occurred in several of the Yugoslav republics. And equal protection under the law will not lead to a thriving and stable democratic society if it helps entrench profound inequalities between national groups.

In areas of mottled population, J. S. Mill argued, national groups have "no course open to them but to make a virtue of necessity, and reconcile themselves to living together under equal rights and laws."[75] This task is best conceived as one of designing institutions so that nationalism is tamed and national conflict takes less dangerous and destabilizing forms—a politics of accommodation rather than an anti-nationalist politics per se. The crucial practical challenge is to devise institutions that guarantee respect for legitimate nationalist aspirations while upholding a commitment to human rights. Donald Horowitz recounts the (perhaps apocryphal) tale of Christmas Island in the South Pacific, which was hurriedly evacuated by the Japanese in 1945, leaving many small arms behind. The island's inhabitants, Chinese and Malays, devised a solution to avert a bloodbath: the Chinese kept the rifles but the Malays kept the bolts, while the Malays kept the pistols and gave the pistol magazines to the Chinese. This tale of reciprocal concessions, motivated by fear, is an instructive one.[76] The effect of the concessions was to make possible a more peaceful and tolerant society, even if

---

74. This point is stressed by Donald Horowitz in *Ethnic Groups in Conflict* (Berkeley: University of California Press, 1985). See also Kumar Rupesinghe, "Introduction," and Martin Ennals, "Ethnic Conflict Resolution and the Protection of Minorities," in *Bulletin of Peace Proposals* 18, no. 4 (1986): 496, 505.

75. Mill, "Considerations on Representative Government."

76. Horowitz, *Ethnic Groups in Conflict*, 563 ff.

those who made the concessions were motivated primarily by self-interest and fear rather than by a wholehearted commitment to civic democracy and human rights.

What are some political strategies that encourage such accommodation? There is no single set of institutions that constitutes necessary and sufficient conditions to ensure the compatibility of nationalism and human rights. Indeed, examining possible institutional arrangements leads to a rather vivid sense of the wisdom of Foucault's observation that "everything is dangerous."[77] Any institutional framework will have its drawbacks and dangers, its potential for failure and misuse. But, keeping this warning in mind, I offer the following suggestions.

The two most important tasks are, first, to seek an appropriate balance between what might be called "nation-respecting" and "nation-undermining" (or "particularist" and "pluralist," respectively) institutions and, second, to deal with communal fear before it becomes dangerous and destabilizing.

Nation-respecting or particularist institutions seek to accommodate the aspirations of particular national groups, while nation-undermining or pluralist ones promote competition within a national group, cooperation between groups, and, more generally, equal citizenship and a sense of belonging for all in a pluralist society.[78] As I argued before, political institutions and processes that are completely blind to national differences may create permanently disenfranchised minorities. It is worth noting, for instance, that the East-Central European government that has most vocally championed a purely civic constitution has been Romania, which has one of the worst records of repression of national minorities. At the same time, mechanisms of group rights that structure the entire political and legal realm along national lines (for instance, consociationalist regimes, which allocate parliamentary seats to national groups, so that each citizen votes for his or her own national representatives)[79] also have drawbacks. In

---

77. Foucault explained that his distrust of "solutions" meant "not that everything is bad, but that everything is dangerous, which is not exactly the same as bad. If everything is dangerous, then we always have something to do." Foucault, "On the Genealogy of Ethics," in *The Foucault Reader*, ed. Paul Rabinow (New York: Pantheon, 1984), 343.

78. For an excellent discussion of strategies for ethnic accommodation, see Horowitz, *Ethnic Groups in Conflict*, chaps. 14–16.

79. The best-known proponent of consociationalism is Arend Lijphart. See Lijphart, *Democracy in Plural Societies* (New Haven: Yale University Press, 1977).

countries with large gaps in power and resources between national groups, group rights may entrench these differences, as they did in the Bantustan system in South Africa. More generally, processes that fundamentally structure political life along national lines tend to deepen the divisions among national groups and hence to exacerbate social conflict. Consociational arrangements, for instance, encourage competition for social resources to be perceived as competition among national groups. They discourage coalitions across national lines and foster an essentialization of group identity—and they place obstacles in the way of attempts to straddle group boundaries or to embrace multiple identities. Politicizing national difference on a grand scale, as required by consociationalism, encourages rigidity.

One technique for balancing nation-respecting and nation-undermining institutions, which has been advocated by Donald Horowitz, is to design electoral systems so that they require politicians to seek support from different national groups. Hence, a presidential system may require winning candidates to amass a certain minimum percentage of the vote in all electoral districts or regions throughout the country, making it impossible for someone to win the presidency who has not appealed at least to some extent to a plurality of national interests.[80]

Another balancing technique involves distinguishing between different levels of governance and administration. So, for instance, while the constitution should articulate fully inclusive principles of citizenship,[81] national groups may be given greater control over public institutions for the expression and transmission of culture, such as churches, theater, and the media, although ideally the segregation produced by such institutions would be balanced by other, more integrated institutions, such as public schools in which children of different cultures studied together.

Exclusion and intimidation often operate most effectively and damagingly at what Foucault called the "extremities" or "capillaries" of governance, hence rights to proportional representation at these levels—on police forces, in the army, in local judiciaries and local administrative bureaucracies—could be mandated by law. Such pro-

---

80. Horowitz, *Ethnic Groups in Conflict*, 15.

81. Julie Mostov offers a powerful critique of national criteria for citizenship in "Democracy and the Politics of National Identity," *Studies in East European Thought* 46 (1994): 9–31.

portional representation could also have the effect of integrating a national elite into the multinational government bureaucracy.

The second crucial task of a politics of accommodation is early response to fear and insecurity within a national community. It is fear that underlies the most dangerous and destructive forms of nationalism. Political sociologist István Bibó offered a vivid description of the vicious circle created by a nationalism of fear in a 1946 essay. He wrote:

> Being a democrat means, primarily, not to be afraid; not to be afraid of those who have differing opinions, speak different languages, or belong to other races; not to be afraid of revolutions, conspiracies, the unknown malicious intent of enemies, hostile propaganda, being demeaned, or any of those imaginary dangers that become truly dangerous because we are afraid of them. The countries of Central and Eastern Europe were afraid because they were not fully developed mature democracies, and they could not become fully developed mature democracies because they were afraid.[82]

Fear and insecurity also easily make national populations the pawns of manipulative politicians. They create the no-win situation of "arrogant majorities" and "militant minorities" that makes a politics of accommodation impossible.[83] They also feed one of the characteristic problems of nationalist politics, its tendency for political overkill, for making ever greater political demands. Early and generous responses to fear and insecurity can help prevent this cycle of accelerated demands, with its potential for destabilization and violence, from beginning. So, for instance, the failure of Croatian politicians to respond when the vast majority of Serbians in Croatia boycotted the elections offers a sobering example of what can happen when a group's fears and grievances (regardless of whether the majority considers them "real" or "imaginary") are ignored.

Dealing with fear may require political innovation at the international level as well. Given the national conflicts in East-Central Eu-

---

82. István Bibó, "The Distress of East European Small States," in Bibó, *Democracy, Revolution, Self-Determination*, trans. András Boros-Kazai (New York: Columbia University Press; Highland Lakes, N.J.: Atlantic Research and Publications, 1991), 42.

83. Mostov, "Democracy and the Politics of National Identity," 21.

rope that could potentially involve foreign governments (for instance, Russia and the Baltics and other former republics; Hungary and the Hungarian minorities in Slovakia, Romania, and Serbia; Albania and the Albanians of Kosovo; Turkey and the Turks of Bulgaria), multilateral efforts to articulate norms, such as minority rights, as well as to mediate conflicts, are very important. East-Central Europe recently offered an extraordinary example of political inventiveness in the roundtables that produced orderly transitions from communism to a multiparty system. This temporary political framework, a "metaparliament," provided a forum for negotiations and collective bargaining between opposition forces and the government. Similar roundtables, perhaps including foreign governments, could be useful in achieving agreements to alleviate group tensions—for instance, securing formal agreement to a border in exchange for explicit guarantees to a national minority. So, for instance, the recent signing of the Slovak-Hungarian Basic Treaty on 19 March 1995 illustrates how the lure of European Union membership may spur East-Central European governments to create formal frameworks that help to alleviate ethnic tensions.

In the end, however, one of the most crucial elements of the struggle to make nationalism compatible with human rights cannot be captured by reference to political institutions. It concerns the need for courageous cultural and social criticism to expose the essentialist illusions and irrational fears that can make nationalism dangerous, while respecting the legitimate allegiances and grievances that make nationalism so compelling. In addition to such criticism, many people—writers, filmmakers, poets, academics, and ministers as well as politicians—need to imagine new communities that encompass old enemies.

Conclusion

A politics of accommodation in multinational societies must carefully balance the universal and the particular. An examination of nationalism suggests that this balance is important for morality and politics more generally. The construction of nations in East-Central Europe in the last century and a half offers a powerful example of the ways in which the boundaries we construct and politicize become naturalized. As Ernest Renan observed, nations are built on collective forgetting—yesterday's invention is viewed as an eternal and inescapable category today. Knowing this, we should be careful about how we politi-cize differences. I do not believe that all politics that grants moral weight to national communities leads inescapably to intolerance. But we should strive, in celebrating differences, to make sure that the moral vocabulary of equality and universality remains vividly avail-able to us—to ensure that we remember why we focused on differ-ence in the first place.

The Next American Revolution

Bruce Ackerman

From Warsaw to Moscow, Johannesburg to Beijing, a specter haunts the world, as if risen from the grave—the return of revolutionary, democratic liberalism. There is, it would appear, only one revolution-free zone that has gained a remarkable historical exemption: the United States of America.

Here all is calm. The United States may welcome the new possibilities opened by world transformation, but it seems curiously untouched. The unmoved mover? The self-satisfied voyeur?

Or could this remarkable turn in world history reinvigorate our own sense of identity? Despite our apparent disengagement, is revolutionary renewal more central to United States that most other polities?

This will be my thesis. One of Marxism's most consequential acts of appropriation in 1917, if not earlier, was its seizure of the idea of revolution. Of course, there were lots more non-Marxist revolutions than Marxist ones even at the height of Leninism's ascendancy. But the Marxists were remarkably successful in getting nearly everyone to believe that their kind of revolution was the genuine article, and that others were sham or worse. Only Hannah Arendt raised a powerful protest against this usurpation;[1] and I will be following her in suggesting that we must rethink the very idea of revolution before we can define America's relationship to it.

This chapter draws from two sources: the Carl J. Friedrich Lecture presented at Harvard University in October 1990, previously unpublished, and remarks scattered through the first three chapters of *The Future of Liberal Revolution* (Cambridge: Harvard University Press, 1992). I am grateful to the questions and comments of participants at the Amherst Conference that allowed me to attempt further clarifications.
    1. Hannah Arendt, *On Revolution* (New York: Viking Press, 1963).

But there is a second stumbling block as well. Modern liberalism has been so traumatized by the struggle with Marxism and Nazism that it has taken a markedly antirevolutionary turn. To reassert the revolutionary promise of human rights, we must rethink liberalism no less than revolution: Should liberal Westerners reserve the idea of revolution to lesser breeds just emerging from tyranny? Are the Marxists right in this at least: that the age of liberal revolution has passed in the capitalist West? Or has it just begun?

I am not using the idea of revolution in a metaphorical sense. That would merely confirm the Marxist claim that their revolution is the only real kind. I want to show how the revolutionary tradition serves as the very lifeblood of the American Republic. More than most modern Western nations, ours can flourish only as long as the prospect of liberal revolution remains genuine.

New Beginnings

Begin with an abstract definition of revolution that can encompass Marxist revolutions in Russia, religious revolutions in Iran, nationalist revolutions in lots of places—as well as liberal revolutions. Only then can we see what, if anything, is distinctive about the last variety. Where, then, to begin?

By remarking upon the distinctive revolutionary orientation to time. First and foremost, a revolutionary proposes to cut time in (at least)[2] two parts: a before and a now. Before, there was something deeply wrong with the way people thought and acted. Now, we have

---

2. It is very common for revolutionaries to divide time into further segments. For example, many have looked back to the day before yesterday—and have found a golden age that preceded a more recent period of catastrophic decline. This three-period schema permits revolutionaries to present themselves as the true conservatives—breaking with the recent past for the purpose of renewing self-conscious commitment to principles and practices of an earlier age.

Given the liberal's distrust of total revolutions, this three-part schema has great attractions. By locating at least some elements of the new order in a remoter past, the liberal suggests that he is not demanding an impossible break, but a critical reappropriation of the best of a common cultural achievement. Cf. J. G. A. Pocock, *The Ancient Constitution and the Feudal Law* (Cambridge: Cambridge University Press, 1957). While it is silly to glorify the perfection of past ages, I shall not allow such "golden age" exaggerations to prevent me from looking back to the remoter past to grasp the transformative possibilities of the present. See chapters 3 and 7 of Pocock.

a chance to make a "new beginning" by freeing ourselves from these blinders.

How does this "new beginning" occur? Through a collective act by mobilized and self-conscious participants. These men and women recognize the validity of new truths and practices—paradigms, if you'll excuse the expression—and proceed to reorganize their collective life by giving new weight to their importance. To put the definition in a single line: A revolution is a successful effort to transform the fundamental principles and practices of a basic aspect of life through an act of collective and self-conscious mobilization.

Note the absence of a key word: I do not insist that a movement induce a *total* change in governing principles to qualify as "revolutionary."[3] This would demand the impossible. Despite rhetorical excess, it is perfectly obvious that there never has been, and never will be, a "total" revolution of all practices at once. Liberal revolutionaries particularly insist upon fundamental limitations on transformative ambition. These limitations will, to the few remaining totalists, make the liberal's revolutionary pretensions absurd.

But I see no reason why we should allow a few extremists to make revolution an impossible concept. In other areas of life, we regularly talk of revolutions without requiring a complete break in continuity. We speak, for example, of scientific "revolutions" without supposing that Copernicus made an absolute break with his predecessors. Nor do we expect revolutionaries in science to move beyond this domain and revolutionize other areas of life.

So, too, with political revolutionaries: it will be enough if they make big changes in the political system, without making sweeping changes in every sector of society. For example, I will consider a change from laissez-faire to a welfare state revolutionary—so long as

---

3. For another protest against totalizing conceptions of revolution, see Roberto Unger, *Social Theory: Its Situation and Its Task* (Cambridge: Cambridge University Press, 1987), 163–64. Unfortunately, Unger embeds his idea of "revolutionary reform" into a larger structure I cannot accept. Adopting an extravagantly romantic ideal of personal development, he mixes irrationalistic notions of social change and the rule of law to endorse a permanent process of "context-smashing" at all levels of social and personal life. Often described in alarmingly violent language, Unger would have us describe his ideal of pervasive and ongoing disruption by the name "superliberalism."

There is poetic justice, I suppose, in this act of stipulative definition. Given the wilfullness of Unger's entire philosophy, why not appropriate the liberal label by an act of will as well? In the unlikely event this gambit succeeds, I guess I'd have to renounce "liberalism" and indulge some neologism of my own.

it is achieved through self-conscious mass mobilization; similarly, an "environmental revolution" may well be in our future, even though many familiar practices will remain more or less the same.

This clarification still allows us to insist that not all big changes come through revolutions. Many, perhaps most, come through evolution.[4] Slowly, without anybody thinking much about the ramifications, a lot of changes add up. But accepting the reality of evolutionary change does not diminish the profound impact of revolutionary mobilizations upon modern life.

How, then, do liberal revolutions differ from other kinds? Must they be violent? Do they have a distinctive life cycle? How has the American experience with liberal revolution differed from other places? These questions define our agenda.

Three Types of Revolution

We have been learning to live with revolution for a very long time. Both in ancient Israel and classical Rome, there were people who set themselves, and their own era, apart from all that preceded it through a collective effort at a "new beginning."[5] And, of course, it is impossible to understand Christianity without confronting the time-splitting consequences of Jesus' intervention in human history. What else divides the New Testament from the Old—but a revolutionary break in time? Fundamentalist movements throughout the Islamic world make it plain that the age of religious revolution has not come to an end.

Nonetheless, most modern revolutions have been more secular. I will distinguish two types. The first is romantic, urging participants to find a new meaning in a mobilized commitment to the language, practice, and symbols of a national culture.[6] Competing with the ro-

---

4. For example, the Industrial Revolution is a revolution only in a metaphorical sense. James Watt didn't get together with other inventor-entrepreneurs and self-consciously decide to inaugurate a new era. In contrast, George Washington or Lech Walesa did make this effort at collective and self-conscious mobilization.

5. On the Jewish conception, see Michael Walzer, *Exodus and Revolution* (New York: Basic Books, 1985); on Roman antecedents, see Kurt Raaflaub and Mark Toner, *Between Republic and Empire* (Berkeley: University of California Press, 1990). While the classical Greeks were perfectly aware of sudden breaks with the past, they were much more pessimistic about their constructive possibilities. See Christian Meier, "Revolution in der Antike," *Geschichtliche Grundbegriffe* (Stuttgart: Kiett, 1984) 5:656–70.

6. For a particularly insightful treatment, see Benedict Anderson, *Imagined Communities*. Rev. ed. (London: Verso, 1991).

mantic nationalist has been a more rationalist type. Here the new beginning is attempted by participants who commit themselves to critical philosophical and scientific principles they believe withstand rational scrutiny.

I am, of course, dealing in ideal types. Revolutionaries may mix rationalistic, romantic, and religious themes into numberless combinations. But it is fair, I think, to place different historical specimens in separate conceptual boxes. If, for example, I wanted to rehabilitate romantic nationalism, I would be drawing my cautionary tales from Nazi Germany; religious transformation, from Iran. Since I will be defending the continuing importance of rationalist revolutions of the liberal type, my cautionary tales should come from Marxism. It is the extravagant oppressions of the Leninist Party that have given rationalist revolution a bad name.

So let me say what was wrong with Leninism from a liberal-revolutionary point of view. First, its science of revolution was normatively impoverished. Rather than organizing their thought and program around critical principles of justice, Leninists believed the whole question of justice unscientific, hence bad. Second, they tried to displace critical reflection on norms with a science of history beyond human capacities. Third, and unsurprisingly given its grandiose pretensions, Leninist science was hideously wrong. Its predictions of postrevolutionary improvement were mocked by the reality of bureaucratic tyranny. Fourth, Leninism remained unrepentant in its scientific pretensions, condemning those with false consciousness to harsh death or unspeakable humiliation. Fifth, the Leninist Party was increasingly dominated by cynical opportunists, without any real commitment to the rationalistic project of social transformation that had earlier motivated the revolutionary enterprise.

The hollowness of this failure is now apparent to all. The only question is what lesson we should learn from it. Should we try to save the ideal of rationalist revolution from the historical debris or cheer its demise?

The Aim of Liberal Revolution

The answer is easy for those who treat "liberalism" as a synonym for laissez-faire capitalism. Surely this understanding does have some support—both in historical practice and philosophical theory.

Nineteenth-century liberalism was sometimes single-minded in its embrace of "free" markets. Contemporary thinkers such as Hayek and Nozick have been vigorous in urging a renaissance of this nineteenth-century tradition.[7] It would be wrong to deny the existence of this laissez-faire strand.

But it would be even wronger to give this nineteenth-century revival undue prominence. At least since John Stuart Mill and Thomas Hill Green, modern liberalism has been trying to put the market in its place—as one, but only one, of a series of fundamental commitments. This is not the place to develop the century-long history—moving from John Dewey through John Rawls to a new generation of liberal theorists who seek to sustain the ideals of activist liberalism. Broadly speaking, activists place four kinds of limitation upon the operation of the free market. The first—expressed in a theory of "market failure"—emphasizes how real-world markets fail to conform to ideal models of perfect competition. This point, when elaborated, justifies a broad range of ongoing state interventions—ranging from environmental control through consumer protection through the subsidized provision of old-age and health insurance.[8] The second—expressed in a theory of distributive justice—challenges the right of one generation of market winners to pass economic gains to their children, without providing equal opportunity for children who were unlucky enough to have poor parents.[9] The third—expressed in a theory of the material and cultural conditions for freedom—emphasizes the crucial importance of education (broadly conceived) in the preparation of each citizen for the exercise of meaningful choice.[10] The fourth—expressed in a theory of equal citizenship—assures each citizen roughly equal

---

7. See Friedrich Hayek, *Law, Legislation and Liberty*, 3 vols. (Chicago: University of Chicago Press, 1973–79); Robert Nozick, *Anarchy, State, and Utopia* (New York: Basic Books, 1974). A more recent contribution is David Gauthier's *Morality by Agreement* (Oxford: Clarendon Press, 1986).

8. Thanks to the work of the last generation of liberal economists, lawyers, and policy analysts, it is increasingly difficult to sustain credibility in practical statecraft without confronting the complexities of market failure. For a useful survey, see David Weimer and Aidan Vining, *Policy Analysis: Concepts and Practice* (Englewood Cliffs, N.J.: Prentice-Hall, 1989); for characteristic applications, see Charles Schulze, *The Public Use of the Private Interest* (Washington: Brookings, 1977); Cass Sunstein, *After the Rights Revolution* (Cambridge: Harvard University Press, 1990).

9. See John Rawls, *A Theory of Justice* (Cambridge: Harvard University Press, 1971).

10. John Dewey, *Democracy and Education* (New York: Free Press, 1916).

political resources despite their different fates in the marketplace.[11] It is only within this larger framework—call it a framework of undominated equality—that activist liberals affirm the enduring value of the free market. Without ongoing efforts to approximate undominated equality, talk of a "free market" degenerates into ideological apologia for the rich and powerful.

Perhaps this conclusion is no news for democratic socialists, who continue to look upon "capitalism" with suspicion. But unlike them, I am genuinely enthusiastic about the free-market ideal. So long as people are guaranteed undominated equality, they have a fundamental right to trade with one another on terms that make sense to them. The challenge for the activist liberal state is to achieve structural conditions for the legitimate marketplace, not to destroy the genuine freedom that the market makes possible.

Large claims, and controversial ones—which I have tried to defend elsewhere.[12] My aim here is to build a bridge between these activist ideals and the enduring significance of liberal revolution. To put the matter simply, laissez-faire liberals like Hayek can think of only one possible role for revolution. It is a moment of mobilized transition from an autocratic regime to a laissez-faire government that contents itself with protecting private property and freedom of contract. While the activist liberal recognizes this "new beginning" as a moral triumph over the false claims of autocracy, he or she does not suppose it represents the end of history. A laissez-faire system is transparently compatible with vast concentrations of inherited wealth, on the one side, and an uneducated, propertyless class, on the other. Such structures make a mockery of the ideal of equal political participation; they are also compatible with a broad range of market failures, from cartelization through environmental degradation to the massive exploitation of consumer ignorance.

Hayek to the contrary notwithstanding, no sensible liberal should remain satisfied with such transparent injustices. Of course, the politics of the last decade has treated these activist ideals with skepticism and contempt. Indeed, this decade of decline does suggest—to me at least—that we will never approach social justice in this country through unconscious evolutionary processes. If Americans are serious

---

11. See Michael Walzer, *Spheres of Justice* (New York: Basic Books, 1983).

12. See my *Social Justice in the Liberal State* (New Haven: Yale University Press, 1980) and *Reconstructing American Law* (Cambridge: Harvard University Press, 1984).

about their liberal principles, they will make progress only through a generation-long effort at political mobilization aiming for a "new beginning." A major move toward social justice would indeed require fundamental changes in American society as we know it. But it would abhor all efforts to use state power to coerce human beings into some narrow political mold. Whatever the failings of liberal revolutionaries, they cannot be accused of sharing the totalitarian ambition that has cursed twentieth-century efforts.

The Resort to Revolutionary Violence

But we have only begun to define the future of liberal revolution. Most obviously, the rich and powerful will not mildly hand over the unfair advantages they now enjoy and propose to pass on to their children. Isn't it likely that they will fight on behalf of the status quo? Won't the ensuing bloodbath lead to a mockery of the modern liberal's utopian effort to reconcile liberty and equality? Therein lies the problem of violence, a second basic source of liberal difficulty with the revolutionary enterprise.

My response is to reject the Leninist equation of revolution with violence. The pathology of violence unquestionably arises from the dynamics of revolution. But once we understand its causes, need they overwhelm us?

The turn to violence arises because all revolutions begin with a relatively small number of true believers, who predictably encounter resistance as they spread the word to others. This larger audience may be unpersuaded of the need for a new beginning. Rather than accepting the liberal's program for more equality, for example, the skeptics look upon it as a cover for envy and greed.

At this point, revolutionary arrogance becomes tempting. So far as the vanguard is concerned, the resisters are victims of false consciousness. If they exercised their critical intelligence in good faith, they would soon find themselves convinced of the need for a new beginning; only sloth or selfishness or worse is keeping them back. So why not force them to be free, and later on they'll thank the vanguard for the therapy!

The liberal revolutionary has learned to beware this gambit; violence is hardly a necessary condition for the mobilization of critical self-consciousness. After all, the vanguard itself achieved this condition not through force of weapons, but through force of argument. Why give up hope that years of committed political activity will fail to lead others—many others—to respond to persuasion?

Violence is simply a shortcut, and one that should be cut short in the name of liberal values themselves. Men and women have the right to be wrong, even when it comes to fundamental questions of social justice. They have a right to demand that we take their objections seriously and that we try to convince them by virtue of the better argument.

The examples of Gandhi and King establish that such a generation-long struggle can yield results that are more profound and sustaining than the quick kills of a Lenin or a Hitler. Perhaps violence may be justified as a last resort, if the power elite responds to liberal demands for social justice by brutally suppressing the revolutionary movement. But it is far, far better if we respond to revolutionary vanguardism—the arrogance of the counterelite—by designing a constitutional system that subjects would-be revolutionaries to a series of fair democratic tests.

Constitutionalizing Revolution

I've called such a constitution "dualistic" because it involves the establishment of a two-track lawmaking system.[13] The lower lawmaking track is intended to register the successful conclusions of pluralist democratic politics—the mix of interest group pressure, regular electioneering, and practical statesmanship that characterizes the democratic polity most of the time.

The higher lawmaking track, in contrast, is designed for would-be revolutionaries. It employs special procedures for determining whether a mobilized majority of the citizenry give their considered support to the principles that one or another revolutionary movement would pronounce in the people's name. Dualists emphasize that while many small movements feel themselves called to the task of revolutionary renewal, few are chosen by a mobilized majority of a nation's citizens.

---

13. This section sketches a larger argument presented in my book *We the People: Foundations* (Cambridge: Harvard University Press, 1991).

As a consequence, the higher lawmaking system imposes a formidable set of rigorous institutional tests before allowing a revolutionary movement to transform fundamental political principles in the people's name. Once the revolutionaries satisfy these rigorous tests, however, the dualist constitution gives their movement's call for a new beginning special status in the legal system. At least until the next successful revolution, the new principles will serve as higher law and trump the outcomes of normal politics.

While all this is terribly abstract, the basic idea should be familiar—since it describes the operating premises of our own system of government. When today's Americans use the original Constitution and the Civil War amendments to test the constitutional validity of normal statutes, they are recognizing the living legacy of the successful revolutions of the eighteenth and nineteenth centuries.

We must resist the conservative invitation to view the Founding Federalists and Reconstruction Republicans as polite gentlemen intent upon preserving the status quo. With Washington in the chair, the Philadelphia convention refused to play according to the rules established by America's first constitution—the Articles of Confederation—providing for constitutional amendment. These rules would have required them to gain the unanimous consent of all thirteen state legislatures for their effort to lead the American people to a new beginning. Instead, our revolutionary Founders asserted that the consent of nine state conventions was enough.[14]

Similarly, the Reconstruction Republicans did not validate the Fourteenth Amendment—guaranteeing all Americans "equal protection"—by playing according to the constitutional rules established by the Federalist Founders in Article 5 of the 1787 constitution. These would have granted ten states the right to veto any proposed amendment. When thirteen Southern and border states solemnly rejected the proposed Fourteenth Amendment, these revolutionary Republicans did not accept defeat. Rather than allowing the South to repudiate its call for a new beginning, the Republican Congress destroyed the rejectionist Southern governments and used the Union army to construct new ones more likely to accept the amendment. Even these reconstructed state governments, however, were not allowed to make a free choice on the Fourteenth Amendment, as the Founding Federal-

---

14. See Bruce Ackerman, *We the People: Transformations*, chap. 2 (forthcoming).

ists intended. Instead, the Republicans refused to admit representatives of the reconstructed governments into Congress until they ratified their proposed amendment. *Reconstruction* was precisely what the word implies: a new beginning in which a mobilized majority of the American People supported the efforts by the Republican leadership to rebuild the Union's identity from the ground up.[15]

Nor did the American exercise in revolutionary renewal end with Reconstruction. Over the past century, the dualist system has repeatedly tested the democratic authority of revolutionary movements seeking to transform fundamental values in the name of We the People of the United States. Sometimes the political vanguard has won the broad and deep popular support required before leaders in Washington are authorized to set the Constitution on a new course; more often the dualist system has only revealed that, despite its inflated rhetoric, the movement's leadership has failed to carry a majority of the country along with its proud vision of constitutional transformation.

The most obvious success story is the New Deal revolution. In contrast to the Founding Federalists and the Reconstruction Republicans, the New Dealers won support for their transformation without great bloodshed. Nonetheless, the New Deal effort to transform traditional constitutional commitments to laissez-faire capitalism did not come easily. It took the Democrats five years to overcome the Supreme Court's resistance to their effort to legitimate an activist welfare state in the United States. Only after repeated victories at the polls, during which the Democrats mobilized broad and deep support for their critique of laissez-faire, did the Supreme Court finally make its famous "switch in time" in 1937. Thus, the New Deal not only suggests the capacity of modern Americans to support the call for a new beginning in our national life; it also points to the possibility of a peaceful, if turbulent, exercise in revolutionary transformation.

The same is true for our most recent success: the Civil Rights revolution. Once again, it is Martin Luther King Jr., not Malcolm X, who spoke for a movement that ultimately gained the support of a mobilized majority of Americans for a new beginning on civil rights.[16]

These successes, of course, should not blind us to our history of false starts. Far more often, a political vanguard's call for a new

15. Ibid., pt. 2 (forthcoming).
16. Ibid., pt. 3 (forthcoming).

beginning only reveals, in the end, that a majority of the American people refuse to go along. Perhaps the most fateful failure was the Populists' failure to carry the country with them during the 1890s. But our recent past has been littered with similar events, the Reagan revolution serving as the last of a series of failed efforts by political vanguards to gain the kind of deep and broad popular support our Constitution requires for a "new beginning."

Many questions can be raised, of course, about the past and present condition of dualistic democracy in America. But one point will suffice here. Once we liberate ourselves from the hold that Marxism-Leninism has had upon the idea, there is nothing odd about the thought of a *peaceful* democratic revolution, nor about a two-track lawmaking system that seeks to place the possibility of such revolutions at the very center of a country's constitutional arrangements.

Revolution and the Limits of Reason

Our inquiry has begun with two moral questions: Does the revolutionary effort at political transformation require the celebration of violence or the brutal transformation of human nature? If so, then liberals are well rid of their nineteenth-century illusions.

If not, however, we can proceed one more step down the path of revolutionary exploration. Suppose, for a moment, that a majority of Americans did indeed mobilize themselves to support a "new beginning," in which our country committed itself to the serious pursuit of genuine equality of opportunity. If this commitment were made, do liberal revolutionaries really know enough to devise a set of state interventions that will do more good than harm? Won't the best-laid plans be swamped by second-order effects that mock the demands for social justice that motivate the revolutionary enterprise? Isn't the world much too complex for our puny efforts at social engineering? Shouldn't we recognize the revolutionary demand for social justice as the delusion that Hayek says it is: a phantasm that will only serve to authorize technocrats to impose a rigid tyranny upon the rest of us?[17]

While laissez-faire ideologists may treat this question as rhetorical, the student of revolution should take it seriously in concrete case

---

17. Friedrich Hayek, *The Mirage of Social Justice* (Chicago: University of Chicago Press, 1976) and *The Road to Serfdom* (Chicago: University of Chicago Press, 1944).

studies. For now, it is enough to glance at the most prominent cases in our own history. Two centuries ago, successful American Revolutionaries thought they possessed a political science sufficiently powerful to establish a new form of republican government. A lot has happened since, but are we prepared to say that they failed?

More than a century ago, Americans fought a war to free the slaves; and at the end of the war, the slaves were freed. Of course, modern Americans may say that their predecessors' notion of freedom was impoverished, but that is a very different point from the skeptical claim that revolutions cannot achieve their professed aims.

Let's examine a couple of more recent cases. The New Deal revolution aimed for social security against the vagaries of old age, accident, disability, unemployment—and today lots more Americans are secure, thanks to this collective act of self-conscious political mobilization. The civil rights movement of the 1950s and 1960s aimed to end apartheid in the American South and to provide more genuine opportunity for oppressed races. While it may be fashionable to ignore this fact in some circles, Americans have today ended apartheid and minorities have won more genuine opportunities.

I do not want to play Pangloss. Obviously, there is a lot wrong with our existing public arrangements and even more wrong with their limited ambition. The American people have not yet been convinced to embrace the full promise of social justice in a liberal state, much less to make it into a living reality. That is exactly why I want to reject the Marxist myth that the age of liberal revolution has long since passed in the modern West. Nonetheless, American history simply does not justify the kind of radical skepticism about the possibility of self-conscious social change now trendy in neoconservative circles.

Liberalism and the Limits of Community

While conservatives have long doubted the liberals' capacity to master the arts of social engineering, a new kind of doubt has gained prominence over the last decade. This, too, scrutinizes the theory of knowledge underlying liberalism. But it does not focus on the daunting empirical inquiries liberals confront in designing programs that will reliably work in the real world. The new doubt goes deeper—to the liberal's theory of moral knowledge.

This critique, now often described as "communitarian," challenges the liberal idea of personhood. The liberal's demand for social justice makes no sense, it is said, without positing the existence of abstract and isolated Egos who are scarecrows of the real-world folk we know and love so well. While a few philosophers may be convinced by abstruse Kantian texts to accept these alienated Egos as the key to personal identity, communitarians are confident that most people will be repelled by such a forbiddingly antiseptic construction. Whatever neo-Kantians may say, most people simply do not think of themselves as abstract choosers whose dignity consists in the possession of equal rights. Instead, ordinary humans gain their identity by sharing in their concrete community's preexisting commitments and traditions. Given this fact, why should normal people sacrifice themselves when the liberal revolutionary calls upon them to join together to guarantee equal rights to all?

I leave this question to my formidable allies who do indeed see in Kant's philosophy the deepest expression of political liberalism. I can only speak for myself, and I am not now, nor ever have been, a member of the Kantian party. In this, I am not alone. Most of the liberal voices of the past take pains to reject the Kantian image of an abstract and isolated Ego. They have emphasized instead the profound ways in which human identity is bound up with the body, the senses, and the experience of society. However different Locke, Hume, Mill, and Dewey are from one another, they are alike in their rejection of the Kantian theory of the self. It is a shallow critique that awards Kant an intellectual monopoly that he has never possessed in modern liberal thought.

If pressed for a counterformulation, I would say that the creature haunting my own thought is not the deracinated self, but the flesh-and-blood people we call strangers. Strangers may live next door, but they are not at all like us. They are doing odd things at odd times, for reasons that deeply disturb. How to respond to this unease?[18]

By loving the strangers as we do ourselves? Only a god could do this; there are too many strangers with too many strangenesses. Or should we persuade these strangers to change their actions and be-

---

18. While the stranger is a recurring figure in modern literature, he/she remains an underappreciated figure in political and legal theory. Some explorations: Robert Burt, *Taking Care of Strangers* (New York: Free Press, 1979); Michael Ignatiev, *The Needs of Strangers* (London: Chatpo & Windus, 1984); Julia Kristeva, *Strangers to Ourselves* (New York: Columbia University Press, 1991).

liefs so that they agree with ours? I myself will never give up on this project. But persuasion and reflection take time: I must listen to the strangers' arguments if I expect them to listen to mine. In the meantime, an abyss remains between us, and we may well die before one of us comes to see the other's truth for what it is.

How, then, are we to conduct our ongoing life? Are we forever fated to repeat the mistake of the ancient Greeks who, finding that others spoke a different language, despised them as barbarians merely because their talk sounded like "bar, bar, bar" to Greek ears? Must we endlessly destroy what we cannot understand?

No, there is an alternative: we must try to become politically self-conscious about the very problem posed by our continuing strangeness. By focusing on it, we may find a political solution. You and I may remain strangers, it is true, but we may find common ground in a politics that protects our equal right to cultivate our distinctive characters without any one stranger calling the shots.

By working with one another to build a liberal state dedicated to our equal right to be different, we may become something more than strangers, if less than friends. We may become liberal citizens, speaking to one another in a distinctive voice. However odd or perverse our beliefs may seem to one another, perhaps we can find common ground in recognizing this: you and I are both struggling to find meaning in the world. We can—we must—build a civilized political life that allows each of us to respect the others' quest.

Self-Restraint

This is the promise of liberal revolution. I do not encounter you in some mythic state of nature, but in the here and the now. I call upon you to mobilize your political energies to work with me to shape a world that gives equal respect to our right to be different. By working out a public understanding of the practical implications of this idea, we may inaugurate a "new beginning" in our relations with one another. We may succeed so well that our children, looking back, will say of us: Thanks to them, we have come to give new significance to the proud American boast that all men are created free and equal.

Or we may fail. It is hard work, liberal revolution. Harder, I think, than the revolutionary exercises proposed by religious and romantic rivals, who can offer a deep spiritual satisfaction that the liberal denies herself. These rivals allow their devotees to proclaim, in a variety of accents: We are the chosen ones, let the rest of humanity go to hell.

Liberal revolutionaries, in contrast, cultivate a principled split between their public and private selves. Publicly, they call out to their fellows: Despite our deep and abiding disagreements, may we not all join together to build a political life of mutual respect and civility—by recognizing each citizen's equal right to be different? Privately, however, they may find that their public encounters only confirm their doubts about the morality of the strangers they recognize as fellow citizens. The tension between private convictions and public tolerance will be difficult to bear. It is so much easier to use state power to suppress difference than to support or endure it.

But managing this spiritual tension is only part of the problem. The practical challenges of liberal statecraft raise special difficulties as well. Other revolutionaries may flirt with totalizing conceptions of the state, using central power to project their religious or romantic idea into the furthest recesses of social life. The activist liberal's relationship to the state is more complex. On the one hand, we must use centralized power creatively to guarantee each of us a fair share of basic resources—wealth, health, and education—as each sets out in her own quest for meaning. On the other hand, we embrace the principle of limited government. It is not the job of the state to answer the fundamental questions of life, but to provide equal resources to all citizens and then to equip all individuals with the tools they need to take responsibility for their own answers.

This double-edged commitment will generate a characteristic search to define a limited set of strategic state interventions in a focused effort to secure initial equality. Progressive taxation and compulsory education serve as classic examples. The challenge is to define new forms of intervention that will make genuine equality of opportunity a social reality. With fundamental entitlements secured, however, the liberal legal order seeks to provide citizens with a broad set of facilitative rights, such as freedom of contract and freedom of association, that enable them to collaborate on their own terms within a just basic structure.

This double-edged program commits the liberal revolutionary to the rule of law. Americans should not be obliged to bow before bureaucrats on bended knee. As citizens of the liberal state, the law guaran-

tees them fundamental rights to an equal starting point in life and a
rich set of techniques for meaningful collaboration. And it is the job of
judges to interpret this law, not appeal to their private notions of
moral perfection in doing justice to their fellow citizens. Revolutionary justice, for the liberal, is provided by a rule of law that guarantees
all their genuinely equal right to be different.

The Revolutionary Cycle

But liberals not only reject the totalizing aspirations of the state and its
officials. They also reject a totalizing conception of revolution. Their
particular target is a notion of permanent revolution that predictably
fascinates more romantic and religious types. For them, the revolutionary moment is a time when the masses are most alive to the national
and religious ideals that make life worth living. It is only natural, then,
that these revolutionaries want this moment to go on indefinitely.

For liberal revolutionaries, things stand differently. The revolutionary moment is indeed one when citizens are most alive to their
problem in political construction: How, given their deep and fundamental differences, are they to elaborate principles of justice that will
give all a fair and equal opportunity to pursue their different lives?
These moments are precious in the life of the polity. They allow liberal
citizens to renew and redefine a common political identity that may
otherwise be drowned out in the cacophony of different voices.

However important this task, it cannot be allowed to displace the
different one each of us faces in answering the simple question: What
is the meaning of my life? While some liberal activists will find the
answer in a lifelong dedication to public service, they cannot be surprised when others turn away from politics for deeper satisfactions
elsewhere.

At their best, then, liberal revolutions are passing events. During
these periods of mass engagement, citizens place the problem of political reconstruction at the forefront of their consciousness. At these
times, they seek to do justice to the problems thrown up by their
historical situation. The challenge for statecraft is to use these precious moments to build new and deeper foundations for liberal
politics—before the opportunity for self-conscious transformation is
lost in the centrifugal whirl of liberal society.

In the best case, a liberal state will experience a distinctive cycle of revolutionary activity over the generations. At time one, a mobilized citizenry will focus its attention upon the political problem posed by their deep disagreements and mobilize themselves for a self-conscious effort to regulate these differences by framing appropriate principles of constitutional justice. If they succeed, most citizens will respond by focusing most of their energies in other directions, leaving the adaptation and implementation of the new political principles to electorally responsible politicians and legalistically inclined judges.

As these periods of normal politics proceed, the proud constitutional ideals of the previous revolutionary period suffer predictable ossification. New forms of difference become central in social life; new historical conditions throw the older revolutionary principles into doubt. Finally, a new generation senses a need to mobilize to transform old vocabularies, confront new differences, and create a new liberal order that does justice to their self-conscious scrutiny. If this effort at revolutionary renewal succeeds, political mobilization will subside as the collective revolutionary achievement empowers most people to explore their differences, rather than their commonalities.

The Varieties of National Memory

But, to put it mildly, the liberal cannot count on the invisible hand to lead the revolutionary impulse down the historical path to the best case. During the past two centuries, the idea of revolution has swept the world, leaving diverse experiences in its wake. These different experiences have had a profound impact upon political memory in different parts of the world. Some political cultures have come to look with fear and loathing upon the revolutionary aspect of their history; others, with hope and expectation.

A thoughtful assessment cannot overlook the range of historical encounters with revolutionary transformation. Our national experience, unlike that of others, suggests that American liberals can more confidently accept the risks of revolution than can liberals in most other places.

In much of the world, the experience of revolution has left behind a bitter residue of cultural suspicion of the very idea that a mobilized people might successfully undertake an exercise in self-conscious political transformation. This was the fate of the first protomodern historical experience: the English Revolution of the seventeenth century. After a generation of bloody conflict, English Revolutionaries saw their hopes for a new beginning destroyed by the Restoration of 1660. From that moment to the present, there has been a deep suspicion of the constructive possibilities of self-conscious political mobilization in English culture—an almost visceral belief that the noisy excitement of revolutionary politics leads to demagogic irrationality, not moral seriousness and rational engagement on fundamental matters of political principle.

This, too, has been the fate of revolution in Germany: one failure after another, capped by the nationalistic madness of Nazi Germany. After 1848 and 1933, there is little wonder that German liberals, and not only liberals, respond to tremors of mass mobilization with unconcealed anxiety. The very notion that it might lead to rational political reconstruction seems almost a utopian dream. From this perspective, the recent upheaval in East Germany is a matter of the greatest importance. Will it generate a new confidence in the constructive possibilities of revolution, or deepened despair?

We shall see. My point here is cautionary. Since modern liberal thought is so indebted to England and Germany, it should not be surprising that so much of it deeply abhors revolution. The liberal skepticism of an Oakeshott or a Hayek expresses, at least in part, the failures of self-conscious mass mobilization in England and Mitteleuropa. For Americans, however, the comparable experiences have left different lessons.

So far as we are concerned, exercises in energetic citizen engagement represent the great creative moments in our political culture. James Madison, Abraham Lincoln, Martin Luther King Jr.—these, and many others, gained political leadership at the head of movements of American citizens mobilized for self-conscious change. After a generation of sacrifice and debate, these movements won the mobilized assent of a majority of Americans to a new beginning in our relationships with one another.

Rather than following Oakeshott or Hayek in their praise of government by a liberal Burkean elite, Americans look upon the everyday adjustments of normal politicians with suspicion more than hope. Without the moral energy supplied by mobilized citizens, normal politicians too easily tend toward vulgar corruption rather than

Burkean prudence. The American Revolutionaries' suspicion of the English Court in 1776 still characterizes our politics, for ill and for good.

In this positive assessment of the promise of revolution, Americans are less like the English and Germans and more like the French. The French, too, look back to their eighteenth-century revolution and find in it the great new beginning of their history. The Declaration of the Rights of Man and Citizen, no less than our constitution of 1787, stands as a token of the good that mobilized and self-conscious political action can accomplish.

But the differences between the American and French experiences are fundamental. Most important, the revolutionary generation in France failed to achieve a permanent political success. A French person whose political maturity began with the storming of the Bastille lived to see the Reign of Terror, Napoleon, and the Bourbon restoration mock the liberal ideals that inspired the early days of the French Revolution. During the same period, an American would have seen a succession of revolutionary heroes from Washington to Monroe demonstrate the continuing vitality of that generation's political achievement. The French failures to institutionalize their revolutionary moments in 1830, 1848, and 1871 have cast a shadow on their political thought, making it more pessimistic about the possibilities of enduring political reconstruction than its American counterpart.

A second difference with the French is no less important. Although the French Revolution certainly had a liberal aspect, it also played a vital part in the birth of modern nationalism. This nationalistic theme is less prominent in our revolutionary tradition. The colonists who separated from England were not trying to preserve a threatened language or indigenous culture. They fought for their rights as Englishmen, to be sure, but these rights were conceived in rationalistic terms as rights to life, liberty, and property—or was it the pursuit of happiness?

Over time, the ethnically Anglo-Saxon aspect of American political culture has weakened. Think back one generation to the civil rights movement, the last outstanding achievement of the revolutionary spirit in America. It was precisely the social marginality of Martin Luther King Jr., John F. Kennedy, and Lyndon Johnson that made their roles especially meaningful. A black, a Catholic, and a Southerner came to represent the mobilized conviction of a majority of

Americans that the time had come to affirm a new and deeper understanding of individual rights and equal opportunity.

In contrast to the French, Americans do not see in this experience of rational revolution a way of deepening their thick ethnic identity. Successful revolutions in the United States allow all of us to place a hyphen after our ethnicities and recognize one another as Irish- or Asian- or African-Americans, working with one another to hammer out fair and equal terms for continued civic cooperation.

We live, of course, at a time when the revolutionary spirit in the United States is at one of its cyclical lows. It is a time when proliferating ethnic, racial, and religious groups glory in their differences, a time when the liberating promise of individual freedom has given way to somber reflections over the paradoxical character of rights.

It is time, in short, for a new beginning.

Contributors

Richard L. Abel is Professor of Law at U.C.L.A.

Bruce Ackerman is Sterling Professor at Yale Law School.

Wendy Brown is Professor of Women's Studies and Legal Studies and Co-Director of the Center for Cultural Studies at the University of California at Santa Cruz.

John Comaroff is Professor of Anthropology and Sociology at the University of Chicago.

Drucilla Cornell is Professor of Law at Cardozo Law School.

Jane Gaines is Associate Professor of Literature and English at Duke University.

Thomas R. Kearns is William Hastie Professor of Philosophy and Professor of Law, Jurisprudence, and Social Thought at Amherst College.

Elizabeth Kiss is Assistant Professor of Politics at Princeton University.

Kirstie M. McClure is Assistant Professor of Political Science at Johns Hopkins University.

Sally Engle Merry is Class of '49 Professor in Ethics and Professor of Anthropology at Wellesley College.

Martha Minow is Professor of Law at Harvard Law School.

Austin Sarat is William Nelson Cromwell Professor of Jursiprudence and Political Science and Professor of Law, Jurisprudence, and Social Thought at Amherst College.

Steven Shiffrin is Professor of Law at Cornell University.

Index